D1559648

Harvard Studies in Business History XXXVI

Edited by Alfred D. Chandler, Jr.
Isidor Straus Professor of Business History
Graduate School of Business Administration
George F. Baker Foundation
Harvard University

Family Firm to Modern Multinational

Norton Company, a New England Enterprise

CHARLES W. CHEAPE

Harvard University Press
Cambridge, Massachusetts
and London, England   1985

Library of Congress Cataloging in Publication Data

Cheape, Charles W., 1945–
    Family firm to modern multinational

    (Harvard studies in business history ; 36)
    Includes index.
    1. Norton Company—History.   I. Title.   II. Series.
HD9503.C59   1985   338.7′67′097443   84-10824
ISBN 0-674-29261-8 (alk. paper)

Editor's Introduction

THE HISTORY of individual business enterprises and persons must remain at the core of business history. Detailed histories of individuals or firms that explain how they carried out different functional activities and executed strategic moves provide the essential information for broader analyses and generalizations concerning the development of business practices, procedures, organizations, and institutions. N. S. B. Gras fully recognized the need for such histories. As the founder and for many years editor of the Harvard Studies in Business History, he concentrated his attention on publishing works that would provide such data. Of the first twenty-two books in the series, all but two were biographies of individuals or firms, and all but two of these twenty dealt with American subjects. Yet none were histories of the large industrial enterprises that have come to dominate the central sectors of modern economies during the past century. Histories of such major firms have been written. Gras himself led the way by making arrangements for publication, outside the series, of the massive four-volume history of the Standard Oil Company (New Jersey), now Exxon. This work, in turn, led to the writing of histories of other oil companies, of railroad corporations, and of a small number of giant industrials. Very few of these, however, carried their story beyond World War II.

Charles Cheape's history of Norton Company brings the series back to one of its basic purposes, for this history of a leading large American industrial enterprise illustrates in careful detail many of the most important aspects of the evolution of large-scale business enterprise in the United States. Like so many of the nation's foremost industrial firms, Norton Company had its beginnings in the 1880s, when its founders perfected a new product vital to the rapidly industrializing economy. Again, as happened in other industries, the entrepreneurs who founded the company created the management team essential to coordinate the flow of materials through the processes of production and invested in a national and then international sales force to market their abrasives, to provide after-sales services, and to assure precisely scheduled deliveries. By 1920 Norton had become multinational by building or buying plants in Germany, France, Japan, and Canada and by using the largest British toolmaker as its agent in the United Kingdom. As in other industries, Norton—the largest firm in abrasives—was the price leader, competing for a substantial share of national and global markets with one large competitor, Carborundum, and a handful of smaller ones. By 1917 its assets placed Norton among the nation's 400 largest industrial enterprises.

Norton differed from many of the new large integrated industrials, however, in that its owners continued to manage. For three generations members of the Jeppson and Higgins families made the critical decisions at the top. The owners not only were able to retain this type of governance longer than most of their contemporaries, they were able to continue their paternalistic pattern of labor relations. From its first years the company relied on Scandinavian and Yankee workers, whose children and then grandchildren often joined the ranks of the working force. By maintaining good wages and a variety of fringe benefits, it continued to enjoy the services of a stable, efficient labor force, one that was almost immune to unionization. In the 1950s two thirds of its workers in Worcester, Massachusetts, its home base, had been employed for more than ten years.

Such personal, family management was able to survive with little difficulty the rigors of the Great Depression of the 1930s and an unprecedented expansion during World War II. Only in the 1960s did the old ways become increasingly difficult to maintain. The new challenges to management resulted in part from continuing postwar expansion abroad and overseas, particularly in Latin America. More serious was the slowing of the overall demand for Norton's major products, as well as a continuing loss in its market share abroad, and eventually at home, to smaller competitors. Management problems were further intensified by a growing commitment to a strategy of diversification into new product lines, a strategy adopted partly because of the declining profits of the older abrasives business and partly because of an increasing popularity in American industry of strategies of growth through diversification. Like many other American companies Norton soon found that because it had few specialized skills or facilities to transfer into new lines, the production and distribution of new products, particularly those obtained by acquisition, proved difficult to manage. The profits of the new lines dropped even lower than did those of the old.

The resulting near-crisis led to the recruitment of professional managers and a shift in strategy. The new executives, particularly Robert Cushman, agreed to building a balanced, diversified product line, one that concentrated on consumable industrial supplies for global markets—that is, on products whose production and particularly marketing were somewhat comparable to the company's original abrasives line. During the economically troubled decade of the 1970s, Cushman developed procedures for a more systematic planning and implementation of strategy and for rationalizing Norton's business at home and abroad. In a decade when many of the nation's leading business enterprises were staggering from intensified global competition, decreasing domestic demand, and overdiversification, Norton Company was able to continue to grow by expanding market shares and profits.

In this history of Norton, then, Professor Cheape provides new and valuable information on the beginnings and continued growth of an American multinational that quickly came to dominate markets at home and abroad. Few other histories provide detailed information of this sort, and none that I have read describes and analyzes on the basis of internal documents and extensive interviews with the participants the ways in which such an enterprise responded to the increasingly turbulent national and international business environment of the sixties and seventies. Writers and teachers of business history will be grateful to Professor Cheape for his careful and exhaustive collection, compilation, and analysis of this most significant record and to the executives of Norton Company for opening their files and their memories for use in such an objective analysis.

Alfred D. Chandler, Jr.

Preface

THIS BOOK was written for several reasons, but not because corporate histories are scarce. Journalists, retired executives, and public relations people have recorded the stories of numerous companies. Rarely, however, is a historian and an outsider given full funding and allowed an unrestricted view from the inside. The opportunity alone was attractive.

In addition, the history of a hundred-year-old New England abrasives company has its own appeal. Regional historians and local residents, employees and officers, retirees and prospective personnel, distributors and suppliers, and others associated with a billion-dollar enterprise that operates worldwide and employs over twenty thousand constitute quite a potential audience. Thus the project has some intrinsic merit.

Norton is also interesting because of its industrial setting. The firm dominated the evolution of the abrasives industry and helped pioneer the development of production grinding machinery. Its grinding wheels and grinding machines soon became crucial for metal making and metal working, especially for the inexpensive, high-volume, precision production of complex metal goods like the automobile that swiftly came to be a hallmark of the maturing U.S. industrial economy of the late nineteenth and early twentieth centuries. In turn the technology of the company's major product, bonded abrasives, was an important determinant in the evolution and character of the enterprise, helping to account for the timing of its appearance, the pace of its growth, and the scale of its operations.

Finally, Norton is intriguing as an industrial firm, in both a general and a particular sense. As a type, it is one of five hundred or a thousand large, integrated, and often multinational companies that have shaped and dominated the core industries of the American economy in the last century. A careful study of Norton's history, then, offers a means to explore and test generalizations about the forces underlying the growth of large-scale enterprises and the patterns of their strategies and structures.

Despite its similarities to other big industrial companies, Norton is an ideal test case because of its obvious differences from other firms during much of its existence. By World War I most large companies were publicly owned and professionally managed, but Norton remained a closely held, family-operated enterprise for an additional half century. The firm was a remarkable anomaly—a transition between the small, regional manufacturing businesses of the nineteenth century, with their self-funding, owner-management, and paternalistic labor relations policies, and the modern, multinational giants of the later twentieth century. In the last two decades the advent of public ownership and professional management amid the challenges of diversification and decentralization common to many industrial companies has revolutionized Norton so that it now resembles many other firms. Nevertheless, its history reminds us that in the evolution of enterprise, as in other fields of history, continuity is often as significant as change.

During five years' research and writing I have accumulated many debts. The greatest of these are to Norton Company, which funded the project with a grant to Dartmouth College and which provided materials, space, and time. The firm granted unrestricted access to all its records, arranged visits to its major operations in the United States and Europe, and scheduled interviews with active and retired personnel. Everywhere, I was received with courtesy and given full cooperation. At the same time Norton agreed in advance to my editorial freedom. The manuscript has been read and criticized by several scholars and senior executives, but the final wording and interpretations are mine.

I am also indebted to scores of individuals, only a few of whom are listed here. A number of people helped with the research. Charles Estus, Kevin Hickey, Kenneth Moynihan, and John McClymer of the Community Studies Program at Assumption College graciously shared their work on Worcester's Swedish community and reviewed the manuscript. Deborah Nabhan researched bibliographic sources. David Corrigan of the Worcester Historical Society and James Hanlan of the Worcester Polytechnic Institute generously loaned materials on the F. B. Norton pottery shop and Norton personnel. The staffs at the Worcester Public Library, the American Antiquarian Society, and the Worcester Historical Society, and the librarians of Clark University and Worcester Polytechnic Institute encouraged the work and recommended sources. Aida Asfour served as general factotum, scheduling trips and interviews, explaining the mysteries of corporate procedure, and generally acclimating me to Norton Company. Chuck Reynolds organized materials and interviews at Watervliet, New York; Red Holmes alerted me to George Jeppson's papers dating from his time as works manager; Wendell Cheney was an invaluable guide to Norton's collection of pictures and did the crucial work of coordinating their preparation; and Ann Swyden carefully preserved several irreplaceable documents.

Many others helped prepare the manuscript. Frank Esposito did the photography, and Emile Gaucher produced the line drawings. Guy Williams of the controller's office gathered the financial statistics essential for several charts. Carol Hillman, vice-president of corporate communications, Dean Wood, director of corporate advertising, and their staff provided the fullest cooperation. Gail Patten patiently typed a number of drafts and corrections while translating my increasingly inscrutable handwriting. Jere Daniell of Dartmouth College, Alfred Chandler of the Harvard Business School, Merritt Roe Smith of the Massachusetts Institute of Technology, and several anonymous reviewers for Harvard University Press read, critiqued, and improved the manuscript. Responsibility for any errors is, of course, my own.

Finally, many people generously gave time for interviews, and most are recognized in the citations. A few made extra efforts and deserve special mention. Robert Cushman took time from a busy schedule for several sessions that were crucial to understanding and documenting the radical changes of the past two decades. Elmer Schacht, Wallace Howe, and the late Donald Kelso graciously entertained me in their homes for repeated valuable interviews. Louis Camarra orchestrated a European tour and educated me about Norton's foreign operations. Despite his duties as chief executive, Donald Melville found time for an important interview and for commenting on the manuscript. Fairman Cowan and Curtis Clark gave me a great deal of their time and an excellent perspective on the changes of the last quarter century. Milton Higgins, who knows more about Norton Company's history than anyone living, patiently endured the many interviews required to impart a fraction of his knowledge.

Three people were most responsible for the conceptualization and implementation of the project. Ralph Gow proposed the study, encouraged it, dictated his own memoirs to give me a vital overview, and granted numerous interviews covering all aspects of Norton's history. John Jeppson, second only to Milton Higgins in his knowledge of Norton's past, introduced and recommended the book to the

Board of Directors, sat through a number of essential sessions, and even opened his family's papers. Finally, Harry Seifert was an invaluable guide who counseled, interpreted, encouraged, informed, arranged, and traveled.

Contents

ILLUSTRATIONS

FIGURES

TABLES

Family Firm to Modern Multinational

Introduction

"WHAT'S A NORTON?" The question, frequently repeated by Norton employees in a semihumorous fashion, reflects the company's relative anonymity. Although Norton Company has a corporate advertising staff, it has no corporate advertising program of the kind that brought North American Rockwell into millions of homes via television. Its name gives no clue to its products and purpose, and its products, which are sold mostly to other manufacturers, are generally unknown to American consumers. The Norton name is often confused with other enterprises such as Norton-Simon, a conglomerate in food, cosmetics, vehicle renting, and other businesses, and with W. W. Norton, the book-publishing firm. A vice-president of a major New York bank once asked Norton's president if the company produced salt.

For a firm so little known, Norton is surprisingly large. In 1980 it employed over twenty-five thousand people in 120 plants in twenty-eight countries. Its $1.28 billion in sales and over $86 million in profits ranked the company 261st among *Fortune*'s list of the 500 largest industrial firms in the United States. Like most big American manufacturing enterprises, Norton is a diversified company, producing a range of goods that include industrial refractories, plastic tubing for sophisticated medical equipment, and drill bits and downhole tools for the oil exploration industry.

Its major product, which was historically responsible for the company's large size and which still accounts for half its total sales, is abrasive materials. These include bonded abrasives—grinding wheels and other shapes composed of natural and manmade abrasive grains cemented together by various clays, resins, and metals; coated abrasives—sandpaper made of abrasive grains glued on a variety of cloth

1

and paper backings; and abrasive grain sold in loose form to polishers, grinders, and other abrasive material manufacturers. Despite their prosaic sound, abrasives are central to the functioning of the world's industrial economy because grinding is a major means of working metal in the twentieth century. Abrasive materials shape, finish, and polish metal for steel and other primary metal industries, for machine tools and other complex producers' goods, and for automobiles and other consumer products industries.

Norton Company is the world's largest producer of grinding materials with 25 percent of the noncommunist market, a share twice that of its nearest competitor. Its size, market, and product qualify Norton for what Robert Averitt has called the "core economy" of the United States—a thousand or so firms in several dozen industries that lead the private sector in sales, profits, and employment and set the pace in innovation, productivity growth, research and development, and labor relations. Or, to put it another way, Norton qualifies as one of 401 global enterprises identified by Alfred Chandler that employ over twenty thousand people and that dominate the leading industries of the free world's economies.[1]

The contrast between the company's relative anonymity and its importance cannot be explained by sudden recent growth. Norton was one of many American industrial firms that grew to size and prominence in the years between 1880 and 1920 and was by 1917 among the 400 largest manufacturing enterprises in the United States. The company also had substantial investments in nonmanufacturing functions resulting from integration backward to mine and process raw materials to produce its own abrasive grain and integration forward to establish a sales department with branch sales offices and warehouses to market its products. By 1920 Norton was already the world's leading supplier of abrasives and had supplemented its worldwide sales and distribution network with plants in Germany, France, Japan, and Canada.

Like so many of the global enterprises that dominate the world's private sector, Norton quickly achieved a leading position, which it has maintained until the present. The process of founding, rapid growth, and maintenance of leadership is the focus of this study. For those readers interested in the Norton story as part of the general business and technological history of the United States, the remainder of this introduction outlines the context and framework for analysis. Those reading Norton's history for its own sake may wish to skip the technical discussion and proceed directly to the account, which begins with chapter 1.

The Framework

Norton Company evolved from the interplay of two types of forces. On the one hand were those special factors that gave Norton its own particular character and traditions, including the circumstances of its creation, the talents, personalities, and values of its founders, its regional setting, and the industry in which it was established. On the other hand were those ingredients that tended to generalize the firm's experience, primarily the technology of its products and production processes and the needs and character of the markets it served, all of which made Norton Company a big industrial enterprise like the many other large manufacturing firms that have dominated the American economy in the twentieth century. The division is neither simple nor mutually exclusive. The processes of particularization and generalization were variously reinforcing, contradictory, and unrelated, and such factors as industrial setting were common to both.

Biography particularizes by definition, and a company history is the biography of a business. The course and character of Norton Company are intimately related to its Yankee and Swedish founders, its Worcester, Massachusetts, and New England location, and its identification with the abrasives industry. Norton was until recently very much a New England enterprise. Six of its seven founders were New England Yankees, and the families of at least three had lived in the region since coming to Massachusetts in the 1620s and 1630s.

The virtues of enterprise, diligence, prudence, and thrift, which long distinguished New England businessmen, were prominent values of the founders, who with their sons and grandsons owned and operated Norton Company for more than seventy-five years. Enterprise had led seventeenth-century Puritan merchants to expand first into fishing and then into foreign trade as they sought markets for the region's exports and exchange for English imports.[2] Diligence meant knowledge and control of one's business not only to collect what was due but to seize opportunity as well. Prudence called for joint ventures and partnerships to reduce risk and for the hiring of offspring to assure trustworthy management. Thrift provided men like Boston's merchant-manufacturer Nathan Appleton with adequate cash reserves for unexpected opportunities and for the unscheduled but inevitable panics and disasters that attended all trade.[3]

Such values were not, of course, unique to New England. Americans' widespread acceptance of work and profit were popularly reflected in Benjamin Franklin's *Poor Richard's Almanac* and carefully documented by such business historians as Stuart Bruchey and Thomas

Cochran.[4] Norton's founders, however, were heirs to the long-standing regional tradition of shrewd Yankee businessmen. These men included the general merchants of the seventeenth century, Nathan Appleton and his Boston Associates of the early nineteenth century, who promoted textile mills in Waltham, Lowell, and Lawrence, Massachusetts, and in Manchester, New Hampshire, and the manufacturers and mechanics who were rapidly developing metal working and machine tool production in the Connecticut and Blackstone River valleys in midcentury.[5]

In numerous New England factory towns during the nineteenth century, producers preached and promulgated their beliefs in a paternalistic effort to establish industrial community, habits, and discipline within their new work force. In Lynn, Massachusetts, growing industrial activity had by the 1820s led rising manufacturers to encourage more stringent application of old values. Established in 1826, the Society in Lynn for the Promotion of Industry, Frugality and Temperance campaigned vigorously for temperance and poor-law and educational reforms, emphasizing self-discipline, productive labor, and repudiation of idleness and waste.[6] Similar efforts were undertaken by the Whitins of Whitinsville, Massachusetts, the Fairbankses of St. Johnsbury, Vermont, and Reed and Barton of Taunton, Massachusetts, among many others.[7]

Located on the Blackstone River, the industrial city of Worcester, where seven partners established the Norton Emery Wheel Company in 1885, reinforced the firm's New England character. Unlike nearby Fall River, Lawrence, and Lowell, Worcester was not a company or single-industry town. With one exception, dozens of small, owner-operated enterprises in a variety of industries—many of them involved in metal working, metal fabrication, and machine building—dominated Worcester manufacturing in the 1880s and continued to do so until the mid–twentieth century. The single exception, the American Steel and Wire Company, was part of U.S. Steel and remained Worcester's largest firm well into the twentieth century. But at the time of Norton's creation and until the merger movement of the 1890s, it, too, was a locally owned and operated enterprise.

Closely allied to the tradition of owner-operation was a definite commitment to owner-control in labor relations and a determined rejection of organized labor. Norton's founders shared these attitudes with contemporary Worcester manufacturers and recruited their work force in an already established industrial city where unionization was weak. Their task was eased by their one Swedish partner, who had close ties to Worcester's Swedish community. Swedes quickly dominated Norton's work force while sharing the founders' values of thrift, diligence, hard work, and antipathy to unions.

An additional link between city and company was the parallel between their fortunes for many decades. Norton grew between the 1880s and 1920s just as industrial Worcester flourished with the rapid growth of the United States as the world's leading manufacturing nation. The maturity and stagnation of the industrial city matched Norton's slow rate of growth and loss of market share between the 1930s and 1960s. The parallel weakens, however, in the last twenty years, as a vigorous Norton Company has expanded, diversified, shed its owner-operation, and acquired a much more national and international outlook.

While Norton Company reflected its location, its history was even more closely intertwined with the abrasives industry as the two grew up together. Like Norton, bonded abrasives were new in the 1880s. Although grinding dates back to primitive man, the development of sophisticated grinding machines and materials for shaping and finishing metal for machinery and mass-produced goods came well after the onset of America's industrial revolution. Like Norton, abrasives production grew rapidly in the twentieth century's first three decades as automobile manufacturing became the nation's leading industry.

Following a familiar pattern, the abrasives business with its dozens of small competing firms in the 1880s matured into an oligopoly by the 1920s when a handful of enterprises led by Norton accounted for most of industry sales, assets, and employment. Basic product and process breakthroughs had been achieved, and future improvements came largely from the research and development departments of Norton and the Carborundum Company, the two largest manufacturers of grinding materials. These firms also established prices, since they were the only companies in the industry that had cost departments to gather and analyze data systematically.

Norton's fortunes were inextricably bound with those of the abrasives business. Company and industry sales and profits plunged in the 1930s depression, soared during World War II, and grew at a decreasing rate in the 1950s and 1960s, eventually falling below the U.S. economy's average rate of growth. Norton's declining market share and lagging profits forced a reevaluation in the 1960s, which led to new marketing techniques, reorganization of its worldwide abrasives operations, and the introduction of a new abrasive grain. More significantly, the company embarked on a new strategy to diversify into more rapidly growing fields such as safety products, plastics, and tools for oil exploration while maintaining its position in the mature abrasives industry.

Whatever Norton's intrinsic interest, the company also has much in common with other large American enterprises, regardless of the industry. The analysis of the firm's evolution—the timing of its founding and rapid growth, the consolidation and maintenance of its power as industry leader, and its recent transformation into a publicly held, diversified, and professionally managed company—is best understood by a comparison with other large manufacturing companies in the United States. The patterns of their experiences suggest the questions and framework for Norton's history. Recent scholarship in business history provides just such a model.[8]

The majority of America's large-scale industrial enterprises appeared between 1880 and 1920. The development of networks of transportation (railroads) and communication (telegraph and telephone) gave dependable, cheap market information and access; rapid urban growth stimulated demand in a society that already led the world in per capita income; and the application of new sources of energy and the development of new methods of metal working generated a continuing supply of technological innovations in process and product. Against this background, large firms arose not only to manufacture but to coordinate the flow of product from raw material processing through manufacturing to distribution. Such multifunctional enterprises succeeded in those industries where the technical complexity of manufacture and product, the volume of distribution, and the need for market service justified the scale of organization and investment necessary for integration.

These firms arose relatively quickly in one of two ways. A minority were vertically integrated through several functions (raw material processing, manufacturing, transportation, and distribution) from the outset. They generally appeared in new industries where the existing distribution network was unable to handle the new product. Classic examples were the meatpackers Swift and Armour, who adapted new refrigeration techniques to process, ship, and distribute frozen meat nationwide.

Most large enterprises, however, resulted from mergers in established industries. These horizontal combinations were efforts to control price and production where new production methods generated excess capacity and increased fixed costs. Early failures—and subsequent government legislation—indicated the futility of attempted monopoly as new entrants with lower overhead provided continuing competition. Where technology and markets allowed, a switch to vertical integration to schedule flows and cut costs proved far more successful, as Standard Oil Company of New Jersey, National Biscuit Company, and many others discovered.

In sum, both types had become vertically integrated firms by World War I. The rapid rise of large, single-industry enterprises, the maturation of their product lines, and the tremendous capital costs of duplication by new entrants generally meant that those industries where the big companies appeared quickly became oligopolies. Professionally trained managers soon replaced owner-operators because of founders' ages, the merger process, and the need for outside capital and financial skills.

Such salaried men differed from owner-operators in that they did not normally own significant shares in the firms they ran. Although owner-managers were not usually professional managers, the two groups were not necessarily mutually exclusive, as Henry Ford II's career indicated. Nor was one group necessarily more able than the other; the term *professional manager* did not mean that owner-operators were amateurs. Salaried administrators have dominated large American industrial enterprises because professional training in colleges, business schools, and business enterprises has historically supplied a more continuous flow of talented, motivated managers than birth and family background have offered.

To manage the multifunctional enterprise, professional managers created highly centralized organizations run by the firm's president along with the heads of various functional departments (manufacturing, sales, transportation, and raw materials processing). They concentrated on organization building to assure the information, product, and cash flows necessary for planning, coordination, appraisal, and profitable operation; on rounding out the product line; and on product and process research and development to cut costs and meet the competition. Frequently, they followed growing sales abroad with overseas plants to hold and expand foreign markets.

Such large, single-industry, multifunctional, multinational enterprises operated by professional managers dominated the American economy until the 1950s and 1960s. Beginning with Du Pont, General Motors, and a few other pioneers before World War II and accelerating rapidly after 1945, however, diversification came to a number of firms, usually following a technology (nitrocellulose from munitions to synthetics at Du Pont and the internal combustion engine from automobiles to diesel locomotives at General Motors) or marketing expertise (such as American Tobacco's expansion from cigarettes into liquors, pet foods, and cereals). Because the highly centralized departmental organization proved ill equipped to handle the diversified firm (Du Pont found it difficult to market nylon, paints, varnishes, and munitions through the same sales network), professional managers created a new decentralized structure. Similar products were grouped into autonomous, fully integrated product divisions, each with a single manager. At the top a general office was organized separately with corporate vice-presidents and staff to supply expertise and guidance to the divisions and to gather information and plan for the future of the enterprise. International operations, which were originally handled in a foreign division, were soon integrated into the decentralized structure as the autonomous product divisions became worldwide product divisions.

The similarity of Norton's experience to the general pattern provides a framework for the analysis of the company's history and suggests the following themes to be developed in the account. First, the timing and rapidity of Norton's rise as a large industrial firm resulted from the growth of the new bonded abrasives industry in the late nineteenth and early twentieth centuries, the need to integrate manufacturing operations backward to improve product quality and assure an adequate supply of abrasive grain by producing new, man-made grains in recently developed electric furnaces, and the necessity of creating a sales department and branch offices staffed with salesmen and demonstrators to educate distributors and customers in the selection and use of the new tool. The continuing application of this philosophy of service and ready supply to meet customer needs in turn necessitated foreign manufacturing plants to satisfy more distant markets.

Second, Norton quickly repeated the experiences of big enterprises in other industries. As the largest company in the abrasives industry, Norton, along with its major competitor, Carborundum, established a pattern of oligopolistic competition in which the leaders developed a full range of abrasives products, including coated abrasives and abrasive grains, set prices, and assumed dominance of product and process innovation in their own research and development departments. To coordinate product and information flows and to administer the new large enterprise, Norton's owner-operators soon established a highly centralized, functionally departmentalized firm and began limited market forecasting.

Third, Norton Company varied from the familiar pattern of American industrial firms by continuing as a privately held, owner-operated enterprise. Family control (which in this case refers to continued operation by descendants of two of the partners) resulted primarily from the careful attention to thrift and cash flow that allowed Norton to finance its own growth. The Worcester tradition of owner-managed firms, the large number of original partners, which provided a pool of potentially talented sons, and the early entry of two partners' sons who grew up with the small enterprise reinforced the opportunity made possible by self-finance and founder-operation. The owners carefully nurtured family control with continued recruitment and training of future candidates and with attentive cultivation of the originally close ties between management and the predominantly Swedish work force. The earlier, informal bonds were institutionalized in a program of labor relations called the Norton Spirit, which formally established in the large firm a paternalistic tradition of owner-management for control and welfare of Norton workers.

Fourth, as owner-management and private control continued with the third generation in the 1940s, 1950s, and 1960s, its burdens became increasingly clear. Continued development of talented family managers grew increasingly difficult. Centralized control in one or two family members encouraged the firm to remain tightly associated with the maturing abrasives industry, reduced opportunities in other industries beyond the capability of family management, and cost Norton the services of talented managers who sought to head their firms. Furthermore, centralized control really covered only the domestic bonded abrasives operations. Foreign plants and domestic coated abrasives manufacturing operated in virtual autonomy, with little monitoring from Worcester.

Fifth, with two exceptions, the forces to change Norton to a publicly held, professionally managed, diversified firm originated from outside the owner-managers and from outside Norton itself. Those changes came not as a result of careful planning but in the ad hoc, opportunistic fashion long characteristic of Norton management. The family firm's limited experience beyond the abrasives field meant a painful trial-and-error process, aggravated by stagnation at Norton and within the abrasives industry and by the coinciding in time of Norton's initial diversification with the great rise of conglomerate mergers (that is, mergers to create a virtual holding company for a number of product divisions unrelated by technology or market and not coordinated by a general office).

Finally, the successful rationalization and completion of diversification reflected the professional managers' clear propensity for planning, order, and system in a decentralized firm with autonomous product divisions. Still, the resulting company is neither a conglomerate nor a diversified enterprise of the Du Pont and General Motors model. Its product divisions share limited common technology and no specific market networks, yet each has been carefully selected to follow a pattern of products of middle-level technology for the industrial market. And while Norton does have a general office at the corporate level, it lacks the large staff for corporate research and marketing typical of the older diversified firms. The Norton Company of 1980, then, reflects several factors at once: the small staff, low overhead, and emphasis on line authority of the thrifty New England family enterprise, the decentralizing influence of conglomerates, and the values of professional managers for an orderly, systematic, controllable operation.

The Structure

Because this study is the biography of an enterprise, the presentation is a chronological one. An organization by functions, with chapters on sales, production, finance, and foreign operation, would obscure the larger issues that fall naturally into four periods or generations. The first was the establishment of the firm and its rise under the founders to a large-scale, integrated enterprise between the 1870s and World War I. The second stage saw the institutionalization of business methods and the administration of the new large company by their sons, who filled out the product line and expanded the firm overseas between the world wars. The challenges of expanding multinationalism, going public, and growth to family ownership and management occupied the third generation after World War II. Finally, in the fourth stage Norton was transformed by professional managers into a modern, diversified, decentralized enterprise in the late 1960s and 1970s.

Periodization avoids a simple narration of facts, for each generation reflects a set of challenges and concerns that identify that period. Furthermore, periodization fits well with the history of a family company. A generational approach parallels the successive layers of management and hence the personalities that dominated and operated the business in each era. The stamp of personalities in top positions played a greater role at Norton than in most large American businesses. Because of the family tie, top Norton executives reached major posts early and held them for two or three decades, a tenure far longer than the five or so years normally served by heads of most large firms.

Of course, the analogy breaks down in the fourth period as salaried professional managers replaced family descendants to operate and control Norton Company. Nevertheless Robert Cushman's fourteen-year tenure as executive vice-president and president spans most of the last era, allowing a continuation of the period approach beyond family management even though the trend toward accelerated turnover at the top will probably eliminate such periodization in the future.

Furthermore, no generation is a perfect fit. Of the seven founders, only four continued in active management throughout the first era, and one of those, Charles Allen, held the presidency through half of the second era. Only two families (the Jeppsons and the Higginses) produced sons to run the company in the second era. Nevertheless, that era unmistakably reflected the leadership of George Jeppson and Aldus Higgins, who assumed control even before Charles Allen's formal retirement. In the third era, John Jeppson's youth prevented a repeat of the Higgins-Jeppson match of the second period, and Ralph Gow paired with Milton Higgins as the first "outsider" to become president until John Jeppson succeeded him. Still, the family character of the company remained unmistakable in Milton Higgins's twenty-year tenure as chief executive officer. And Jeppson's brief term as president served as a transition to the fourth era, today's diversified, multinational, decentralized enterprise under professionally trained managers.

1.

From a Bet on a Bucket of Beer: The New Firm in the New Industry

NORTON COMPANY'S RISE, so typical of many large U.S. industrial firms in its rapidity and timing, took place in two stages: the growth of the successful small enterprise in the new abrasives industry during the last part of the nineteenth century and the mushroom development of the large integrated industrial company in response to new product technology and the demands of the automobile industry during the first two decades of the twentieth century. Success followed the Norton Emery Wheel Company almost from its founding in 1885. The new firm paid steady annual dividends in all but one of its first fifteen years while reinvesting profits to multiply its capital fifteen times to $306,000. By 1900 Norton was the largest company in the industry.

The early prosperity and growth resulted from a combination of factors both within and without the enterprise. The bonded abrasives industry emerged in the 1870s and 1880s with dozens of small competing firms but no large or powerful companies to dominate it with extensive financial resources, market share, or patent control. Norton's predecessor, an adjunct of the F. B. Norton pottery company, provided its successor with a strong position in the industry, excellent location near major markets, superior product technology, and key personnel for production, administration, and marketing.

The 1885 incorporation freed Norton from the constraints of the old pottery firm to meet the growing demands for bonded abrasives in the machine tool and metal-working industries. A new partnership combined a variety of entrepreneurial, administrative, sales, and production skills with a remarkably homogeneous set of values. Together, the partners built Norton's already established position into industry leadership, expanded its product line, and extended its re-

12

gional distribution to national and international scope. Finally, they established a set of values and traditions, including a system of paternalism and owner-management, that characterized the company's labor relations, finance, and operations for most of its history.

The New Market: Grinding Machinery

The modern abrasives industry originated in the last half of the nineteenth century as the industrial revolution stimulated the use of grinding to cut and shape metal. In a broader sense, of course, grinding has long been a valued technique.[1] Abrading, a process of rubbing, tearing, and wearing as well as cutting, dates from prehistoric times. Well before the time of Jesus abrading was extensively used on stones, bones, metal, and gems. Grinding allowed man to shape the hardest substances for his own use, to sharpen tools for better cutting, and to polish or put a fine finish on stones, gems, and metal for ornamental and practical use.

Such sharpening and polishing required only hand tools or simple machines using grinding material formed by nature, and changes in tooling and abrasives were few and slow. Until the nineteenth century, grinding was generally a manual process employing sandstone, a naturally formed composite of quartz crystals bonded with silica and iron oxide. Water and animal power had supplemented human energy in turning sandstone wheels by the fourteenth century, but not until the early sixteenth century did Leonardo da Vinci conceptualize a fully mechanized grinding process—an artificially powered machine that also held the work.[2] Actual construction of machines for metal grinding followed slowly until the nineteenth century, when the use of coal and steam for power and the development of new technology for iron making rapidly expanded the use of metal.

Between 1780 and 1850 grinding machinery appeared in a number of industries. By midcentury machines ground clock parts, gun barrels, spindles for textile machines, and saws, and specialized machinery had evolved for surface, disk, and cylindrical grinding.[3] The real impact of the industrial revolution on grinding and the abrasives industry came after 1870. Until then the grinder's purposes had continued to be sharpening, finishing, and polishing, and in cases such as the draw grinding of gun barrels, the new machines still used grinding wheels of sandstone. But while natural stone and a few simple shapes sufficed for light cuts and polishing, they were inadequate for the increased demand to cut hardened metal parts into precise dimensions. Advances in metallurgy after 1860 and the rapid advent of precision grinding machines called the new abrasives industry into being.

To shape metals in the industrial revolution's early stages, machinists had relied heavily on such machine tools as the lathe, drill, and planer. Each used a single point or edge made of hardened carbon steel to cut iron, steel, and other, softer metals to relatively precise dimensions measured in hundredths of an inch. Although some parts had to be reheated and hardened, with inevitable distortion, their number was limited and they could subsequently be hand-filed to proper shape.

The increased use of hardened parts and the development of new steel alloys outstripped the old process. Nineteenth-century metal workers well knew that adding carbon to and reheating steel produced a "harder" steel that wore more slowly. In 1855 Franz Koller of Austria and in 1868 Robert Mushet of England successfully hardened steel by adding tungsten, and in the next thirty years metallurgists produced new hardened steel alloys with chromium, manganese, and nickel.

Adoption of the new steels was quite rapid. Beginning in the 1870s Samuel Osborn of Sheffield, England, introduced Mushet's special tool steels for the edges and cutters of lathes, planers, and milling machines to workshops around the world, and in the 1890s engineers and armorers employed James Riley's nickel steel for armaments and prime movers. By the century's close, hardened steel was widely used for parts and dies with high stress and wear, including railroad tires, splitting knives and headers in the nail industry, pointing for screw and bolt manufacturers, ball bearings and races for bicycles, and needle bars for sewing machines.[4]

Grinding machines capable of doing precise work and producing light, small parts developed as quickly as metallurgy and the demand for wear-resistant and sometimes interchangeable parts. The rapid pace depended both on the experience with nineteenth-century crude grinding machines already alluded to and on the adoption of *"mechanisms* and *precision . . .* already developed for other machine tools, especially the lathe" (italics in original).[5] In what Nathan Rosenberg has called technological convergence, the high precision, rigid beds, fine crossfeeds, and improved head and tail stocks pioneered for lathes and other refined cutters in the previous fifty years were quickly adapted to grinding machines.[6] In the 1860s and 1870s Charles Moseley at the Nashua Watch Company in Nashua, New Hampshire, and Ambrose Webster of the American Watch Company of Waltham, Massachusetts, built small grinders to supply precise and finely finished watch and clock parts. After contracting to manufacture sewing machines for Willcox and Gibbs in 1858, the Brown and Sharpe Company of Providence, Rhode Island, had to modify lathes into grinding machines to produce precise needle bars, foot bars, shafts, and other hardened parts. The machinery firm patented and sold some thirty such "grinding lathes" in the next few years.[7]

The mechanical inadequacies of the grinding lathe and its inability to do many types of grinding led Brown and Sharpe to design and manufacture a universal grinding machine capable of a wide variety of precision grinding jobs. First advertised in 1875 and demonstrated at the Philadelphia Centennial Exhibition in 1876, the universal grinder was a genuine breakthrough. Henry M. Leland, then a foreman at Brown and Sharpe and later the builder of Cadillac and Lincoln automobiles, thought it "Mr. Brown's greatest achievement," and the historian of grinding machinery argued in 1958 that "the modern machine . . . is still basically the universal grinding machine as Joseph R. Brown conceived it."[8] After the universal grinder demonstrated the ready adaptability of "precision mechanical elements" to grinding machines, Brown and Sharpe and other firms followed in the 1880s and 1890s with a number of specialized precision grinders, including tool and cutter, surface, cylindrical, and internal grinding machines and attachments.[9]

By 1900 the significance of grinding as a metal-working method and of the grinding machine as a precision machine tool was well recognized. Joseph Horner, expert machinist and machine tool historian, wrote in 1902 that "grinding machines have become a highly differentiated class, just as have the milling machines and gear cutters, the operations done on which were also at one time performed on lathe and planer." Horner argued that "the workmanship put into high-class grinders is second to none employed in the construction of machine tools, and it is superior to most." He went on to point out that

> the lathe, planer, shaper, and milling machines are now largely preparatory, and subservient to the work of the grinders . . . No work as it leaves these machines is perfectly accurate, using the term in its shop meaning, and . . . the fine dimensions demanded in high-speed mechanisms are unattainable excepting by corrections following the work of the machines of the cutting-tool types. The emery-wheels supply the place of corrections otherwise effected by hand-work on unhardened surfaces, while on hardened surfaces they produce results which are in some cases otherwise performed by the mutual grinding of cylindrical or conical surfaces.[10]

But Horner quickly reminded his readers that the general adoption of grinding was a quite recent phenomenon and implied that it was part of the emphasis on scientific management, cost cutting, and increased throughput in factory management in the 1880s and 1890s. Two economies, "increased accuracy and time saved, result from the use of grinding machines. And the labour saved is skilled labour, while low-priced labour may in many cases be employed to operate grinding machinery." Although "precision grinding machines" were "not very recent . . . the general extension of their use is." Tool grinders were also "rather old, but their extended employment is on the increase." In fact "improvements and developments have produced what are practically new machines, in recent years, by comparison with their more crude prototypes." As a result "the grinding department of the modern factory is now something entirely distinct from the machine-shop and turnery, instead of being, as of old, a small and subsidiary adjunct of the same."[11]

Important to the pace of development was not only the use of precision grinding on new and harder metals in toolrooms, but the evolution of production grinding for the volume manufacture of metal goods and machinery as well. Although interchangeable parts in metal goods originated with gun manufacture in antebellum America, extensive application for high-level output began in the 1880s. As one historian of technology has recently shown, hand filing and fitting gave way to fully mechanized production of Singer sewing machines in Elizabethport, New Jersey, and of McCormick reapers in Chicago only after 1880.[12] The emerging demand for volume grinding encouraged Norton Company's predecessor to open a branch store in Chicago in the 1880s, and the firm's administrator singled out midwestern farm equipment manufacturers as a major market in 1886.[13]

The New Product and the New Industry: Bonded Abrasives

Despite the improvements in universal and specialized grinding machines, they were still no better than the grinding wheels they used. Though little understood at the time, abrasives in wheels and other forms were actually cutting tools. A grindstone consisted of a bonding agent cementing thousands of abrasive grains which acted as cutting points. When rubbed against metal, wood, or some other material, each point dug, scratched, and cut small amounts, just like the point of a lathe. As the abrasive grains on a stone's surface dulled and wore, they gradually fell away and were replaced by fresh, sharp grains underneath until the stone itself became too small to use.

Determining the proper combination of factors to reduce friction and heat and to increase cutting speed and efficiency, particularly in the metal-working industries, was the challenge for abrasives firms in the last third of the nineteenth century. Expensive, complex new grinding machinery designed to work new and harder metals faster, more precisely, and with less operator skill than had previous cutting machines demanded a wheel with uniform, predictable character to be run at optimum speed. As late as 1885, James Hobart observed that "when a machinist has a job of emery grinding to do, he is pretty apt to sit right down and hate himself."[14] Experience was the only guide for selecting a wheel of the proper grain size, bond type, and hardness and for determining the appropriate speed. The mechanic had to hope that the wheel's cutting properties were uniform around its circumference and throughout its diameter.

Also troublesome was the tendency of wheels to fly apart when unbalanced, when improperly trued and thus with sides not parallel, when inadequately bonded, or when run too fast. Breakage at high speeds (up to 3,000 surface feet per minute in the 1880s) hurtled lethal fragments across the shop. An amateur historian of the industry remembered his grandfather's story of working at a Providence, Rhode Island, screw machine company in 1850 when a wheel burst and "took the head off of a man standing nearby." And although he was a man of great strength and courage, the grandfather feared ever after "a skunk and a grinding wheel."[15]

Given the uncertainties, a Gresham's law of grinding evolved: bad wheels drove out good ones. Mechanics soon learned to hoard good wheels of known character, using them sparingly for the finest and most crucial precision work. Hobart argued that with the foibles of grinding machines and wheels of 1880, the special jobs of grinding should be left to one individual especially skilled at the task. "Emery grinding is just like gear-cutting or carving. Man and machine have got to be in sympathy, and 'both jump together.' "[16]

Although Brown and Sharpe and others brought greater precision and ease of operation to the machine in the 1880s, wheels remained a challenge. Producing wheels in the necessary quantities and varieties and with adequate skill to ensure uniform and predictable character was beyond the abilities of machine shops and metal-working factories. Instead, commercial production appeared in a new industry to satisfy the needs of the new machine tool and the new process of precision grinding.

By midcentury naturally formed abrasives, on which the world had relied since prehistoric times, were clearly inadequate, especially for the task of industrial metal working. The cutting properties of sandstone wheels were neither uniform nor standard. With the exception of gun barrel grinding, they were little used on the grinding machinery developed for the nineteenth-century metal industry. Annual domestic output of grindstones, dominated by the Cleveland Stone Company of Berea, Ohio, grew slowly from $500,000 in 1880 to $581,000 in 1901 as sandstone grinding was largely confined to such traditional tasks as sharpening and edge work, the dry grinding of castings, and the abrading of logs for the pulp paper industry.[17] Buhrstones, once used in large quantities to grind grains, cereals, paints, cements, chemicals, and other nonmetallic products, were largely replaced by the roller system in continuous process mills.

The industry producing small natural stones for hand grinding was a minor exception to this general decline. Composed of novaculite, a fine-grain stone quarried largely in Grafton County, New Hampshire, near Hot Springs, Arkansas, and in Orange County, Indiana, and called whetstones, rubstones, oilstones, and scythestones, these pocket stones were popular with farmers and mechanics for hand sharpening edge tools. By the 1890s, the Pike Company of Pike, New Hampshire, virtually monopolized a domestic market that was less than $200,000.[18]

Although natural stones were largely limited to sharpening and hand work, manmade products grew rapidly after 1870 to meet the need for precise and rapid grinding in the new grinding machines. Such products—abrasive materials taken from nature and bonded artifically—fell into two categories. The first group, called coated abrasives or sandpaper, had a paper or cloth backing to which flint, emery, or garnet were glued. First produced in the United States by the Baeder-Adamson Company of Philadelphia in 1828, coated abrasives were largely consumed by the woodworking, hat, and shoe trades. By 1899 nine firms manufactured products valued at $1,175,000, but their impact on the metal trade and the development of metal-working machinery came largely after 1920 and will be taken up in chapter 4.[19]

The second category was bonded abrasives, wheels and other shapes made of naturally occurring abrasive grains (largely emery and corundum) and bound together artificially with various glues, clays, and gums. These abrasives had a much greater impact on the development of precision and production grinding, especially in the metal-working industries. The first artificial wheels, called composition wheels, were employed on the crude grinding machines developed in the eighteenth and nineteenth centuries. Handmade by mechanics and other users, the wheels had iron or wooden centers sometimes edged with leather. Emery grains were then embedded or glued along the edges.[20] The abrasive layer was neither strong nor deep and the short-lived wheels were best used for light cuts and for sharpening.

Longer lasting, solid emery wheels, henceforth called emery wheels and composed only of the abrasive grain and a bond, provided greater precision. Since emery grains were distributed throughout the wheel, emery wheels, unlike grindstones and composition wheels, could have uniform cutting properties around the edge and across the diameter. Furthermore, the selection and sizing of emery grain, along with more careful control of bond composition and of the bonding process, gave greater predictability and uniformity of action as empirical data grew from manufacture and use.

Such emery wheels first appeared in the early nineteenth century, but commercial production awaited the rise of precision and volume grinding after 1870. In the United States the output of emery wheels quadrupled from $322,022 in 1880 to $1,381,685 by 1899.[21] With no serious patent controls, a ready supply of raw materials, and no major capital requirements, the industry expanded in classic fashion from eleven firms in 1880 to triple that number by 1899, while average (and probably inflated) capitalization per enterprise was less than $50,000 in 1890.[22]

Early manufacturing was largely by hand and required only an oven or kiln, some molds and kettles, and a few simple tools to stir the mix and shape the finished wheels. The Detroit Emery Wheel Company started in Gilbert Hart's kitchen, the Sterling Emery Wheel Company with a single potter, the Waltham Grinding Company in one room of a machine shop, and the American Emery Wheel Company in a second-story loft.[23] Founders included mechanics like Gilbert Hart and Henry Richardson, who had previously made their own wheels in machine shops and watch companies, and potters such as Swen Pulson, experienced in mixing and firing clay bonds.[24]

Their companies clustered largely in the Northeast, especially near the Connecticut and Blackstone River valleys, which was home for the many machinery, machine tool, and metal-working firms they served. Even a notable exception like the Detroit Company was established by Gilbert Hart, a Vermont mechanic who migrated west after the Civil War.[25] The generally shorter moves by such artisans diffused knowledge and contributed to the clustering. The Swedish potter Swen Pulson, who produced his first emery wheel at F. B. Norton's potting shop in Worcester, Massachusetts, in 1873, later helped establish the Sterling Grinding Wheel Company of Sterling, Massachusetts, the Norwich Emery Wheel Works of Norwich, Connecticut, the Springfield Emery Wheel Company of Springfield, Massachusetts, and in 1892 the Abrasive Material Company of Philadelphia.[26]

While the industry at first included a zany variety of bonds and abrasives, relatively stable patterns had appeared by the 1880s. Wheel makers had tried flint, quartz, and garnet, as well as such exotic items

as crushed milk bottles, but they quickly settled on emery and to a
lesser extent corundum, its purer form, after public trials in the 1860s
clearly established emery's overwhelming superiority to sandstone
for grinding metal.[27] Emery—a grey or blue-black rock whose cutting
properties result from its aluminum oxide (corundum) content—was
found in nature as a mechanical mixture with iron oxide, magnatite,
and other impurities. Emery was known to the ancient Greeks but
rarely appeared in a natural stone formation pure and uniform enough
to be shaped like sandstone.

By midcentury emery was readily available to American manufacturers. While emery-bearing rock is common in the world, the relatively few deposits with the purity levels of 60–70 percent corundum
necessary for effective grinding were concentrated in Turkey and on
the Greek island of Naxos. The rock came in ballast (though a limited
amount was shipped as grain) to western Europe and the United
States, where brokers and importers sold it to processors to be crushed,
sized, and sold to wheel manufacturers.[28] Domestic deposits, mined
by the Hampden Emery and Corundum Company near Chester, Massachusetts, were small, and given the superiority of Turkish and Greek
emery, imports usually accounted for at least two thirds of total consumption.[29]

The Hampden Company did have a virtual monopoly, however,
on the supply of corundum, the cutting ingredient in emery. It mined
rock of 80–90 percent purity at Corundum Hill, North Carolina, and
Laurel Creek, Georgia. Competition came only from Indian corundum
imports in the 1890s. With its greater purity, corundum was far superior to emery in cutting and uniformity, but the limited supply and
a higher price (in the 1890s corundum sold for 10¢ a pound when
emery sold for 5¢) meant that corundum usually appeared in wheels
as a mix with emery rather than in its pure form.[30]

Although wheel manufacturers were virtually unanimous in their
choice of abrasives, the selection of bonds was more varied. The New
York Belting and Packing Company began using a vulcanized rubber
bond in 1867, and the Northampton Emery Wheel Company introduced an animal glue binder in that same year. Gilbert Hart's Detroit
Company manufactured wheels with a silicate of soda bond in 1872,
and Henry Richardson's Waltham Emery Wheel Company pioneered
shellac or elastic bonded wheels in 1880.[31]

Such binders ultimately captured only a fragment of the market,
and the dominant bond soon became (and still remains) a mixture of
clays heated until they achieved vitrified or glass form. So prevalent
was the vitrified clay bond that in 1915 veteran manufacturer Walter
Gold estimated that vitrified wheels were 75 percent of the business

and argued that Americans dominated the emery wheel business because Europeans had "only lately" turned to vitrified bonds.[32]

Weaning the New Business: The F. B. Norton Pottery Shop

Further evidence of the vitrified clay bond's importance was the early success of the Norton Emery Wheel Company. Its predecessor, F. B. Norton & Co., was among the first firms to manufacture vitrified clay wheels. The F. B. Norton firm and its successor grew rapidly, and by 1890 the Norton Emery Wheel Company was probably the industry's largest enterprise.

Frank Norton entered the industry by accident and never fully appreciated its potential. Yet by a combination of chance and design, the grinding wheel adjunct to his pottery business established a location, developed a product technology, and attracted personnel crucial to the success of Norton Company and the evolution of the grinding wheel industry.

Frank Norton and Frederick Hancock were partners in a Worcester firm manufacturing varied stoneware items including open and covered pots, beer bottles, pitchers, jars, and jugs when their employees began experimenting with grinding wheels in the 1870s.[33] Both had come to Worcester in 1858 from Bennington, Vermont, where Norton's grandfather, John Norton, had manufactured pottery in the eighteenth century and where John Norton's descendants and the closely related Fenton family continued through the nineteenth century as well-known pottery manufacturers. In Worcester on Water Street Norton and Hancock ran a small family firm employing three of Norton's sons, his son-in-law George Rice, and a few journeymen potters, and by the late 1860s annual sales reached $7,000.

When the depression that followed the crash of 1873 dampened sales, limited production, and reduced the work force, two of Norton's potters tried grinding wheel manufacture for additional income. Peter Van Cleek, an old Dutch potter, mixed glue, emery, and leather findings and shaped them into a wheel that he dried on a stove and then tested (with little success) on the steam engine shaft in the pottery. Van Cleek's work and a Gilbert Hart silicate wheel seen in Boston then stimulated Swen Pulson, one of several Swedish immigrant potters employed at Norton since the 1860s, to experiment further.

According to company legend, Frank Norton bet a bucket of beer that Pulson could not duplicate the Hart wheel. Since Norton was looking for more items to fire in his kiln and since he probably bought the Hart wheel, he may have offered the beer as a prize to Van Cleek, Pulson, or any potter who developed products to supplement his depressed pottery output. At any rate Pulson filched some of Van Cleek's emery, mixed it with some pottery slip clay, and fired three wheels, one of which came from the kiln as a successfully vitrified-bonded emery wheel.[34]

The firm's lack of interest in Pulson's success testified to the product's novelty and as yet unappreciated market potential, as well as to Frank Norton's haphazard involvement with grinding wheels. His partner, Hancock, was firmly committed to potting and opposed to further development, and Pulson's failure rate of 67 percent no doubt dampened Norton's enthusiasm.

For several years Pulson continued to experiment at his own expense in vain attempts to produce and sell a practical product. His many challenges included selecting the right mixture of clays, determining the proper ratio of emery to clay, and deciding on the proper time and temperature for firing the product. He purchased emery at a local hardware store, worked clay and emery mixes at home with a glass bottle and his coffee mill, and fired the results at the Norton kiln. Two emery sticks made for the Winslow Skate Company performed so poorly that Pulson received no payment, and two large wheels made for the same firm cracked in the kiln. In nearby Ashland, Massachusetts, where the Vitrified Emery Wheel Company had struggled unsuccessfully since the 1860s to manufacture first vitrified and later silicate wheels, he contracted in 1875 to sell his technique for $137.50 and his services at $4.10 a day, dependent on a successful demonstration. To ensure proper firing, he invited his brother-in-law John Jeppson, a skilled potter and kiln setter from Taunton, Massachusetts. But the clay bats that supported the wheels melted and ran across the wheels and the kiln. The company terminated the agreement and Pulson returned to Norton.[35]

Pulson's return and the continuing depression eventually persuaded Frank Norton to add the wheel line after all. He bought out the still protesting Hancock in 1876 and patented Pulson's wheel in 1877. When commercial production finally began at the pottery by 1878, the frustrated Pulson had already departed for nearby West Sterling, Massachusetts, where he continued to experiment while making earthenware and flowerpots at Snow and Coolidge, thus beginning his odyssey of technical diffusion noted earlier.[36] To manufacture his grinding wheels, Frank Norton first employed another Swedish potter, Otto Soderberg, and then John Jeppson when Soderberg left for Bangor, Maine.

Norton's hesitant but eventually successful move into commercial production illustrated several important characteristics of the new industry. Manufacturing fell to new people and not to firms like Pike and the Cleveland Stone Company that dominated the production of natural abrasives. The older enterprises had merely quarried and shaped their output. They lacked the manufacturing skills and experience required for the new product, including the proper selection of bond and abrasive, their mixture in correct proportions, and their bonding at proper temperatures.

Furthermore, the new industry's techniques derived largely from potting itself and thus offered an advantage to firms like Norton.[37] The vitrified bond's popularity and success posed no special problems of material supply, for clay mines were numerous and widespread, but both pottery and vitrified grinding wheel manufacture depended on the selection and working of clay. Both relied essentially on manufacture by hand and required considerable skill. In potting, clays had to be mixed to a proper consistency before being thrown or shaped on a potting wheel. In grinding wheel manufacture, Jeppson mixed and stirred emery and clay by hand (later with a wooden paddle) in a large tub and added water and sawdust until the mix felt right. He used a big sugar scoop to transfer the mixture into an iron mold on a plaster bat, and then shaved it to proper dimensions. The shaving, not unlike the shaping done by potters, was in fact performed on a potter's kick wheel until the twentieth century. Jeppson then fired or vitrified the wheels in the Norton kiln along with the firm's pottery products at temperatures of about 2,300° F.

Like the potter, the expert wheel maker needed two major skills in addition to his ability to mix and shape. Crucial to the quality of the final product in each case were kiln setting and firing, skills that Pulson lacked. Temperatures varied widely in nineteenth-century kilns and location helped determine color (vital for sales purposes) and hardness (a major determinant of the wheel's grinding quality). Improperly located wheels failed to bond adequately. Some cracked while others did not heat sufficiently to vitrify the clay. In either case the flawed wheel flew apart at high grinding speeds and could not be sold.

While the use of vitrified bonds directed the Norton Company to a product that accounted for a majority of industry sales, the recruitment of John Jeppson provided for its leadership in that segment. Unlike his brother-in-law Swen, Jeppson was skilled at setting and firing kilns. An accomplished potter, he had emigrated from Hoganas, Sweden, in 1869 and eventually joined Pulson and a few other Swedes at the Norton potting works. After migrating during the 1870s depression in search of work, Jeppson rejoined Pulson at the Snow and Coolidge firm in West Sterling where Pulson presumably taught him wheel-making techniques.[38] When he returned to Norton in 1879, then, probably no one in the United States equaled Jeppson's combination of kiln-setting and firing skills and wheel-manufacturing knowledge.

Furthermore, Jeppson's sober, industrious character complemented his skills to make him even more valuable to F. B. Norton. As Norton's entire wheel department, he worked beyond the firm's normal eleven-hour day and averaged eighty to ninety hours a week. He hand-loaded and carefully located two stacks of wheels for each kiln setting. The Swedish immigrant then fired the kiln with cordwood and worked for twenty-four-hour stretches when handling the ticklish job of burning off a kiln. Jeppson also anticipated the job-shop nature and service requirements of the new product. His son George remembered his father's studying the job for which a wheel was intended, making the needed measurements, manufacturing the wheel, and delivering it. In some cases he hand-carried wheels to Worcester customers, mounted them on machines, and advised on proper speed selection.[39]

While the happy mix of vitrified wheel production and the recruitment of John Jeppson provided F. B. Norton with a superior product, two additional ingredients helped account for the firm's rapid success: its location and the development of a distribution system. The Worcester setting placed Norton close to its raw material sources. Clay mines were scattered throughout the Northeast, and emery could be readily purchased from the Chester mines, Boston importers, and processors like the Washington Emery Mills Company in nearby North Grafton.

For distribution the Worcester address placed Norton in the heart of a city and a region whose metal-working and machine tool manufacturers were the firm's major market. Shortly after the 1876 centennial, *American Machinist* titled Worcester "the machine-tool-building center of the nation."[40] A manufacturing city whose trade and industry grew with the railroad, Worcester's population reached 25,000 by 1860 and then more than quadrupled to 118,000 by 1900. That growth depended on the proliferation of dozens of machine- and metal-manufacturing firms supplying consumers' and producers' goods for America's industrial revolution.

Here Lucius Pond, Parritt Blaisdell, Samuel Hildreth, A. F. Prentice, Fred Reed, E. N. Boynton, and other skilled artisans produced lathes, drills, planers, punches, shears, and gear-cutting machines. Located in Worcester were Washburn and Moen Manufacturing Company (wire manufacturers), Curtis and Marble Machine Company (textile machinery), Crompton and Knowles and its predecessors (loom manufacturing), Bradley Car Works (stagecoaches, railroad and street railway cars), Coes Wrench, Morgan Spring Company, the Worcester Boiler Works, F. E. Reed (lathe manufacturing), and many others.[41]

In addition the city boasted the Worcester Free Institute of Industrial Science (later known as Worcester Polytechnic Institute, Worcester Tech, or WPI), an early vocational college for training mechanics and engineers. Its Washburn Shops provided hands-on training for students while manufacturing and selling a wide variety of machinery, including grinding machines.[42] Within one day's easy travel were Robbins and Lawrence and the machinery companies of Windsor and Springfield, Vermont, in the Connecticut River valley to the north. To the east were the Providence Tool Company and Brown and Sharpe in Providence, Rhode Island; in Hartford, Connecticut, to the south were Pratt and Whitney and the Colt Armory; and to the west lay the Springfield Armory in Springfield, Massachusetts.[43]

What carried Norton wheels beyond John Jeppson's hand delivery in Worcester were the sales efforts of Walter L. Messer. Born in Troy, New York, in 1844, Messer was a traveling merchant who sold grinding wheels and other small items on commission to hardware distributors. In 1880 a chance encounter with Norton wheels so impressed him that Messer became Norton's general sales agent—with immediate results. He set up a distribution network across the industrial Northeast and Midwest, including Harlan Page in Philadelphia, N. F. Patten in Providence, E. M. Drollinger in South Bend, and McIntosh, Good, and Huntington in Cleveland. Norton stores with salaried managers were located in Chicago and New York, and John Sloan was appointed Paris agent for overseas sales which by 1886 were described as "large."[44]

Messer pushed sales with easy terms and an eye for volume accounts to develop the new market. He readily understood the need for service to overcome customer resistance to what was still a new product from an unknown firm. Messer offered a liberal returns policy, amounting to more than 20 percent of wheels shipped. In the grinding industry where wheels were only a minor item compared with capital investment in grinding machines themselves and where the consumable nature of wheels promised reorders and long-running, volume accounts, customers had to be appeased. Buyers could normally return unused wheels, and they expected that the many extra wheels left for trials or sales inducement were also returnable. Primitive knowledge of wheel action and manufacture also necessitated frequent return of wheels that were the wrong size or hardness or that simply did not perform properly for reasons unknown.[45]

Other sales promotion techniques depended on commissions, advertising, and credit. To attract distributors Messer offered large discounts, running as high as 60–70 percent off list price. Loring Richardson, an accountant reviewing the company in 1885, commented that "enormous amounts" had been spent for advertising and introducing the business.[46] Richardson also noted that only 20–25 percent of sales were for cash, that is, on terms of forty to sixty days. The remainder averaged six to seven months and derived largely from long-running open accounts with such large users as machine tool, stove, and agricultural implement firms that made frequent partial payments. "The longest standing accounts, as a rule, produce the most money and profit."[47] Finally, Messer made Norton more attractive by expanding its line. In 1884 he contracted with the Washburn Shops of WPI to sell their output of bench and floorstand grinders and other grinding equipment.[48]

So fundamental were Messer's efforts in establishing Norton that Richardson identified him as "one of the originators of the business."[49] The flood of orders resulting from his sales work began swamping the firm by 1881 and forced rapid, if limited, expansion. The company built another kiln that year to handle the load. To expand production F. B. Norton added other Swedes, including Swen Pulson, Nils Nymberg, John Roslund, and Philip Styffe, and in 1882 appointed John Jeppson superintendent of production.[50] In late 1881 when the office work exceeded Frank Norton's capacity, he hired Charles Allen, a 23-year-old Worcester high school graduate with clerking experience, who was soon handling orders, billing, keeping books, answering inquiries, labeling, and packing in the thriving business.[51]

By 1885 the wheel business had far outstripped the old potting enterprise. Wheel sales in 1882 surpassed $42,000, or 82 percent of total revenue, and although the figures declined slightly in 1883 and 1884, grinding wheels accounted for 79 percent of the firm's business between 1882 and 1884. In that period net income from wheels alone topped $25,000, an annual average larger than the pottery's gross receipts of a few years earlier. Norton sales probably accounted for 10 percent of industry output, making the company one of the industry's largest.[52]

Establishing the New Firm: The Norton Emery Wheel Company

Even more rapid growth awaited different ownership. A new partnership formally signified that control of the growing firm fell to men who saw the potential for the grinding wheel industry and who were willing to supply the capital, time, and effort to exploit that opportunity. They successfully led the growth of the small company to industry leadership by 1900, and they subsequently presided over the rise of the large multinational enterprise by 1920. They established basic values and traditions, many of which characterized the company until private ownership ended in the 1960s and some of which endure to the present.

At first glance it seems odd that Frank Norton decided in 1885 to sell the business for little more than one year's net income (which removed the entire Norton family from the abrasives business, leaving only the name that identifies the enterprise to this day). Yet, in many ways the grinding wheel business had always been Norton in name only. Frank Norton, though not so unalterably opposed to manufacturing grinding wheels as his former partner Frederick Hancock, had never been in the forefront of the business. He had delayed several years before patenting Pulson's work, had entered commercial production hesitantly and in desultory fashion, and had made no effort to keep the talented Pulson. Norton's success was due almost entirely to outsiders, newcomers who recognized the market for the new product and pushed aggressively to develop that market. John Jeppson's continued work to improve bonds and the firing process created a better product; Walter Messer's efforts expanded Norton sales from local to interregional and international scope; and Charles Allen organized the small firm's administration.

Indeed, by 1885 there were really two enterprises sharing the kilns and the Norton name. They occupied opposite ends of the same Water Street building with separate addresses. Early pictures and reminiscences suggest that the work force divided naturally and completely.[53] Frank Norton, his sons, and a few native-born helpers continued to manufacture pottery, while Charles Allen, his close friend John Jeppson, and a few Swedes who had emigrated from Jeppson's hometown in Sweden handled exclusively the grinding wheel business. There were even separate salesmen: Albert Stockwell for pottery and Walter Messer for wheels.

Under such circumstances friction was almost inevitable. The Norton family had for generations practiced the potting craft, and Charles Allen recalled that Frank Norton and his sons "were always more interested in their old trade of pottery than in wheels."[54] As expanding wheel orders competed with pottery for kiln space and promotion of grinding wheels pushed stoneware products out of local Norton advertisements, Stockwell urged Frank Norton to get rid of "this nuisance."[55]

On their part the Jeppson-Allen-Messer triumvirate grew increasingly impatient with Norton's methods. Younger, more ambitious, and more organized than the potter, they thought him slow, sloppy, and shortsighted. Charles Allen remembered years later the "lax" work routine that allowed up to an hour's break in the morning for pipe, beer, and yarns, and John Jeppson told his son George that

The shop divided against itself: the F. B. Norton pottery in the early 1880s.
Pottery workers are on the left and abrasives workers on the right.

Allen's arrival meant he would now be paid regularly.[56] Years later
George Jeppson recalled that Frank Norton had "irregular habits"
and "was a man whom liquid spirits annoyed."[57] Dun and Bradstreet's
Worcester correspondent concurred that Norton had "hab[it]s con-
vivial and rather extravagant" and noted by 1884 that arthritis and
other ailments left him "sick a good deal." The potter's ill health put
the business increasingly in the hands of his "capable Bookkeeper"
and a son. By 1884 hard times compounded Norton's difficulties, for
the firm was long on accounts receivable and short on cash.[58]

   Thus, when Jeppson, Messer, and Allen asked Frank Norton to put
a price on the business in 1884, his ready and generous response of
$10,000 for the entire wheel operation excluding the premises was
hardly surprising. His illness would kill him in two years, and the
firm still carried a $3,000 mortgage from the 1876 purchase of Han-
cock's partnership. Selling a business in which neither he nor his sons
were interested raised cash to pay the mortgage and care for his wife.
Furthermore, while the sales agreement provided that the wheel business could temporarily continue to use the Water Street building and

the pottery kilns, it also presaged the eventual physical separation of the two contending enterprises.

Raising enough cash to pay the $10,000 purchase price and provide working capital was beyond the trio's limited means and forced them to expand the partnership. Neither Jeppson nor Allen had large savings or property holdings. Allen was renting, and although John Jeppson had a generous monthly salary of $75, Mrs. Jeppson still took in sewing to supplement the family income.[59] To raise additional funds, Messer went to Milton Prince Higgins, head of the Washburn Shops.[60] Higgins, who had used Norton wheels for several years and who sold his grinding machinery exclusively through Norton, readily appreciated both the grinding market and the quality of the Norton wheel. He had already sought to purchase the business, and as he told his daughter years later, "we and 'our crew' . . . were just mighty lucky to be around in the beginning of the age. Somebody else would have snapped up the opportunity that grinding wheels offered, if we hadn't."[61]

As a result, the Norton Emery Wheel Company was born in May 1885 after some months' negotiations. Seven partners capitalized the firm at $20,000 (half of which was working capital) in two hundred shares. Milton Higgins joined Jeppson, Allen, and Messer and brought in George I. Alden, his long-time close friend and professor of mechanical engineering at WPI. Either Messer or Higgins approached Fred Harris Daniels, chief engineer and later general superintendent at Washburn and Moen in Worcester, and Daniels and Horace Young, Washburn and Moen's master mechanic who happened to be in Daniel's office at the time, joined the enterprise. When the partners chartered the company on June 20, 1885, Higgins had sixty shares, Walter Messer forty shares, George Alden thirty shares, Horace Young and Fred Daniels twenty shares each, John Jeppson sixteen shares, and Charles Allen fourteen shares.[62]

Of the seven original partners only four directed the Norton Emery Wheel Company in its rise to a large firm. Horace Young and Fred Daniels left the Board of Directors in 1892, and although Daniels returned briefly before his death in 1913, both were content to make profits without determining strategy. Walter Messer left the board even earlier in 1889 and joined with Swen Pulson and distributor Harlan Page to establish the Abrasive Material Company of Philadelphia, the first of several competitors started or aided by Norton alumni.[63] Jeppson and Allen, who as the smallest stockholders were not on the original board, replaced the three departed men, and the team of Higgins, Alden, Allen, and Jeppson then ran the firm for many years.

The founder-managers (left to right): John Jeppson, Charles Allen, Milton Higgins, and George Alden, about 1910.

Teamwork and cooperation rapidly became a Norton hallmark. The company was never a one-man operation. For the founders and their succeeding generations, sharing top management among two, three, or four men blended abilities, values, and interests to establish the firm's course and character. Certainly, the original quartet of top decision makers included varied personalities, talents, and backgrounds as two academics joined the bookkeeper and the immigrant artisan.

President Milton Prince Higgins, an inventor, businessman, and educator, was the most wide-ranging, aggressive, and enterprising of the group.[64] At the Washburn Shops, he had developed pilot valves for a hydraulic elevator that was quite successful until the advent of taller buildings (the hydraulic elevator required a shaft running into the earth equal to the height it traveled) and the improvement of electric elevators. The invention contributed largely to the almost one-million-dollar surplus at the Washburn Shops in 1895, and after leaving WPI in 1896, Higgins and Alden bought the rights and ran the successful Worcester Plunger Elevator Company until subsequently selling out to Otis Elevator Company. Besides the Norton and Plunger Companies, Higgins also successfully launched the Worcester Pressed Steel Company and the Riley Stoker Company.

In addition, Higgins was throughout his life an inveterate supporter of vocational education. He taught at WPI and headed the Washburn Shops for twenty-eight years, served as a consultant at Georgia Tech and at Miller Training School in Crozet, Virginia, helped found Worcester Boys Training School, and proselytized tirelessly for vocational education with shop training.

About his partner and close friend, George I. Alden, less is known. Alden, who joined WPI with Higgins at its founding in 1868 and who left with him in 1896, married Mrs. Higgins's cousin and was a partner in several Higgins ventures.[65] He served as Norton's treasurer from 1885 until 1912 when he succeeded his friend as president after the latter's death. While Higgins constantly bombarded Allen and Jeppson with ideas for new equipment, bonds, or abrasives and fought hard to establish a research laboratory at Norton to test wheels and to follow up on the experiments and ideas that he found in *Scientific American* and other journals, Alden's direct contributions are obscure.

He was a scientist and theoretician rather than an inventor and characteristically was best known in the grinding industry for his "grain-depth-of-cut theory." Published in 1914, the theory employed diagrams and simple trigonometry to explain the relationships of work speed, wheel speed, rate of cut, and wheel wear. His work underpinned long-used empirical rules but had little if any impact on wheel design and manufacture. As president, Alden was far less active than Higgins, and a 1917 organization chart showed the line of authority running through General Manager Allen's office and placed the president's office on the side with no functions and no one reporting to it.

Alden's figurehead presidency confirmed the separation of top officers from administration which obtained from Norton's founding. The company was reminiscent of early nineteenth-century textile firms in New England where the president and treasurer resided in Boston and made weekly visits to rural mills administered by a superintendent.[66] Both Higgins and Alden continued as full-time teachers for eleven years after the 1885 incorporation, and Higgins was active in establishing other firms and in vocational reform after that. Neither had the time, expertise, or knowledge required for daily operation, which Jeppson and Allen continued to direct as they had in Frank Norton's time.

The importance of experienced wheel men was clear from the beginning. Richardson's 1885 review of the business praised Allen's "very clear understanding as to conducting the business on sound business principles" and emphasized John Jeppson's role in taking "proper care" to select the "best materials" and direct "judicious mixture by the experienced hands now employed." And, as we have seen, he argued that Messer's work as salesman had made him one of the business's "originators."[67]

Throughout the industry, direct manufacturing experience was highly valued and even crucial. As a reward for their experience, Jeppson, Allen, and probably Messer were given options for additional shares of stock equal to the number they could purchase outright.[68] Messer was on the original board and Allen, while not a member, served as clerk and attended all the meetings. Messer's departure came only after it was clear that Allen could administer sales. Both Allen and Jeppson went on the board and Allen was formally appointed general manager.

Striking social differences also separated the four men that directed the firm and seemed to split them into two groups. Jeppson and Allen were close friends who called each other Charlie and Jepp and at one time lived across the street from each other.[69] They had worked together since 1881 and had grown up with the business. Alden and Higgins were academics and long-time friends with no direct knowledge of the wheel industry who moved in a social class distinctly apart from Allen and Jeppson. Both were New England Yankees who traced their roots to early colonial settlements. Alden was a descendant of John Alden of Plymouth Colony, while two Higgins ancestors had traveled on the Mayflower and another, Richard Higgins, had settled in Plymouth in 1633. Both came from relatively well-to-do backgrounds. Higgins had graduated from Dartmouth College and Alden from Harvard University.[70] The contrast with Allen, a high school graduate who started as a shoe clerk, and Jeppson, the immigrant Swede, was clear.

More significant for the firm's operation, however, were the qualities the four men shared. Each had a strong personality and respected the others' abilities. Higgins's sons remembered him as "an aggressive man of indomitable will" and little tolerance for error.[71] He and Alden unhesitatingly ended their twenty-eight-year teaching careers at WPI after a dispute with the trustees over the educational value of the Washburn Shops. As treasurer, Alden's reports persistently criticized Messer and presaged his early departure.[72]

Jeppson and Allen were often described as quiet, gentle men, but both had the considerable amount of iron necessary to maintain respect. George Jeppson remembered Allen as "calm, quiet, but always persistent."[73] Allen's ascendancy as general manager over Messer and the salespeople was an early example of his strength. And Jeppson's widespread respect among brawny Swedish workmen rested in no small part on his ability to keep the peace on the factory floor.

Their respect for one another was clearest in their insistence on owner-management, a tradition that endured until the 1960s. Contrary to the practice in nineteenth-century textile mills, both the daily administrators, Jeppson and Allen, and the top executives, Higgins and Alden, decided major questions of strategy and policy on the Board of Directors. Early board minutes indicate few dissenting votes and note on several occasions that no vote was taken until the group was of one mind.[74]

Their ability to agree turned on the partners' extensively shared values. Allen, Higgins, and Alden (and Young and Daniels as well) were New England Yankees who prized success earned by hard, honest work and steady accretion. Higgins's daughter Olive remembered that her father rejected pretense. He preferred "mister" to "professor," and when she asked him to decorate their home, "one of the ugliest houses in Worcester," he told her that "what we *are*" was more important than "what we *have*" (italics in original).[75]

John Jeppson's Swedish background led him to value the same traits. He and many other Swedes in Worcester were ambitious and upwardly mobile. As part owner of Norton, Jeppson was like the many Swedes who established their independence with small manufacturing and service enterprises of their own, including the Worcester Ornamental Iron Works, Johnson Steel and Wire Company, and the O. G. Hedlund Coal Company, as well as numerous groceries, drugstores, and musical instrument shops.[76] His experience as superintendent paralleled many other Worcester Swedes who either rose rapidly out of the laboring ranks to lower level supervisory positions as foremen and assistant foremen at Washburn and Moen and later at Norton Company, or who prospered as skilled workmen. Like the New England Yankees, John Jeppson and other Swedes were a godly people, Protestants who quickly established and supported their own churches while maintaining a long-standing antipathy for Catholics, especially the Irish immigrants. Politically, the Swedes like the Yankees were generally a conservative group who valued social order, joined the Republican party, and supported or tolerated Prohibition.[77]

All four men, then, could work together easily despite different backgrounds, income levels, and social classifications. Like New England merchants in the seventeenth century, they believed that business required careful attention, enterprise with close scrutiny and risk avoidance, and growth by reinvestment while maintaining a strong cash reserve.[78] The classic values of diligence, prudence, and thrift were very much a part of Norton enterprise and could be found in production, labor relations, sales, and finance as well as in the company's strategy. Indeed, they shaped a strategy of owner-control and moderate growth for the small firm and guided the quartet in the rise of the larger enterprise.

New England Enterprise: Production

Enterprise tempered by diligence, control, and care was a Norton hallmark from the outset as the partners relocated in a new plant and worked to standardize their product and manufacturing process. The new plant was in several ways a bold undertaking by the new firm. Representing a $12,000 investment, the two-story building with about 17,000 square feet was the largest abrasives plant in the United States and may have been the first one designed and built for grinding wheel manufacturing. Even more striking was its distant location from central Worcester. Milton Higgins wisely selected Barbers Crossing (later called Greendale), an undeveloped spot at the city's northern edge, which offered space at low cost (one and a half acres for $450) and two railroads for transportation.[79]

But Norton's owners tempered action with caution. At Water Street nearly a year passed before Higgins and Alden persuaded Young and Daniels of the wisdom of the new plant. To protect themselves, the directors advertised for rent what they thought would be unused space and planned to manufacture pottery to keep the two kilns filled. To help hold down the costs, Higgins supplied WPI students to survey the land and design the plant. And the year's delay allowed the firm to virtually self-finance the project. In 1886 the owners forewent a dividend for the first of only two times in Norton history, paid half the $12,000 investment from profits, and still retained a respectable cash reserve. Horace Young supplied an additional $5,000 secured by a real estate mortgage, and W. H. Sawyer, the contractor, accepted a $1,000 note for the remainder.

In fact, the cautious owners underestimated their own needs. Increased sales readily canceled their indebtedness and forced the firm to use the entire building. In April 1887, four months after occupation, Norton started constructing a third kiln, and night work began in May.[80]

The new plant needed only modest mechanization and design to improve the process of production. To replace the bags and barrels of emery grain that cluttered the Water Street shop, bins were de-

New home for the new firm: the first Barbers Crossing plant.

signed with gravity chutes to deliver grain directly to the mixing kettles. Higgins, Young, Daniels, and Oakley J. Walker, who founded the machine shop in 1890, designed or modified simple machinery for the manufacturing process, including a variable speed, electric-powered mixer with wooden blades to replace Water Street's hand-mixing with a tub and paddle.[81] Other innovations included a modified potting wheel to shave grinding wheels, several machines to face or true wheels, and a high-speed tester. Alden and Higgins helped keep the plant abreast of the latest technological advances: electric lights and a dust-collecting system were soon installed. By 1900 the dust collector reportedly recovered some fifty tons of emery per year.

Not all inventions worked, and their failure helped confirm John Jeppson's control of production. Despite Jeppson's objections, Milton Higgins enthusiastically and incautiously insisted on transferring mechanization and other techniques for greater speed and efficiency from metal working to the ceramics industry. Giant fans in the drying rooms worked too fast and cracked the wheels. An attempt to du-

Mixing and pouring.

plicate the bins and chutes for clay storage failed because the pul-
verized clay lumped or bridged and refused to flow. When George
Jeppson banged the chute to dislodge the clay, the powder broke
loose in a rush and covered everyone.[82]

More important than mechanization for wheel quality and increased
sales were the diligent efforts by Superintendent Jeppson and his
Swedish workers to standardize and control the product. Some changes
came with the new plant and firm; others probably dated from Frank
Norton's days as empirical data accumulated. Continuing the potting
domination of wheel manufacturing, Jeppson designed coal-fired,
downdraft kilns for the new plant after studying pottery manufacture
at Trenton, New Jersey, in 1886.[83] The new Lawton or "beehive" kilns
provided more uniform and controllable heat than the old-style wood-
burning, updraft kilns of Water Street. In addition, Jeppson used clay
rings (probably dating from Water Street) to help measure kiln temperatures more accurately. When workers at Water Street realized
that wheels that came saucer-shaped from the kilns broke easily, the
wheel company built machines to true not only the wheel's face or

circumference but its sides as well.[84] Later, at Barbers Crossing, Jeppson went further and tested all wheels at twice their recommended speeds to protect against the hazardous accidents of breakage.

While truing and speed testing largely eliminated the dangers of fracture from manufacture, the major challenge in the 1880s and 1890s continued to be the production of wheels with uniform, predictable action. The factors affecting performance were numerous, some were unknown, and not all were immediately remediable. The variation in the composition and ratio of impurities to aluminum oxide in emery was beyond Norton's control. Like its predecessor, the new company did little crushing and continued to buy processed grain. Scarce and expensive corundum supplied only 5 percent of total grain requirements and was usually mixed with emery, depending on customer order and wheel purpose.[85]

Nevertheless, Jeppson and Allen took all reasonable action to assure raw material quality. The firm shifted from Turkish to Greek to Chester emery and from Georgia to India corundum as deposit compositions varied. Workers carefully cleaned imports of nonabrasive mate-

Truing.

rial, and to get the uniform sizes so important to wheel behavior, they shoveled the grain through screens with wire mesh varying in twenty-one sizes from coarse to fine. By the 1890s the firm also roasted its emery, which for reasons then unknown improved bonding and reduced wheel cracking.[86]

Norton's most important control over wheel behavior stemmed from increased knowledge of bonds and the bonding process. The differing abilities of bonds to hold emery grains in a wheel was common knowledge among wheel manufacturers and users by the 1880s. Several firms, including Tanite, Hart, and Northampton, marketed wheels of soft, medium, and hard grades.[87] Soft wheels were those whose bonds held abrasive grains loosely. Grinding action quickly pulled the emery grains from the wheel and rapidly wore it down. Conversely, in hard wheels the bonds gripped tightly and the wheel eroded slowly.

In response to Loring Richardson's criticism about the high rate of returns and in order to cut costs, Allen and Jeppson began collecting wheels returned for unsatisfactory performance as well as the stubs of successful wheels sent back for duplication. Jeppson soon realized that by diligent work and careful record keeping he could greatly increase predictability of wheel action and refine the crude, three-category grading system into an alphabetical scale ranging from A for softest to Z for hardest. Experimentation with bond mixes, firing time, and kiln setting allowed him to produce a wheel to a given grading standard. As he put it:

> We first made our vitrified wheels to fit the jobs they were to do. They were tailor made for the work they were to do. A record was kept of the grain and hardness sold a customer, and pretty soon . . . it became a natural thing to line up soft to hard on an alphabetical scale. Our first grading standards were successful stubs brought back from satisfied customers. Our vit[rified] bonds were numbered to bring out the desired grades—and finally a set of standards were produced.[88]

Norton's grading system gave the firm a significant advantage over competitors and was a major contributor to sales growth. Although its lettering code and scale were soon copied by other manufacturers, the crucial difference was Norton's continued ability to supply—and resupply—wheels that came closest to meeting users' standards. Throughout its history Norton, like its competitors, has closely guarded the bond formulas so central to wheel behavior. After John Jeppson became superintendent, charge of the mixing department and bond formulas fell to Nils Nymberg, a fellow Hoganas Swede who joined the business in 1881 and was still there over forty years later.

The grading process itself was a skill rather than a secret. Measurement simply consisted of digging a screwdriver-like tool into a wheel's side to "feel" its hardness as compared with the hardness felt in the old wheel stubs that served as grading standards. The grader then reversed the tool and used its wooden handle to rap the wheel. Feel and ring determined hardness and therefore letter grade. Volume orders of the same grain, grade, and size required only the ring test. So critical was grading that until the early 1890s all wheels were classified by Superintendent Jeppson and General Manager Allen before shipping. As the business grew, Jeppson trained another Hoganas Swede, Hjalmar Styffe, to head the one-man grading department. Styffe categorized wheels, trained assistants, and was chief grader for more than forty years.[89]

Despite Norton's efforts to regulate grain, grit, and grade, other influences on wheel action such as speed and proper mounting depended on the education of users by the sales department. Beginning in 1885, however, Jeppson and his associates gathered empirical data, at first in informal testing to solve customers' grinding problems and after 1898 through the Department of Tests, to provide general knowledge and guidelines for wheel behavior.[90]

The Department of Tests, like the mixing and grading departments, was indicative of the shift from shop to factory. When Norton moved to Barbers Crossing in early 1887, a work force of thirteen accompanied the single wagon that held all the equipment. By the mid-1890s the labor force had swollen to more than a hundred and production spilled across several multistory buildings. To handle thousands of orders annually, a small bureaucracy arose in the 1890s, reflecting both an internal need to routinize and specialize for greater control and productivity and an exogenous trend toward scientific factory management.

Rationalization helped improve the company's position. Herbert Dodge was appointed head of a new inspection department to maintain quality. Norton established an order department and employed a ticket or voucher system to schedule and track orders. When Charles Allen wanted tighter control of expenses, he ordered Henry Duckworth to establish a cost department. Duckworth, hired as an office boy from Washburn and Moen, rationalized the ticket system with one item per check and ruled spaces for each department. The quantities of material and labor recorded by departments for each item were then tabulated by the new cost department to calculate primary costs. Duckworth also began allocating overhead costs based on his reading of the new cost-accounting literature written by Frederick W. Taylor and other promoters of scientific management and on careful studies conducted by himself and the cost department.

As the one bonded abrasives firm with a cost department before 1900, only Norton knew the cost of each of its thousands of standard items, and only it could determine rationally the price of the thousands of special orders so characteristic of a job-shop business.[91] Its knowledge of costs and its sales volume soon established Norton's price leadership in bonded abrasives. Expense data also helped the firm focus its cost reduction efforts and increase its market position. By 1899 Duckworth began investigating piecework incentive systems which were installed shortly after the century's turn.[92]

At the same time inventory control forced the creation of a stores department, and Duckworth began scheduling raw material flows to ensure adequate supplies. Indian shellac for elastic wheels had to come in the winter, for it blocked and stuck if shipped in the heat. On the other hand, he had to fill clay bins in the summer because the numerous small operators dug carload lots in the warm weather and lived off the proceeds during the bitter New England winters.[93]

New England Enterprise: Labor Relations

While mechanization, product improvement, and factory management reflected careful and conscious efforts to control costs and gain competitive advantages, labor relations at Norton evolved in an ad hoc fashion because of John Jeppson's personality and his position in Worcester's Swedish community. By the 1880s Jeppson was already a leader, one of the first six Swedes in Worcester and an active participant in Swedish organizations. He was a founding member of a male quartet, the first Swedish organization in Worcester, and as treasurer for the Gethsemane Lutheran Church he raised funds and materials for the building of the first Swedish Lutheran Church in Worcester.[94]

Like many others before and after, he used his position as superintendent to help his own people. While at F. B. Norton, he had hired John Roslund, Nils Nymberg, and other Swedish immigrants, especially those from his hometown of Hoganas, and the pattern continued after the formation of the Norton Emery Wheel Company. Since the Swedes were godly and orderly western Europeans respected for their industry, and because Alden, Higgins, and the other directors left daily operation to Allen and Jeppson, the superintendent had a free hand in the recruitment of factory labor. Allen, who looked upon Jeppson as an older brother or father, willingly assented.

For Allen and the directors the vital result was a strong, stable work force. Muscular, hardworking Swedes were prized in a labor-intensive business that involved much lifting and carrying of heavy wheels.

The beehive kilns, for example, were too small for ready use of block and tackle, and wheels, plaster bats, and sand had to be hand-loaded to get maximum volume per firing.

Furthermore, Norton Company could draw on a ready supply of immigrant Swedes with no recruitment costs to itself. Swedes had migrated to the United States in large numbers after 1840, and a second wave beginning in the 1880s was largely urban bound. Between 1876 and 1910 Worcester's Swedish population swelled from 200 to more than 8,000 as hundreds poured in to work at the rapidly growing Washburn and Moen wire mills. In Norton's early days, John Jeppson could simply recruit among workers who, like himself, were looking for better jobs after first laboring in the mills. Of Norton's 113 twenty-five-year veterans in 1925, fewer than 20 had started their careers at Norton, suggesting that Norton Company was a first job for a small portion of the work force.[95]

Eventually the process developed its own momentum, and a kind of unofficial recruitment extended back to Hoganas. Early employees wrote to brothers, cousins, and friends in Sweden and elsewhere in the United States of the special opportunity for Hoganas Swedes at Worcester's Norton Company. Emil Styffe, for example, was the first of four brothers who joined Norton between 1887 and 1898. Jeppson's position as part owner and superintendent also contributed to Norton's reputation and attraction. One veteran worker later recalled that shortly after the century's turn Norton Company was known in Hoganas as "Jeppson's shop."[96] By 1899, 152 of the firm's 208 employees were Swedes and factory notices appeared in English and Swedish.[97]

What kept the process going and kept Swedes at Norton was their satisfaction with the work. In the factory those jobs associated with the new industry of wheel manufacture were largely Swedish. Swedes held 99 of the 101 positions in the elastic, mixing, shaving, molding, truing, crushing, kiln, power, and emery-milling departments, while native-born Americans appeared in the older, nonabrasive areas of operation such as the machine shop, carpenter shop, and shipping department.[98] In addition, for a select number of Swedes fast growth offered an excellent opportunity for advancement as the Styffes, Nils Nymberg, Carl Ahlstrom, and others filled the increasing ranks of foremen and supervisory personnel in the plant.

Jeppson, sometimes with Allen's support, eased the transition to urban industrial life in a new land. Both helped establish a mutual benefit association, insuring illness, injury, and funeral expenses. The superintendent aided his countrymen in obtaining citizenship papers, and as Worcester's leading Swede, his testimony in court was all the character witness any judge required. He helped them with language

Jeppson's shop: the entire company in 1887. John Jeppson is left of the door-
way. Behind him to his left are Charles Allen and Walter Messer.

problems and cultural adjustments. Edward Anderson still remembered years later that John Jeppson had taught him to tip his hat only
to ladies and not to the men he considered of superior rank.[99] The
superintendent also dragged drunken Swedes home from saloons on
Saturday nights, delivered part of thirsty Swedes' pay directly to their
wives, settled family squabbles, and loaned money to needy workers.[100] He paid Carl Ahlstrom's way to night school and then hired
him as Norton's first apprentice in 1891.[101]

   The plant itself became a focal point for many Swedes as they
established a community in Greendale. Company-sponsored Christmas dinners were major social events and included singing, dancing,
entertainment, and a mix of American and Swedish yule customs.
After the work force grew too large for a dinner, the firm gave a
Christmas turkey to each employee, a tradition still celebrated in
Worcester, and substituted an annual excursion to a nearby park or
lake on June 24, Swedish Midsummer Day. The 1900 outing to Mount
Wachusett transported 375 employees and their families for races, a
baseball game, songs, dances, and marches.[102] A company band headed
by Anders Tahlin played at Christmas parties, picnics, and the dances
or socials that frequently followed Mutual Benefit Society meetings.

   By 1900 the early affiliation that existed between John Jeppson and
his fellow immigrants had evolved into a pattern of paternalistic labor

relations. The benefit society, the outings, and the band were only minor amelioration for long hours (ten or eleven hours daily and half-time on Saturday) and arduous physical labor for daily earnings ranging from $1.50 to $2.25, but even these considerations were attractive by the standards of the time.[103] In 1902 Norton was singled out by *World's Work* as an exceptional example of employer concern for its workers.[104]

The relationship's origins were ad hoc and domestic. Although nineteenth-century visitors to John Jeppson's Hoganas remarked about the favorable treatment of ceramics workers and coal miners in his hometown, Jeppson did not establish the Norton welfare policy by himself.[105] The partners jointly granted piecemeal approval based on their familiarity with similar plans and because of the particular circumstances of Swedes in Greendale.

By the late nineteenth century, many American industrial firms offered some form of corporate welfare, including profit-sharing plans, company housing, libraries, restaurants, club houses, and recreational facilities. Such practices were especially common among rural New England textile manufacturers such as the Howland Mills of Bedford, Massachusetts, and the Ludlow Manufacturing Associates of Ludlow, Massachusetts. The inextricable link between welfarism and paternalism for social regulation and greater productivity can be traced to the early Lowell textile mills where owners required company residence, regular worship, curfews, and abstinence for the recruitment and control of their famous New England mill girls.[106] Worcester's Mechanics Hall, opened in 1857 to educate artisans and inculcate the appropriate values of discipline and industry by lecture and reading, was a civic landmark to the paternal creed.

For Norton's founders the immediate stimulus was the need to recruit a productive work force. Although Swedes readily suited the company's purpose, Greendale was relatively undeveloped and distant from Worcester's original Swedish community. As Norton grew and workers moved near the plant, the company naturally assumed social responsibilities because of Jeppson's ties and because rapid growth outstripped public action. The owners never voted a formal policy but simply accumulated a program for the expanding Greendale Swedish community. In some cases the company sponsored activities directly, such as the summer outing; in others, such as the benefit society, it loaned facilities and encouraged private action by its employees; and in still others it contributed to (and later practically underwrote) local organizations such as the YMCA.

The approach was admirably suited to and quite typical of the partners' methods. The small firm's owners had little need for and less interest in systematic management. Their ad hoc techniques of direct problem solving reduced the need for bureaucracy, held down costs, and kept control tightly centralized. The one exception was Henry Duckworth's financial department. Detailed knowledge of finances and costs were essential not only for market leadership but also for proper monitoring of operations to maintain the centralized owner-operator control that the founders valued so highly.

In the case of labor relations, the ad hoc creation of a paternalistic welfare policy administered largely by Jeppson and Allen meant clear benefits even if they could not be recorded on a balance sheet. Norton had from the very beginning a remarkably stable and loyal work force. In normal times turnover rates were low, and after layoffs in hard times the company often regained valuable, skilled employees like Joel Styffe, Carl Ahlstrom, and Edward Anderson who returned as soon as work was available. In the firm's early days when skills such as wheel grading were rare and bond formulas were highly prized for the advantages they conferred, Jeppson was able to lead the company from shop to factory operation and still retain the confidentiality of manufacturing secrets and pride of workmanship characteristic of craft production.

As an additional advantage, the predominantly Swedish work force seldom challenged the Jeppson-Allen leadership. The Worcester Central Labor Union's effort to establish a union at Norton in 1901 and shorten the ten-hour workday sputtered along for several months until the firm took a stand. When it condemned the organization and refused to rehire several workers fired for union activities, the Swedish workers ignored agitation for a strike and abandoned the alliance.[107] In labor relations as in manufacturing, diligent attention and prudent if small investments paid generous dividends.

New England Enterprise: Marketing

In sales as in production, the Norton Emery Wheel Company grew by careful modification of patterns already established by the F. B. Norton company. Small, inexpensive, consumable products like screws, bolts, drill bits, and other hardware items that went to thousands of customers were normally handled by specialized middlemen, hardware and mill supply jobbers, who bought in bulk and sold in small quantities. For Norton as for many incipient industrial giants, the promotion of a new product, the job-shop nature of its market, and the service and education required for proper application forced the firm to maintain its own sales organization.[108]

As a result, Norton continued to market primarily through distributors served by its own small, traveling sales force, which also contacted major customers directly. By 1888 the company had stores in Chicago and New York and twenty-two distributors located mostly in the midwestern, northeastern, and middle Atlantic states which contained most U.S. manufacturers. As late as 1900 the firm's more than fifty distributors were handled by only four salaried traveling salesmen.[109]

Even more characteristic of the new company was its sales expansion with minimum investment and lowered costs as Charles Allen replaced sales head Walter Messer. Messer's policy of volume at the expense of profit margins and his emphasis on sales over manufacture fitted poorly with his partners' goals and values, as Richardson's comments on high sales costs portended.

Criticism came early. Levi Best, whom Messer had recruited to operate the New York City store, kept poor accounts, confused orders, and failed to cooperate in efforts to reduce returns; his replacement was no better. Treasurer Alden's trip to Chicago in August 1885 uncovered additional slackness. Alden wrote that salesman George Smith had been sent out only 154 days in eleven months and "the rest of his time has been spent here lying about waiting for money and helping in the store."[110] The poorly supervised sales force generated expenses about equal to orders in Chicago in the summer of 1885. When Messer visited the trouble spot, Allen wrote asking "if you could find the time to turn your attention a little toward the expenses as well as sales."[111]

Expenses were never Messer's special interest. Although his $1,500 salary was the firm's highest, he impudently sought a $300 raise. To promote sales he often consigned wheels to distributors like Philadelphia's Harlan Page, pursued an ever-growing trial order policy, and was slow to push collections.[112] Consignment compelled the manufacturer to carry inventory costs rather than having distributors buy stocks, and the generous returns policy only increased those charges. Messer's failure to insist on prompt payment had contributed to a cash flow problem at F. B. Norton, which Allen, Alden, and Higgins determined to resist.

The conflict simmered for several years until Messer left in 1889. Allen centralized bookkeeping in Worcester, closed the New York and Chicago stores, reduced consignments, and sped up distributors' payments. Messer was also piqued when the directors chose to market Milton Higgins's two-dollar wheel dresser instead of his own one-dollar dresser, a small issue that bared the salesman's different approach.[113] The dresser, a simple tool used to clean a wheel's face by scraping away dulled emery grains and embedded bits of metal, was a necessary minor item for any grinding machine operator and was commonly marketed by grinding wheel manufacturers. Messer wanted to sell a cheap dresser at little or no profit to encourage abrasive sales, while his fellow directors insisted on maintaining a profit margin on a higher quality item. As George Alden put it, Norton "could make some money on them but it would ruin the dresser business and take away the profit to sell any lower." He and the other directors refused "to break the price," fearing it would "create further antagonism, which was poor policy."[114]

At the same time the firm joined with other grinding wheel companies for form the Emery Wheel Manufacturers Association and establish price maintenance agreements which Norton publicly announced in its catalog.[115] The decision accorded well with the directors' values and their experience in production rather than sales. Henceforth, as a leading manufacturer Norton would stand for an orderly market. Its goal was to make quality products to be sold at premium prices. Price cutting and price wars the directors associated with fly-by-night firms and shoddy goods.

For Messer the estrangement was virtually complete. His frequent road trips continued to undermine his position since he missed many directors' meetings where policy was discussed and voted. He sold his stock and resigned as director in January 1889, but continued as head salesman. In the following year he refused to submit itemized expenses as Allen requested, was accused of "apparent neglect of duty," and discharged for "unsatisfactory conduct."[116]

To Norton's first head of sales, itemized expenses were the final ignominy. Until the late nineteenth century, merchants and salesmen rather than manufacturers had dominated commerce in America and elsewhere. They supplied credit and market data, organized the trade, and even set product specifications.[117] Trained in the tradition of independent wholesalers and general sales agents, Messer rejected itemized accounts as an attack on his integrity. They were something he had never done and refused to do.

Charles Allen's trip west to fire Messer symbolized his ascendancy as well as the preeminence of production over sales in the firm. Following Messer's departure, Allen's salary rose to $2,100, the company's highest, as he consolidated his hold on sales as well as administration. The savings effected by terminating the branch stores, selling direct to distributors, reducing returns from 20 percent to 10 percent of sales, and eliminating Messer's and Best's salaries allowed Allen to reallocate sales expenses more directly toward merchandising and servicing the product while cutting or at least holding down total costs.

If marketing was subordinate to manufacture and administration, Allen did not neglect its significance. He, like Messer, was careful to see that salesmen were well paid. Veteran George Smith's salary was raised to $1,500 in 1890 and $1,800 in 1892, and in 1895 he was the first employee allowed to buy Norton stock.[118] Whatever advantages the Swedes had in the factory did not extend to the office or the sales force. For such salaried positions which involved direct contact with the trade and the business world, Allen carefully recruited native-born Americans who would not offend any ethnic prejudices. In the 1899 company census there were no Swedes in sales and none in administration outside the plant.[119]

The Norton Emery Wheel Company's catalogs reflected most clearly the directors', and especially Allen's, emphasis on sales service and education. The first catalog carefully apprised the reader of the variety available to him in bonded abrasives. He could select wheels of emery and corundum with ten different faces or shapes, twenty-six grades, and twenty-one grits. Standard wheels came bushed to order in fifteen thicknesses and twenty-three diameters with maximum speeds ranging from 735 rpm for large wheels to 18,000 rpm for the smallest shapes.[120]

In addition to its standard wheels, Norton offered to quote a price on any special order. It even included an extensive line of wheels designed especially for particular grinding machines. The elaborate list of grinding machine model numbers for such firms as Pratt and Whitney, Brown and Sharpe, and Gould and Eberhardt was ample reminder that grinding wheels were classified as consumable accessories. A machine tool company's recommendation to its customers was a valuable way to expand business, and satisfactory wheels often led to repeated reorders. Norton, like other firms, carefully catered to the machine tool firms. Norton salesmen served Brown and Sharpe directly and offered plant tours to their representatives, no small favor when all abrasives manufacturers jealously guarded bonding and process secrets. When machinist Charles H. Norton at Brown and Sharpe redesigned the universal grinding machine and built a special machine to grind the triple cylinders of Westinghouse air brakes, Charles Allen spent days in Providence consulting about grinding wheel behavior and Brown and Sharpe's requirements.[121]

Service took many forms. In catalogs and pamphlets Norton sought to educate customers often bewildered by the intricacies of grinding. It offered charts and rule-of-thumb guidelines for wheel selection and speed. It lectured on wheel safety and illustrated proper wheel-mounting techniques. The job-shop nature of the orders required

Early advertising of the new product and new firm.

much individual investigation by special correspondence. In response to a Jones and Laughlin order, Charles Allen wrote that

> we would like to have you advise us more particularly what kind of work the wheels are to be put to. In making the above we have taken for a basis the $22 \times 3\frac{1}{2}$ wheel sent you April 10th which was coarse being #20 grade but it may be that you will require a finer grade, especially if it is for tools or that class of work. We enclose a few slips for your convenience in ordering and if you will be particular to state the *number of emery* and describe the work you wish to do, we will give your orders all possible attention. (italics in original)[122]

In other cases the customer simply expected Norton to select the correct wheel. David Spencer of Waynesboro, Pennsylvania, wrote for the price of "a very coarse Emery Wheel for grinding soft iron or steel that will not wear away fast and cut like thunder."[123]

The job-shop nature of the grinding wheel industry placed the greatest service burdens on the firm. Variations in grit, grade, size, and shape created more than a million possible combinations among Norton's standard products. These choices, along with customer predilection, the absence of standard machines, and the varied composition of materials to be ground made standardization and large-batch manufacturing nearly impossible, especially for a new industry. A sample of thirty orders in 1891 indicated that twenty-seven wanted only a single item, and of the thirty-three items ordered twenty-one were one of a kind.[124] Norton's response was to stock the world's largest grinding wheel inventory and to carry excess kiln capacity for special orders.[125]

As careful service and better product quality expanded Norton sales, Allen continued to widen sales efforts. The firm advertised extensively in metal, woodworking, glass, and machinery trade magazines as well as in leading industrial and engineering journals, including *Engineering News*, *Engineering Record*, *Iron Age*, and *American Machinist*. The company participated extensively in the expositions so common in the era, including the World's Columbian Exposition at Chicago in 1893, the International Universal Exposition at Paris in 1900, and the Pan American Exposition at Buffalo in 1901. Norton's Columbian exhibit alone included 50,000 wheels (weighing twenty tons) arranged in five emery-wheel towers with two multiwheel arches.[126] When expanded volume among the stove, steel, and implement manufacturers of the Midwest exceeded the ability of its Chicago distributor, the firm reopened its store there in 1897 and the one in New York in 1904.

Increased volume also stimulated greater interest in Norton's foreign trade. Although the company had used John Sloan's Paris agency, most of its overseas sales were handled by exporters buying directly from Norton. In 1891 prosperity and Allen's reorganization of sales led the board to send him to Europe "in the interest of our foreign trade."[127] In two months he negotiated contracts that gave Norton distribution throughout the continent. Buck and Hickman of London purchased $2,000 in wheels, half paid in cash and the remainder in two quarterly installments. The new distributor signed a two-year agreement to sell Norton wheels in England, Scotland, and Wales. To handle continental sales Allen contracted with Schuchardt and Schutte of Germany, perhaps the most prestigious distributor of machine tools in Europe.

Norton's willingness to consign rather than sell $20,000 in wheels testified to its desire to attract the German firm, but the agreement offered the abrasives company a great deal. All sales over $20,000 were for cash, and Schuchardt and Schutte further agreed to market Norton wheels through their outlets in Germany, Austria, Belgium, Sweden, and Russia.[128] The deal firmly established the Worcester company in Europe and made it a major competitor with English and German firms such as Universal and Durschmidt, based largely on American leadership in vitrified wheel manufacturing. And when the crash and depression of 1893 hit the American economy two years later, George Jeppson recalled that only export sales kept Norton profitable. Even in more normal times after the turn of the century, foreign sales were 20–30 percent of gross revenue.[129] The overseas business soon became large enough to justify plants outside the United States, a subject treated fully in chapter 5.

Allen also contributed to sales growth by building on Messer's earlier efforts to establish Norton's leadership and offer a full range of products. Norton began manufacturing shellac- and silicate-bonded wheels for the cutlery industry, wet tool grinding, gear grinding, and saw gumming, as well as oilstones which it distributed through the Pike Company. The first catalog carried a variety of grinding machines and accessories manufactured by the Washburn Shops, Diamond, Barnes and Gould, and Eberhardt, including tool and cutter, bench and floor grinders, dressers, and grinder pedestals. In 1890 at Milton Higgins's urging, Norton employed Oakley S. Walker to head its own machine shop and took a license for Walker's patent to manufacture its own tool and cutter grinder. Walker, who had developed his grinder between 1887 and 1890 while working for Higgins at the Washburn Shops, was a brilliant machine tool man. His tool and cutter grinder and his magnetic chuck were staples for decades. In addition to manufacturing machinery, Walker redesigned Norton's truing machines and other equipment to protect them from the emery dust that pervaded the plant.[130]

New England Enterprise: Management and Finance

Charles Allen's success in sales and administration established him as Norton's chief operating man. Following his successful European trip, the directors made him general manager in 1892, a title he held for more than forty years. The appointment formally recognized Allen as chief administrator and gave him a position equal, if not superior, to Higgins and Alden, the major stockholders.

Prior to that appointment, the division between daily administration and policy making remained cloudy. In theory Jeppson ran the plant, Messer the sales force, and Allen the office, while the directors determined major questions of strategy and investment and approved the administrators' performance. In fact the directors were soon involved in daily questions.[131] George Alden sought to negotiate overseas sales contracts, and because of their expertise, Alden, Young, Daniels, and Higgins all began designing machinery, dust collectors, buildings, and heating, power, and light systems. Soon they tried to prescribe product standards, including recommended wheel speeds.

Director involvement quickly generated conflicts of interest and personality. Higgins felt "slighted" because Alden and Young neglected to consult him about designing exhaust fans. Not only did Higgins and Messer battle over the adoption of a dresser; they also expected the company to purchase their patent rights as well. The president was quite piqued when the directors offered him $75, instead of the $200 he asked, and Messer was unhappy because the firm chose not to market his dresser. Alden missed a European trip at Norton expense when the directors refused to send him as sales representative.[132]

More serious problems resulted from President Higgins's position as head of both Norton and the Washburn Shops. The use of WPI students to survey land and design buildings and a contract making Norton the exclusive agent for Washburn grinding products drew public criticism. An investigating committee composed of WPI trustees, at least some of whom were unfriendly with Higgins and opposed to the Washburn Shops in principle, reported that "the contracts appeared to be all regular, and the prices paid for the work were as large or larger than was had elsewhere."[133] Higgins continued to hold both positions until WPI terminated the shop operation in 1896.

A formal allocation of functional responsibilities among board members failed quickly. Alden persuaded the Board of Directors to create one-man committees for real estate, buildings, motive power, machinery, and selling, each designating a chief responsibility for its director-member. But directors were too often absent when action was required. As Charles Allen wrote Messer about the president and treasurer in Norton's very first month, "they are very busy at the school with examinations etc. and I see little of Higgins and Alden."[134] Three years later the president was away for twelve months while consulting at Georgia Tech. In the absence of the proper director-specialist, another director or, more frequently, Allen and Jeppson had to act.

The final resolution of authority was an informal process. Norton's owners had little interest in viewing management systematically, and they were content to let Messer's departure and Allen's ascendancy settle their immediate problems. Since Daniels and Young no longer served any real function, they left the board in 1892 when Allen joined Higgins, Alden, and John Jeppson (who had replaced Messer in 1889). The ambiguity of Higgins's and Alden's positions remained. As the major shareholders they had been elected and remained the firm's top executives, its president and its treasurer. Yet in fact they executed little and deferred to Allen on most administrative matters, while all four deliberated and voted formally as directors on major issues and firmly established a tradition of active owner-management and highly centralized operation.

Aided by personality and prosperity, the arrangement worked well for the remaining twenty years of Higgins's presidency and for Alden's seven-year succession. Much of the credit goes to Charles Allen as the ideal managerial type who sought cooperation over conflict. The "gentle" but "persistent" general manager handled people very well. As calm, quiet men who had known each other since the firm's days as a pottery, Allen and Jeppson worked together efficiently. Allen listened carefully to the outspoken Higgins and was quite willing to take advice from his talented president. For their part, the shrewd Higgins and his quiet friend Alden learned to accept polite but determined refusals from an able administrator who guided the business to success after success.

By 1900 Norton was the industry's largest and most successful firm. The tiny 1885 enterprise of a dozen men now exceeded two hundred. Sales had doubled, redoubled, and doubled once more to $423,000 giving Norton 30 percent of total bonded abrasives sales. The company turned a profit every year, including 1893, the year of a disastrous panic and depression, and paid dividends annually except 1886 when the firm built its first plant at Barbers Crossing. By 1893 the enterprise had returned over 750 percent on the original $20,000 investment and paid almost one third of the return (240 percent or $48,000) in dividends. In 1894 Norton declared a 400 percent stock dividend at par, increasing the stock to $102,000, and in the next five years it paid out an additional 105 percent on the new capitalization. In 1900 another stock dividend tripled the capital to $306,000.[135]

Indeed, success outran the owners' highest expectations. When Henry Duckworth reported to Treasurer Alden that the previous month's sales had totaled $7,000, the professor, who still owned a cow and peddled milk to his neighbors, made Duckworth recompute the totals. "There isn't demand enough in the whole world to use $7,000 worth of wheels," he insisted until Duckworth convinced him the totals were correct.[136]

The Alden anecdote reflected the prudence and thrift that characterized Norton finance and persisted throughout the small firm's life. While the owners enjoyed large returns, they used their profits cautiously. To hold down costs, neither President Higgins nor Treasurer Alden drew a salary until 1892 when success was assured. As a private, closely held company Norton had no need to water its stock or pay dividends at the expense of reinvestment. In fact the firm's book value consistently understated its real worth and its dividends averaged about 39 percent of profits—very conservative practices in an era noted for railroad booms and industrial mergers.[137] The careful owners kept the rest for reinvestment and cash reserve.

Maintaining a ready cash reserve, a technique typical of their seventeenth- and eighteenth-century merchant forebears, was especially prudent, for fluctuating abrasives sales followed the erratic metal and capital goods industries. In the boom-and-bust business cycle of the nineteenth-century economy, violent and unexpected swings were common. In six of the fifteen years after 1885, sales increased 33 percent or more over the previous year. In five other years, they increased less than 4 percent, including two years of decreased revenues.[138]

In addition to supplying reserves for hard times, the directors' thrift allowed them to finance rapid expansion in the 1890s. By 1889 Norton's growing business forced it to build an addition to the "oversized" plant opened two years earlier, and more additions were made in 1893 and 1897. In 1896 the company built a second plant and within three years had to expand it. In that same decade the firm also added a two-story office building, a power plant, and in 1900 an abrasives plant.[139] Self-finance avoided debt burdens in hard times like the 1893 depression and assured the owners' privacy and independence. They opened their books to no bankers and brought no financial men onto the board. Like the early New England merchants, they kept their own counsel.

New England Enterprise: Liabilities and Assets

Although prudence, diligence, and thrift contributed largely to Norton's success, the firm's cautious policies also had their limitations. In 1896 the owners' determination to stick to what they knew cost the company the services of Oakley Walker and the chance to manufacture his very successful magnetic chuck. Walker had developed the chuck while working in the Norton machine shop.[140] In this case Charles Allen, who knew only abrasives, probably overruled Milton Higgins, the experienced machinist who had recruited Walker in the first place but who was distracted in 1896 by his rancorous parting from WPI and by the establishment of his plunger elevator company. When Norton refused to manufacture his invention, Walker took what was to become an outstanding tool to Bryant Chucking Grinder.

If the Walker opportunity was missed because it fell outside the abrasives industry, much more puzzling was Norton's refusal to invest in the fledgling Carborundum Company, whose new product, a manmade abrasive grain, helped revolutionize grinding and made the new firm Norton's biggest competitor. Edward Acheson began experimenting in the late 1880s with electric arc furnaces which delivered more concentrated energy and higher temperatures than previously possible.[141] When he sent an electric current through a mixture of clay and powdered coke in 1891, he produced hard crystals that scratched glass and, according to Acheson, diamonds. He named the new material carborundum, based on the erroneous conclusion that he had made artificial corundum, the aluminum oxide crystal that was the abrasive in emery and corundum. In fact he soon discovered that his manmade abrasive was actually silicon carbide, a substance even harder than aluminum oxide.

The new product had tremendous significance. For the first time the manufacture of artificial abrasives was commercially feasible. And since carborundum was manmade, its characteristics could be controlled to produce a uniformity of behavior and properties not found in nature. Acheson began commercial production in the Carborundum Company in 1892 at Monongahela, Pennsylvania, marketing the grain as polishing powder to jewelers and manufacturing tiny dental wheels with it. When the first Niagara Falls power plant opened the following year to supply cheap electricity, Acheson quickly decided to relocate his power-intensive operation there.

His search for funds and his efforts to market his new grain sent

Acheson to Norton's owners to whom he offered Carborundum bonds and Carborundum grain at discounts not approved by his own board of directors. In the absence of records, the reasons for the owners' refusal to accept Acheson's offer are conjectural, but they probably turned on several points. Acheson's willingness to undercut the Carborundum board in his own behalf was certainly foreign to Norton's experience. If he betrayed one set of partners, any Norton partnership must always be unstable. Acheson also characteristically underestimated his capital needs. Hundreds of thousands more dollars would be needed in addition to the $50,000 investment, probably exceeding Norton's ability to self-finance.

Furthermore, Norton had no guarantee that it would be Carborundum's sole customer. Acheson thought that only Norton and Carborundum would make wheels but he doubted that his firm would "actually bind itself to such conditions."[142] In fact, the uncertainty was too great. Norton had to invest large sums without the prudent controls and risk reduction that had so characterized its history thus far.

Although the directors judged Carborundum's immediate future correctly, in the long run their misjudgment cost them a major opportunity. After failing to get Norton financing, Acheson turned to investment bankers Richard and Andrew Mellon, who steadily poured funds into the struggling firm until they gained control at the century's turn.[143] Acheson was a better inventor than businessman. He paid little attention to management, and while the company struggled to learn the intricacies of bonding abrasives, he burdened it still further with an expensive foray into coated abrasives.

Despite cheap Niagara power, silicon carbide grain remained expensive, twice the cost of emery, and its applicability was limited.[144] Unlike aluminum oxide, which ground steel and materials of high tensile strength, the hard but brittle silicon carbide worked best on glass, fibrous woods, leather, low-tensile metals, and other relatively soft materials. Carborundum Company's wheels gave Norton little competition until Acheson's departure and a reorganized management under the Mellon-appointed Frank Haskell put the business on its feet after 1901 and rapidly made it the industry's second largest firm. By that time Norton was fortunately able to develop its own artificial abrasive.

Luck was of course an important ingredient in Norton's success. The act of founding had given the firm an excellent product and a superb location. The accidents of recruitment had assembled such talent as Jeppson, Allen, and Messer, and after Messer's departure, Norton happily avoided the potentially crippling loss of the others.

Jeppson lacked the wanderlust that characterized his brother-in-law Swen Pulson, and Allen, whom Acheson tried to recruit as a general manager in 1898, apparently decided that he was incompatible with that erratic genius and stayed with Norton for more than fifty years. In addition, Norton suffered none of the crippling fires that plagued many grinding wheel firms, and it benefited from the absence of large companies and powerful, wealthy entrepreneurs who might have blocked the small company's progress.[145]

Luck was only part of the story, however, for Norton's good fortune was shared by many other firms. Such companies as the Abrasive Material Company, the Vitrified Emery Wheel Company, Sterling Emery Wheel, and numerous others enjoyed early starts and good locations in an open, growing industry without achieving Norton's success. Prosperity resulted largely from a combination of opportunity and enterprise.

The abrasives industry had evolved as a late response to the industrial revolution. In the last half of the nineteenth century, the need to work metal, especially hardened steel and new steel alloys, more quickly and precisely had stimulated the development of both universal and specialized grinding machines. In turn the new machinery required new forms of bonded abrasives, manmade for greater uniformity and predictability.

Of the dozens of firms that entered the new industry, Norton met the demand most successfully. Capitalizing on their excellent Worcester setting, the company's founders represented a remarkable blend of talents and values. Entrepreneurship, the creation of a new enterprise in a new field, was a joint venture that combined scientific knowledge, ceramist's skills, administrative ability, and marketing expertise. Despite their differences, the founders shared a deep commitment to the values of the work ethic—enterprise, prudence, diligence, and thrift—so highly prized in nineteenth-century New England. Implementing those virtues meant the development of policies central to the small company's success in the short run and to the enterprise's character and traditions in the long run.

Such policies provided a fine balance between enterprise and control. Self-finance, large cash reserves, and careful cost analysis assured independence and the ability to respond to new opportunities. Owner-operation and ad hoc, centralized management provided flexibility and held down costs. A paternalistic labor relations program and competitive wages promoted worker productivity and discouraged unions. Special emphasis on product and process along with premium pricing encouraged growth and stability for the firm and the industry. Careful attention to sales service and education along with national and international distribution reinforced the goals of expansion and order.

By 1900 Norton was the tiny but integrated and successful leader of the new bonded abrasives industry. In many ways it closely resembled dozens of small New England firms that appeared in the metal-fabricating and machinery-making industries after 1890 and that became Norton's neighbors and customers. As James Soltow has noted, most were founded by men with technical backgrounds, owner-operated, self-financed, avowedly independent, paternalistic, predicated on a new product or yet unfulfilled need, and located primarily on the basis of founder rather than customer preference.[146] Unlike most of the others, however, Norton predated the rise of huge industrial companies and did not adopt a conscious strategy for success as a little firm among giants. When the opportunity occurred, it became instead a large enterprise based on the character and policies of the small business.

2.

The Rise of the Big Firm

DESPITE ITS GROWTH AND SUCCESS, the Norton Emery Wheel Company at the turn of the century was only the biggest firm in a little industry. The revenue of the entire abrasives industry was smaller than the annual sales of many American enterprises, including the Pennsylvania Railroad, the New York Central Railroad, U.S. Steel, and Standard Oil of New Jersey. Annual abrasives sales were also smaller than those of such recondite industries as the artificial feather and flower, blacking, billiard table, net and seine, lead pencil, and whip businesses. At that time George Jeppson wanted to enter the booming steel industry because abrasives were only "fourth rate fire works."[1]

New technology and rapidly expanding markets brought swift change. As Charles Allen later recalled, "It was when the wonderful automobile came down the pike that grinding got its great impetus."[2] The automobile and subsequently World War I greatly expanded the use of grinding, and this in turn brought forth a number of heavy duty, energy-consuming, specialized machines for production grinding. Plain, internal, cylindrical, and centerless grinders shaped larger parts from increasingly harder metals to finer tolerances with more speed and at less cost.

The new markets and machines vastly increased abrasives consumption, and industry growth in turn made possible Norton Company's rise as a large integrated firm. The expansion of Norton (closely followed by Carborundum Company) and the abrasives business was part of the rise of big enterprise that transformed American industry between 1880 and 1920. In those areas where growing markets and technological developments offered economies of speed and scale, large enterprises arose to coordinate internally the flow of materials from the raw or semiprocessed state through production and distribution to consumers or marketers.[3]

58

The majority grew by merger through horizontal consolidation of producing facilities and then integrated forward into sales and backward toward raw materials. Other big firms, especially in such industries as meatpacking and electrical equipment whose products were new and demanded special services, integrated vertically through internal development. In the areas where they appeared, such large companies quickly dominated their industries, which were characterized by oligopolistic competition among the few big enterprises.

For Norton, industry growth, the rise of the large firm, and the advent of oligopoly included a series of challenges. Rapid market expansion challenged the company to hold and increase its share as such powerful finance capitalists and investment bankers as Charles Flint and the Mellons promoted serious competition. The new potential for production grinding led to major diversification as Norton pioneered the manufacture of plain and cylindrical grinding machines. To meet the demand for heavier cuts to produce rapidly and cheaply finer tolerances in harder metals, Norton began manufacturing artificial abrasives with more uniform and predictable behavior. Artificial abrasives in turn required large investments in the new electric furnace technology and the mastering of electrochemistry. Finally, to assure a steady raw material supply, Norton integrated backward and competed with the giant Aluminum Company of America in bauxite exploration and mining. To counter successfully the greater risk and uncertainty resulting from rapid growth and more capital-intensive investment in new fields, Norton's founders drew on their previous experience, their strong market position, and their New England values.

Expanding Markets: The Automobile and Precision Production Grinding

Grinding remained at the century's turn a relatively restricted field.[4] As late as 1893, Appleton's *Cyclopedia of Applied Mechanics* argued that emery wheels were necessary but costly substitutes for other steel-cutting tools when working edges and smoothing surfaces.[5] Grinding machines remained light and small as their primary tasks were finishing cuts on small parts after the lathe's capability had been exhausted. Achieving tolerances of .001 inch on frail machines required all the experienced machinist's skill and artistry. Charles H. Norton, who was to join the Norton partners, recalled that at Brown and Sharpe "every workman could not grind plugs. You have got to select the artist and the artist studies his speed. He does it unconsciously, he looks after all those things, and he learns how to grind; he studies the depth of cut."[6]

In fact, the grinding machine was little more than an extension of the lathe. To work a metal piece to a .001-inch tolerance, a lathe operator turned the part slowly and smoothly to about .002 inch. He then took it to the grinder for a final light cut or "refining finish," after carefully tapping the slide "just right" and truing the face of his narrow wheel to a sharp edge similar to the cutting point of a lathe. Precision to .001 inch required such expertise and time that it was practical only for "very slow" tool work and a "very limited line of machine parts." Precision grinding was also restricted to pieces with $\frac{1}{2}$-inch to $1\frac{1}{2}$-inch diameters and 6-inch to 10-inch lengths (though Charles Norton conceded a 3-foot maximum), which the frail machines could handle.[7]

The pace and cost of precision grinding, then, was ill-suited to volume production. As noted in the previous chapter, pre-1900 production grinding concentrated largely on such tasks as finishing sewing machine needle bars, polishing stove parts, and putting edges on agricultural implements. Precision production machinery for grinding hardened bicycle ball bearings and bearing races was not fully developed until the late 1890s, and even those machines were confined to light parts.[8]

In industries such as railroading, where heavy precision grinding of car wheels and car axles might have come earlier, its development was delayed by industry tradition, mechanics' conservatism, and an unfounded fear that emery particles would contaminate the metal. Charles Norton remembered that except for machine shops, railroads were "the only markets for grinding machines in those days" and recalled that he toured railroad shops in 1900 when designing his first heavy production plain grinder.[9] But the promise always exceeded actual sales, since railroad men rejected Norton's argument that using grinding machines only for fine work cost time and money.

The real development of precision production grinding and the consequent expansion of the abrasives industry stemmed from a new product and a new industry. For its manufacturers the automobile and its internal combustion engine posed an unprecedented challenge in metal working and assembly. Its parts were more numerous, heavier, and larger than the parts of sewing machines, bicycles, and agricultural machinery. To withstand heat and wear in the engine and drive train, auto manufacturers used more pieces composed of hardened steel alloys—including carbon, tungsten, nickel, chromium, and vanadium steels. Precision assumed a new meaning. Standard tolerances reached .00025 inch in volume production, instead of the .01 to .001 inch that had previously sufficed.[10]

The challenge was commercial as well as mechanical. As Henry

Ford and William C. Durant soon made clear, the automotive industry's success required volume production to combine low cost and
dependability. That formula made the auto business the largest industry in the United States within twenty-five years. In the words of
a recent historian, "By 1925 an industry that had barely existed in
1900 ranked first in the value of its product, the cost of its materials,
the volume added to manufacture, and wages paid. Moreover it became overnight a major market for steel, rubber, plate glass, aluminum, nickel, tin, copper, felt, leather, paint, and other products."[11]

The relationship of the automobile and production grinding was
symbiotic. The new industry's rapid growth established precision
grinding as a standard production method in U.S. metal-working
plants, and in turn precision production grinding was a necessary
condition for the new industry's success. A leading historian of technology explained that "the grinding machine in this form [as a heavy
production machine] became indispensable to the emerging automobile industry because it provided the only technique, at this time,
of precision machining of the strong, light alloy steels which played
such a prominent part in automobile components."[12] Only grinding
could produce gears, brake drums, pistons, piston pins, piston rings,
cylinder blocks, crankshafts, connecting rods, camshafts, ball bearings, steering knuckles, axles, and valves to precise tolerances from
hardened metals quickly and cheaply enough to permit volume production. As Henry Ford reputedly put it in 1920: "The abrasive processes are basically responsible for our ability to produce cars to sell
for less than a thousand dollars. Were it not for these processes these
same cars would cost at least five thousand dollars, if indeed they
could be made at all."[13]

In turn the auto industry vastly expanded the field for abrasives
and Norton Company's sales. It soon became Norton's major customer, and the firm located a store in Detroit in 1919 to supplement
a branch sales office opened early in the century. A Norton publication
estimated that by 1927 grinding helped shape 95 percent of the auto's
moving parts, while higher speeds, wider wheels, and harder metals
increased abrasives consumption. Production grinding techniques pioneered or popularized in auto plants soon spilled into other industries, including the manufacture of trucks, airplanes, and tractors as
well as reaping, harvesting, threshing, and other agricultural machinery. By 1927 in the airline industry alone, nearly a hundred parts
required precision grinding.[14]

World War I accelerated dissemination of new grinding techniques
and abrasives consumption. Production grinding helped expand output of internal combustion engines for military purposes—tanks, air-

planes, and other vehicles—and of agricultural machinery for food production. By 1916 form grinding—the use of wide shaped wheels for single or plunge-cut grinding in automotive manufacture—was adapted to the manufacture of shrapnel, shells, and rifle barrels. With European sources of hardened steel alloys cut off or diminished, U.S. production soared. By 1919 the former importer was a net exporter of ferrotungsten, ferromanganese, and ferrosilicon.[15] In response to the new techniques and expanded high-speed metal working, grinding wheel sales doubled between 1914 and 1918.[16] Wartime demand capped twenty years of the industry's most rapid growth and carried output to a much higher level for the postwar era. Bonded abrasives production increased more than twenty times from $1.3 million in 1899 to more than $30 million in 1919, while employment grew more than 1,000 percent, energy consumption more than 1,300 percent, and value added more than 2,100 percent over the 1899 figures.[17]

Finally, both the automobile industry and the war sped the growth of the American machine tool industry, always a significant user of abrasives. Most important for abrasives consumption was the development of specialized production grinding machines between 1900 and 1925 in response to the automotive industry's needs. By 1905 James Heald had established a plant in Worcester and had begun manufacturing internal grinding machines, first for piston rings and later for cylinders. In the same year the Landis Tool Company began marketing auto crankshaft grinders and machines to grind rolls for the sheet steel mills that produced steel for auto bodies. And by the early 1920s L. R. Heim and the Cincinnati Milling Machinery Company developed centerless grinders, which rotated the work held between grinding and regulating wheels without independent support. The new machines were soon adapted for grinding valve stems, push rods, and piston pins.[18]

Expanding Markets and Enterprise: The Norton Grinding Machine Company

Norton's founders were promoters as well as beneficiaries of production grinding. Beginning in 1900 they joined with Charles H. Norton (who was unrelated to Frank Norton) to establish the Norton Grinding Company and to pioneer the development of precision production grinding. Charles Norton was a veteran machinist whose experience in the previous fifteen years had convinced him of the need for and the practicality of production grinding. Partnership with the Norton people offered the chance to implement his ideas, while for Norton Company the new firm was a logical means to expand its abrasives markets.

Yet despite the logical fit, entering the machine tool business was both a departure and a challenge for Norton's owners. Four years earlier the company had refused to manufacture Oakley Walker's magnetic chuck and had confined its machine production to small, simple bench, floor, and tool and cutter grinders. The machine shop had only a lathe and a few other simple machine tools and lacked a force of trained, experienced mechanics. Furthermore, the partnership with Charles Norton came at his, not Norton Company's, instigation. Consistent with their previous prudence and concentration on the abrasives business, the founders gingerly accepted what seemed to be a very risky proposition.

Risk stemmed from Charles Norton's radical ideas and not from any lack of expertise and experience. Born in Connecticut in 1851, Norton had trained in local machine shops and joined his father and uncle at the Seth Thomas Clock Company in 1866, where he later became superintendent of machinery.[19] After coming to Brown and Sharpe in 1886, he had redesigned Brown's universal grinder into a more rigid, dependable machine, added an internal grinding attachment, and then developed a special machine to grind triple cylinders for Westinghouse air brakes. In 1890 he teamed with Henry M. Leland, former head of Brown and Sharpe's department for manufacturing Willcox and Gibbs sewing machines, to design and build machine tools at Leland and Faulconer before returning to Brown and Sharpe in 1896.

By the 1890s his know-how led Charles Norton to begin advocating construction of a production grinder. The new machine was to be a sharp departure from past practice: it embodied the principles that opened the field for inexpensive, high-volume production from a precision grinder, and it eventually established Norton as the father of precision production grinding. He wished to transform the light, spindly grinder of the late-nineteenth-century toolroom into a large, heavy production machine for the factory floor. As he put it, he wanted *"more investment* for [a] machine to utilize *more power* during a *shorter period of time* . . . in order to secure the product in a *shorter time for labor"* (italics in original).[20]

Norton was very much a man of his time, and his new machine reflected broadly the principles of scientific management, mechanization, and economies of speed so popular among American engineers and factory managers in the late nineteenth and early twentieth centuries. What he proposed would reduce the emphasis on individual skill and judgment in grinding and build those qualities into a more capital-intensive machine. Norton recalled that at Brown and Sharpe from "1877 until the birth of Norton Plain Cylindrical Grinding Machines in 1900, cylindrical grinding was understood to be a method of securing a greater degree of refinement than could be secured with the same labor cost by the older methods [for instance, hand filing], and by many mechanics it was regarded as useful only in cases where unusual refinement was necessary, and especially for the working of hardened pieces."[21]

After returning to Brown and Sharpe in 1896, Norton designed a plain grinding machine free of those limitations. To handle big parts accurately he planned a heavy, three-point base with rigid, steady rests to support the work. To perform faster, deeper cuts with the grinding wheel, the machine required fifteen horsepower instead of the two or three horsepower currently used. To further speed the operation he advocated wider wheels with a faster work traverse. A wheel with a 2-inch face would replace the $\frac{1}{8}$-inch to $\frac{1}{2}$-inch wheels customarily used. Followed to their logical conclusion, wider wheels eventually led to single or plunge-cut grinding in which the wheel face equals the length of the area to be ground. To obtain the necessary precision, Norton figured that "if a machine was heavy enough, and the mechanism was heavy enough, we would make an actual accurate micrometer out of the machine itself, and when the operator moved the index .00025 it actually reduced the piece .00025."[22]

In the late 1890s, however, the potential for production grinding remained largely in Norton's head. At Leland and Faulconer his ideas received no support, and he left after a dispute over a milling machine. Efforts to find financial backing for his own firm failed during the depression of 1894 and 1895. And at Brown and Sharpe after 1896 his plans for a production grinder sparked refusal along with ridicule, lectures, and predictions that "a lot of dire things would happen." His proposals for wide wheels and plunge-cut grinding "nearly caused a riot." Years later he bitterly recalled the scornful response when his promotion of a heavy precision machine challenged the Brown and Sharpe assumption that only "lightness" and "small, beautifully made mechanisms" could produce accuracy:

> Why! Mr. Norton, consider the fact that a grinding *wheel is so delicate,* its cutting particles so microscopic, Why! You can never make a grinding machine a metal removing tool . . . *The grinding machine is a Delicate tool for Delicate refining* work. Why! Mr. Norton, machines so heavy as you suggest to remove stock like that, would be so clumsy that you could never adjust them delicately enough to size nearer than many thousandths from the desired size. (italics in original)[23]

While Charles Norton's uncorrected reminiscences are the sole evidence for the opposition at Brown and Sharpe, his repeated proselytizing and debates in such journals as *Iron Age* and *American Machinist* in the late 1890s and early 1900s suggest that the resistance was real enough. The opposition within the machine tool industry forced him to look at grinding wheel companies as the next candidate for partnership, and the Norton Emery Wheel Company, as the industry's largest wheel manufacturer and a producer of some grinding machinery, was a logical choice. Its Worcester location was close to Providence and, as noted earlier, was in the center of the northeastern tool, machinery, and metal-working firms to which Norton would seek to market his grinders.

As another and perhaps the most important attraction, Charles Norton had a long-time personal tie with the Norton Emery Wheel Company. Charles Allen and other Norton people had cooperated with him for more than a decade to improve grinding. Allen had taught him the importance of wheel grades, guided him in grit selection, and supplied him with information on the effect of bonds, speeds, and balancing on grinding wheel action. Charles Norton even credited Allen's work on wheel selection as an inspiration for his concept of direct grinding from rough forging.[24]

Although Norton Company's Worcester location and diligent customer service had paid an unanticipated dividend by attracting Charles Norton, the magnitude of the dividend was doubtful in 1900. With their typical prudence, the founders agreed to partnership in a new enterprise only after considerable discussion. Competition with Brown and Sharpe threatened the fine relationship with a respected machine tool firm and a valued wheel customer. Charles Norton delayed his move twice because of "the good will of Brown & Sharpe, [and] the acquaintance between the two concerns."[25]

The long-standing Charles Allen–Charles Norton friendship was the key to Norton Company's acceptance. The inventor's ability to approach his old friend directly with his proposal of partnership helped ease any opposition from the man who had been chief administrator when the firm refused to manufacture Oakley Walker's grinder and who had always focused Norton Emery Wheel Company's energies on the abrasives business.

Of the remaining three directors, Norton's new machine most intrigued Milton Prince Higgins, the major stockholder and the company president. Unlike Jeppson and Allen, the well-read and inquisitive Higgins had considerable experience outside the bonded abrasives industry and was more attentive and receptive to opportunities in other areas. He had been building grinders and other machinery since his appointment as head of the Washburn Shops in 1868 and had sponsored Walker's work on tool and cutter grinders at the Shops. Higgins's interest in the new venture induced him to join Charles Norton in visits to railroad shops where the two surveyed the market and determined proper machine dimensions. One source even credits Higgins with supplying the start-up funds for the new company.[26]

For Allen, Higgins, Alden, and Jeppson there were of course other considerations. Charles Norton had a tremendous reputation. According to the *American Engineer and Railroad Journal*, he was "an acknowledged authority upon the subject of machine grinding," well known for his work at Brown and Sharpe and for his frequent publications in *American Machinist, Iron Age, Engineering Record*, and other journals.[27] As already noted, his machine and the development of production grinding promised to increase considerably the market for grinding wheels. In addition, the previous Norton-Allen cooperation suggested that preeminence in grinding machine engineering was closely tied to better understanding wheel behavior and to an improved product.

Partnership was also facilitated because Charles Norton shared the New England background and values that characterized the Norton Emery Wheel Company's owners. He was New England born and, like Alden and Higgins, valued the shop culture with its hands-on experience. Like the Norton founders, he was a Republican with a strong religious sense who valued continued progress in an orderly society. He prided himself as an engineer who worked to discover exact truth or "God's immutable laws" and to create "the wonders of our present civilization."[28] Such progress met the world's material needs and encouraged art, education, and refinement for mankind's better side.

Shared values were most evident in starting the new venture. The founders' thrifty policy of retaining earnings provided a large surplus to finance the infant firm. By 1909 the Norton Emery Wheel Company had loaned it more than $263,000 in cash, equipment, and services.[29] The original partners prudently took all possible means to reduce the initial cost and risks of the new enterprise. They chartered it in 1900 as a separate entity, called Norton Grinding Company, to avoid compromising the wheel company, and each of the five partners in the new firm—Alden, Allen, Jeppson, Higgins, and Norton—shared equally in the $10,000 stock that capitalized the enterprise.[30]

Cost cutting was evident in both production and sales. The directors located the new operation in the basement of one of the wheel company's plants and built subsequent mills near the wheel operation where they could be salvaged if the machine company failed. Job work helped defray expenses and the owners starved the fledgling firm for equipment. When removing his first machine from the basement required a whole day, Charles Norton fumed that "where I come from they could do this in five minutes."[31] Sales literature and distribution were handled through existing Norton Emery Wheel Company distributors, and at first prospective customers examined machines at the Norton Grinding Company plant or Charles Norton himself diligently sold machines and supervised installation.

The double challenge of promoting production grinding and a new grinder was difficult despite the machine's excellent qualities. By 1901 Charles Norton had designed several models, and he assembled two machines from pattern pieces made in Worcester shops. As advertised in the Norton Emery Wheel Company catalog, the biggest model held work 18 inches in diameter and 8 feet long on dead centers. The 9,500-pound machine rested on a three-point base with rigid steady rests to allow precision grinding of long, frail pieces without springing. The automatic micrometer cross-feed could handle pieces up to 1,200 pounds with accuracy to .00025 inch—half the diameter of human hair and quadruple the previous .001-inch standard. The machine featured speed and flexibility. The work could move the width of the 2-inch wheel face in one work revolution instead of the customary .01 to .1 inch, which allowed rough grinding at the rate of six to twelve feeds per inch rather than the normal sixty to one hundred feeds per inch. Norton offered eight work speeds, six wheel speeds, and sixteen table speeds, each changeable independently.[32]

The new Norton plain grinder was a genuine production machine capable of high-volume, rapid, and precise metal working never be-

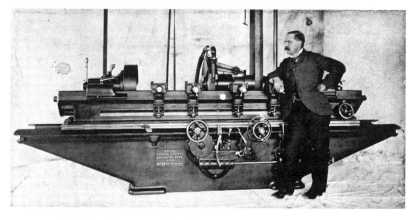

Charles Norton and his first production grinder, 1901.

fore achieved in manufacturing. As Charles Norton later remarked, the grinder was now a true "metal cutting tool" and the lathe a "roughing tool only." He explained that economical operation now permitted a lathe operator to take a quick, rough cut from $\frac{1}{32}$ to $\frac{1}{10}$ inch and the grinder would take the final sizing cut to .00025 inch. Using the new machine and the new technique increased the metal removal rate from $\frac{1}{16}$ cubic inch to 1 cubic inch per minute. It reduced the cutting time for locomotive piston rods from five or six hours to one and one-half hours, for hydraulic cotton press plungers from "several hours" to ninety minutes, and for piston rods from seventy-five to fourteen minutes. As machinist Joseph Horner put it, "The Norton grinder combines the generally antagonistic qualities of reducing time and cost of labour, and giving great accuracy."[33]

Novelty and cost, however, made marketing difficult. A year passed before Charles Norton sold his first machine, and total orders for 1901 were only sixteen machines. As was often the case, potential users were fearful of, ignorant of, or slow to recognize the new product's possibilities, and marketing the innovation fell to its developer.[34] As his own chief demonstrator and salesman in the first few years, Norton found that many manufacutrers took only a shortsighted look at initial capital cost rather than a more considered look at the potential economies in total production cost.

> I had great difficulty in inducing the listener to wait until he learned about the virtues of the machine and its value before I told him the price. He would continually interrupt me and ask what this machine cost and finally when I had talked about other things as long as it was possible and was obliged to name the price—when he heard the price I simply heard a long, sharp whistle, with the remark that $2500 didn't grow on every bush and no one could ever make a grinding machine costing $2500 profitable.[35]

Conservatism among manufacturers and machinists was especially disheartening. Early grinder sales included such metal-working firms as Hoe Rotary Press, the Draper Machine Tool Company, the Ingersoll Sergeant Drill Company, and Westinghouse Electric and Manufacturing Company, but none went to railroad shops as originally planned.[36] Even after Norton designed special grinder attachments for car wheels and car axles, railroad sales were slow. As late as 1926 turning on a lathe accounted for twice as much railroad repair work as did grinding, and much of the grinding was light, off-hand work done at bench and floorstand grinders. And in many plants in and out of the railroad industry, veteran machinists obdurately continued to depend on the lathe on which they had been trained.[37]

Opposition from the shop and factory floor stemmed as well from the machine's impact and Charles Norton's personality. Because Norton had built his "brain work" into the machine, the ability and judgment required from the operator was correspondingly reduced.[38] The trend continued as Norton added automatic feeds, automatic wheel balance, and automatic steady rests. As he and other machine designers simplified and automated machines, they inevitably reduced operators from skilled machinists to semiskilled machine tenders. The shift was an essential part of the rise of scientific management and mass production to reduce factory costs, and machinists and their organizations not unnaturally opposed the changes.

Norton aggravated the problem with his own impatient, overbearing approach. George Jeppson, a son of John Jeppson and later head of wheel production, called him "a rather difficult man to get along with," and his office boy remembered him as a tough taskmaster.[39] Norton publicly argued that labor movements were ignorant of the "real laws of progress and of growth in the Mechanical World" and constantly sought "the thinking mechanic" like himself who found satisfaction in fine work.[40] As a result, accidents, stupidity, and outright sabotage dogged his efforts. When he installed his triple cylinder grinder at Westinghouse in 1886, workers tampered with the machine and substituted inferior wheels. His early plain grinders suffered from being operated at the wrong speeds with too little coolant and improperly trued wheels.[41]

Conservatism, ignorance, and oppositon, however, only slightly slowed the introduction of production grinding and the Norton grinder. The inventor promoted his machine and production grinding in demonstrations, speeches to the National Metal Trades Association, and numerous articles in *American Machinist* and other engineering periodicals. The advent of high-speed steel and the Taylor-White high-speed lathe tool complemented the plain grinder. The Taylor-White machine was designed for rapid, rough cutting of the new tungsten-steel alloy manufactured to hold its temper despite the heat generated by high-speed turning. High-speed grinding to finish the work followed naturally and economically.[42]

Norton also had considerable success in Europe. Three trips to England and the continent between 1902 and 1908 effectively demonstrated the grinder's capability and boosted sales. In London, after the inventor had ground a bar from rough steel to fit precisely through an onlooker's ring, Norton received orders for seven machines. In Germany a demonstration that the Kaiser judged flawless (*tadellos*) preceded a "considerable amount" of orders and "set the shop to work again."[43] The German market soon accounted for 18 percent of sales.[44]

Modest success for the Norton Grinding Company paralleled the grinder's acceptance. Although the disheartened partners had offered to sell the business to the Morse Twist Drill and Machine Company for $171,417.53 in July 1904, sales exceeded $350,000 by 1906, including over $259,000 for 155 plain grinder orders. In March 1906 Ludwig and Loewe contracted to manufacture and sell Norton machines throughout Europe. In the following year Norton Company (which had already begun to acquire control of the grinding company by purchasing Higgins's, Alden's, Allen's, and Jeppson's shares) bought Charles Norton's 20 percent interest for $10,000, five times its par value, and voted him an annual salary of $3,000 in addition to a 2 percent royalty on all plain grinder sales (worth $7,400 annually for the next five years).[45]

Real success for production grinding and the new firm, however, had only just begun, and ironically, it grew initially from the firm's jobbing business. When the five directors founded Norton Grinding Company in 1900, the automobile business was in its infancy, with only 4,100 sales. In the early years the small enterprises were mainly assembly companies that bought from or subcontracted to independent producers their complicated metal parts. As a metal-working center, Worcester soon attracted a good deal of the business. Wyman, Gordon forged crankshafts, axles, and gears as early as 1902, and the neighboring Heald Company internally ground cylinders and piston rings.[46]

Norton Grinding Company entered the auto business in September 1901 when it ground steel and brass rods for the Overman Automobile Company. In the next several years the firm received a number of job contracts for cylindrical grinding from automotive companies, including orders for 169 shafts and 51 axles from the George N. Pierce Company of Buffalo and 250 axles from the Ford Company.[47]

The firm's expertise and machinery soon led it to specialize in automobile crankshafts. The crankshaft, which transfers the engine's energy from the piston to the drive shaft, is a complex, solid metal shaft on which crankpins, bearing bodies, and side walls have to be machined. In addition, since metal rotates around metal at high speeds, precise tolerances to .00025 inch and smooth surfaces are necessary in hardened metal. Early crankshafts required five hours to turn, file, and polish. The Norton machines, which operated first with blocks attached at each end with holes bored in them as centers and later with a double head machine, had reduced grinding time to fifteen minutes by 1910. By 1905 Norton ground crankshafts for much of the automotive industry in a special crankshaft department headed by S. H. Amsden, and crankshaft grinding was soon part of company advertising.[48]

In that same year what had become a profitable jobbing business became an even more lucrative machine tool market. Automobile firms with larger volume such as Locomobile, Pope, Haynes, and Thomas Flyer began buying 10-by-50-inch plain grinders to machine their own shafts. By the following year Norton had designed a special crankpin attachment with a wide wheel for single-feed or plunge grinding of the crankpins. By 1915 at least 85 percent of all crankshafts were ground.[49]

The crankshaft business was the initial stage of Norton Grinding Company's success. Cylindrical grinding became a crucial part of automobile manufacturing, and its importance grew as automobile volume increased and manufacturers like Ford moved toward mass production. Charles Norton followed in 1910 with a special camshaft-grinding attachment for his plain grinder that formed cams directly from solid stock without milling. By 1917 he estimated that Norton Grinding Company and Heald, located across the street, produced perhaps two thirds or three quarters of the world's master and model cams, as well as its cam-grinding equipment.[50]

The close tie had become almost commonplace by 1914 when Ford placed a $30,000 order for 35 machines with Norton Grinding Company. Some ground camshafts, others handled crankshafts, and still others ground rear axles to .001 inch at the rate of one a minute.[51] In 1912 the company sold 464 grinders, almost triple its 1906 figure, while gross sales had more than doubled to approach $750,000.[52]

For Norton Grinding Company, just as for production grinding, the automobile industry had a dual impact. By the 1920s it accounted for a hefty portion of total sales. In 1927 one Norton specialist estimated that the industry, which bought some 55 percent of Norton Grinding Company output, had over sixty-eight thousand grinding machines, in contrast to fewer than one hundred a quarter century earlier.[53]

Furthermore, cylindrical grinding techniques developed for cars were applicable in other markets. Charles Norton chortled that "automobile makers have taught us a lesson in the efficient use of modern machine tools."[54] When World War I broke out, the inventor easily modified his plain grinder and wide-wheel plunge feed to grind munitions. By 1915 at least ten Norton machines at Bethlehem Steel and E. W. Bliss Company ground shells and shrapnel for the French and English at a rate exceeding one hundred per hour. The Bliss machines were modifications of the 10-by-24-inch special-purpose machines sold to Ford in 1914.[55]

America's entry into the war further expanded the new market. Salesman George Park recalled a sale of sixty or more machines to E. W. Bliss alone. Norton also produced attachments for grinding Liberty Motor crankshafts, gun tubes, bayonets, and rifle barrels, and the firm even ground shells and other projectiles as job work. So great was the wartime grinding market that Norton Grinding Company shared with Norton Company the $5,000 salary of Colonel Paul Hawkins, whom they stationed in Washington as a lobbyist and agent.[56]

As a result of the wartime boom the grinding company's 1913 sales quintupled to more than $3.7 million in 1918, and annual orders for plain grinders averaged 1,500 between 1915 and 1918.[57] And while peacetime inevitably weakened demand, the slump was softened by expanded markets for Norton grinders in the sewing machine, office machine (cash register, adding machine, and typewriter), agricultural machinery, wood-working machinery, and linotype machine industries.[58]

By 1919, Norton Grinding Company's last year as an enterprise legally separate from Norton Company, the firm was a mature, successful operation and an acknowledged leader in grinding machine manufacture. Its thirty distinct models and more than two hundred combinations of machines and fixtures included universal, tool and cutter, roll, and surface grinders, in addition to its plain and cylindrical grinders whose total sales exceeded six thousand.[59] Manufacture had left the wheel plant's basement and now occupied six buildings covering 300,000 square feet, while the labor force had jumped from a handful in 1900 to 1,000 in 1918. As early as 1910 Superintendent John Spence oversaw twenty-two foremen.[60]

Furthermore, as the last statement suggests, growth had driven the company by 1915 into a functional bureaucracy that included three major departments for manufacturing, sales, and engineering, along with smaller traffic, cost, and office forces. As chief engineer, Charles Norton, assisted after 1914 by Howard Dunbar from Western Electric, headed the engineering department, which designed machinery built by John Spence's manufacturing department.

The sales organization under C. O. Smith in 1910 included five men who demonstrated machines and contacted the network of distributors that marketed Norton equipment. In 1915 the firm inaugurated a training school for grinder operators whom it helped place in plants around the country to expand its own markets.[61] In Europe the company terminated its contract with Ludwig and Loewe in 1910, selling its German patent rights for $15,000. Distribution for England and France fell to Alfred Herbert, a company established in 1888 and already renowned as a manufacturer of capstan and turret lathes and as a machine tool distributor. Schuchardt and Schutte, the wheel company's premier European distributor, handled Germany, Austria, and the rest of the continent. In addition, the machine company employed two men in Europe as missionaries and demonstrators.[62]

Though nominally a separate enterprise, Norton Grinding Company was really part of the wheel firm, since renamed Norton Company. Except for Charles Norton their boards of directors were identical. Like Norton Company, Norton Grinding Company was closely held and privately financed. By 1907 Norton Company had purchased all Norton Grinding Company stock from its founders.[63] The merger of the two companies in 1919 merely ratified what had always been unified control. It generated some tax advantages and eventually helped clarify administrative control, which, although formally assigned to George Alden as general manager, had actually fragmented among Charles Norton, Spence, and Smith.[64]

Norton Company and its owners derived considerable dividends from their venture into the machine tool business. The original $10,000 investment in the grinding company had grown by 1918 into assets conservatively valued at more than $1.5 million. The automobile market, which had nurtured the grinding firm and been nurtured by it, had become the wheel company's major customer, consuming $8 million in wheels annually by 1927.[65] The growth of the grinding machine business and its impact on the wheel market had contributed largely toward making Norton Company part of American big business.

Furthermore, the machine business helped maintain Norton's leadership in the abrasives industry while expanding its reputation. Charles Norton worked closely with Norton Emery Wheel people in studying machine and abrasive behavior. Their joint efforts demonstrated conclusively through microphotography that a properly synchronized wheel and machine was a true cutting tool with thousands of cutting points. Charles Norton's work also firmly established the importance of coolant in grinding. Water had long been used to draw off heat and preserve metal temper. The inventor's labors now underscored the importance of temperature control to improve wheel efficiency, and the dispensers on his machines supplied water (mixed with soda to control rust) at rates up to forty gallons a minute.[66]

Wider wheels, faster speeds, better temperature control, and increased understanding of wheel action combined with the power, strength, and precision of Charles Norton's machines to make grinding crucial to mass production of metal parts and products in the twentieth century. In 1925 the Franklin Institute voted the inventor the John Scott Medal, already awarded to such innovators as Orville Wright, Edward Acheson, Thomas Edison, and Madame Curie, in recognition of his contributions.

In addition, Charles Norton's work and the development of production grinding stimulated the abrasives business by encouraging higher standards and greater output. Major capital investment in grinding machines (such as Ford's $35,000 order) made predictability and uniformity of wheel action even more crucial. A poorly selected or poorly made $2.50 wheel could ruin the production capability of a $2,500 machine. Norton Company and other firms began manufacturing wider wheels with bonds specially suited to particular tasks in efforts to meet the precision, high-volume production rates of which the new cylindrical, internal, surface, and centerless grinders were capable.

Expanding Enterprise: The New Abrasive

The most obvious area for improvement, however, was the abrasive grain itself. The use of emery and corundum found in nature continued to limit control over grain composition and behavior. The solution was an abrasive grain manufactured to precise requirements. Carborundum, the silicon carbide grain produced in electric furnaces by the Carborundum Company, was just such a product, but as noted earlier, it had limited use for iron, steel, and other high tensile strength metals. What wheel manufacturers and their customers needed was artificial corundum.

Norton Emery Wheel Company developed artificial aluminum oxide to replace emery and corundum, but not simply because of Charles Norton's work in production grinding and Carborundum Company's work with electric furnace grain. In fact, the firm pioneered the manufacture of artificial corundum (or Alundum as the company trade-named its product) simultaneously with Charles Norton's arrival at Norton Grinding Company. And when Norton began electric furnace work in 1901, Carborundum had made a significant but still small dent in the abrasives market.

The force for innovation was a more immediate challenge. By 1900 supply problems began to threaten Norton Company and encouraged it to master electric furnace technology and to move into raw material processing. American supplies of high-quality emery and corundum were fast dwindling. By 1906 both U.S. corundum mines were exhausted and closed, and domestic emery production was one quarter of 1899 output.[67]

The foreign sources on which the industry was increasingly dependent were uncertain. Shipments of corundum from India were costly, inadequate, and insufficient. The Naxos and Turkish emery mines, still the world's major suppliers, were erratic. Located in a politically volatile and technologically backward area, the distant mines were always subject to shutdown. As the Turkish exporters wrote one U.S. processing firm, "The ore should have reached us long ago, but did not on account of the scarcity of camels. Please ask your friends to wait a while."[68]

Furthermore, as suppliers grew fewer the trade was increasingly subject to monopoly control, especially when the great trust movement for horizontal combinations of raw materials processors and manufacturers grew so popular in the 1890s. At the century's end Charles Jenks, whose father had originally developed the North Carolina and Georgia corundum mines, obtained options on all significant domestic emery and corundum production. To get additional funds he joined with such finance capitalists as Charles R. Flint, popularly known as the "father of trusts" and founder of such industrial consolidations as U.S. Rubber, American Woolen, and National Starch, Ohio C. Barber of Diamond Match, Frank Rockefeller, and B. F. Kimball. They established the International Emery and Corundum Company and took fifteen-year options on all Turkish and Naxos ore. The grain monopoly then sought to combine with a number of wheel manufacturers. Although Jenks and Kimball soon lost control in 1902–03, when credit grew tight and sales declined as wheel manufacturers consumed stockpiles built in anticipation of the trust, the combine continued its control over natural grain supplies through the Ashland Emery and Corundum Company and Alden Speare and Sons Company.[69]

Anticipating the consolidation, Norton had already begun production of artificial corundum and was able to refuse Jenks's offer of combination. With their typical thrift, diligence, and prudence, the firm's founders were able to seize an opportunity when offered. Thrift supplied the capital for development, diligence characterized the long, arduous process of product evolution, and prudence helped Norton negotiate a most advantageous agreement to get control of the new product from its original developers.

No other single development, including the advent of the automobile market and the evolution of production grinding, had a greater impact on Norton's growth. Artificial abrasives marked a turning point in the abrasives business and in the rise of large enterprises to dominate the industry. Manufacturing artificial corundum forced Norton into bauxite mining and into the new electric furnace technology, thereby expanding its manufacturing processes beyond their pottery derivations. Alundum grain and Norton bonds yielded wheels suitable for the new precision production grinding machines and the auto industry.

With its new product and its expertise, Norton fended off Carborundum, its only serious early challenger in the artificial abrasives field. As the abrasives industry grew 2,000 percent to a $30 million business between 1899 and 1919, Norton not only defended its position but outstripped all its competitors for new business. The firm's share of abrasives production reported by the U.S. Census rose from 29.8 percent in 1899 to 34.3 percent in 1919; its portion of total sales reported by the Grinding Wheel Manufacturers Association was about 44 percent in 1919.[70]

Norton was the innovator but not the inventor of artificial corundum. Production moved beyond laboratory experiments with the advent of Clerc's electric furnace in 1879, which provided energy levels heretofore unavailable and which eventually nearly doubled temperature levels in commercial furnaces from 1,800° C to 3,500° C. The higher temperatures generated reactions between previously inert chemical ingredients to produce calcium carbide, metallic silicon, cyanide, graphite, nitric acid, and such alloys as ferrosilicon and ferrochromium.[71]

The new furnace and its higher energy levels also encouraged work with bauxite, an ore with a high amorphous alumina (aluminum oxide) content. Until the 1890s bauxite was largely a source for alum production by such firms as the Pennsylvania Salt Manufacturing Company of Philadelphia. In the mid-1880s, however, when Charles Martin Hall and Paul Heroult independently used electric furnaces to manufacture aluminum by reducing alumina from bauxite through electrolysis in molten cryolite, bauxite's potential market expanded enormously.[72]

The interest in bauxite, the electric furnace, and the need for artificial corundum culminated in a number of experiments in the 1890s. Crystals with useful abrasive character came first from Charles Jacobs's work in Ampere, New Jersey, in 1897. Jacobs, a former General Electric chemist, learned to produce aluminum oxide crystals by first fusing bauxite in an electric furnace and then regulating the cooling rate and the process of crystallization. Working for the Ampere Electrochemical Company, a seminal experimental firm in electrochemicals, he was soon joined by Charles Bradley, whose earlier work fusing ores in electric furnaces had led to a long and successful patent battle with the Pittsburgh Reduction Company (later renamed the Aluminum Company of America or Alcoa).[73] To develop their process, the two experimenters sold 51 percent of their interests to Stone and Webster and with Edwin S. Webster, Frederick S. Pratt, and W. Cameron Forbes, incorporated the General Electro-Chemical Company. Stone and Webster put in limited funds to promote the venture while Bradley and Jacobs conducted further experiments at Rumford

Falls, Maine, where electric power was cheaper. They then sent samples of the new material, which they called Alundum, to the Norton Emery Wheel Company and other emery wheel producers.[74]

At Norton, President Milton Higgins, and subsequently his son Aldus, appreciated the potential of Jacobs's work and led the firm into the practical commercial development of the new product. Alundum was a tougher grain than Acheson's silicon carbide, and its wider grinding applications included high tensile strength materials such as carbonized, alloyed, and high-speed steels, malleable iron, wrought iron, and tough bronzes. The inquisitive elder Higgins avidly read *Scientific American* and other periodicals for recent developments in grinding and metal working. When Charles Allen displayed the Jacobs sample as a curiosity piece, Norton's president quickly realized the need to act, and with either George Alden or John Jeppson visited the General Company's operations.[75] Despite his disappointment that promoters already controlled the invention, Higgins and his son made several trips to Rumford Falls and initiated protracted discussions that led to an exclusive Norton license for Alundum in 1900.

While a year's delay for negotiation and investigation reflected the New England firm's prudent care in entering a new field, the founders also risked overcaution, which might have allowed another company to outbid them. In this case, however, Higgins and his partners rightly estimated that the new product's unknowns considerably diminished its attractiveness. Lengthy negotiations allowed Norton to learn more about the new product, reduce its own risk, and drive an excellent bargain for itself.

The absence of any serious competitors for Alundum suggests the uncertainty of the new product. Before Norton contracted with the General Company in August 1900, no one had produced a commercially successful artificial corundum grain. In fact, as far as can be determined, no one had even manufactured a wheel using artificial corundum. With one exception, Norton's rivals in abrasives were basically ceramics firms producing grinding wheels. None had any experience with bauxite and electric furnaces, and none had Norton's capital surplus to finance the furnace construction, experimentation, and promotion necessary for Alundum development.

Carborundum Company, the single possible exception, was certainly experienced in electric furnace abrasives, and the Mellon family provided ample financial resources. But by 1899 Edward Acheson, the one man with the curiosity and experience to undertake the project for Carborundum, was only a figurehead president, estranged from the Mellons and their operating men.[76] For their part, the Mellon people were too busy rationalizing operations, stemming losses, and promoting artificial silicon carbide to consider serious investment in still another unknown product.

Neither General nor any other nonabrasives company indicated serious intent to enter the field. Such a potential investor not only faced the challenges confronting Norton and other wheel firms but also had to learn wheel bonding, manufacture, and sales as well. Those tasks, which had cost Carborundum a decade and hundreds of thousands of dollars, held little attraction. General's owners, the most logical candidates to enter the market, intended only to promote, not to manufacture. Although they capitalized their firm at $100,000, Webster, Pratt, and Forbes raised less than $10,000 cash.[77] Their limited funds served only to finance primitive experimental production, first at Rumford Falls and later at Niagara Falls. Milton Higgins visited the Niagara operation and wrote Aldus in July 1900 that the owners were "hard up."[78]

Bradley and Jacobs were no more operating men than Webster, Forbes, and Pratt were manufacturers. Jacobs was a chemist who soon sold out his interest, and Bradley was in Higgins's words "the leader of plans and ideas—and does not attend to details."[79] His previous electric furnace work in fusing metals had led only to broad patents that he had quickly sold to the Cowles Electric Smelting and Aluminum Company for exploitation.

The absence of serious competitors and General's straitened circumstances and uncertain intent allowed Norton to negotiate advantageously. When Stone and Webster offered to sell its process for $100,000 and a $\frac{1}{2}$¢ per pound ($10 per ton) royalty on all Alundum produced, the Worcester firm refused and suggested that the General Company might manufacture grain for Norton's use.[80] General then completed the Jacobs patent and relocated in an abandoned Union Carbide plant at Niagara Falls, where it could obtain cheap power in large quantities unavailable elsewhere.

But the move and the need to design a suitable electric furnace consumed time and General's capital while Milton Higgins negotiated a Niagara site and a power contract for Norton. On August 17, General willingly turned over development rights to the abrasives company for an unknown consideration. The agreement included a Norton option for an exclusive license during the patent's life in Canada and the United States at a royalty of only $2 per ton of finished Alundum.[81]

Alundum soon proved far superior to emery and even natural corundum for most grinding purposes. After building its own Niagara plant in 1901 and completing several years' experimentation and field testing, Norton began commercial sales of wheels and other Alundum abrasive products in 1903. In January 1904 the company exercised its option for an exclusive license, and in 1906 it renamed itself Norton Company instead of Norton Emery Wheel Company to signify its wholehearted use of the new product.[82]

Henceforth, the firm marketed bonded products using electric furnace grains almost exclusively. Subsequently, Norton also developed markets among jewelers, polishers, and sandpaper manufacturers for direct sales of grains, although it seldom sold grain outright to competitors. By 1910 manufactured abrasives, Norton's Alundum and Carborundum Company's silicon carbide, were challenging natural emery and corundum to "an alarming extent," and by 1914 manufactured abrasives exceeded total raw emery and corundum ore imports, a ratio that had been 1 to 3 eight years earlier.[83]

The Jacobs patent, however, was only partially responsible for the Norton prosperity and growth resulting from Alundum. Neither the license nor Norton's sales policy assured the company's exclusive use of the new grain. The patent expired in the United States in 1917 and in Canada in 1919, but competition came much more quickly as rivals developed other processes to manufacture artificial corundum.[84] Commercial manufacture fusing powdered aluminum and metal oxides began in France in 1903. And, since the Norton license applied only to Canada and the United States, Carborundum Company and other competitors were soon using the Jacobs process to manufacture Alundum in Europe.

In the United States several competitors appeared before World War I. In 1905 Carborundum adapted a European process to manufacture artificial corundum from fused emery instead of bauxite. In 1912, the Alden Speare Company, representing the old emery monopoly, developed an alternative method of production and organized the Exolon Company in February 1914 to furnace artificial corundum. In the same year, the Hamilton Emery and Corundum Company and the American Emery Wheel Works established the General Abrasive Company to manufacture corundum by modified Jacobs techniques developed at the Massachusetts Institute of Technology.[85]

World War I accelerated the diffusion of electrochemical manufacture of grain. By 1915 shipments of Naxos and Turkish emery to the United States became increasingly rare as Europe consumed a larger share of mine output and shipping grew more hazardous. Several new firms, including the International Abrasive Company and D. A. Brebner Company, rapidly entered the field. Furthermore, because none of the alternative processes produced artificial corundum equal in quality and cost to Norton's Alundum, furnace competitors soon began to threaten infringement of the Jacobs process. When the General Electro-Chemical Company, which functioned only to receive Norton royalties, refused to act, Norton bought General in 1916 for $40,000, the amount of the remaining royalties due for the patent's life, and then sublicensed the Carborundum, Exolon, Brebner, and General Abrasive companies. The sublicensing headed off infringements and costly litigation, expanded America's artificial corundum capacity to meet wartime needs, and paid Norton more than 400 percent.[86]

Expanding Enterprise: Mastering the New Technology

Norton could readily afford to sublicense in 1916 because Alundum manufacture had gone well beyond the Jacobs technique. The exclusive license merely gave the firm a head start in maintaining its leadership amid growing competition. Far more important were product and process development. Mastery of the electric furnace technology and control of the characteristics of artificial grains assured superior products and premium pricing. In turn those advantages soon supplied the volume and profits that created the large enterprise. Not by accident, Norton Company and Carborundum Company, the first bonded abrasives firms to integrate electric furnace operations with wheel manufacture, became a duopoly that dominated the U.S. abrasives industry and established large markets in Britain, Germany, and other major industrial countries as well.

Thus the personnel Norton hired from General were as vital as the license itself, for the abrasives company had no experience with the electric furnace technology central to Alundum production. Although one historian has recently pointed to the significant interlocks among early electrochemical companies as a means of technological diffusion, in this case at least, there is no evidence of any direct cooperation among firms.[87] Indirect data suggest the opposite. Norton and other wheel manufacturers jealously guarded bonding secrets and except for the later development of resinoid wheels, the bonded abrasives industry had no tradition of significant patent licensing. After acquiring the Jacobs patent, Norton Company pioneered its furnaced abrasives products and processes internally and independently of the Carborundum, Ampere, and General Companies. Important furnace patents remained exclusive during their lifetimes, and Norton licensed the Jacobs patent to others only near the end of its life, in wartime and long after its contents were commonly known and practiced.

Migration of scarce, knowledgeable experts like Lewis Saunders and Ray Hill White, rather than interfirm cooperation, facilitated Norton's innovation of commercial techniques for furnacing artificial corundum. Saunders, who joined Ampere shortly after graduating in chemical engineering from the University of Rochester in 1897, had worked with Bradley at General's Niagara plant. There he was joined by Ray White, a graduate of MIT's first class in electrochemical engineering.[88] The two men, along with Phillip Schultz, and experienced furnace man hired from nearby Alcoa, assumed technical control of research and operations under Superintendent Aldus Higgins. Robert Ridgway, one of Saunders's later colleagues, described his mentor's role as providing the "chemical and metallurgical engineering for the control of composition and quality of the furnace products."[89]

Establishing technical control was quite a challenge. Alundum production was so new that manufacturing and research were virtually indistinguishable. White and Saunders created a small research department, but technical and quality control consumed more time and resources than did pure research. Simultaneously, much research took place on an ad hoc, empirical basis in the plant itself. As one technical man subsequently put it, "The plant has been considered a research laboratory on a large scale."[90]

A twofold process of innovation naturally separated and specialized the research. The Niagara Falls plant focused on perfecting the electric furnace and the new grain, while Norton's Worcester operation concentrated on bonding Alundum and on its applications. Joel Styffe, George Jeppson's laboratory assistant in Worcester, spent 1903 in Niagara observing Alundum manufacture. Subsequently, he and his assistants under Jeppson's direction were responsible for testing various grain compositions for their bonding stability, grinding behavior, and special applicability. When the first Alundum wheels produced surfaces like alligator hides, for example, John and George Jeppson and the Worcester laboratory developed a grain-roasting technique to ensure better bonding.[91] Work on actual grain characteristics such as hardness and toughness remained at the furnace plant. The two groups communicated by a series of regular reports and intermittent conferences.

At Niagara, Higgins, White, and Saunders faced two challenges: determining optimum product composition and structure and then establishing technical control to assure efficient, uniform production. Two decades of empirical evidence in the grinding wheel business and Charles Jacobs's work had already provided some clues for product character. By 1900 abrasives experts had begun to understand that hardness was not the sole determinant of an abrasive grain's effectiveness.[92] Silicon carbide was harder than corundum, emery, and Alundum, but its applications were not nearly so broad. More im-

portant were a grain's temper or toughness and its fracture characteristics.

Toughness, which Norton Company defined as "that property of
a body by which it retains strength under strain," and fracture, "the
condition of surface left after the breaking off of particles," were
central to grinding efficiency.[93] Retention of strength and proper renewal of sharp cutting edges allowed the grinding wheel to work
faster while consuming less energy. Microphotography from comparative tests in Worcester showed that grains with proper toughness
and fracture cut ribbons or chips of metal. Other grains needed more
power and time to grind because they burned the metal and produced
tiny melted globs.[94] In sum, a grain had to fracture to provide continually sharp edges, but pace was important. Slow fracture left dull
edges that consumed energy, generated heat, and distorted metal
temper, while too rapid fracture crumbled the grain and used up the
wheel uneconomically.

Charles Jacobs had already learned that stirring the fused bauxite
and varying the cooling rate influenced crystal size and grain temper.
Saunders's and White's work soon disclosed that Alundum with 92–
95 percent aluminum oxide content gave optimum results. Grinding
tests at Worcester disclosed that some impurities, such as aluminum
carbide, were unstable and disintegrated under grinding heat and
pressure. Other inpurities, such as silica, titanium oxide, and iron
oxide, either as residuals of bauxite fusion or as additions to the mass,
helped form a slag to bond the crystals in a grain and provide proper
fracture.[95] Less important to grinding action but vital to commercial
success was constant color by control of contaminants. Buyers insisted
that regular Alundum be brown and its sister product, 38 Alundum,
be white.

After establishing 93 or 94 percent aluminum oxide as optimal for
regular Alundum, Saunders began experimenting with variations for
special jobs. By far the most successful was white or 38 Alundum,
developed by 1908 at Niagara and then tested for bonding and grinding character at Worcester under George Jeppson.[96] White Alundum
was fused from pure alumina rather than from bauxite to produce an
abrasive with 99.5 percent aluminum oxide. Because sodium vapor
perforated the crystals to make the grain softer acting than regular
Alundum, the new product was especially suited for various tool
steels and hardened steel alloys. Commercial production began in
1910 and continues to the present. Subsequent variations had less
commercial success; the ranges for regular and 38 Alundum covered
most grinding jobs requiring artificial corundum.

Devising efficient manufacturing processes was as crucial as identifying and developing products. At first glance, manufacture seemed relatively simple. Furnace operators placed calcined (dried) bauxite in an electric furnace between two carbon electrodes. They then passed current across the electrodes and through the bauxite, generating temperatures to 3,700° F for twenty-four hours to melt or fuse the raw material. Impurities were drawn off and the residual Alundum mass left to crystallize as it cooled for several days. Subsequently, workmen broke the massive abrasive pig into smaller chunks for milling and screening.

Aldus Higgins, White, and Saunders soon appreciated that manufacture demanded "considerable experience and skill" to control the numerous process variables and to create a standard product at a stable, efficient cost.[97] Between 1901 and 1920, White and others established "technical control" as they experimented to determine and regulate proper feed rates of bauxite and other materials into the furnace and the optimal level of energy input per pound of raw material. They fixed a cooling rate for maximum yield of useful grain sizes per pig and substituted graphite for carbon electrodes to avoid aluminum carbide contamination of the product. They learned to specify bauxite containing 58–65 percent aluminum oxide with the lowest iron and titanium content consistent with low silica content in order to reduce energy consumption.[98]

Because of the energy consumption necessary for manufacture, furnace design was probably the single most outstanding process innovation. Bauxite is a good insulator and its melting point exceeds 3,600° F; therefore, 450–500 kilowatts per hour were required for small volumes of material in the furnace design inherited from Charles Jacobs. This design was costly, inefficient, and short-lived. A small container of brick and steel lined with carbon blocks enclosed fixed electrodes, while the furnace hearth operated on a plunger. During the melting, the hearth slowly lowered as operators fed in more bauxite, thus ensuring that the entire charge passed close to the electrodes to get maximum heat for fusing. After cooling, the furnace had to be disassembled to remove the charge and replace the burned out carbon blocks. Any leak among the blocks was very dangerous, for at 3,700° F the fused bauxite exceeded the melting points of steel (2,800°) and firebrick (3,100°).[99]

Superintendent Aldus Higgins, aided by Assistant Superintendent Samuel Hall, quickly made modifications to cut costs significantly.[100] Higgins watched workers spray hot spots or break-out points with water to avoid complete meltdowns and realized that hot spots never recurred in the same place. In other words, chilled Alundum was its own best insulator and the elaborate brick and block structure was unnecessary. Higgins designed instead a conical steel shell circled at the top by a perforated pipe that sent a constant stream of water down the shell's outer side. The fused Alundum hit the shell, was chilled by the water, and established an insulating ring. After melting was completed, the shell was simply lifted off and the pig moved away for cooling. The old shell, which was easily patched and relatively inexpensive, could then be quickly lowered onto a new hearth for another cycle. Subsequent changes, including a mobile hearth, better design, and self-regulating electrodes, further improved the basic Higgins furnace and more than doubled individual furnace capacity by 1913.[101]

Savings were considerable. The original Higgins furnace alone reduced costs 40 percent from $89.73 to $53.27 per ton between 1902 and 1904.[102] Aldus Higgins received the John Scott Medal in 1914 for his work, and his furnace became standard at Norton (and subsequently throughout the industry after his patent expired). It remains in use today. By 1906 Norton doubled its output to yield three tons of Alundum daily.[103]

Mastery of electric furnace production of Alundum encouraged Norton to offer a full line of manmade abrasives. Saunders's experience, supplemented by consultant Francis Fitzgerald who had previously worked with Carborundum Company, allowed the firm to move quickly into silicon carbide production after Carborundum's patents expired. Silicon carbide was made from silica sand and carbon in an open resistance furnace whose end walls held 3-foot carbon rods to carry current, rather than in the arc-type furnace used in Alundum manufacture.[104]

Still, the two processes had much in common. Both consumed a great deal of energy in high-temperature operations conducted in electric furnaces. Both also required similar careful technical controls to ensure uniformity, chemical and ceramic stability, and efficient costing. Silicon carbide furnaces had 740-kilowatt capability, compared with 550 kilowatts for Alundum, and as in Alundum manufacturing, uniform temperature and charge were crucial. Saunders discovered that a range of only 400° F existed between the formation and decomposition of silicon carbide.[105]

Full-scale commercial production came quickly in 1911 after test work was conducted at Niagara and Worcester in 1908 and 1909.[106] In 1910 Norton built silicon carbide furnaces across the river from Niagara in Chippawa, Canada, where power was cheaper and more plentiful. The company trademarked its new product Crystolon and soon competed seriously with Carborundum, the original developer.

Expanding Enterprise: Assuring a Raw Materials Supply

By this point, the process of expansion and change that produced the big enterprise had begun to develop its own momentum. Solving problems led to growth and to new obstacles, whose solutions again enlarged the firm. The search for assured grain sources and a better product had led Norton into electric furnacing of manmade abrasives. Investment in new techniques of grain manufacture now raised new supply difficulties and serious challenges from outside the abrasives industry. The founders' logical solutions then further expanded the company.

Fusing bauxite carried Norton back into raw material processing, forced it to confront the powerful Alcoa, and offered opportunities for broad diversity. As noted earlier, Norton had previously purchased its raw materials from processors. Clay supplies were plentiful and widely held, as were emery and corundum deposits before 1900. Bauxite deposits were many, but few had the purity necessary for aluminum and artificial corundum production. The founders' prudent desire for a domestic supply to avoid the uncertainties that had attended Greek and Turkish emery shipments further restricted its choices. The company noted proudly at the outset of World War I that "in all its supplies it has tried to be as independent of the broker or the foreign producer as it has been of the money-lender."[107]

After Hall's and Heroult's work, the expanded production of aluminum and aluminum alloys initiated commercial mining of good-quality bauxite in Alabama and Georgia in the late 1880s and 1890s.[108] Limited supplies and the continued growth of users soon extended exploration into Saline and Pulaski counties in Arkansas, which became after 1900 the major domestic source of commercial bauxite. The market was a small one, including the Pittsburgh Reduction Company (Alcoa), which consumed more than half the output, the Pennsylvania Salt Manufacturing Company, the General Chemical Company, and a few other chemical firms.

Because bauxite with low concentrations of iron oxide, silica, titanium oxide, and other impurities was scarce, there were few suppliers, numbering primarily the Republic Mining and Manufacturing Company, the Southern Bauxite Company, the Georgia Bauxite and Mining Company, the American Bauxite Company, and the General Bauxite Company. Concentrated ownership of its vital raw material induced Alcoa to begin buying holdings to assure itself of a steady supply. In the 1890s it acquired the Georgia and the Southern Bauxite companies, which had major holdings in Georgia and Alabama, and its 1905 purchase of the General Bauxite Company from the General

Chemical Company gave Alcoa a major stake in the Arkansas fields.[109]

When Norton began commercial production of Alundum in 1903, its desire to assure a stable, independent bauxite source generated a major confrontation. Limited known sources were heavily dominated by the powerful Alcoa, and its 1905 purchase of General Bauxite suggested that the aluminum company might well tie up all major domestic supplies. Dependence on Alcoa was not attractive. After investigating its operation, Lewis Saunders wrote that "the handling of other ores than those for their own use is distinctly a side issue."[110] Even worse, Alcoa was held by Richard and Andrew Mellon, who were primary owners of Norton's major abrasives competitor, Carborundum Company.

Security resulted from quick action and shrewd bargaining by Aldus Higgins to stake out Norton Company's position among the few independent sources left. Higgins was the natural choice for the job. He was young (32 when he traveled to Arkansas in 1905) and with his father had been the most active of all the Norton owners and their sons in Alundum development. Aldus had investigated Ampere's Rumford Falls operations and superintended Norton's Niagara plant since its opening. Though not a technical man, he knew the product and its requirements, and his formal training as a lawyer equipped him for the elaborate negotiations, contracting, and ownership transfers necessary to acquire the remaining valuable bauxite holdings.

Higgins quickly established for Norton a position of strength from which it would negotiate with Alcoa.[111] In October 1905 he skillfully purchased for $14,000 a 116-acre tract from Cornelius Vreeland and William Higgins in Saline County, Arkansas, triumphing over a claim by the General Bauxite Company, an Alcoa subsidiary. In the summer of 1906 he bought the American Bauxite Company and rights for three other bauxite properties in Pulaski County from Walter Berger for $75,000. In the same summer he obtained an option (which Norton exercised in February 1907) to buy 75 percent of the Republic Mining and Manufacturing Company for $75,000. Republic had begun bauxite mining at Hermitage, Georgia, in 1888 under William G. Neilson. Neilson and his two sons, Winthrop and William L., had expanded operations until their firm was the largest and most successful independent, holding 6,700 acres outright and 1,000 leased acres in Georgia and Alabama.[112]

Within two years and for less than $200,000 Higgins had made Norton the second largest bauxite producer in the United States. He quickly consolidated all holdings in the Republic Company, which the Neilsons continued to operate. Prudence again helped reduce the risks of partnership. Norton Company had bought bauxite from Republic since 1901, and the founders as well as Aldus Higgins respected the Neilsons' experience and integrity. His negotiations left Aldus "more than ever convinced" that the Neilsons were "absolutely square, honest and broad-minded as to the character of their dealings," and he thought it "very advantageous" to combine with them.[113]

Furthermore, as he reviewed his work for Charles Allen in late 1906, Aldus felt he had accomplished more than just securing a raw material supply through partnership with men who shared Norton values. Young Higgins was an optimistic man whose career had begun with artificial abrasives. He believed strongly that Norton's knowledge of and experience with bauxite, aluminum oxide, and the electric furnace, along with its raw material holdings, offered major opportunities outside the abrasives industry. Refractories, including firebrick and other heat- and chemical-resistant products, were a "promising field for bauxite."[114] The Laclede Fire Brick Manufacturing Company of St. Louis was already an important customer for Norton bauxite. Perhaps Alundum and silicon carbide had refractory potential as well.

An even larger and more lucrative field was the young aluminum industry. As Higgins told Charles Allen: "I left Arkansas feeling that we had accomplished the purchase of some very valuable properties and when combined with the Neilson properties, it will place us in a very strong position for whatever industry using bauxite we care to embark in. I believe there is enough bauxite in the Arkansas and Georgia-Alabama properties to justify going into the Aluminum business on a large scale, if desired, and it certainly makes us a very strong fractor [sic] in the field and strengthens our position enormously with the Pittsburgh Reduction Co."[115]

Whatever the opportunities, Norton never realized them. Within three years it sold the Republic Company and all but forty acres of its bauxite holdings to Alcoa. While it did begin commercial production of Alundum and silicon carbide refractories by 1913, that business was always a small sideline that produced little profit and concentrated instead on supplying the company's own requirements for kiln furniture. Norton never seriously considered aluminum manufacture and as part of the Republic sale, it expressly agreed not to enter that industry.

Although new technology and markets had provided the opportunity for Norton Company's rise to large-scale enterprise, the founders' values set the limits to its expansion. No direct evidence exists on what was a watershed in the firm's history, but indirect data suggest that further diversification was beyond the owners' abilities, funds, and desires. In fact, given their deeply held assumptions, the possibilities may well have seemed so remote that the choice was made by failing even to consider any alternative seriously. There was no large, diversified American enterprise to serve as a model. Most big companies concentrated their activities in a single industry, and the few exceptions, such as Armour Company, the meatpacker, had only such tiny sidelines as glue and sandpaper manufacture to handle by-products.[116]

Further expansion threatened the character of the closely held, owner-operated company that the founders had so carefully nurtured. Bauxite mining was fast becoming more capital intensive. Originally, Republic workers had manually scraped away brush and topsoil or overburden to surface mine bauxite ore. Processing involved merely crushing and calcining the ore in kilns to drive off the moisture, which constituted up to a third of the material. Mining required more investment, however, as the company exhausted surface deposits and looked deeper for better quality ore. It then needed huge steam shovels and other mechanical earth movers to dig open-pit mines and rail lines and later powerful trucks to haul the product.[117]

Whatever the potential of Norton's bauxite, serious competition with Alcoa in the aluminum industry was certainly beyond even the New England company's comfortable resources. Alcoa was a $27 million enterprise that virtually monopolized crude and semifinished aluminum production.[118] Norton's owners would need millions for manufacturing facilities, a distribution network, and product and process development in order to battle the powerful, established firm backed by Mellon money. Raising funds from outside sources would inevitably bring financial people onto the Norton board, diluting the founders' precious independence.

Simultaneous operation of machinery, abrasives, and aluminum companies would end owner-control. By 1909 George Alden, Milton Higgins, and John Jeppson were all at least 65 and poorly prepared for the burdens of major diversification. Higgins and Jeppson were already grooming sons as successors, and their plans for continued family operation stood little chance in the publicly financed and professionally managed company required for further growth.

In addition, the move into Alundum manufacture, electric furnace technology, and bauxite mining was largely a Higgins undertaking, as noted earlier. Charles Allen and John Jeppson, Norton's chief operating men, had grown up with the abrasives industry, and while they were willing to undertake artificial abrasives manufacture to protect the grinding wheel business, they showed little inclination to go beyond the business they knew. The machinery company was strain enough.

Furthermore, a dispute between the Higgins family and the other owners over stock ownership was already distracting attention and threatening to drive a serious wedge between the founders.[119] When Horace Young, one of the original seven partners, died in 1909, the firm at first refused to buy his securities, arguing that his estate had overvalued them. Milton Higgins's subsequent efforts to purchase the stock and secure control of the company for his own family alarmed the other owners and started a wave of ill feeling that lasted for several years. Charles Allen led the formation of a stock trust to prevent the sale of additional shares to Higgins, and both Milton and Aldus ceased attending board meetings. Lacking a quorum, the board never formally assembled in 1911, and the company operated with the directors and officers elected the previous year. Through Aldus's intercession, the founders soon smoothed over the split. The Young stock was distributed among all the owners and Milton Higgins was reelected president in 1912, but by then the chances for further expansion had passed.

Whatever the reasons for not entering the aluminum business, Norton's strength forced Alcoa to buy the New England company out of the bauxite industry in a remarkably generous settlement. Although the Mellons controlled both Alcoa and Carborundum, Arthur Vining Davis, the aluminum company's chief operating man, had continued conducting a vigorous campaign to tie up bauxite reserves and keep potential competitors out of the aluminum business. Agreements with the General Chemical and Pennsylvania Salt Manufacturing companies in 1905 and 1907 turned their bauxite holdings over to Alcoa and provided that neither party would enter the other's industry.[120]

In April 1909 Alcoa made Norton a similar offer to neutralize its last serious threat.[121] Alcoa paid $312,500 for Republic Mining and its bauxite holdings, and the aluminum and abrasives firms agreed not to compete. Although a 1912 consent decree instigated by the U.S. Department of Justice subsequently nullified the formal noncompetition agreement, Norton's sale of Republic had in reality ratified its decision to stay in the abrasives industry. The company did conduct further explorations for bauxite in the British, French, and Dutch Guianas between 1915 and 1919, but its efforts lagged well behind Alcoa's, which quickly tied up the rich deposits.[122]

Although the 1909 contract closed off further diversification for Norton Company, its liberal terms confirmed the enterprise's dominance of the bonded abrasives industry. Norton's subsequent failure in South America was of little consequence because the contract had already guaranteed a bauxite supply. Alcoa agreed to ship Norton Company annually up to fifty thousand tons with specified purity at $5.50 per ton for forty years. Norton did not require that tonnage until World War I, and only in the 1920s did annual consumption begin to reach that figure consistently. In 1909 the fixed price equaled the market rate Norton had previously paid its Republic subsidiary, but it soon fell below bauxite's market value. By 1928 Aldus Higgins estimated that the abrasives company had saved over $850,000, and the contract did not expire until 1949.[123]

In addition, Norton was allowed to keep the forty-acre Arnold Heir tract whose clouded title had been claimed by both parties. Located in the heart of Alcoa's Arkansas operations, the tract contained large deposits of high-purity bauxite. Norton merely held the land as reserve and mined it only during peak demand in World War I and World War II. Later executives likened it to a kind of dowry, prudently tucked away by the New England company.

Alcoa also sweetened the pot with a long-term contract for alumina and with a patent exchange. The alumina assured Norton of adequate material for commercial production of 38 Alundum, which began the next year. The patent exchange merely sublicensed the Jacobs patents to Alcoa in exchange for vital process patents held by Charles M. Hall.[124] The difficulty with fused bauxite was drawing off the impurities. The hardness of the outer chilled Alundum shell made tapping impossible. Hall had learned to add carbon to the fused bauxite to reduce the metal oxide impurities and form a ferrosilicon button that precipitated at the furnace's bottom. The remaining iron particles

The big firm: Worcester operations in 1916.

Table 1. Norton Financial Data, 1885-1919.

Year	Net Sales ($ thousands)	Net Income ($ thousands)	Total Investment[a] ($ thousands)	Return on Investment (%)
1885	32[b]			
1886	57	11	36	30.6
1887	77	11	44	25.0
1888	80	18	59	30.5
1889	108	9	60	15.0
1890	144	32	85	37.6
1891	157	33	109	30.3
1892	169	34	129	26.4
1893	156	5	130	3.8
1894	148	13	135	9.6
1895	204	43	157	27.4
1896	236	46	183	25.1
1897	243	47	210	22.4
1898	324	59	248	23.8
1899	412	91	314	29.0
1900	423	55	338	16.3
1901	497	80	381	21.0
1902	596	101	452	22.3
1903	656	149	572	26.0
1904	661	94	634	14.8
1905	892	206	783	26.3
1906	1,355	221	882	25.1
1907	1,468	233	954	24.4
1908	1,055	44	970	4.5
1909	1,882	384	1,685	22.8
1910	2,508	687	1,800	38.2
1911	2,332	478	1,922	24.9
1912	3,107	633	2,233	28.3
1913	3,383	599	2,559	23.4
1914	2,734	449	2,793	16.1
1915	5,679	1,760	4,515	39.0
1916	10,871	3,829	8,805	43.5
1917	15,171	4,545	13,968	32.5
1918	16,643	5,322	17,376	30.6
1919	13,902	3,379	19,524	17.3

Sources: Norton Company, "Annual Report," 1910; Norton Company, "Brief to Commissioner of Internal Revenue," June 16, 1928; Norton Company's annual reports of condition to the Commonwealth of Massachusetts, 1916–1919.

Note: Figures do not include the Norton Grinding Machine Company's data for 1901–1905 or the German plant's data for 1910–1919.

[a] "Total investment" (Norton's term) apparently includes original capital plus reinvested earnings for the years 1886–1915. Figures for 1916–1919 are gross assets as reported to the Commonwealth of Massachusetts.

[b] Sales for 1885 cover about seven months of that year.

suspended in the mass were easily removed by magnets. Hall's technique for purifying fused bauxite soon became and still remains an abrasives industry standard.

By World War I Norton Company had become a big business by employing the techniques of the prosperous small firm. In 1917 total assets of nearly $14 million ranked the enterprise 386th among all U.S. industrial companies, and employment exceeded four thousand.[125] Three years' rapid expansion pushed assets to more than $21 million and increased the work force periodically to five thousand. As table 1 indicates, growth came quickly and steadily. Norton's annual net sales more than doubled every five years in the two decades after 1900 to exceed $18 million by 1920, while annual return on investment averaged nearly 28 percent. Wartime demand raised sales of all products (abrasives, refractories, and machines) and established a new plateau for company revenue as annual sales in the 1920s averaged nearly $14 million.

Throughout Norton's evolution as a big business, its owner-managers controlled its expansion. Hard work, careful attention to business, and healthy retained surpluses allowed the founders to seize the opportunities offered by the development of production grinding, the automobile, and electric furnace abrasives. Norton Company was a diversified firm manufacturing abrasives, machinery, and refractories. It was multiunit and multifunctional with bonded abrasives production in Worcester, electric furnace plants in Niagara and Chippawa, and a bauxite calcining plant in Bauxite, Arkansas. And the company had even become multinational by establishing wheel plants in Germany in 1909 and in Canada, France, and Japan by 1920. Yet control remained in Worcester where Charles Allen administered, the board directed, and the New England family firm endured.

3.

"Catching Up": Administering the Large Firm

By WORLD WAR I the problems facing Norton Company were in leadership and administration. Advancing age and death had removed most of the founders from guiding positions, and the challenge of replacing them was a dual one. Successors needed the knowledge, skills, and experience required to manage any large firm. In addition, the roller coaster effect of rapid growth during World War I followed by a serious depression in 1921–22 especially emphasized the necessity for younger, capable leaders to handle the multiunit, multifunctional, multinational enterprise.

The founders' determination to preserve the company's special character complicated the replacement process. The diligence, prudence, and thrift of the founding generation had all aimed at control. The traditions and maxims of earlier New England enterprise and of the small Worcester firm from which Norton sprang had centered on owner-operation as the best means for assuring continuity of values, efficiency, and prosperity. The answer, then, was continued family operation, common enough in small companies but quite unusual in the evolution of American big business. In short, Norton's founders and their successors had to find some way of maintaining the nineteenth-century firm amid the development of the modern, twentieth-century enterprise.

The solution lay in establishing adequate administrative techniques and structure for the big business. In a rapidly maturing industry, pricing and competition were more stabilized. Product development came in smaller steps, without startling breakthroughs comparable to electric furnace abrasives. Growth came more slowly and opportunity shifted increasingly from industry expansion to competition for market share. As an earlier Norton historian phrased it, the period was a time for "catching up."[1]

Catching up may have been less exciting than building the big enterprise, but initially, at least, it required real innovation. Nor was the challenge unique to Norton. Elsewhere, managers of the large-scale companies that had risen so rapidly since 1880 to become the core of America's industrial sector faced the challenges of consolidation and rationalization. Administration meant institutionalizing the actions often performed ad hoc by the original entrepreneurs or builders. Like other leaders, Norton's top executives had to establish a bureaucratic structure with clear lines of communication, authority, and responsibility to handle a large labor force, geographically scattered operating units, and the variety of functions, such as sales, finance, purchasing, and transportation, that supported the enterprise's original manufacturing business.

At Norton the same boom-and-bust cycle that made the leadership transfer so urgent also rushed administrative innovation. World War I complicated manufacturing by more than quadrupling orders, disrupting supplies of energy and raw materials, shortening delivery times, and gobbling up the labor supply. Rapid fluctuations in demand between 1914 and 1923, coupled with increased capital investment in raw material processing and manufacturing, soon required careful forecasting to coordinate operations for maximum, stable throughput. And rapid growth of an increasingly militant and unstable work force demanded a conscious, consistent labor relations policy and an organization to administer it. Finally, preserving Norton's dominance, meeting competitors' new products, and responding to new metals and grinding tasks in the stable industry that followed the war compelled the company to institutionalize innovation in a full-scale laboratory for research and development. The changes made in the World War I era determined Norton's leadership, character, pace of growth, and direction of development for the ensuing generation.

Stabilizing the Environment: Organizing the Industry

World War I marked the maturing of the bonded abrasives industry. Technological changes after 1920 were largely modifications or improvements of existing wheels. Resinoid bonds and diamond abrasives were exceptions, but none of the changes equaled the impact of vitrified bonds in the 1880s or of electric furnace abrasives after 1900. Markets continued to grow but not at the previous rate. Production of furnaced Alundum and silicon carbide exceeded emery for the first time in 1914. Natural abrasives never recaptured their lost leadership, as artificial abrasives accounted for most of World War I demand. While consumption of natural abrasives by value rose 33 percent in 1917 over 1916, the increase for artificial abrasives was by 177 percent to more than 115 million pounds.[2]

Sales also flattened, as figure 1 indicates. Industry output doubled four times between 1899 and 1919 but grew only 26 percent in the next twenty years. Auto sales leveled between three and four million units after 1923 and although the application of production grinding continued to expand to airplane manufacture and other industries, none equaled the automobile business in size, rate of growth, and impact on metal working.

Patterns of competition within the industry reflected similar stability. By 1920 all the major grain producers—Carborundum, Norton, Exolon, General Abrasive, International Abrasive, and the Abrasive Company—produced electric furnace abrasives. The major patents on grains had expired, and the initial Higgins furnace patent ended in 1921. Competitors quickly hired technicians from Norton and Carborundum, the veteran producers. Norton's Ray Hill White went to the Abrasive Company, H. A. Collins to General Abrasive, and N. Clif Hilton to Manhattan Rubber's Abrasive Wheel Division, while Carborundum's Thomas Allen went first to General Abrasive and then to the Abrasive Company.[3]

Despite the profusion of electric furnace manufacturers, Norton and Carborundum remained the wheel industry's leaders and its only integrated firms, except for the Simonds Abrasive Company, the successor to the Abrasive Company, which manufactured only aluminum oxide and which was never a major competitor. The two dominant companies' early experience, rapid growth, and success had preempted the field. Other wheel manufacturers lacked the volume and range of products required to justify installing their own furnace operations, and furnace manufacturers did not have the bonding expertise and marketing network to compete successfully with the two leaders.

As in so many industries at the century's turn, mastering new technologies and servicing new markets had simultaneously produced large integrated firms and established barriers to entry that protected early leaders in what quickly became a stable oligopoly. In 1920 Norton was the industry leader with $15 million in sales (excluding machines), and Carborundum was second with $11 million (including refractories).[4] Their combined market shares certainly exceeded half and may well have equaled two thirds of the total output of the industry's sixty companies. Both rank and market dominance have endured into the 1980s. The only major threat to the domestic duopoly was a challenge in the 1970s to Carborundum's second position from the Bay State Abrasives Company (today a division of Dresser Industries), founded in the 1920s and long operated by ex-Norton people.

The creation of a permanent industry association, the Grinding

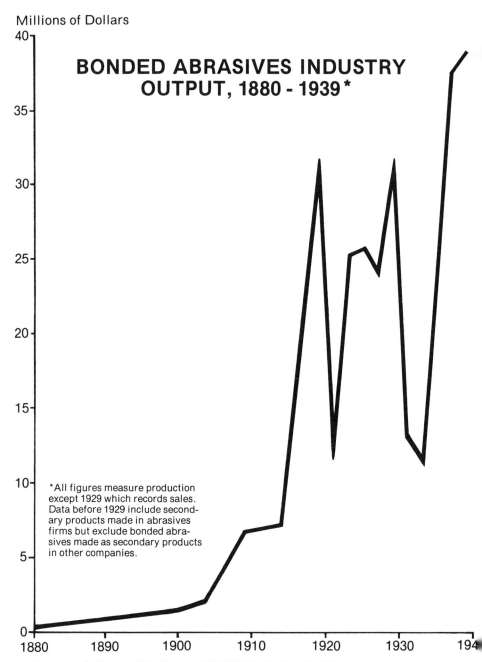

Millions of Dollars

BONDED ABRASIVES INDUSTRY
OUTPUT, 1880 - 1939 *

*All figures measure production
except 1929 which records sales.
Data before 1929 include secondary products made in abrasives
firms but exclude bonded abrasives made as secondary products
in other companies.

Source: U. S. Bureau of the Census, CENSUSES OF MANUFACTURES, 1905-1939.

Figure 1

Wheel Manufacturers Association (GWMA), in 1914 resulted from efforts to assure price stability and product standardization and further reflected industry maturity. Norton had participated in previous industry efforts to fix prices in 1888 and 1901, but both were unenforceable and short-lived. The timing of successful organization and price control in 1914 helps explain the prior failures. The ease of entry and lack of product standards in the new industry had prevented manufacturers from excluding fresh competition. Reliable cost data were lacking and the intense secrecy that shrouded bond formulas and manufacturing processes had discouraged the sharing of other information among companies. Before 1900 only Norton had a cost department, and by 1914 only Carborundum had added one.

Furthermore, those two firms were unable to compel or persuade others to share their standards until the industry matured. As the only fully integrated enterprises after the acceptance of artificial abrasives, Norton and Carborundum had tremendous market power. And while the capital costs for simple manufacture of grinding wheels still remained low, consumers' increased familiarity with wheel performance and standards made significant competition by cut-rate outsiders more difficult.

The threat of price cutting in the 1914 recession provided the final impetus to organize under Norton and Carborundum leadership. New industry price lists based on data from Norton's and Carborundum's cost departments soon raised prices as growing demand inspired by World War I reinforced the integrated firms' strong position. Careful consultation with Philander C. Knox, former attorney general from the Taft administration, cleared the association of antitrust difficulties. Promulgation and enforcement were handled by the GWMA's Price List Committee, which was always dominated by top Norton and Carborundum salespeople.[5]

The Price List Committee performed a variety of functions. It gathered sales and cost data, provided reliable market share statistics for members, oversaw trade practices, arbitrated protests and abuses, and supervised catalog publication.[6] Even after Fedral Trade Commission and federal court decisions led to its dissolution in 1923 and later replacement by a Merchandising Committee in 1931, continued industry price stability testified to successful control. The association had one printer produce all member price lists from the same galleys, leaving the heading blank so that company names could be inserted separately.[7] Assuring standard discounts to complement uniform list prices violated antitrust law and was handled informally. Carborundum and Norton agreed on discounts by customer classification, and smaller firms were expected to stay within a 5 percent range of those figures. At least one small manufacturer remembered that Norton "put the whiplash on us and we agreed to meet Norton Company's prices" after he had increased sales with overly generous discounts.[8] The system endured successfully until antitrust action in 1947.

Standardization of products was the second need that generated the GWMA and reflected the industry's growth and power. In 1913 grinding machine manufacturers persuaded the general manager of the National Machine Tool Builders Association to call a conference of fourteen machine builders and bonded abrasives manufacturers to standardize wheel grades. Led by Brown and Sharpe's chairman, W. S. Viall, machinery manufacturers decried the variety of grades, grits, and labels.

A joint committee's investigation determined that uncontrollable variations precluded uniformity among wheel manufacturers, but its recommendation that machinery people standardize spindle size revealed how much conditions had changed since the 1880s.[9] Machine tool companies were still large and valued customers, but they were now matched by the power and size of the large, integrated wheel manufacturers. The solution would be handled by discussion among equals—wheel manufacturers, machine builders, distributors, and major end users—and not by dictation from the veteran machinery producers, once the lords of the trade.

Continued growth of wheel use and the rise of a national movement for product standardization eventually led to simplified wheel shapes. By the early 1920s machine builders and wheel manufacturers recognized that "interest in standardization in other lines had increased with rapid strides."[10] They heard frequently from such powerful customers as Ford and other auto makers about "the confusion which prevailed in the plants of the [user] manufacturers."[11] Five years of study by a GWMA committee for standardizing wheel shapes led to a grand conference of major manufacturers, users, and distributors that reduced 414 customary bonded abrasive shapes to 144. It also appointed a standing committee with two representatives each from users, distributors, machinery manufacturers, and wheel makers to implement and oversee the plan and further simplify wheel shapes. The plan, which was quickly accepted by 80 percent of the wheel and machinery manufacturers, cut standard inventory from 715,200 to 255,800 stock sizes, slashing inventory costs and shortening delivery times for stock items.[12]

Inventory control, like price regulation, was another clear sign of the wheel association's growing power in a stable industry, and its influence quickly spread to a variety of other functions, including the standardization of wheel speeds and grading symbols, the formation of the Abrasive Grain Association in 1934, the enactment of safety codes in thirty-six states, and guidance in collective bargaining.[13] The association also served as the wheel manufacturers' representative to the federal government, especially during the code writing for the New Deal's National Recovery Administration and for preparedness and organization of war production during World War II.[14] Reorganized as the Grinding Wheel Institute and stripped of its pricing functions after a 1947 antitrust consent decree, the association continues today as the industry's spokesman and coordinator.

Preserving the Family Firm: The Transfer of Power

While maturation brought cooperation and stability to the industry, it challenged Norton Company with two new problems: transfer of leadership and administration. Age and death had by 1920 thinned the ranks of Norton's founder-managers. Milton Higgins died in 1912 and George Alden, his successor, retired as president in 1919 at the age of 75. John Jeppson remained Norton's superintendent of manufacturing until his death in 1920, but he had ceased active daily management before World War I.

Of the original owners, only Charles Allen, elected president at 60 in 1919, remained. Operating and guiding the large company was too much for one man. At this stage in many large American enterprises, professional managers assumed the top positions. They owned little or none of the enterprise, but they had trained and advanced within the firm as salaried career men. By World War I they made almost all middle-level administrative decisions, such as pricing and scheduling of production, and dominated stragetic planning and policy-making for resource allocation. If owners and outside financial people acted at all, they exercised a negative role.[15]

In sharp contrast, Norton's owners chose founders' sons for top management, as shown in figure 2. When Allen became president in 1919, George Jeppson succeeded him as secretary and Aldus Higgins replaced him as treasurer. Along with Allen, they were the most powerful men in the firm and were clearly destined to succeed him as its head. The elections of 1919 symbolized a changing of the guard; a second generation of owner-managers replaced the founders and assumed the challenges of managing the large enterprise while preserving its nineteenth-century New England character.

In fact, the 1919 changes were not the abrupt watershed they appeared to be. Allen remained chief executive for fourteen years and counselor for twenty years. Both Jeppson and Higgins already had two decades' experience with Norton, and as noted in the previous

NORTON COMPANY'S
OWNER-MANAGER FAMILY TREE

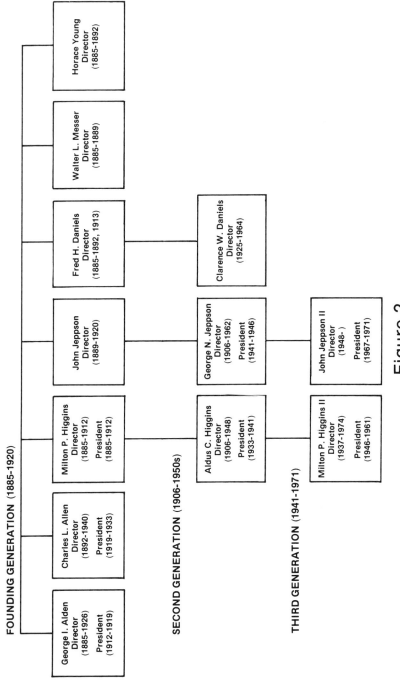

Figure 2

chapter, they were directly involved in building the large firm. They had been recruited and trained as a deliberate policy by the founders. Charles Allen had offered George Jeppson a generous salary and a position as assistant superintendent to deflect him from a career in the steel industry.[16] And although Aldus Higgins subbornly pursued a law career, he soon found that legal work requested by his father had virtually made him company counsel.[17]

Both men quickly passed a series of challenges that tested their ability and the viability of family management. Between 1900 and 1910 Higgins negotiated an inexpensive, exclusive lease of General Electro-Chemical's Alundum patents, oversaw the establishment of electric furnace operations at Niagara Falls, acquired impressive bauxite reserves for little cost in the southern United States, and in 1909 represented Norton in its settlement with Alcoa. In the same period George Jeppson mastered Worcester operations, established the firm's first laboratory, directed the development of Alundum wheels, and helped his father oversee Norton foremen and the manufacturing departments.

By 1910 the four founding directors—Higgins, Alden, Allen, and Jeppson—had clearly accepted Aldus and George as their successors who would operate Norton until midcentury, first with Charles Allen in a transition period and then on their own. The directors voted both onto an expanded board in 1906 and charged them with several major operations. When Norton Company established a manufacturing plant at Wesseling, Germany, in 1909, Aldus did the legal work while George oversaw plant construction. In the following year they established silicon carbide operations at Chippawa, Ontario, and in 1911 they supervised the planning and construction of a third plant in Worcester. By 1911 Aldus's and George's $9,000 salaries exceeded the $7,000 annual pay of President Higgins, Treasurer Alden, and Superintendent John Jeppson, and most of the board's committee work fell to the two sons and Charles Allen.[18]

The two sons' complementary interests and personalities made them a good team. George quickly succeeded his father as the firm's manufacturing head, while Aldus was clearly destined to replace Allen as the office man. A handsome man with the erect carriage of military school training, George was the more aggressive and outgoing. He knew most of the employees and talked with them easily and comfortably. His son remembered George as "a no-nonsense kind of character as well as a fellow who could have a pretty good time."[19] He was "Mr. Jeppson" to all but a handful of early associates.

Though personally a systematic man and a conscious planner, Jeppson was never bound by organization charts. He readily and sometimes impetuously badgered department heads about their operations if something displeased him. When Norton Company had difficulty selling camshaft Bakelite wheels, George wrote Aldus that "Sales Engineers and Laboratory have muffed the ball," and the sales engineer responsible "either makes good, or he gets out." He wanted the laboratory people "put squarely on their keels" and the two departments "antagonistically intimate."[20]

His constant interest and vigorous advocacy reinforced the emphasis on plant and product at Norton. Research Director Wallace Howe thought George Jeppson was a "sparkplug" who generated intriguing but difficult ideas and then charged others to develop them.[21] He strongly pushed such pet projects as 38 Alundum, segmental pulpstones, continuous process manufacturing, and zirconia-alumina abrasive, which became major Norton breakthroughs.

Aldus Higgins, who was only a year older than George Jeppson, was a thinker where Jeppson was a doer. In a curious reversal, the younger Higgins's personality echoed Charles Allen's and John Jeppson's, whereas George was more like the elder Higgins. Aldus's protégé, Ralph Gow, recalled that "Aldus Higgins was the kind of fellow who would kind of roll along and play for opportunities."[22] Unlike the more autocratic, outspoken Jeppson, Higgins avoided confrontation and "always did [things] in low key." Fellow executives marveled at his ability to listen and to ask perceptive questions to bring out others' ideas. Yet he never equaled George Jeppson's charm with employees, although he certainly cared as much for them. While George was careful to greet each one by name, Aldus might absentmindedly shuffle past with a nod. Finally, although George had attended college in Sweden, Aldus was probably more sensitive to the firm's New England parochialism. Gow thought Higgins "a very broad gauge fellow" who consciously encouraged his son, Milton P. Higgins II, and Gow to train in a variety of departments both in and out of Worcester.[23]

Despite their differences, the New England Yankee's son and the Swedish immigrant's son got along well with each other and with Charles Allen. Milton Higgins II recalled that early in their careers Aldus and George had one serious argument—possibly the 1910 battle over Horace Young's stock—after which they worked in harness, bound by their commitment to Charles Allen and to the preservation of the New England family firm.[24]

To both men Allen was a kind of second father whom they respected and obeyed. In the early years Charles Allen was always the boss and did not hesitate to criticize either of his younger colleagues, who addressed him as "the manager" or "Mr. Allen." As Allen aged, they supplanted him and gently moved him into the largely ceremonial position of chairman when he turned 75 in 1933. Both continued to consult him as titular leader, a role that they insisted he retain. When the old man, embarrassed with his age and frailty, attempted to resign in his eightieth year, the two sons resisted. Aldus's letter betrayed affection despite the stiff, New England formality that had always defined their relationship. He firmly but gently told Allen that he and George wished "to assume entire responsibility for the decision" to retain him as chairman. To put it on a company basis, Allen represented "some of the finest traditions that the Company has" and his retirement "would be a calamity," for "we all admire and love you."[25]

The two sons' rise as Allen's successors was due to a process of attrition as well as to their abilities. Although George Jeppson and Aldus Higgins may have had an inside track, since their fathers were among the four main Norton directors, other offspring could have perpetuated family management. Yet other owners' children were either unable or unwilling to endure the term of training and proving on which the owner-managers continued to insist. Horace Young's family showed no interest in the business and eventually sold his stock. Charles Allen's only child was a daughter, which automatically disqualified her from serious consideration. Of the male descendants, George Alden's stepson J. Herbert Johnson and Fred Daniels's son Dwight worked for Norton, but both left within a few years before attaining any major position. Clarence Daniels, Dwight's brother, joined the firm in 1913, became plants engineer in 1915, and eventually rose to vice-president and director, but he was never chief executive or a policymaker like George and Aldus.[26] Milton Higgins provided other businesses for his second son and his sons-in-law. Aldus's brother, John Woodman Higgins, headed the Worcester Pressed Steel Company; R. Sanford Riley, husband of daughter Katherine, was president of the Riley Stoker Company; and Lewis Prouty, husband of Olive Higgins, was briefly a manager at the Carr Fastener Company.

George Jeppson's and Aldus Higgins's promotions established more than family management. They virtually assured that their successors would come from within their own families. Of the seven original founders, Messer and Young had sold out, and Allen's daughter had no children. Descendants of collateral Higgins, Jeppson, and Daniels branches generally followed their parents' role as securities holders who ratified directors' decisions.

Aldus Higgins and George Jeppson realized that maintaining family management entailed continued recruitment, selection, and training for the third generation. A number of descendants from several founding families worked in low- and middle-level management jobs but left within a few years. However, Aldus's son, Milton P. Higgins II, was a willing and dogged recruit who left Harvard in 1928 to join Norton full time. Aldus carefully guided his son into all branches of the business, beginning as an employee and rising through the managerial ranks. By World War II he had worked in sales as a sales engineer and market research manager; in research as a laboratory man, technical secretary to George Jeppson, and assistant manager of Abrasive Products and Research; in production as a wheel maker and as resident manager at Chippawa; and in finance as Norton's treasurer after 1941.[27]

George's son, John Jeppson II, had to be recruited, much like his father and Aldus. George brought John along with encouragement but not force, holding weekly family and business reviews with his teenaged son and encouraging him toward college and professional business training. And when his son entered Amherst with vague plans for a law career, George continued to mail him letters and data about Norton Company until John gradually decided on a Norton career and attended Harvard Business School. After graduation in 1940 he joined the firm as a methods engineer until entering the Navy in 1942. George continued sending John company material throughout his military career to ensure his convert's return at the war's end.[28]

As their careful recruitment, selection, and training suggests, Norton's owners prized family management. Family management and employment was a tradition in Norton employee ranks, within the industry, and in the mercantile enterprises that had dominated New England business until the nineteenth century. Family management symbolized local control and assured stability and preservation of values in America's rapidly changing industrial world at the century's turn. Operation by the founders' descendants continued and deepened Norton Company's special character among America's big industrial enterprises. Owner-operation was the vital element in preserving the small, nineteenth-century New England business within the framework of the large twentieth-century firm.

Familial relationships were also prevalent outside owner-management. Kinship ties among Norton workers dated from the company's outset and endure to the present day. The pottery enterprise from which Norton sprang was a family business in the tradition of craft manufacturing. Norton Company's early dependence on Swedes who migrated from Hoganas and southern Sweden and its longevity as a major Worcester employer provided job opportunities first for employees' brothers, cousins, fathers, and uncles and later for sons, daughters, nieces, and nephews.

In the absence of systematic data, examples have to serve as evidence. The Styffes and Johnsons are extreme but illustrative cases of long careers and family employment. Three Styffe brothers, Hjalmar, Joel, and Herman, and a cousin, Phillip, followed Emil who came to Norton in 1887. By 1929, fifteen Styffe kin from three generations had joined the company, including a sister-in-law, a wife, eight sons, a daughter, and granddaughter.[29] Brothers Olaf and Ed Johnson were among many Johnsons employed at Norton Company before 1900. Olaf worked for thirty-eight years, his son Frank for forty-two years, his brother Ed for forty-five years, Ed's sons Edwin for forty-five years, Arthur for forty-seven years, and Harry for forty-seven years, and Harry's son Harold for nineteen years.[30]

Kinship was also found in management outside the owning families. William L. Neilson, son of the founder of the Republic Mining and Manufacturing Company, Norton's bauxite subsidiary, was vice-president of sales and head of the foreign division. His son, William, Jr., was a traveling representative to Norton's foreign plants. Irving Clark was the firm's first physician and his son, W. I. Clark, Jr., was secretary of Behr-Manning Company, a subsidiary. Pierre Baruzy, manager of Norton's French plant, was a nephew of Georges Bouillon, a company demonstrator in Europe, while Otto Schutte, head of the German plant, was a nephew of Alfred Schutte, Norton's major European distributor. Thomas Green, Aldus's brother-in-law, ran the French plant and was treasurer at Behr-Manning, and his son, Thomas Green, Jr., served as a Norton vice-president. Many other examples could be mentioned.

Norton's family management was not unusual among abrasives firms. Like so many small enterprises, the tiny companies of the industry's early days included kin among their leaders. Muriel Collie's 1951 industry history discussed seventy-seven firms and identified the personnel of sixty companies. Nearly 75 percent (forty-four) of those sixty enterprises had family administration. Father and son managers accounted for one half (twenty-two) of the group and brothers for one quarter (eleven).[31] Family operation even characterized Carborundum Company, the industry's other large firm. Ownership was concentrated in the Mellon family, but the company was headed for many years by President Frank J. Tone, whose son F. Jerome Tone became vice-president of sales, and by Vice-President and Sales Manager George R. Rayner, whose son became manager of sales administration in 1948.[32] The persistence of family operation at Carborundum, Norton's chief but seldom threatening competitor in a stable duopoly, then, reinforced and eased the continuance of family management at Norton.

Timing also helped account for the founders' interest in and perpetuation of family management. Although family operation later became quite exceptional among large American industrial firms, it was not at all remarkable when Norton's owners first began recruiting their sons at the close of the nineteenth century. Family firms, of which farms are the most numerous examples, have appeared throughout American business history and have persisted as long as business enterprise remained relatively small and simple.[33] Potters and other craftsmen passed their patrimony onto sons. The general merchants who dominated American business into the nineteenth century relied on blood ties to ensure trustworthy management at distant points when limited communication and transportation prevented careful oversight. Before 1900 professional managers ran only the tiny fraction—notably railroads—of American businesses that had become large, capital intensive, and complex. Their entry into the emerging large industrial firms had only just begun.[34]

Furthermore, family operation, so common among New England farmers, craftsmen, and merchants, ensured for Norton owners local control, stability, and preservation of the traditions and values of the earlier small firm. Timing here was especially crucial, for the founders made their move toward family management just as the great industrial merger movement of the late 1890s accelerated consolidation of numerous independent plants in a variety of industries. The most notable effect in Worcester was the merger of its largest enterprise, Washburn and Moen, first into American Steel and Wire and then into the giant U.S. Steel combination.

Few machine tool companies were absorbed, however, and most Worcester firms, like Norton, continued to pride themselves on local control by owner-managers closely associated with the community. Norton owners maintained deeply felt attachments and pride in their Worcester ties, a feeling that Milton Higgins II and John Jeppson II still hold very strongly.[35] Until the 1970s at least, Norton would always be a Worcester-centered firm.

Family management also helped transmit to the large enterprise traditional techniques and values. The new Aldus Higgins–George Jeppson team, which specialized, respectively, in the commercial and manufacturing segments of the firm, continued the two-man administrative leadership of Superintendent John Jeppson and General Manager Charles Allen. In the plant George Jeppson fell heir to his father's position as leader of the Swedish workers and the Swedish community. Workers turned to him, as they had to his father, for advice, intercession with authority, and emergency funds. George also headed or served on numerous local and national Swedish organizations and received the Order of Vasa from the king of Sweden, just as his father had.[36]

Like his partner and the founders, Aldus Higgins felt a deep affection and responsibility for the Worcester company and its people. He told protégé Ralph Gow that "we have three responsibilities. We want to make money for our stockholders. But I don't want big fast growth; I want steady growth. And we won't do that unless we satisfy our customers. But second we have a responsibility to our employees. They have devoted their lives to the company and they mean a great deal to us. And third, we have a responsibility to the community of Worcester. The company was formed by Worcester people in Worcester, and most of our employees live in the Worcester area."[37] Both George and Aldus were firmly committed to Norton's primacy as an abrasives company with owner-management and financial independence.

The new team's commitment only partially accounted for the continuity between the small firm and the large enterprise. Much of Charles Allen's, George Jeppson's, and Aldus Higgins's success centered on their ability to fit their controls and ideas with the emerging standard form of big business administration. Between 1900 and 1920 most large integrated industrial companies adopted a highly centralized structure based on functional departments.[38] Modified from railroad administrative structure, the new organization carefully delineated a line of authority downward from the president and the executive committee of the board of directors. Daily operation was handled by middle and lower level managers organized into functional departments for production, sales, finance, purchasing, transportation, and research and development. General managers or vice-presidents headed the major departments, and along with the chief executive, corporation counsel, and a few others, they comprised the Board of Directors' Executive Committee. Corporate staff handled such service functions as legal needs, personnel, and advertising, and interdepartmental committees helped coordinate activity among the functional departments.

Although professional managers established and headed the new structure in most industrial firms, Jeppson, Higgins, and Allen found it quite congenial to family management. The structure concentrated power in the top three (or two, after Allen's departure) owner-managers who served as president, works manager, and treasurer. From this vantage they could plan, oversee, and directly administer most operations of the Worcester-centered company, which remained stably concentrated in two product areas after World War I. The decision to expand Worcester operations instead of building a midwestern plant, even though eastern sales were less than a third of total business, helped retain central control.[39]

Figure 3 indicates that the structure grew naturally from the small firm. As the senior manager and the only active founder, Charles Allen retained his position as general manager of the entire business. Works Manager George Jeppson headed all wheel-manufacturing operations, including the foreign plants, research, and raw materials. As treasurer and general counsel, Aldus Higgins watched over the legal and financial departments. Although General Sales Manager Carl Dietz was nominally equal to Higgins and Jeppson, his Sales Department was in fact overseen by Allen and Higgins, who managed the "office" portion of the business. Following Dietz's departure in 1921, the sales position was further weakened because his successor, William L. Neilson, was frequently abroad in his second capacity as foreign manager.

When Norton Company formally absorbed the grinding machine company in 1919, the partners tightened their hold by simply allocating the machinery enterprise's functions within the wheel company's framework.[40] Thus, machine Sales Director Howard Dunbar reported to Carl Dietz (and later to William L. Neilson), who in turn answered to Allen and Higgins. Although figure 3 shows John Spence, works manager for machinery, reporting to Charles Allen, Spence also answered to George Jeppson, a relationship that was subsequently formalized with Jeppson's promotion to vice-president of production.

The three owners retained all final or real authority for themselves despite the formal allocation of control to the Board of Directors. The directors had expanded the board in 1921 to include the top salaried departmental heads—John Spence, superintendent of machine manufacturing, William L. Neilson, vice-president and foreign manager, Assistant Treasurer Henry Duckworth (who had first been elected in 1914), and Lewis Saunders, vice-president and director of research and raw materials.[41] (Carl Dietz, vice-president and general manager of sales, left the company before the election.) As the older owners died or retired, the Allen-Jeppson-Higgins team and the salaried managers made up most of the nine-member board. When the board expanded to sixteen in 1937, an executive committee composed of the two owner-managers and the functional vice-presidents was created to preserve centralized power. In weekly meetings the smaller group provided continuous and direct operating control.

In fact power was even more highly concentrated. Since Allen, Jeppson, and Higgins were major stockholders and the chief administrators who selected and appointed Norton's professional managers,

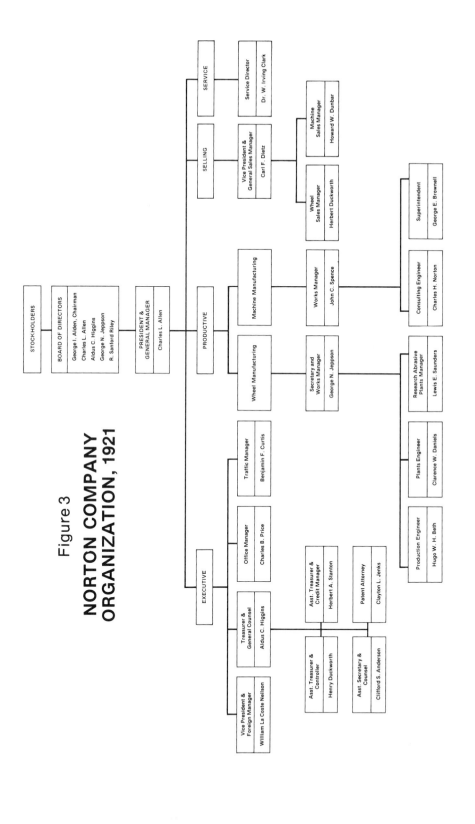

Figure 3

NORTON COMPANY
ORGANIZATION, 1921

STOCKHOLDERS

BOARD OF DIRECTORS
George I. Alden, Chairman
Charles L. Allen
Aldus C. Higgins
George N. Jeppson
R. Sanford Riley

PRESIDENT &
GENERAL MANAGER
Charles L. Allen

EXECUTIVE

Vice President &
Foreign Manager
William La Coste Neilson

Treasurer &
General Counsel
Aldus C. Higgins

Office Manager
Charles B. Price

Traffic Manager
Benjamin F. Curtis

Asst. Treasurer &
Controller
Henry Duckworth

Asst. Treasurer &
Credit Manager
Herbert A. Stanton

Asst. Secretary &
Counsel
Clifford S. Anderson

Patent Attorney
Clayton L. Jenks

PRODUCTIVE

Wheel Manufacturing

Secretary and
Works Manager
George N. Jeppson

Production Engineer
Hugo W. H. Beth

Plants Engineer
Clarence W. Daniels

Research Abrasive
Plants Manager
Lewis E. Saunders

Machine Manufacturing

Works Manager
John C. Spence

Consulting Engineer
Charles H. Norton

Superintendent
George E. Brownell

SELLING

Vice President &
General Sales Manager
Carl F. Dietz

Wheel
Sales Manager
Herbert Duckworth

Machine
Sales Manager
Howard W. Dunbar

SERVICE

Service Director
Dr. W. Irving Clark

Top management in 1921: the owner-managers and their assistants. Seated clockwise: George Alden, Aldus Higgins, John Spence, Herbert Duckworth, Clifford Anderson, William L. Neilson, Henry Duckworth, Carl Dietz, George Jeppson, and Charles Allen. Standing left to right: Herbert Stanton, W. Irving Clark, M.D., Arthur Butterfield, Wallace Montague, Clarence Daniels, Albert Fritts, Lewis Saunders, and Charles Price.

they were always first among equals.[42] They also retained for themselves a variety of tasks that would have been more systematically delegated in the average firm. As Ralph Gow later described the process, "there was a lot of reliance on individuals rather than firm procedures and rules."[43]

The company's community service largely reflected the trio's strong personal and Worcester biases, even after Norton established manufacturing operations in Canada, Japan, Germany, and France. Corporate contributions had focused heavily on the Swedish workers during the small firm's early days and attracted little attention in the already established industrial city. Norton's success naturally expanded both assistance and influence. Generous donations went to the Worcester Boys Trade School, which Milton Higgins had helped found, to Worcester Polytechnic Institute where Higgins and George

Alden had taught and where Aldus Higgins had trained, to Worcester's Swedish Lutheran churches, and to the Greendale YMCA, which Aldus, George Jeppson, and Charles Allen strongly supported.[44]

With the firm's growth, its owners—the Jeppsons, Higginses, Danielses, and Charles Allen—had quickly joined Worcester's civic leadership. Charles Allen headed the Bancroft Realty Company, builders of the Bancroft Hotel, Worcester's largest and an emblem of civic pride. Both Higginses served as trustees for WPI, while George Alden donated funds to establish its Alden Laboratory. Aldus Higgins was president of the Worcester Art Museum, counselor of the Worcester-based American Antiquarian Society, and a cofounder of the Golden Rule Campaign. In addition to his work in the Swedish community, George Jeppson served on several World War I committees in Worcester such as the YMCA War Work Fund, was a WPI trustee, and helped direct the Golden Rule Fund. He was a Republican member of Worcester's Board of Aldermen and its Common Council, while Aldus Higgins chaired the Republican City Committee in 1909.[45] The uncertain boundary between the owner-managers' personal charities and community service and their donations as representatives of Norton Company served to strengthen the tie between company and community. Their encouragement of community participation by top Norton salaried officials only broadened and deepened those ties, but in a typically personal or unsystematic fashion.

The owner-managers exercised their informal power in other ways as well. Selection and guidance of talented managerial prospects always rested with the top two or three. Charles Allen had reached out to encourage Jeppson and Higgins, and they in turn supported their own candidates in addition to their sons. Aldus Higgins guided young Ralph Gow almost from the time he joined the firm as a graduate of the Massachusetts Institute of Technology in 1925.[46] George Jeppson encouraged the career of WPI engineer Andrew Holmstrom in a similar fashion. Salary decisions and advancement were always the owner-managers' prerogative. Top-level promotions simply grew out of informal discussions between George Jeppson and Aldus Higgins, each of whom assumed managerial appraisal as a personal responsibility.[47]

Especially indicative of this unsystematic approach was the awarding of stock options to favored employees. Like many chief executives in other firms, Norton's heads soon realized that stock holding could serve as additional remuneration and incentive to key personnel, and by World War I the directors realized the need for a stated, if informal, policy. They argued that "the growth of Norton Company has been so rapid and its activities so scattered and extensive that much of the responsibility of its conduct and management has been placed in the hands of heads of departments and branches." Norton had thereby "built up . . . a group of loyal, earnest men," and it seemed "wise . . . to foster and encourage this spirit of loyal co-operation" by allowing "those carrying these responsibilities to become Stockholders."[48]

The actual procedure was quite simple and the selection always remained in the hands of Higgins and Jeppson. The company set aside small amounts of stock to be offered in "special instances . . . as the Directors may see fit." Norton Company arranged for a low-interest bank loan to cover 10 percent of the stock's purchase price at book value and provided that the purchaser could pay the remaining 90 percent from dividends. The directors carefully stated that they intended no "radical change" in ownership.[49] To preserve the closed company, employee purchasers could sell the stock only to Norton Company, and all buyers and their heirs were obliged to sell their shares back to the company at retirement or death.

Initial offers were made to top sales, financial, and manufacturing people, but typically, George Jeppson and Aldus Higgins never established precise guidelines for size of offers or for selection of recipients. They made individual choices ranging from department heads to long-time secretaries. While the number of shares and recipients always remained a small fraction of total stock issue and total employees, the figures grew into thousands of shares and several hundred workers in the ensuing decades.

As the directors' statement acknowledged, Norton's owner-managers were forced to assign some authority as the firm expanded. Yet they were always careful to delegate in a fashion that assured maximum centralized control and preservation of the owners' ideas of what the company should be. Major investments outside Worcester were originally projects overseen by sons, much as early New England merchants had used relatives to handle business at distant points. When the founders thought that initial uncertainties had been resolved and operations routinized, trusted salaried men replaced the sons. Aldus Higgins established the Niagara Alundum operation and superintended it for ten years until his technical man, Lewis Saunders, was ready to replace him. George Jeppson built and headed the German plant through its first year before giving way to William L. Neilson. Higgins acquired and held the southern bauxite properties until he felt certain that the Neilson family could be left to manage them.

The project approach soon became a traditional way of handling extraordinary tasks at Norton. A committee or task force served as a convenient way to handle new ventures, pet programs, or those jobs that failed to fit within a neat departmental structure. Following World War I, project teams set up manufacturing operations first in Canada and France and later in England. An extensive committee system, including Experimental, Mechanical, Abrasive Production, Refractories, and Abrasives committees, coordinated inter- and intradepartmental projects.[50] After detailed studies of new undertakings, such committees reported directly to the chief executives, who retained final authority and decided when a project should become part of the regular organization.

Assuring Leadership and Control: Finance and Sales

Within the regular departmental structure, the cautious selection of salaried managers for delegation of authority helped maintain owner control and values. The original owner-managers and their sons promoted experienced men who agreed with or at least accepted the owners' outlook and who were quick to obey the owner-operators' wishes.

Henry Duckworth, assistant treasurer and controller, is a particularly good example. He had advanced from his original position as office boy under Charles Allen's close scrutiny and, as noted in chapter 1, established systems for expediting orders, inventory control, cost accounting, and raw materials management. Control had always been highly prized by Norton's owners, and Duckworth's work was critical to maintaining the owners' knowledge and power in the rapidly growing firm. His close attention to cost reduction made him especially attractive to the thrifty New England owners. In Norton's job-shop business, an inventory in excess of one million wheels accounted for one fourth of all assets, and its regulation was crucial for economical operation.[51] Cost data were vital to preserving adequate profit margins and effective price leadership.

By dint of self-training, Duckworth continued to elaborate the simple system of order tickets he had established for the small company in the 1890s to record direct labor and materials costs. By 1907 he had built an extensive, up-to-date cost-accounting program.[52] His department accurately tracked each item's direct costs, which reflected labor, materials, and department overhead, and also recorded and allocated general overhead, which it divided into plant expenses and sales and administration costs. Based on careful data gathering, Duckworth determined formulas to measure quickly departmental and factory expense as a percentage of more easily determined direct labor expense.

His data readily allowed Norton to establish per item list prices with calculated profit margins for its hundreds of thousands of products, a complex job essential for success in a job-shop industry. As Duckworth explained:

> We try in every case to determine what expense the product is affected by, and then try to find a logical basis on which to apportion it . . . If it is necessary to sell it for less than it costs, we should do so with full knowledge of the facts. We should not charge more than its share of expense to a profitable product in order to lighten the burden of a product which shows little or no profit. The practice is liable to result in large losses because of low prices made as a result of fictitious costs and also to restrict the sale of the profitable article because of the higher prices necessary to absorb the additional expense referred to above.[53]

His cost accounting ensured high profit margins and maintenance of generous cash reserves in the hectic period of rapid growth and helped Norton owners to monitor their expanding bureaucratic enterprise. Return on investment, which had varied between 16 percent and 28 percent between 1911 and 1914, jumped to a range of 39–51 percent in the next four years, while average profit on sales rose from 25 percent to over 44 percent for the same periods.[54] Duckworth also perpetuated the founders' policy of liquidity and careful reinvestment of profits to avoid outside ownership or long-term debt. His controls and short-term loans from Worcester, Boston, and New York banks supplied the funds that quadrupled capacity between 1911 and 1918, while Norton stock split six for one and average dividends exceeded 20 percent annually.[55]

The few exceptions to self-finance resulted from unusual and unexpected events—a $630,000 bond issue in 1913 to help finance employee homes and a $2,500,000 bond issue in 1917 to anticipate constraints in short-term credit during World War I. Outside financing was also necessary when Norton failed to predict the bite of new federal income and excess profits taxes during World War I. Norton's owners reluctantly issued $6 million in nonvoting preferred stock in 1919, for which they quickly accumulated reserves for liquidation in 1925.[56]

While the loans helped finance extraordinary growth, Duckworth's system of financial reports helped regulate that growth. Systematic depreciation and budgeting provided more accurate knowledge of capital assets.[57] Careful financial controls allowed Allen, Higgins, and Jeppson to judge the performance of salaried managers in Worcester's burgeoning operations and especially those working beyond direct oversight in the United States, Canada, and Europe.

A strong Financial Department and influential financial men soon

became an enduring Norton tradition, reflecting the owners' emphasis on thrift and control. Duckworth, who stayed on for more than
half a century, was the first nonowner elected to the Board of Directors. He oversaw the purchasing, cost, and stores departments in
addition to his accounting and auditing functions for Worcester and
all foreign plants. He and his successors, William Magee, Edwin
McConnell, and William Perks, jealously guarded their cost figures
and their role in setting prices, and they were always included in the
owner-managers' inner councils.

Furthermore, Duckworth's financial organization reinforced secrecy, centralization, and owner-control. In the early years balance
sheets and statements of company performance were shared among
the seven founders and those relatives who held Norton stock. Such
unpublished reports supplied much of the data used in table 1 in
chapter 2. In the second generation, however, since only George
Jeppson and Aldus Higgins were active as top managers, they saw
no need to share such statistics with absentee owners who merely
collected dividends. By the 1920s and 1930s annual meetings of stockholders became largely ceremonial affairs at which Duckworth and
his successors announced dividend levels. Data on gross revenue,
net income, and return on sales were known only to the owner-
managers, their top financial man, and a few of his assistants. As a
result, systematic records of profits have not survived, and such data
only became available again when the company went public in the
early 1960s.

While the Sales Department was never so strong as Finance, its
development clearly reflected Norton's expansion and the effort to
carry the policies and traditions of the small business into the large
enterprise. The big business's needs were most evident in the sales
force's increase in quantity and quality. The four-man salaried sales
force of the 1890s had become sixteen in 1907 and nearly forty by
1915.[58]

Better training accompanied expansion. George Montague had no
formal preparation when he was assigned to sell oilstones in 1897,
wheels in 1898, and grinding machines in 1902. He recalled that in
response to his protests of ignorance Charles Allen confidently replied, "You know enough to take a piece of metal against a wheel
and know if it's hard or soft by the looks of the metal, don't you?"[59]

In typical Norton fashion, formal instruction of wheel salesmen
grew out of desultory educational experiments with a few new recruits. Charles Jinnette remembered that in about 1903 he and Otto
Lof spent time in each department of the business from raw materials
through manufacturing to shipping before going on the road. Weekly

Saturday meetings with Charles Allen and John Jeppson allowed them to appraise both Jinnette's and Lof's performance and the program.[60] Success soon encouraged the owner-operators to institute annual wheel sales conferences to explain new developments and to stimulate veteran salesmen, and in 1914 an educational department provided new wheel and machine salesmen with formal courses and two years' experience in all elements of wheel and machine manufacturing.[61]

Their education considerably increased the salesmen's understanding of their product and their ability to specify proper wheels for customers, a crucial service for maintaining Norton's industry leadership. Joe Cannon, an early trainee, recalled that the training was "a great thing for the salesman. It enabled me to look right down into the wheels and [know] how it was constructed and what you would expect it to do and so on. I built my knowledge of how to specify wheels on that beginning."[62]

By 1920 Norton had created a full-fledged sales bureaucracy. General Sales Manager Carl Dietz and his assistants Herbert Duckworth (for wheels) and Howard Dunbar (for machinery) presided over a domestic sales department that exceeded eighty salesmen and demonstrators. Two thirds were in the bonded abrasives section (75 percent of gross sales) and nearly one third in the machine section (20 percent of sales), with the rest handling abrasive grain and refractories. The wheel and machine divisions were divided into territories, which gave Norton Company national coverage. The twenty-one wheel districts and fourteen machine districts were each headed by branch office managers whose monthly reports provided valuable market information on a regular basis. Warehouses or branch sales offices were located in New York, Chicago, Detroit, Philadelphia, Cleveland, and other large industrial centers.[63] Central administration at the Worcester headquarters included the order and stock divisions, the training program, and such support operations as sales engineering, sales service, and publicity.

Despite growth and bureaucratization, sales continued many patterns established in the small firm. Because abrasives remained largely a job-shop business of mainly small orders and very few high-volume items, distributors serviced by Norton salesmen continued to handle most sales to end users. Norton sales people generally supplied and helped distributors, selling directly only to large accounts and those that required special handling. By 1923 Norton had 125 exclusive agencies and many smaller dealers scattered across the nation.[64] Following the pattern established by Charles Allen in 1885, distributors and dealers purchased their stock outright, although Norton might occasionally consign a large "service" stock for a special customer.

Pricing policies that dated from the company's early days helped regulate the distribution system while maintaining Norton leadership and profits. Theoretically, all pricing was done by cost. An item's list price included 40 percent for manufacturing costs (on a 100-wheel standard base), 30 percent for sales and administration, and 30 percent profit. In fact the formula was kept flexible for competition and the conditions of trade. An elaborate discount system (ranging from 30 percent to 70 percent) separated direct and dealer accounts and varied among customers and dealers on the basis of annual volume. List prices remained fixed to avoid frequent reprinting of large catalogs, and fluctuating discounts permitted quick price adjustments per item for changing markets and costs.[65] Norton, like most oligopolists, preferred to avoid price competition just as it had as a small firm. Carborundum had similar costs, and in the relatively stable abrasives business after 1922, price cutting could not drive it out of business. As Milton Higgins II put it, "This idea of killing competitors off is for the birds. You can't do it. All you do is end up by making less money."[66]

Norton Company's long-time position as industry leader and its conservative business methods reinforced that view. Norton had marketed premium products from the beginning, and its owners had argued (just as had Charles Norton in his case for production grinding) that performance per unit cost was more important than initial cost. Good performance for a fair price assured repeat sales, which were the heart of a consumable industrial supply business. As Aldus Higgins explained, "Customers may be sold the first time but they purchase the second time and thereafter." To Assistant Sales Manager Howard Dunbar, price cutting was "the argument of the weak, incompetent and incapable" who competed by selling inferior products at lower prices.[67]

Norton's leadership underpinned its ability to set industry prices, and as it had in the past, that leadership continued to depend on service as well as superior goods. In addition, customer aid and product quality were closely intertwined. The large volume that resulted from its premium products gave the company crucial advantages over competitors, including a standard inventory with thousands of wheels, which would have to be special-ordered from smaller firms, and the extra kiln capacity to handle special orders more quickly. Volume also defrayed the maintenance of a trained sales and engineering staff that was responsible for the education of users, a critical part of service. As H. K. Dodge, Norton's first sales manager, explained in 1907, "In a majority of the various lines, it is possible for the customer to decide the worth of the goods for sale, from the appearance, or sense of feeling, but it is not so with grinding wheels." Demonstration and detailed knowledge of the conditions of wheel use were "very essential."[68]

The big firm merely institutionalized what Charles Allen, John Jeppson, and others had done on an ad hoc basis earlier. After 1900 Norton advertised extensively in metal and other industry journals and printed numerous manuals and pamphlets to explain the process of grinding, the mysteries of wheel selection, and the determination of proper wheel speed. *Grits and Grinds,* a Norton trade organ begun in 1909, became a monthly twelve-page bulletin sent free to salesmen, distributors, and customers. By World War II worldwide distribution in six languages disseminated clearly illustrated articles covering new developments in grinding machinery, wheels and abrasive techniques, valuable safety procedures, and the principles of proper wheel selection.[69] Other educational efforts included a school for agents' salesmen and a grinding course for machinists from all over the United States.

Finally, the big sales organization reflected the early firm in a more general sense. With George Jeppson in charge of production and Henry Duckworth heading company finances, Norton Company remained a conservative abrasives-manufacturing firm for many decades. Informal centralized operation by owner-managers undercut potential Sales Department strength. Norton Company made limited use of its regular sales and market data. Careful market research began only in the late 1920s and remained sporadic before World War II.[70] The Sales Department did not even control prices, which were set in a give-and-take consultation with the financial people and which could be established or changed only after approval by the Board of Directors. Despite its size and crucial functions, the Sales Department never dominated Norton Company.

Assuring Leadership and Control: Production

Growth's largest impact on administration occurred in manufacture, the key to the company's success. This function was headed by George Jeppson, first as works manager and later as vice-president of production. Raw materials processing became a full-fledged department with operations spread from Worcester to Bauxite, Arkansas, Niagara Falls, New York, and Chippawa, Ontario. The two-man Department of Tests became laboratories in Worcester, Niagara, and Chippawa, employing fifty and handling raw material analysis, product testing, and rudimentary research.

In addition, the expanded work force and workspace in Worcester necessitated a more elaborate factory staff. In 1914 Norton hired three efficiency experts from Western Electric, a leading exponent of scientific factory management. B. A. Hildebrant headed the Methods Department to oversee the production process and the piecework system. Harold Dunbar operated a Planning Department to route orders and coordinate flows within the plant, while his brother Howard did similar work for the Grinding Machine Company. Under Clarence Daniels, Plants Engineering became a major constructor, building four mills for machine manufacture, two abrasive plants, storage facilities, and a power plant. Thure Larson's Mechanical Engineering Department separated from the Methods Department to study and improve technical methods and machinery.[71]

World War I, which accelerated management challenges and expansion, bared two special problems: coordination of product flow and labor relations. Wartime shortages sporadically disrupted supplies of coal, high-quality bauxite, electric power at Niagara and Chippawa, alumina for 38 Alundum, and railroad cars to transport raw materials. The virtual closure of Greek and Turkish emery supplies coupled with inadequate domestic sources threw an additional burden on artificial abrasives. To meet special wartime needs and substitute for emery shortages, Norton produced a variety of sizes and types of Alundum grains, including regular, 21, 26, 38, and 66 Alundums, as well as a cheaper Alundum from alunite, a bauxite substitute.

The raw materials disruption and multiplication of grain types produced a bewildering variety of complex mixtures and substitutes. Irregular spurts in industrial production and the uncertainty about America's entry into war and about its duration complicated problems by alternately causing shortfalls and surpluses. Coal shortages in early 1918 became an overstock in December, while George Jeppson complained that excessive clay stockpiling had produced "very respectable clay mines" in the yards. Shortages of 21 Alundum, a special product for the lens-grinding industry, led Norton to establish an impromptu mill and to produce such large quantities that Jeppson wondered if "we will ever grind any more optical abrasive."[72] Nor did the difficulties of coordinating production and demand end with the war. Large cutbacks in work force, inventory, and production in early 1919 left the company running flat out by the year's end to catch up with the economy's unexpected spurt.

Elementary responses and planning eased some of the difficulty. In January 1917 Norton began weekly inventories of ore and grain, and George Jeppson consolidated responsibility for management of all Norton raw materials in Lewis Saunders. Tom Green from the

Grain Department proposed eight-week reports of wheel and grain inventories, orders, and scheduled production, and by late 1919 the Cost Department was making six-month forecasts of grain need based on inventory and consumption in the previous quarter.[73]

But the disruptions continued. When George Jeppson complained in mid-1919 that Norton had a five-year supply of 66 Alundum but was short of regular and 38 Alundums, Wallace Montague responded that after "careful" consideration by representatives from the sales, research, manufacturing, and planning departments, "it is impractical, if not impossible," to forecast consumption "accurately enough to keep us out of difficulty . . . We really cannot anticipate the demand for our abrasive products."[74]

The 1921 depression strikingly bared the firm's inadequacies and compelled forecasting and budgetary controls to coordinate production and demand. The sharp collapse of the economy, which began in late 1920 and bottomed out a year later, was the nation's worst since the 1890s and the first serious depression since large integrated firms had come to dominate U.S. industrial production. Few were prepared, and the combination of lengthening inventory build-ups, credit shortages, and the high fixed cost burden of large-scale enterprise was devastating. The automobile, machine tool, and metal-working industries were especially hard hit. General Motors scarcely avoided bankruptcy and Ford survived by forcing its dealers to take cars.[75]

At Norton the impact was so great that old-timers still think of this collapse, rather than the 1930s debacle, as the great depression. By December 1920 Aldus Higgins despaired that "I have never seen anything like it." Production had plummeted to 30 percent of October's level. Six months later Charles Allen wrote that "we are running only about 4% in the machine end and from 15 to 20% in the wheel end." For 1921, abrasives industry sales fell 70 percent and Norton sales dropped 78 percent from the previous year.[76]

Because grinding was part of the metal-working cycle, Norton had suffered from previous downturns in the 1890s, 1907, and 1914. But this was the big company's first collapse and it was poorly prepared, for unlike the case in previous domestic recessions, foreign sales did not cushion the impact. The French plant operated at 5 percent capacity, and the new Japanese and Canadian operations were all back to "bed rock." Only the German plant profited, and it wanted more credit.[77]

To make matters worse, Norton had been running flat out like the rest of the economy before the crash. Total sales for 1920 were a record high. In addition to establishing three overseas plants, the company had allocated $600,000 in the spring of 1920 for machinery division construction and equipment and had set up five branch stores. It had "a large stock of grinding wheels on hand," which it did not begin to reduce until early 1922. As Aldus Higgins put it, "We were greatly overbuilt, overstocked, and generally inflated."[78] Furthermore, in contrast to previous times, the firm faced $420,000 in annual interest payments on its preferred stock, and failure to pay would shift voting control from the owner-operators to the preferred stockholders.

The short-range response was a ruthless paring. Allen, Jeppson, and Higgins slashed the work force 80 percent from more than four thousand to less than eight hundred. They closed operations at Bauxite, Niagara Falls, and Chippawa and gave an "indefinite leave of absence" to all but twenty-five men in the machinery division.[79] The remaining plant employees worked three-day weeks, and office employees took three 10 percent pay cuts. The directors skipped a dividend for the second time in the firm's history.

Despite rumors to the contrary, Norton was never near bankruptcy. The paring was severe and even Aldus Higgins had to stop construction on his new home. But he privately wrote William L. Neilson in June 1921 that "we are in very excellent shape. Our cash resources are ample" even though no recovery was projected "for a number of months," or even "a year." Preferred stock dividends went out on schedule, and after the upturn came in 1922, Norton declared a two-for-one split in its common stock.[80]

The crunch's impact left an indelible impression on George Jeppson and Aldus Higgins. Both appreciated anew the founders' thrifty financial policies of large cash reserves and prudent investment at a cautious pace. They liquidated the preferred stock as rapidly as possible, and there was no major outside long-term financing for four decades. Twenty years later, when Norton was running full blast in World War II, George Jeppson and Aldus Higgins amassed cash reserves exceeding $22 million, refused to rebuild the machinery division despite obvious tax advantages, and agonized over the coming postwar depression.[81] During the 1920s and 1930s the cautious managers eschewed diversification, slowed foreign expansion, and stuck to the abrasives industry they knew.

Not only was the entrepreneurial spirit diminished, but economizing had devastated the organization. The tremendous waste of resources and personnel occasioned by roller coaster demand between 1913 and 1923 was injurious to long-run health. Numerous skilled personnel in the wheel and machinery divisions had been laid off, and the research department had shrunk 80 percent to eight people. While many returned, the company did lose some real talent, including Carl Dietz, vice-president and sales manager who left for Bridgeport Brass, and researcher Orello S. Buckner, who, along with Leonard Krull and George Bullard, left to establish the Bay State Abrasive Products Company in nearby Westboro, Massachusetts.[82]

The depression also compelled Aldus Higgins to recognize a crucial shift in demand. "Our business has within the last few years depended perhaps more than any of us realized upon the automobile trade, either directly or indirectly. I suppose that 60 or 70 percent of our business is dependent upon the automobile trade. This was not the case in 1914 when there was a general business depression."[83]

The greater concentration of markets that accompanied expanded demand paradoxically facilitated forecasting. Although Norton was even more deeply and permanently tied to the machine tool and metal-working cycles and although its dependence on the automotive industry—a consumer durable business—threatened to make its market fluctuate even more erratically, predicting the course of relatively few industries meant greater knowledge of future demand.

Norton's desire for greater certainty was also eased by efforts in other industries after the 1921 depression. At General Motors, Du Pont, and other large industrial firms and in associations of large manufacturers such as the National Industrial Conference Board, top people recognized that some kind of planning or forecasting was essential. The waste generated by wide fluctuations in large enterprises with high fixed investment was too great to tolerate. Forecasting helped smooth out the bumps and allowed such firms to run steadily and run full for maximum use of resources.[84]

Henry Duckworth, the controller and assistant treasurer under whom Norton's costing had evolved, encouraged planning and enthusiastically quoted Donaldson Brown, who had established an elaborate forecasting mechanism for General Motors. "Forecasting and planning [Brown explained] are nothing more or less than a system of control whereby production, purchase of materials, and the employment of capital are coordinated with sales requirements . . . The focal point of the system is the sales outlet."[85] Simultaneously, the encouragement of trade associations and standardization by Herbert Hoover's Commerce Department was tending in the same direction. The government's data gathering and collation provided interested firms with statistical pictures of the economy's behavior and were a vital tool for forecasting.[86]

At Norton as at other large companies, the actual development of forecasting techniques came from middle-level, salaried experts. Stephen Foster, a statistician with the National Industrial Conference Board, was hired in 1920 to help with coordination of grain supply,

wheel production, and sales. In 1923 he set up a Business Analysis
Department with L. D. Dorney, who had handled statistical work in
the Sales Records Department, while John Truelson returned from
the German plant to administer a budgetary control system.[87] In the
1920s the Business Analysis Department drew on branch sales managers' monthly reports to gather, collate, and record sales data in
eighty different reports. These reports, divided according to time,
product, customer, district, and salesman, permitted short-range forecasting and more careful appraisal of salesmen's and managers' performances.

Norton forecasting began for bonded abrasives in 1927 and for
machinery in 1928. It focused, as Donaldson Brown had suggested,
on sales projections and then coordinated production and inventory
with them through budgeting.[88] The sales forecast depended on three
sources. Foster assessed the general business situation through "the
movement of commodity prices, stock prices, freight car loadings,"
the business index, and other indexes in the federal government's
Survey of Current Business. The *Survey*, special trade services, industry
journals, and business conferences also supplied production statistics
from the abrasives industry's customers, particularly the automobile,
steel and iron, agricultural implement, and machine tool industries.

Foster then correlated past Norton abrasives industry sales (reported by the GWMA) with the general economy, with particular
industries, and with time. The time studies revealed patterns based
on seasons and general economic performance. Given Norton's market share and the grinding industry's and Norton's ratio of sales to
a customer industry's output as the economy moved, Foster then
calculated that industry's demand for Norton products by wheel type.

The forecasts were drawn up each December in quarterly periods
for the next year. After making inventory projections, production
levels were set and scheduled by the planning engineer and quarterly
production budgets were established. Revisions, based on adjustments between projections and actual performance, were also made
quarterly. Administration fell to the Wheel Division Inventory Control
Committee, which comprised the Planning Department's head, the
stock supervisor, and the statistician and which reported to George
Jeppson, the vice-president of production. The committee was formally "charged with the duty of maintaining even production by
balancing increase or decrease in inventory against fluctuations in
incoming business [and of providing] economical manufacture, good
service and a minimum amount of money invested in inventory."[89]

Forecasting for the machine division was a similar, though more
difficult, process. The Machine Schedule Committee, which com-

prised the sales manager, superintendent, planning engineer, and statistician, planned with monthly sales forecasts and quarterly production, inventory, and budgeting units. Because of the greater lag time for production, sales were measured by shipments rather than orders. Inventory control turned on the number of stock mechanisms, or subassembly units including bases and parts, per product.

Although forecasting did smooth fluctuations, the formal system was not as great a departure from the informal centralized firm as it appears at first glance. Forecasting never became long-range planning, statistics were never a rigid guide, and final control still rested with the owner-managers. Norton's managers found that accumulated adjustments invalidated the original forecasts after six or nine months. Duckworth, who pronounced wheel forecasting "satisfactory" in 1929, included in that judgment two 10 percent quarterly rate adjustments for 1928. Machine forecasting was less accurate. Machine sales in 1929 were up 30 percent over their six-month projection, although changing inventory moderated operating adjustments to 6 percent.[90]

In exceptional periods the forecast was less accurate. The 1937–38 recession left Norton with "by far the largest stock" in its history, in part because of its desire to keep workers on the payroll beyond production needs.[91] Ralph Gow, who served as works manager before World War II and as executive vice-president and president between 1948 and 1966, argued that even in stable times "we were adjusting to reality always." Milton Higgins II observed pungently that "running the abrasives business is a pain in the ass . . . because the inventory is quite changeable and it swings. You get quite a lot of swings. How much it is going to swing toward one size [of abrasive grain] as against another size, is very difficult to determine."[92]

From the outset Duckworth warned that Norton did "not merely forecast from figures." Projections were "tested against judgment," and "the final forecast is the result of statistical evidence and business judgment."[93] That judgment, which was based on years of experience with the industry, remained at the top. Schedules and projections were approved and modified by Henry Duckworth, George Jeppson, and Aldus Higgins until 1945 and by Ralph Gow and Milton Higgins II, in the ensuing twenty years.

Finally, given forecasting's limited effectiveness and the owner-managers' conservative determination to stick with what they knew, they had no incentive to expand forecasting into long-range planning. Such planning became essential for firms like General Motors and Du Pont, which diversified into a variety of businesses and whose complex decision making and capital allocation were beyond the abilities of a single executive or even a small group of top men. At Norton career executives like Aldus Higgins, George Jeppson, Milton Higgins II, and Ralph Gow had little trouble overseeing and guiding a firm concentrated on a single industry that they knew thoroughly.

Expansion and Turmoil: The Work Force

Labor relations gave George Jeppson a great deal of trouble during World War I when an increasing overall demand for industrial workers coincided with Norton's rapid expansion. The factory work force at the Norton wheel and grinding companies more than tripled from 900 in 1914 to 3,000 in 1918.[94] Competition with Worcester's booming machine tool, machinery, and metal-working industries limited the supply of skilled and steady workers, while Norton's rapid growth and a decline in immigration restricted Sweden's ability to supply labor as in the past.

Relaxed standards and recruitment from new sources failed to satisfy fully the firm's requirements. Instead of carefully selecting strong, healthy men with stable backgrounds, the company began accepting almost anyone who sought work. As Norton physician W. Irving Clark put it: "Is he breathing? Well, then let him work."[95] Full employment and high wages induced by the war accelerated labor independence and mobility. Turnover rates ran as high as 90 percent to 158 percent annually as workers moved among firms looking for the highest wages for the least work. Recruiting non-Swedish immigrants did little to improve loyalty and stability, and the Swedish component fell to 24 percent of the work force by 1917.[96]

Ethnic clashes heightened tensions in the plant. The veteran Swedes dominated the low-level supervisory and skilled ranks. The Catholic Irish and Italians, for whom the Lutheran and Baptist Swedes had little respect, found themselves concentrated in the outdoor, low-paying, and physically arduous jobs. Dissatisfaction over discrimination in favor of Swedes encouraged many to move on. High turnover, inexperienced workers, and the lost sense of family shop resulted in increased manufacturing costs as breakages and off-grades grew and production rates slipped. Henry Duckworth complained that "years ago . . . we had a lot of old reliable men here who were above padding their piece work records. Now it is entirely different, and almost every day we find evidence of a new scheme that has been devised to beat us."[97]

Recruiting women for the plant added some stability but generated a variety of conflicts between the sexes. Women had worked in the Norton office force as secretaries, typists, telephone operators, and clerks since the 1890s, but their employment in the plant came only in 1917 when U.S. entry into the war further tightened the labor supply. George Jeppson carefully reviewed the experiences of local firms and was assured that the majority of successful Norton applicants had already had manufacturing experience.[98] At Norton Company, at least, there was to be no wholesale transfer from housewife to factory worker.

Within six months, the company employed more than 140 women in the plant, and the number eventually reached 260. Strength limitations and respect for female "delicacy" assigned most to such light tasks as inspecting and testing small wheels, light shaving, tracing, and drafting. Women proved to be steady, dependable workers with one-fifth the turnover rate of male employees. Mrs. Emil Styffe served as company matron to maintain "the moral atmosphere surrounding our girls," and difficulties over restroom, locker room, and eating facilities were gradually adjusted.[99]

Not surprisingly, the knottiest problems were equality of wages and benefits. In the interests of plant harmony, Jeppson conducted no cultural revolution. He simply supported women workers' applications for admission to the Norton Mutual Benefit Association, but failed to act when the association insisted on "males only." Likewise, he ducked the pay issue by segregating tasks by sex to avoid comparisons and by continuing the pay differentials that already existed in Worcester and the rest of the United States.[100] Despite their performance, Jeppson apparently viewed women plant workers as a temporary expedient. The layoffs following World War I and accompanying the 1921 recession removed all women from the plant.

Conflicts by ethnicity and sex, high turnover rates, and apathy finally combined with increased labor militancy and potential sabotage to compel Jeppson, Allen, and Higgins to address directly the problem of an unstable and unsatisfactory work force. Across the United States strikes, agitation, and other labor conflicts after 1907 disrupted the comparative peace that had followed the 1890s. The growth of the radical International Workers of the World, the bloody massacre at the Colorado Fuel and Iron Company's Ludlow works, and the bitter textile strikes in Paterson, New Jersey, and nearby Lawrence, Massachusetts, were only a few of the more prominent examples.[101]

By 1915 Worcester—and Norton Company—had become part of that turmoil.[102] Led by skilled mechanics and machinists and aided by J. H. Gilmour of the International Association of Machinists, workers at the Reed-Prentice Company, the Leland-Gifford Company, the Whitcomb-Blaisdell Company, and other firms agitated for a 5 cent per hour pay raise and for reduction of the workday from ten to eight hours and of the work week from fifty-five to forty-eight hours. Activity began with small companies in already unionized trades in March and moved to large enterprises in the summer. By September workers at Norton Grinding Machine Company were making similar demands. When the grinding company refused shop committee demands and laid off twenty protesters, approximately one hundred fifty workers met Friday evening, October 8, but at Gilmour's and other leaders' urging, postponed a strike decision.

Norton reacted ruthlessly. Its founders vehemently opposed union activity, which threatened their control of the plant and the work force, and George Alden was president of the Employers Association of Worcester, the local open shop organization. Unhappy with the growing unrest and fearing its spread to the abrasives company, the leaders decided to force a confrontation which Superintendent John Spence called "the dumping out of the cause of most factory troubles." On Saturday, October 9, Spence asked each worker to sign a card pledging "not to strike or in other ways injure the Norton Grinding Company." Only 245 of 565 employees signed cards and reported for work on Monday. Most of these were supervisors and unskilled workers—"foremen, inspectors, helpers, chippers and sweepers."[103]

When the 320 nonsigners appeared on Monday to reclaim their tools and to picket with signs and wagons, Norton's owners were carefully prepared to restrict their activity. Police officers stopped all nonsigners at the entrance to Norton property, a quarter mile from the grinding company, and admitted only five "discontents" without placards at a time. Spence told them that "if they communicated with any men working in our plant, except the guide that I would furnish each one, that we would not hesitate to knock them on the head with a chunk of steel and throw them out of the window." By noon all had regained their possessions and returned to the public street with "no parade and no demonstration."[104]

The ensuing strike lasted many months but with little effect. Worcester lacked a strong union movement and worker solidarity was weak. The organizers neglected to appeal in native tongues to immigrant workers, who comprised at least half the area's work force. Although more than three thousand struck in the city, many workers stayed on the job, and others, who would not scab their own trade, changed trades. The strikes were sporadic, and the machinists' union and the Central Trade Union were no match for the well-organized and well-supported Metal Trades Association, which acted as an employment bureau and tracked strikers and protesters. Many workers simply left the city, and employees from firms less affected by the World War I boom took their place.[105]

Norton Grinding Company easily rode out its difficulties. Spence sent foremen into the surrounding country towns to hire workers and within two months had recruited a full force. The Massachusetts Board of Conciliation and Arbitration found the firm guilty of discouraging unions. President Alden's warning of October 9 clearly revealed the tension in Norton paternalism between benevolence and an iron resolve for owner-control. Norton Company did "not propose to allow Mr. Gilmour or any outside person or interest to interfere with its business, tell us how to run it, or interfere with our honest endeavor to have a happy working family of all of us employed by this company."[106] Alden's speech, the oath, and the lockout certainly disrupted industrial peace and interfered with the workers' attempts to organize, but the state's reprimand had no teeth.

The strike was the only labor protest of any consequence in Norton's history in Worcester and its occurrence at the grinding machine company reflected real differences between it and the abrasives firm. The relatively new abrasives industry lacked the heritage of mechanics' organizations so common in the older machine tool industry. The abrasives company had a larger percentage of Swedes and benefited from Superintendent John Jeppson's decades as a Swedish father figure.

The machine company's management was less sensitive. Charles Norton was a hard-nosed taskmaster who detested unions and espoused the bootstrap theory. John Spence was an uncompromising, no-nonsense Scot who was reluctant to concede even small favors to workers, lest they compromise his authority. He categorically rejected George Jeppson's 1919 suggestion for eight-hour shifts as pandering to the American Federation of Labor's desire of something for nothing.[107]

George Jeppson readily recognized the differences. He argued that "the traditions of the machinists go back much further than the makers of grinding wheels," and he confidently offered as evidence the differential in per capita output on similar jobs.[108] He also urged Spence to moderate his policies and encourage company-supported athletics and other forms of corporate welfare. Jeppson even lectured the machine manager personally to relax and enjoy some physical activity so that he would be "better satisfied with himself and his job."[109]

Nevertheless, the hectic pace and rapid expansion were creating problems for Jeppson as well. In 1916 and 1917 there were isolated incidents of worker protest in the abrasives company. Hard working conditions, especially in the dusty clay plant and truing room, inflation, the recruitment of Irish and other employees less respectful of authority, and widespread labor dissatisfaction amid a plentiful supply of jobs combined into a general malaise. Jeppson urged Charles Allen to increase pay rates "in order to settle unrest which is liable to come to the surface at any time." Yet, even he acknowledged that "with the class of men that we hire now and the temper they are in when they come to work, it is difficult to satisfy them."[110]

Careful monitoring of potential discontent and weeding out of protesters was a partial solution. Foremen reported malcontents and potential subversives to Jeppson and the employment department where records of behavior were kept. "Agitators" who flagrantly defied authority were promptly fired; temporary suspensions punished less serious offenders. As might be expected, campaigns for strikes, efforts to organize, and other defiance of owner-control were dealt with by instant dismissal. Carelessness or personal failure such as absenteeism and drinking often merited less severe discipline.[111] Grumblers were removed in the periodic layoffs that followed business slowdowns. Discrimination between citizens and noncitizens and between the loyal and the disloyal in employment, raises, and promotions were an additional discipline.

As another form of worker control, the company turned to labor spies, primarily because it feared sabotage.[112] When the United States entered World War I in April 1917, Norton Company and its leaders were caught up in the enthusiasm and hysteria of total war. Parades, band rallies, flag-raising ceremonies, donations, speeches, and numerous other events typified a lighter spirit. Such efforts also publicly proclaimed the firm's patriotism despite its German plant and helped disassociate it from a national perception that Swedish-Americans were pro-German or isolationist.

The firing of those considered unpatriotic and the hiring of detectives to monitor the Norton work force, particularly its twenty-eight Germans, reflected a darker side. Many Germans had been interned in 1914 and 1915 from German ships chased into American ports by the British navy and subsequently seized by the U.S. Government. Some had joined Norton in 1915 and 1916 after working in New Jersey near the famous Black Tom explosion. This disaster and other explosions in munitions plants sharpened fears of sabotage and tightened security at factories involved in the war effort.

Norton's reaction, led by the virulently anti-German Charles Allen, resulted from that anxiety and from labor discontent.[113] As early as 1915 guards checked those entering Norton property, and the company issued employee identification badges. At the same time George Jeppson, at Allen's direction, hired six men from the Boston branch of the William Burns Detective Agency, prominent for its industrial spying. The agents, posing as Swedish, Finnish, or German workers, were planted in various parts of the abrasives and machinery companies, primarily to spy on the German workers but also to report on worker behavior and pinpoint trouble spots.

The project was a costly, tawdry episode of petty tale bearing that lasted six months with no results. The spies were incredibly inept and soon recognized by much of the work force. Ironically, their major defenders were the homesick German workers who readily befriended those who spoke their native tongue and who steadfastly refused to believe the spy charges. Norton paid $6 a day plus expenses to have agents drink beer, loaf on the job, and pad their daily reports with petty tales of "vile language" and "dangerous associates," often inaccurate or contrived. The detectives found no serious worker unrest (even though it was there), and even their biased view disclosed a harmless group of lonely, homesick Germans who were simply content to take good pay and sympathize with the fatherland.

After a fruitless $2,200 expenditure, a scornful George Jeppson persuaded Allen to terminate the Burns contract. As an immigrant's son who stood apart from Worcester's Yankee culture, he had little patience with super patriots, "the narrow minded chatterers" who were "about as dangerous as the Germans themselves."[114] He wearied of repeated inquiry about such loyal men as Production Manager Hugo Beth and Sales Manager Carl Dietz. From the outset he had supreme confidence in his own lines of authority in the plant—the network of foremen, supervisors, and veteran loyal employees who as good low-level managers kept a careful eye on workers as well as work. Jeppson thought the spies' reports were "mostly taffy," and he offered to "give more for the foremen who were watching these men than all the J-8's [spies] we could hire."[115] As early as April 5, the works manager wrote Allen that "there is absolutely no indication that they [the Germans] are liable to give us any trouble. I would consider them as safe as any other group of men."[116]

Stabilizing the Work Force: The Norton Spirit

The effectiveness of Jeppson's cadre of loyal, experienced Swedish workers and supervisory personnel also revealed the solution to his general labor difficulties. He realized that better labor relations required a renewal of the loyalty, good feeling, respect, and care that had characterized the bonds between worker and owner in the small firm. If a haze of nostalgia obscured or exaggerated the early day fellowship, proof of its effectiveness was the core group of a thousand or so seasoned employees who continued to be Norton's backbone. Although no individual could replace John Jeppson or duplicate in the big company what he had accomplished over thirty years in the smaller firm, a conscious, continuous effort, directed by George Jeppson and implemented by the veteran core, did much to stabilize workers, improve attitudes, increase productivity, dampen agitation, and in general restore what was soon called the "Norton Spirit."

As early as 1910 the Norton Spirit began replacing John Jeppson as the owners-managers labored to transfer the values and traditions of the small business into the large-scale enterprise. The term itself had arisen from unknown origins by 1909, and in the following year, a booklet celebrating Norton's twenty-fifth anniversary defined it as the "spirit of co-operation and enthusiasm which inspires every one to do their utmost in behalf of the Norton interests and to always cheer the Norton banner."[117] Aldus Higgins's observations in a 1912 management conference suggest that top managers had already adopted the concept for labor relations:

> Efficiency must not be had at the cost of the men who should be the primary beneficiaries from efficiency . . . A workman would be less than a man if he did not resent the introduction of any system which deals with him in the same way as a beast of burden or an inanimate machine . . . [Improved plant operations] can only be handled successfully through the creation of a real living, breathing, sympathetic and broadminded spirit—a spirit which is bringing employers and employees closer together every day.[118]

By 1917 the idea of Norton Spirit (or Norton family as it was sometimes called) was so pervasive that George Jeppson could readily refer to it when lecturing foremen about a decline in skill and performance. "How are we going to get into them [the workers] what we call 'Norton Spirit' so that they will have a pride in the place they work and the work they do."[119] Good wages were only part of the answer. Fragmentary data suggest that Norton wage rates ranked in Worcester's middle range in 1915, and in later years Norton pay and fringe benefits followed settlements at American Steel and Wire, the city's largest employer.[120]

The company's labor relations policy evolved as a typically informal hodgepodge of separate programs until the formation of the Service Department in July 1918. Headed by Norton's physician, W. Irving Clark, the new agency combined most of Norton's corporate welfare functions, including programs or committees for health and sanitation, safety engineering, employment, catering and cafeteria operations, housing, transportation, naturalization, and the company newspaper (aptly titled the *Norton Spirit*).

Under Clark's analytical guidance, the new department's function was to extend the principles of scientific management into employee relations for greater efficiency and higher output. He argued that the department's "business is to give the same attention to the needs of the company's workers that the selling departments give to the needs of the company's customers. It promotes loyalty and cooperation; it diminishes sickness and accident; it promotes thrift and health; it diminishes misunderstanding and discontent. It tries in every way to make the factory a good place in which to work."[121]

Clark's statement reflected the health care program he had administered at Norton since 1911. Originally hired by Charles Allen to investigate links between artificial abrasive dust and tuberculosis in both Norton's and its customers' employees, the physician pioneered in industrial medicine and in monitoring tuberculosis and other lung infections. Research by Clark and others eventually determined that while prolonged, heavy concentrations of aluminum oxide and silicon carbide dust did cause bronchitis and minor lung infections, they did not contain the free silica associated at first with tuberculosis and later with a similar lung disease, silicosis. Norton's and Carborundum's tuberculosis rates were little higher than that of the community at large.[122]

At the same time Clark persuaded Allen to establish a Norton hospital. Examinations and x-rays of potential employees screened out those with tuberculosis and reduced Norton's potential liability. A hospital provided excellent emergency care in the event of accidents and thus cut injury costs. But most important, proper industrial medicine performed the positive function of improving worker efficiency. Periodic exams, preventive medicine, and counsel against "the minor vices" of oversmoking, late hours, and "sprees" reduced accident rates and lost time while improving health and productivity.[123]

Just as the title of a Clark article—"Keeping Workmen in Repair"— indicated, the physician was almost a caricature of the efficiency engineers who transferred scientific management techniques from production processes to labor relations. As he so clearly put it in another statement, "The ideal of production is a continuous output which can be raised or lowered at will to meet the demand and which will at [all] times be of uniform quality. If all machines were automatic such an ideal could be accomplished but there are many disturbing elements all due to the necessity of employing men and women to run the machines. As soon as the human element enters, uncertainty enters also. When thus considered the personnel assumes great importance and it is generally recognized that the more stable and efficient the personnel the closer to ideal is production."[124]

Clark's health care was productive. Lost time was halved; thousands of exams screened unfit workers and identified physical characteristics for proper job matches.[125] The savings quickly convinced Allen to establish the hospital and the examination program permanently. But the doctor's mechanistic approach was hardly conducive to the warm relationship that the Norton Spirit implied, as a startled worker revealed:

> I also had to undergo a Doctors examination. To judge after the thoroughness they must expect all their employees here to be ready to take Keyser Wilhelm's job after he has worried himself to death. I never saw anything like it. It takes about two hours and two Doctors. First they measure you, then they weight you, then they start to hammer all over and you are stripped of every stretch [*sic*] of clothing. Then a most severe Eye Test and so on and still further. Those two Doctors was more fit to be Veterinairs than human Doctors so thorough they are. Well I got over everything, only I got order to come and have my teeth fixed. So that is all over with.[126]

As in the case of forecasting, the owner-managers' insistence on centralized control overrode the potential for cold, rigid bureaucracy. Although Clark administered the Service Department, policymaking was reserved to a Service Committee on which he, George Jeppson, and John Spence of the Machine Division served. George Jeppson always insisted that managing people was a responsibility for line authority and was not to be delegated to staff. As works manager he met regularly with his formen and continually emphasized their primacy in maintaining a contented, productive work force. Although hiring and firing and employee record keeping were taken from general foreman Joel Styffe and centralized in an Employment Department under E. H. Fish in 1915, Fish left after complaining unsuccessfully that the foremen continued to usurp his functions and that he could implement personnel policies only if George Jeppson stood behind him.[127] Jeppson replaced him with John Erickson, a Swede who got on well with the predominantly Swedish foreman and who kept the employment office out of the plant.

Jeppson's dominance of the Service Committee allowed him to work around Clark, whom he thought a poor "people man," and to shape personnel policies consistent with his plant management. So vital an area justified direct intervention to assure line and staff coordination. Centralized control through the line held down staff bureaucracy and cost and reinforced the ad hoc, personal approach so typical of top Norton management.

The evolution of fringe benefits such as retirement clearly illustrates the technique. As in many firms, pensions were an informal attempt to resolve a widespread conflict between values that emphasized individual responsibility and the realities of an urban, industrial society where old workers could no longer earn their keep. Beginning at least as early as 1900, Norton workers received, but never earned, pensions. Decisions were made on an individual basis, and awards were based on service, character, physical condition, the worker's obligations to or support from his family, and his financial position.

Where possible, Norton preferred a working retirement that assigned the pensioner to light duties. The difference between his diminished productivity and his salary was paid from an allowance fund and charged as pension. Typically, Jeppson refused Clark's suggestion of a light work department for all pensioners; the plan smacked too much of staff interference with line authority. In extreme cases, the company paid pensions for full retirement or to indigent surviving spouses, but often tempered these grants with offers of employment for children or other relatives.[128]

A worker was always expected to care for himself when possible. Norton encouraged savings bond life insurance and membership in the Mutual Benefit Association for sickness and accident insurance. As a result of self-help and family support, the company's burden remained fairly small. Of more than 2,500 employees in 1925, 52 received pensions and only 16 of these were fully retired.[129] With the local American Steel and Wire pension as a model, awards typically ranged from $5 to $20 weekly with periodic reviews. Systematic coverage came relatively late, after the New Deal had established Social Security and rapid unionization was expanding fringe benefits. Formal retirement and insurance plans, funded jointly by employer and employee contributions, appeared only in the 1940s.

The Norton Spirit helped inculcate and spread founder values as well. Paid vacations based on seniority rewarded stability. The Norton Credit Union and the Mutual Benefit Association both encouraged thrift. The firm also considered but abandoned profit sharing as a work incentive and stimulus to thrift because the required public disclosure violated the more deeply valued private company. An education program, which included training courses, machinists' apprenticeships, citizenship classes, instruction in rudimentary English and mathematics, and WPI scholarships to Norton employees and their children, emphasized the opportunities available through individual initiative.

Most prominent, however, was an extensive recreation program. Norton's leaders responded readily to Clark's argument for improved worker productivity; athletics produced healthy minds and healthy bodies. As one official put it, "Healthful, happy play is fundamental in any community that wants to achieve industrial efficiency and social happiness."[130]

George Jeppson sought a more specific effect. Recreation would provide "a splended opportunity to know a great deal more of our workers than we do now." He continued to feel strongly that "the big job in a large place like ours is to keep in contact with our people."[131] His solution was to mix veteran line people with the newly hired, including the "many young men who come here as immigrants and are away from a home or church influence, and who are ready material for the radical."

> Let their American born fellow employees assist them in their recreation . . . In these days our greatest danger is from the young men who are not seasoned by experience and ignorant Europeans who have nothing to base their ideas of government on . . . Get all the young men into some healthy recreation where they come in personal contact, outside of work, with their superintendents, foremen and other steadying influences, and they will probably gain the friendship of these men. They will understand them better.[132]

Jeppson's prosecution equaled the vigor of his prose. Company-sponsored athletics expanded from baseball and soccer in its earliest days to include track, rowing, swimming, volley ball, tennis, quoits, basketball, and trap shooting. For those less vigorously inclined there were quieter hobbies—dancing, gardening, photographic contests, pig farming, and stamp collecting. When Norton's recreational movement peaked during the Red Scare of 1920, the Norton Athletic Association, which administered all such activities, had 2,600 members, more than two thirds of the work force, and nearly 1,100 participated in some athletic program. Among the more peaceful pursuits, gardening on company-provided plots alone involved at least 800, though the campaign by Herbert Hoover's World War I Food Commission helped swell the ranks.[133] The firm even published a special newspaper, the *Norton Athlete*, to cover all activities.

The natural corollary to the program of company-sponsored activities was employee identification with the firm. As George Jeppson put it, "I do not believe it would be possible to strike a shop in [which] you have all the young men with you."[134] The enterprise remained a center of social as well as economic life for Norton families. Norton Beach on nearby Indian Lake and Norton Boathouse on Lake Quinsigamond became family activity centers for picnicking, boating, and swimming during the day and dancing and outings in the evening. The gala Harvest Day in the adjacent New England Fairground was a major holiday, where competitions displayed the results of gardening, photography, and other Norton-sponsored hobbies. The annual

Healthy play makes healthy attitudes: swimming at Norton Beach.

festivity, which began in 1913 as the Swedish Folk Fest and eventually became the Family Outing, attracted as many as 20,000. The *Norton Spirit*, founded in 1914 as the company newspaper for employees, reported social events, personal items, athletics, marriages, births, and deaths, as well as company news with names and pictures of hundreds of employees.

Norton rhetoric emphasized the company as an institution to which one belonged, not a business for which one worked. Athletes were awarded the Norton "N", the Norton banner led parades, and the firm regularly honored long-time employees, those with ten, fifteen, twenty-five, and later fifty years on the job, with speeches, banquets, and medals. In its new office building the company included Norton Hall, a large auditorium dedicated to its employees and decorated with murals celebrating the evolution of abrasives and a sprawling, painted tree listing all twenty-five-year veterans.[135]

Like so much of the Norton Spirit, such identification sprang easily from the small firm when Norton had been a Swedish community center. The Harvest Fest simply replaced and magnified the family

Entertainment: parading to open the folk fest and family outing, 1916.

outings of the 1890s and early 1900s. Without the twentieth-century American's careful distinction between home and work, employees naturally measured their lives by work experience, and honoring the twenty-five-year patriarchs was quite appropriate.

Rewarding that cadre, maintaining a stable work force, and attracting new workers stimulated company housing, the most extensive and elaborate example of Norton paternalism. The construction of homes for sale rather than for rent, the typical purpose of industrial housing, again reflected the owner's values of thrift and property. The first batch of fifty-eight dwellings, built on Indian Hill adjacent to Norton operations, was designed "to make it easy for foremen and more progressive workmen to obtain for themselves homes of taste and convenience, likely to make the employee happy and contented with his personal work, to improve his taste, [and] stimulate his ambition."[136] The company expected to select or encourage foremen and potential leaders to buy homes.

Few needed encouragement, for the project was a garden city of varied, tasteful, well-built dwellings and not the tenement or row

housing typical of many company towns. Norton hired Grosvener
Atterbury, who had recently been the architect of Forrest Hills, New
York, to lay out attractive homes in harmonious patterns and varying
angles to roads curving across the hillside. A choice of floor plans
included three bedrooms, living room, dining room, kitchen and bath
with electricity, indoor plumbing and coal-fired steam heat, and op-
tional finish.

The company was as careful with financing as it was with the
design. Since few workers in America could afford required down
payments of 25 percent or more, Norton owners used company clout
and credit to ease the way. Employees paid 10 percent of a purchase
cost ranging from $3,000 to $4,000, while Norton's subsidiary, the
Indian Hill Company, carried a mortgage for 90 percent. Workers had
twelve years to make deposits at one of five cooperative savings banks
in order to accumulate 30 percent of the cost. After twelve years the
home owner could then continue the savings bank plan or refinance
with another institution.[137] The $380 initial payment and $20-25 monthly
payments were well within the reach of skilled workers earning $1,200
annually. The homes sold as fast as they were built until inflation
and war stopped construction in 1916.

Success generated much bolder planning for the future. A 1917

Homes for the loyal: Indian Hill, about 1920.

conference among Atterbury, George Jeppson, Aldus Higgins, Charles Allen, and Clarence Daniels produced a housing plan situated on Indian Hill by ethnicity, job, and income. At the bottom were concrete block apartments in double and triple deckers to be rented to Italians, Poles, and other immigrants holding unskilled jobs at $20 a week. Above these were modest private dwellings for purchase by skilled workers earning $30 a week, and finally, at the hilltop would be better homes for foremen and office employees earning $5,000 or more annually.[138]

Inflation and unexpected costs scotched the social engineering. After the war Norton Company built Norton Village, a batch of ninety-two smaller homes, which proved less attractive and ended Norton's venture into employee home ownership. The company rented many dwellings when the 1921 depression killed any hope of sales, but even after recovery, the firm still had to rent homes and in 1926 finally reduced prices to sell the remainder. By the 1920s stable operation removed the stimulus for company housing, and losses and the unexpected responsibility of being landlords persuaded Jeppson, Higgins, and Allen to avoid future ventures.[139]

The 1921 depression, which signaled the end of Norton's two decades of rapid growth, also terminated its innovative work with the Norton Spirit and labor relations. The desperate economies of 1921 disrupted some athletic and recreational programs and terminated others. The wholesale layoffs allowed the owner-managers to concentrate on retaining stable Swedish and native-born workers and reduce the number of eastern and southern Europeans, whom they associated with disruption and radicalism. The relative calm that followed underscored the importance of what had occurred. Although the owners had no direct statistical evidence, the maintenance of a stable force of productive, loyal workers reflected a major accomplishment. By 1923 half of all workers had at least three years' experience, and in 1930 three fourths did.

While Norton Company's labor relations program was not unique among large American enterprises, the firm was certainly an early practitioner of the corporate welfarism practiced by a small fraction of American businesses. Its programs began by 1910 and had peaked by 1920 when corporate welfarism was just hitting its stride in other businesses that practiced it. Norton leaders never hesitated to examine and borrow from the programs of other firms, and although the company's housing plan was a model program, its other techniques—pensions, company newspaper, education courses, and athletics—and its motives—increased worker productivity and avoidance of unions—had numerous counterparts in American industry.[140]

What made Norton's labor relations program unusual was the overwhelming owner paternalism that evolved from the small company. John Jeppson (and to a lesser extent Charles Allen) had "looked after" fellow Swedes, and after 1910 Allen, George Jeppson, and Aldus Higgins continued to oversee their people. Paternalism not only helped improve satisfaction and productivity; it also served to inculcate such highly prized values as thrift, order, and property ownership. Its ultimate aim was not to blend democratic ideals with bureaucracy and technology, as some have described corporate welfarism, but to maintain the control so cherished by founders and their descendants.[141]

Thus the Norton Spirit was not simply another corporate welfare program. It extended the paternalism so common in New England manufacturing firms and industrial communities of the nineteenth century into twentieth-century, large-scale enterprise.[142] Both sought dominion and efficiency, but with different emphases. Paternalism stressed direct inculcation of values by owner-operators for greater control, whereas welfarism accented social engineering by a staff organization to assure greater productivity. Norton's owner-operators married the two techniques to facilitate the continuation of the particular traditions and character of the small business within the framework generally evolving for modern industrial companies.

Their program succeeded and persisted far beyond most welfare policies, which slowed or ended in the 1920s, because of its timing and its central importance to the definition of the firm. In the late 1920s only 25 percent of Norton's Worcester employees owned cars, and the plant remained an important social center.[143] The 1930s depression made workers even more dependent, at least before New Deal reforms took effect. Norton workers understood then that the company nurse would not only track down absentees but would serve as a social worker as well, establishing care, notifying relatives, making funeral arrangements, and providing other services. Pensions helped ease old age and retirement, education offered opportunities, and recreation programs furnished entertainment and facilities when government programs were inadequate.

The owners' persistent desire for control helped the paternalistic approach develop its own momentum by the 1920s and endure well into the 1950s. The founders had worked hard to instill this value in their descendants and their top salaried managers, just as they had inculcated thrift, prudence, and independence to preserve the family firm. By the 1920s and 1930s Aldus Higgins and George Jeppson were preaching the virtues of paternalism and the Norton Spirit to Milton Higgins II, John Jeppson II, Ralph Gow, and other future leaders of the third generation.[144]

Among employees, diligent efforts and careful selection had recruited a permanent cadre that accepted and expected paternalistic management. In normal times the second and third generations of Norton management presided over an extraordinarily stable labor force. In 1948 more than 60 percent of all workers had at least ten years' experience.[145] Despite Norton's location in the heart of industrial Massachusetts, the Worcester operation remained without unions. Even in the 1930s and 1940s amid the national rise of industrial unionism and the United Steelworkers of America's organization of Worcester's American Steel and Wire plants, union sentiment was never sufficient to warrant even a vote at Norton.

Institutionalizing Innovation: Research and Development

As in forecasting and labor relations, the big firm's rise also routinized product development. Although Norton's laboratory dated from 1898, routinized research and development did not come until the 1920s. The delay was not uncommon. Other pioneers in industrial research began around the same time—General Electric in 1900, Du Pont in 1902, American Telephone and Telegraph in 1904, and Eastman Kodak in 1912—but acceleration came in the 1920s. At General Electric, Willis Whitney's laboratories were responsible for quality control, patent protection, product development, and pilot plant operations until World War I.[146]

Norton stood outside the pioneer industries—communications, electrical machinery, and chemicals—where the development of scientific knowledge was not preceded by powerful craft traditions. In Norton's case laboratory and craft evolved together because of the peculiar ownership mix. While John Jeppson led the transfer of craft skills from pottery shop to wheel-making factory, the value of research and testing was readily appreciated by his college-educated son and by old Milton Higgins and George Alden, former engineering professors at WPI. In 1906 Higgins wrote Charles Allen that while Norton's testing work was "good," the results were "by far too meagre," and he strongly urged an expanded experimental department to test new products and methods. His private notes record his certainty that research "will put the Norton Company further in advance of all other wheel makers."[147]

Early work, however, still emphasized product testing rather than research. Centralized, methodical experimentation began in 1912 when Norton hired Ross Purdy, a professor of ceramic engineering at Ohio State University and a leading American ceramist, as research engineer. Purdy established and systematized scientific procedures and headed a Worcester operation combining the Department of Tests (or

Mechanical Laboratory) which handled the special grinding problems of Norton customers, the Analytical Department which tested Norton raw materials, and the Ceramic and Organic Laboratories which did bonding, chemical, and quality control work for vitrified, rubber, and shellac products. By 1918 the Worcester laboratory had thirty-nine workers, and its expanded functions included crystalline analysis of grain and bonds by petrographer Albert Klein, examination of competitors' products, and manufacturing control.[148] Purdy also watched for promising clay and bauxite sources and wrote that new product development "occupies a very large portion of the laboratory's attention."[149]

He probably meant the creation of such minor refractory products as Alundum and Crystolon cements, baffles, muffles, and other laboratory and furnace ware. Most of Norton's new abrasives products at this time were merely adaptations of different grains developed at Niagara, and none was of significance. Product development in bonded abrasives referred primarily to variations in the mechanical mixture of grain and bond and in manufacturing methods. As late as 1919, both Purdy and Charles Allen thought of Norton research operations as "control laboratories."[150] Further change came after 1919 when Allen combined most Norton research work under Lewis Saunders, vice-president and director of research. Reporting to him were R. H. White and later Robert Ridgeway, who headed operations at Niagara and Chippawa, and Milton Beecher, who succeeded Purdy in Worcester. Only research in machine manufacturing remained separate.

Until the 1920s Norton people made little effort to understand the chemistry and physics of grinding. Company employees performed tests of uncertain reliability for physical properties and produced products whose qualities they could not entirely explain. Norton had roasted grain since the 1890s to improve bonding but no one knew why. One veteran researcher recalled that laboratory workers ran useless grain capillarity tests to measure bonding because "they didn't know what else to do." Clay plasticity tests "were done for donkey's years [and] they didn't mean a damn thing."[151]

Purdy himself admitted about Worcester's and Niagara's impact and compression tests of grain character that "neither are trustworthy in furnishing [a] basis for positive conclusions and final deductions."[152] Not for nearly a decade did researchers understand that sodium vapor caused perforations and gave 38 Alundum its special character. Purdy's recognition of basic ignorance in 1914 remained true in the early 1920s: "Some expressions of opinions have been made, but all of us apparently are beginning to realize we cannot appreciate what a grain really does undergo in grinding." As for the differences between aluminum oxide and silicon carbide, "No one knows why these two materials have their distinct fields as abrasives. We simply know that they have."[153]

Uncertainty remains despite a great deal of work, and recent explanations of grinding action still fail to explain all actual behavior.[154] Dr. Newman Thibault, a leading Norton researcher for more than forty years, recalled that when he first joined Norton he studied regular and 38 Alundum in detail, "trying to answer the whys to my satisfaction. Well, frankly, I got kind of discouraged. After a while I just really didn't spend too much time on that, feeling that I would get further ahead by an Edisonian approach, frankly."[155]

Nevertheless, there is today a much better understanding of the physical and chemical action of grinding than in Purdy's time. Much of that advance has resulted from applied research and its sometimes theoretical by-products in the laboratories of Norton and Carborundum Companies, the industry's leading researchers. Since university and government research have only recently become a factor, most knowledge and research was internally generated. Norton people visited ceramics and refractories firms with similar processes, scrutinized competitors' patents, analyzed their products, read technical journals and attended meetings of the American Ceramic Society, the Electrochemical Society, and other relevant professional associations. But basic and applied research had to come from within the firm. There was little patent sharing and no discussion of research with competitors through the GWMA. As one researcher put it, "You couldn't very much buy help."[156]

Norton's contribution began after recovery from the 1921 depression, when Milton Beecher, Albert Klein, and an existing nucleus were joined by such men as Rennie Washburn, Lowell Milligan, Wallace Howe, Baalis Sanford, and Robert Ridgeway, who had formally trained in the physical and chemical sciences for degrees in petrography, ceramics engineering, electrochemistry, and other specialties. The modern Norton laboratories for systematic research and product development were born, and simultaneously Isabelle Chaffin rationalized and expanded what had been a hodgepodge of books, pamphlets, and catalogs into a well-stocked industrial research library.[157]

Since the laboratory's manufacturing control and analytical functions were vital to Norton's continued leadership and to George Jeppson's centralized control of manufacturing operations, Ross Purdy reported directly to him. Jeppson carefully monitored Purdy's expenses and insisted on final approval for any research articles and pictures. He badgered his research director for quick, simple solutions to manufacturing problems and did not hesitate to prod: "I want some real ACTION, PEP and the gas masks taken off some of your experts down there so that they can see what they are doing. At the present time there is an enormous business in these wheels and we are not getting any of it."[158]

Authority for general allocations of laboratory resources remained with Aldus Higgins, George Jeppson, and Charles Allen, who in 1916 ordered "a complete study of our present abrasives, to determine the reasons for their efficiency in various fields . . . Conclusions should be drawn as to what can be done to either improve the old abrasives or what new attempts should be made to create new ones."[159] Purdy left in 1919 when reorganization failed to establish an independent, experimental department.

Even after Lewis Saunders assumed formal control in 1919, Jeppson continued to influence laboratory work. The division between manufacturing control and research remained confused until the 1930s. As owner-operators, George Jeppson and Aldus Higgins allocated funds and dominated decisions when Saunders sent his people before the Board of Directors to plead for special projects. Jeppson had running battles with Saunders over research performance and never hesitated to establish special teams and personally push such pet projects as pulpstone manufacture, continuous process manufacture of wheels, and the development of new abrasives.[160]

The comfortable assumptions of centralized control made the project approach as popular for the evolution of products and processes as it had been for establishing new operations. By the late 1920s, when researchers were developing B-bond wheels and controlled structure, a new wheel-manufacturing process, there was a three-step standard procedure for laboratory direction of innovations. The first stage included "the technical aspects of the problem which must be thoroughly investigated in a careful manner before any consideration is given to the direct commercial application." In the second or semicommercial step, the laboratory continued "to safeguard . . . [and] direct the development" during its adaptation to plant manufacture. Finally, after a year's pilot production, the product or process was turned over to line authority.[161]

Owner-control also meant that most research was directed toward bonded abrasives development. Individual researchers were of course free to pursue small projects, but major research allocations and instructions to Saunders and to Robert Ridgeway and Milton Beecher, who headed research in Chippawa and Worcester, focused on abrasives. Ralph Gow recalled that "although we would play with the idea of doing research on new, radically different products, almost all work . . . involved . . . making better grinding wheels, newer grinding wheels, controlling their quality and also doing the same thing with crude abrasive and with coated abrasive."[162] Researchers at Chippawa and Worcester felt "you could work on anything you wanted as long as it was round and had a hole in it."

The concentration was not without cost. Norton virtually ignored refractories, an area of research that Gow rated "very incidental," but a business that Carborundum carefully and profitably cultivated. In particular, Newman Thibault recalled that Norton passed up such by-product developments as fusion cast refractories, electrical ceramics, and synthetic graphite. Less noticeable were the potential products never sought. Wallace Howe did not look for spin-off products because "I think I was too much married to our existing line and the problems that we had with those."[163]

Focused research helped make the owners' desire for single-industry operation a self-fulfilling prophecy. At times it even obscured important bonded abrasives developments. With its long-time strength in vitrified abrasives, the company was slow to develop adequate Bakelite or resin bonded wheels, which grew popular in the late 1920s and 1930s. Norton had experimented with Bakelite bonds just before World War I, but abandoned the work when prevailing hot press techniques produced only dense wheels.

In the mid-1920s, Carborundum, working with Lawrence Redman of the Bakelite Company, developed cold-molding techniques for resin bonds of tremendous strength in thin reinforced wheels that ran at double normal speeds and quickly replaced saws for the cutting off or grinding of glass, metal, and plastic tubing and bar stock. In the 1930s they supplanted vitrified wheels for snagging or cleaning castings in the foundry industry. Although Norton took a Carborundum license and soon began to manufacture resin bonds, it trailed Carborundum, de Sanno, West Company, and other pioneers in that large market for decades.[164]

Focused research also implied that Norton's managers avoided serious debates over applied and theoretical work. Given the owners' practical bent, directed work meant applied work, although in many cases solving problems of application did provide basic knowledge about the nature of grinding and grinding wheels. The laboratory's major product and process contributions between World War I and World War II resulted from direct, concrete stimuli. All but two were responses to customer needs, and none evolved primarily from an abstract, theorectical consideration of possible improvement.

Both exceptions were process improvements, and neither was a theoretical development. Charles Hudson's mixer replaced the kneading-type mixer, designed thirty years earlier by Milton Higgins. Still in use today, the Hudson mixer uses rotary blades in a large pan to coat grains thoroughly without crushing them.[165] Easy cleaning avoided contamination, and mixing time was cut from twenty minutes to three. The replacement of the old beehive kilns with tunnel kilns resulted from Ross Purdy's contacts with the ceramic industry and Charles Kirk of the American Dressler Kiln Company. Unlike the beehive or periodic kilns, which had to be cyclically loaded, heated, cooled, and unloaded, tunnel kilns, which had been used in ceramic production since the nineteenth century, operated continuously. Extending several hundred feet, they had heating and cooling zones through which cars loaded with product passed at automatically determined speeds.

Credit for their implementation clearly belongs to the laboratory. Research by Purdy and Hudson overcame objections from Hugo Beth, the production manager, and persuaded George Jeppson and Charles Allen to buy and modify tunnel kilns for Norton's use after World War I. The savings were impressive and labor conditions were vastly improved. Firing time and unwanted temperature variation were halved, while Lowell Milligan's pyrometric rings replaced older style cones for more accurate temperature measurement. Workers no longer had to load and unload by hand in 150° F temperatures, surrounded by sand whose free silica content constantly threatened silicosis.[166] Tunnel kilns eventually replaced most periodic kilns for volume production.

Responses to customer needs brought many product and process innovations. Chippawa developed two standard Alundum grain shapes. E-1 was a dense, blocky, strong grain well suited for snagging wheels, while the slivery, needlelike E-17, which was sharper and fractured more easily, was better suited for coated abrasives and fine grinding. When electric-powered grinders replaced turbine-driven machines in pulp paper production during the 1920s and made sandstone wheels obsolete, the Norton laboratory developed huge, segmented artificial wheels with greater strength and width to handle larger logs at higher temperatures and pressures. A superior product and the efforts of Donald Chisholm, an experienced pulp engineer hired from the paper industry to install wheels and educate users, helped Norton Company dominate by the 1930s the national pulpstone market (which it still holds) and move abroad in the 1940s.[167]

Advances in metallurgy triggered two new Norton products. Cemented tungsten carbide, first developed commercially in Germany during World War I and extensively used in metal-working tools by the 1930s, was too hard for Alundum, and silicon carbide was not very efficient. Norton's first response was boron carbide, which it tradenamed Norbide.[168] Robert Ridgeway developed the new material, then the hardest manmade substance, at the Chippawa laboratories, only to discover that its weak grain structure and low oxidizing temperature disqualified Norbide for bonded abrasives. However, high pressure and temperature molded small shapes for gauges, nozzles, and dies whose wear resistance far exceeded existing materials. As a powder it readily replaced more expensive diamond dust for lapping cemented carbides.

Norbide's failure led the company to develop diamond wheels.[169] As the hardest substance known to man, diamonds had long served as an abrasive. Jewelers used diamond dust to polish gems and machinists employed diamonds to true grinding wheels, but prohibitive costs and inadequate bonds had prevented the development of diamond wheels. At the neighboring Heald Company's request in 1930, Norton researcher Baalis Sanford had made a small wheel using the new resin bond and tiny diamond chips or bort for internal grinding of tungsten carbide dies.

Costs and the wheel's modest success delayed further work until it was clear that neither Norbide nor tungsten carbide wheels were suitable. By 1934 Sanford's additional research work produced diamond wheels capable of grinding .022 inch of tungsten carbide in ten minutes, whereas the best Crystolon removed only .001 inch of stock after hours of trying. Subsequent research directed by Edward Van der Pyl produced sintered metal and vitrified bonds capable of withstanding higher pressures and temperatures and expanded the diamond wheel market into granite, marble, and glass grinding. Like the pulpstone, the diamond wheel became a real money maker for Norton as the company jumped into leadership of what rapidly became a major field. Between 1936 and 1942 production grew 5,200 percent, and by 1952 diamond wheels accounted for 20 percent of all sales by value.[170]

The two remaining innovations stimulated by customer problems, B-bond and controlled structure, were developed simultaneously in the mid-1920s and clearly signaled the triumph of the laboratory and scientific methods over craft production. B-bond was an iron-free bond with borax added for strength. Lowell Milligan, a Ph.D. from Cornell University, directed the project after field complaints that axe and snagging wheels were breaking because of improper annealing. The new bond matured at a lower temperature and avoided slag transfer from abrasive crystals, which caused cracks or crazing in the bonds. The absence of iron oxide helped avoid swelling, and since the new bond's coefficient of expansion matched that of the abrasive grain, internal strains or crackling were reduced.[171]

Controlled structure grew out of even longer standing difficulties. Factory people had always realized that uncontrolled factors remained in wheel production. Periodically, off-grades rose and there was hell to pay in the field, the laboratory, the factory, and the furnace plant until some combination of changes reduced rejections. Joel Styffe insisted on using Indian Lake water in mixing; others tried roasting the grain; still others checked the grading standards and pressured graders to ease up. The problem grew worse as different shaped grains were used and became more crucial by the 1920s when high-production crankshaft and camshaft grinding required precise wheel duplication for best results.[172]

Controlled structure resolved the issue by pressing fixed amounts of abrasive and bond into a predetermined volume, thus standardizing or controlling the ratio of grain, bond, and air space. Originally, all vitrified wheels were puddled or open structure. Pressing wheels to get desired density began about 1910 with the use of silicon carbide abrasive. A third process, the jolting or Y-process (named for the Swedes' pronunciation of jolting), was begun after World War I by Charles Hudson to get proper density in segments and cylindrical shapes whose molds could not be closed and pressed. Jolting simply meant shaking the mold to settle the mix.

Researcher Wallace Howe, who had come to Norton from MIT in 1923, conducted jolting experiments until he realized that vibration caused a standard consolidation and hence a standard density. Testing indicated that a number of factors affected density, including grain shape, bond wetness, variations in the physical process of mixing, and the amounts of water and sawdust added. Control of such factors had long remained an art. From John Jeppson's time until the 1920s, experienced wheel makers added water and sawdust to the wheel mix by feel or taste in the way a veteran cook adds ingredients to a batter. They learned to trowel the mix in a special way to distribute air bubbles properly. Although the skilled makers did not understand the rationale, their techniques provided the proper ratios of grain, bond, and air that in turn determined a wheel's grade. Howe's solution was to control production scientifically by closing the mold and pressing to a fixed, predetermined volume.[173]

B-bond and controlled structure permitted faster output of better quality, more uniform wheels. Their implementation, along with the adoption of the more precise tunnel kiln, represented greater mechanical and scientific regulation of the production process and the passing of craft techniques that dated to John Jeppson and F. B. Norton's pottery. The laboratory supplanted veteran wheel makers to establish ingredient ratios to provide predetermined grades. Milligan's work with bonds and modulus of elasticity produced a machine that graded by impact and a sonometer that precisely measured wheel ring or pitch.

Implementation came within a few years, but not without a struggle. Vestiges of the craft practices endured for decades as defenders of the old shop culture resisted the scientific controls imposed by the laboratory. Seasoned mixers swore by their cherished puddled process and complained that reduced amounts of water produced dry, crumbling mixes that hurt their piece rates. Chief grader Hjalmar Styffe, a forty-year veteran, refused to accept the new standards and Charles Hudson's statistical quality control that soon followed. If a controlled structure wheel failed to meet his grader's standards, it was rejected.

The new, young technicians simply worked around him. Norman Monks persuaded graders to ease up, and hid the rejected wheels until he could send them through again to get a second, acceptable grade. Nevertheless, sporadic hand grading endured into the 1950s and 1960s as a sign of the shop culture's defiance of or indifference to laboratory standards. In some cases the old skills were a shortcut in using the new equipment. Because of the inconvenience of transporting big wheels up several flights to the sonometer, grader Bob Werme continued to ring them with his hand-grading tool and carry the pitch in his head up three flights where he would measure it against the machine's ring.[174]

Routinized product research and development along with the other administrative changes helped maintain a successful, if somewhat less exciting, company. Milton Higgins II put it bluntly: "People that had research made progress; people that had no research didn't make any progress in the grinding wheel business."[175] The introduction of diamond wheels, B-bonds, controlled structure, and other innovations helped Norton preserve its leadership in the abrasives industry, although its 34 percent share of the wheel market (as measured by the GWMA in 1939) meant a six-to-ten-point diminution since 1919, resulting from late entry into the resin bond business.[176]

Testing the New Organization

The relative ease with which Norton met the 1930s depression reflected its successful transformation from the small enterprise to the large, centralized, bureaucratic firm. Their long training and leadership allowed George Jeppson and Aldus Higgins to retire Charles

Allen in the midst of the depression and begin to install their own team of top managers to replace aging executives. Assistant Treasurer Henry Duckworth gave way to William Magee; Milton Beecher supplanted Lewis Saunders as director of research; Tony Clark took William L. Neilson's place as head of sales while Herbert Stanton displaced him as manager of foreign operations; and young Ralph Gow became works manager.

Despite the changes, policies remained constant. Prudent operations, new products, and national sales efforts maintained market leadership and a continuous cash flow throughout the Depression. Average annual sales, based on the statistics in table 2, were almost $14 million in the 1920s, but they rose to almost $18 million in the 1930s in spite of hard times. (When sales for the Behr-Manning Cor-

Table 2. Norton Consolidated Sales, 1920–1939.

Year	Sales[a] ($ millions)
1920	18.8
1921	4.3
1922	8.5
1923	13.6
1924	11.1
1925	15.2
1926	15.9
1927	13.7
1928	17.7
1929	20.3
1930	11.8
1931	11.2
1932	8.0
1933	10.7
1934	15.0
1935	19.4
1936	24.5
1937	30.8
1938	21.6
1939	26.7

Sources: Norton Company, "Comparative Net Sales Growth, 1885–1932" (for 1920–1930); Assistant Controller Guy Williams to the author, December 29, 1982 (for 1931–1939).

a. Figures do not include foreign plant sales for 1920–1930, which apparently never equaled 10 percent of total reported company sales.

poration, a 1931 coated abrasives acquisition to be discussed in chapter 4, are subtracted, average sales revenue in the depression decade still exceeded the 1920s by more than a million dollars annually.) Large cash reserves helped offset losses in 1931 and 1932 and allowed Norton to maintain dividends and spend more than ten million dollars in the late 1930s to rebuild its two oldest wheel plants, install three big tunnel kilns, mechanize product flow, and retool and reorganize the Machine Division.[177]

Forecasting helped cushion the more than 75 percent drop in bonded abrasives and machinery sales between 1929 and 1932 (60 percent of the newly acquired Behr-Manning's sales are included for 1932) and the 30 percent drop in the 1937–38 recession and helped avoid repeating the panic cutbacks of 1921. In contrast to the 80 percent layoff rate in the previous depression, 50 percent of workers remained on the payroll between 1929 and 1932 with a staggered work system and shorter workweek.[178] Finally, continued corporate welfare helped maintain a stable work force and avoid later strife and unionization. Although it had not come without costs, centralized family management had profitably weathered rapid internal change as well as external economic disaster.

The patterns of strategy and structure common to large industrial firms in the United States had reinforced efforts to preserve the small company within the big enterprise. The emergence of oligopoly provided stability. Concentration on a single industry allowed two or three men to master the business effectively, and the evolution of the centralized, functionally departmentalized structure extended owner-control. Within this framework Charles Allen, George Jeppson, and Aldus Higgins had institutionalized the values and traditions of the Worcester-centered firm and simultaneously continued its leadership and profitability, thus sustaining the large multinational enterprise with its avowedly New England character and base for nearly a half century after World War I.

4.

Challenges to the Family Firm: Inertia and the Management of Other Lines

ADAPTING THE OPERATIONS of a large enterprise to family management did provide the control and continuity desired by Norton Company's owners, but in the decades following the 1921 depression Aldus Higgins and George Jeppson counted the costs as well in lost people and opportunities. How was the company to retain top executive talent who naturally expected to head an enterprise? How could high-level family owners with long tenure be challenged with fresh ideas? And what prevented even able owner-operators from staying at the top when past their prime?

The general pattern of evolution of large American industrial enterprises did not always reinforce efforts to preserve Norton's special character. The limitations of owner-management became most clear when Norton Company emulated other firms to develop a full product line and foreign markets. Owner-operation meant that Norton remained, and in fact became even more, a Worcester-centered abrasives company. It passed up opportunities in other industries and in other countries. It sacrificed a pioneering position in grinding machinery production. The company's major strategic move—the acquisition of the Behr-Manning Company to enter the coated abrasives industry—resulted from good judgment, good luck, and good timing. But Behr-Manning's success was almost entirely independent of Norton management. Ironically, the cost of tightly centralized family control was almost complete autonomy for those parts of the business that Jeppson and Higgins could not directly oversee or had not completely mastered.

Inertia at Norton

During the interwar years, "catching up" increasingly gave way to routinization and even stagnation as Norton Company reflected the stability and slower growth of the abrasives industry and the decline of Worcester itself. The city's course followed the general slide of eastern industrial centers and was exacerbated by the deterioration of New England's economy. Textile, clothing, and shoe firms, important customers for Worcester's machines, suffered heavily from foreign and southern competition. Sales in the automobile industry, another major market for Worcester machinery and metal products, leveled off in the 1920s. Leadership in automation of machine tools fell increasingly to non-Worcester firms, such as the Cincinnati Milling and Landis Tool Companies.[1] Finally, of course, the 1930s depression disastrously reduced all markets for the city's metal-working, machinery, and machine tool companies.

Worcester's population mirrored the maturation of its economy. It had advanced more than 40 percent per decade in the last half of the nineteenth century, and the pace continued at 23 percent per decade between 1900 and 1920. Slower industrial expansion and the shutdown of immigration after World War I reduced the gain to 9 percent in the 1920s, and in the 1930s the population actually decreased.[2] Construction slumped and Worcester stagnated and declined.

At Norton Company, although the 1909 contract with Alcoa first signaled the limits to Norton's expansion, lost dynamism was especially evident after the shocking 1921 slump. Allen, Jeppson, and Higgins continued to run the firm but found increasing time for outside activities and Worcester civic service. Allen built his camp at Petersham, Aldus Higgins his big house in Worcester, and George Jeppson his farm in nearby Brookfield. Jeppson and Higgins traveled frequently, and annual European inspection tours also included vacation trips from a Paris base.

Family control meant that owner-managers remained in top executive positions for long periods despite their declining energy, and stability reinforced the trend. In many large industrial enterprises, time spent working up the career ladder and mandatory retirement at 65 limited a major executive's tenure to five or ten years. At Norton, owner-operators came early and stayed late. Milton Higgins was president for twenty-seven years; George Alden was treasurer and president for thirty-four years; and John Jeppson remained superintendent from the firm's founding until his death in 1920. Charles Allen was Norton's chief administrator for forty-eight years, and George Jeppson and Aldus Higgins had assumed by 1910 the executive positions they were to hold until nearly midcentury.

Although the lengthy exercise of power was quite congenial to Allen, Jeppson, and Higgins, their longevity meant the continued loss of good people. The problem is familiar in any large organization where talented people feel stifled by bureaucracy, and Norton's family control, which barred the position of chief executive to others, aggravated the difficulty. Losses were especially concentrated in sales and research since the firm emphasized abrasives manufacturing. Orello S. Buckner, Leonard Krull, and George Bullard, all from sales or research, left in 1921 to establish the Bay State Abrasives Company. At the same time Vice-President and General Manager of Sales Carl Dietz left to head Bridgeport Brass Company, reportedly after he was told that he could not become top man.[3] During the 1930s, Earl Hughes, a talented assistant general sales manager discouraged by lack of further opportunity, left to join Bay State, which he subsequently guided into third place in the industry.[4] Finally, Norton lost Tony Clark, still another sales manager, who became president of Carborundum Company after World War II.

In addition, owner longevity at the top reduced the opportunity for newcomers' challenges to established patterns, a process that had been so crucial in the firm's earlier growth. Allen and Jeppson had expanded F. B. Norton's staid pottery and wheel operation; Milton Higgins and Charles Norton had led the firm into machinery manufacturing; young Aldus Higgins had played a central role in the development of Alundum; and young George Jeppson had institutionalized the Norton Spirit and the corporate welfare program.

Their capacity for adventure, which had always been balanced by the owners' emphasis on prudence and thrift, was severely diminished after Milton Higgins's death. Charles Allen puttered along as president through the 1920s, increasingly set in his ways until Aldus Higgins and George Jeppson nudged him into the largely honorary position of chairman of the board at 75. Aldus Higgins, who was most aware of the dangers of inertia, was a much subdued man after his first wife's death in 1911 and was in later years periodically incapacitated by ill health. George Jeppson remained vigorous and active for decades, but his focus, like Allen's, was always on Worcester abrasives manufacture.

The labor force had stabilized after the end of rapid expansion in 1921, and Norton could once again rely largely on Swedes and native-born workers. Moreover, the Swedes had established their own access to power and no longer depended so heavily on Norton Company. By 1916 when Pehr G. Holmes was elected mayor, a local historian notes that "there were two Swedes on the School Committee, three on the Common Council, three on the Board of Aldermen and one in the state House of Representatives."[5]

Stagnation was also reflected in overseas operations. Foreign expansion, which had leapt ahead with the acquisition of wheel-manufacturing plants in Canada, France, and Japan in 1919 and 1920, virtually ceased. Norton abandoned 1919 plans for a factory in Leicester, England, and sold the Japanese operation. It added no other foreign plants until changing tariff laws finally forced an English factory in 1930, and the Italian and Australian operations, the only other foreign acquisitions before World War II, were virtually thrust upon the company.[6]

Expansion into other industries became almost as insignificant as foreign growth. Exploratory by-product lines in refractories, tiles, and floors were disappointing minor operations by the 1920s. Refractories, an industry in which Carborundum Company became very successful, had appeared quite attractive in 1910. Norton's kiln experience meant considerable expertise in high-temperature work, and the firm's consumption of bats, saggers, and other kiln furniture provided some product volume. As a secondary consideration, refractories were to help consume some of the growing stockpiles of fine Alundum and silicon carbide grains, too small and too numerous for wheel use.

Bonded Alundum and Crystolon refractories proved superior to older clay refractories, especially for the newer, high-temperature electrical furnaces in industrial use. They had higher melting points (up to 2,100° C), low coefficients of expansion, thermal conductivity twice that of older porcelains, and relatively high resistance to acids and alkalis. Thus, they made excellent porous tubes, crucibles, filters, extraction thimbles, combustion boats, muffles, and other containers for chemical reactions, especially those of higher temperature. They also made excellent brick and cement for furnace linings.[7]

In addition, refractories were an attractive by-product because they had some manufacturing and marketing parallels with bonded abrasives. They were mostly producers' goods, which like grinding wheels went to industrial customers. Sales were primarily of a job-shop nature: special orders with very few higher volume standard items. Like wheels, refractories were composed of grains and binders that were mixed, molded, and burned.

Electric furnace abrasives also had desirable properties for floors and stair treads. After he watched Charles Allen slip on a wet bathroom floor, George Jeppson remarked that Alundum grain would be nonslip and was as wear resistant as any material other than diamonds.[8] Again, surplus fines and waste from the truing, bushing, and shaving of wheels could readily be bound into aggregates for concrete floors and precast stair treads or molded into ceramic mosaic tiles.

Both refractories and floors evolved slowly through the special project approach so common at Norton. Special interdepartmental committees handled the new products and markets until regular production and sales departments could assume control of a mature product with specified manufacturing procedures and steady markets. By 1917 the refractories department had a six-man production team and annual sales of $80,000. In the same year Norton established a small special sales department to replace what had been a mail order business.[9] By the early 1920s there were catalogs, advertisements, and separate salespeople for both floors and refractories.

Neither product amounted to much. Wartime demand for wheels hindered vigorous development, and the marketing of floor tiles was a challenge. The porous tiles resisted wear but accumulated dirt. Architects had to be importuned to specify Norton tiles and contractors persuaded to use Norton aggregates, and no inspection system monitored compliance. Public buildings and public works such as the New York City subway system offered large potential sales, but Norton people, accustomed to dealing with industrial suppliers and customers, never mastered the art of lobbying, payoff, and patronage necessary for municipal contracts.

However, the real failures came from within the firm itself. Norton's owners were never fully committed to either product and insisted that both fit the mold of the abrasives company. Accordingly, both refractories and tiles were manufactured as premium products. High overhead charges added to already expensive manufacturing costs simply priced Norton floors beyond much of the market. Few buildings required floors to resist 30 million pairs of feet, and tiles costing one fourth of Norton's $2-per-square-foot price were adequate substitutes.[10]

There were similar problems in refractories, with which Norton was more familiar. High overhead charges and steep profit margins priced Norton's product at double the best grade firebrick. Ross Purdy, head of the Worcester laboratory and a ceramics expert, was convinced that Norton was "most favorably fitted to enter [the market] in a large way," but the firm's desultory advertising, stiff pricing, and inadequate sales efforts persuaded him that Allen, Jeppson, and Higgins were "indifferent whether our refractory business is developed."[11]

Only inertia and the need to supply Norton kilns kept the company in both businesses. Purdy proposed a partnership to operate an independent refractories plant at Niagara Falls, but the owner-operators were unwilling to share control or to decentralize operations. Norton Company continued to produce refractories primarily for itself and never threatened Harbison Walker or other leading refractory manufacturers. Floor sales continued until the 1960s, although annual sales peaked at $203,000 in 1926 and were always "well under $100,000" between 1931 and 1944.[12] Combined sales of by-products remained less than 5 percent of total business.

Apathy not only precluded full development of potential by-products; it also frittered away a pioneering position in grinding machine manufacture. By the 1920s the grinding machine division needed a strong hand, new products, and careful reorganization. Charles Norton, primarily an inventor and developer, was an indifferent administrator.[13] His small-shop approach, which built one machine at a time, was ill suited to the volume production of machines and parts necessary to satisfy automotive and wartime demand after 1910.

Typical of Norton Company's strategy was expansion by piecemeal construction of separate, nineteenth-century-style mill buildings. Their galleries and bays fitted well with separate departments for lathe work, stamping, grinding, and other functions, as customarily found in small-scale machine tool manufacture. When supervision of the departments and their foremen grew beyond the inventor's interest and capacity, John Spence, a dour taskmaster, became superintendent while Norton headed engineering and development, and Howard Dunbar, a methods engineer from Western Electric, established a Planning Department to help rationalize production.

Nevertheless, administration remained fragmented and production uncoordinated. George Alden, president of the machine company, exercised little if any administrative authority, and Charles Allen was too busy with the abrasives company to pay close attention to the machine business. Actual operation, then, fell to Charles Norton, John Spence, and C. O. Smith, head of machinery sales, but the inventor, who was no respecter of organization, interfered in production, sales training, and administration. The 1919 merger and reorganization, which retired Alden and made Charles Norton a consultant, only partially resolved the problem. The machinery company's functional departments were divided to suit the organization of the abrasives firm, and no one had charge of all machine operations—research, production, and sales.

Product development was also a weakness. By the 1920s Norton Company was no longer an innnovator of production grinding machines. Instead, competitors like Landis, Bryant, and Cincinnati Milling became leaders in developing automatic feeding, chucking, and sizing mechanisms to speed operations and reduce skilled labor costs.[14]

Aldus Higgins noted in 1928 that Charles Norton's plain grinder "has been built for practically twenty-eight years with only slight modifications and improvements in minor details of construction."[15] Machines became obsolete, gaps appeared in the product line, and the parts business deteriorated.[16]

A major turning point was the company's failure to establish itself in the burgeoning field of centerless grinding. Norton's cylindrical machines held the work on centers at each end of the piece. Centerless grinders, which were pioneered by L. R. Heim and later the Cincinnati Milling Machine Company, operated without centers to hold the work. The piece to be ground rested atop an angular blade and rotated between a guiding or regulating wheel and a grinding wheel. By the late 1920s Cincinnati had produced automated, centerless, external grinders that outstripped Norton cylindrical grinders in speed and economy, while Landis and Heald were adding thread and internal centerless grinding machines.[17]

Stagnation in the firm's grinding machine division did not, however, result simply from the errors of an aging inventor who refused to admit the possibility of centerless grinding. Problems dragged on long after Charles Norton's virtual retirement in 1919; they reflected the owner-managers' fundamental commitment to abrasives manufacturing and relative lack of interest in machinery building. George Jeppson and Aldus Higgins were not machine men, and neither they nor Chares Allen were ever closely associated with the machinery business. Nor was there a strong leader and spokesman from within the Machine Division after old Norton's departure. John Spence was little more than a day-to-day administrator, and sales head Howard Dunbar, who had both ideas and ability, was isolated from operations and reported to Norton Company's vice president for sales.

After the 1921 depression literally shut down the entire machine operation and for the first time exposed the owners to the burden of high fixed costs and a cyclicality even worse than abrasives manufacture, support for machinery development was limited and opportunities were passed. Despite Charles Norton's opposition to centerless grinding, Norton Company did buy the Detroit Machine Tool Company, an early developer of centerless machinery, but when the Cincinnati Company eventually won a patent suit, Norton sought no license to allow it to stay in the business. Robert Lawson, a fifty-year veteran and eventual head of the Machine Division, still feels the failure was a "bad mistake," because centerless operations "became a big part of grinding and we just dropped completely out of it."[18]

Furthermore, the centerless grinding instance was only one of several defeats. The company failed to continue improving the surface and roll grinders that it had built before World War I. It manufactured rotary table surface grinders but never produced the rotating table type that became so successful. When a conjugate camshaft machine, whose sixteen 60-inch wheels simultaneously ground all points on a camshaft instead of the usual one item at a time, failed in a spectacular accident at the Ford Motor Company, Norton also ceased development of conjugate crankshaft grinding and allowed the Landis Company a ten-year lead in that lucrative field. By 1928 the product line had so deteriorated that Charles Norton's plain grinders accounted for 85 percent of sales and 90 percent of profits.[19]

Howard Dunbar eventually stopped the decline after he replaced John Spence in 1928.[20] Engineers redesigned the line and introduced fourteen new machines. The parts business was rationalized. After acquiring the Bethel-Player Company in 1927, Norton Company manufactured a line of excellent mechanical lapping machines, designed to produce a final polish or superfinish on surfaces by rubbing ground surfaces with loose abrasive. Mechanical lapping became especially important in the automotive, appliance, and aircraft industries, where it reduced undulations and friction in tight-fitting, fast-moving metal parts.[21] Dunbar instituted a new wage and incentive system, scrapped aging equipment, and redesigned production with a floor plan adopted from the auto industry that emphasized a continuous flow from materials through parts to machines.

The successful reorganization won an *American Machinist*'s award in 1931, and in the following year Dunbar became general manager of the Machine Division as sales were finally reunited with research and production.[22] Dunbar's work, however, was more stabilization than restoration. Norton Company remained a manufacturer of excellent cylindrical grinding machines but never recaptured the premier position that Charles Norton had originally established in production grinding. The division generated large profits in wartime and held its own in peacetime, accounting for about 20 percent of Norton sales. Because of the division's indifferent performance in the 1920s, Jeppson and Higgins continued to channel most resources into the abrasives business, and Dunbar's reorganization had to be fitted to the old, two-story mill buildings. His bosses refused to build the new plant he designed even though they spent $10 million in abrasives plant reconstruction in the 1930s.

Although financial conservatism continued to characterize Norton Company in the 1930s, maintaining a careful surplus did not preclude some prudent reinvestment. In the early 1930s Higgins and Jeppson invested to preserve the assets they already had in the Machine Division, but not to recapture what they had lost. They financed abrasives plant construction while building costs were cheap, and they acquired firms to fill out the product line while their stock values were low.

The 1932 acquisition of the Pike Manufacturing Company was such a purchase. In the thirty-five years since Pike had first contracted to sell Norton's output of sharpening stones, the company had languished, and the relationship was an unsatisfactory one after the erratic E. Bertram Pike succeeded his father as head in 1908. When Pike died in 1926, the firm was in serious financial difficulty. Norton wanted to continue its profitable line of stones whose annual sales were several hundred thousand dollars, but it lacked the New Hampshire company's contacts with hardware stores and other retail outlets. The 1932 acquisition of Pike assured Norton of better operating control and a small sales network. The business, however, remained small, and 1949 sales were less than half a million dollars.[23]

Pike's sales were handled by the Behr-Manning Company of Watervliet, New York, purchased in 1931 as Norton's first major acquisition. The investment, which filled out Norton's product line by adding coated abrasives or sandpaper manufacture, was a major exception to the conservative routine that characterized Norton Company between the world wars. It was the most profitable venture of the Jeppson-Higgins era, and it moved Norton into a field that grew rapidly until the 1950s while bonded abrasives' expansion slowed. The Behr-Manning merger also exposed the limits of Norton's strategy of centralized owner-management. While cash resources and Aldus Higgins's judgment permitted Norton to take advantage of an excellent opportunity at bargain prices, success derived from Behr-Manning's management and excellent position in an already established industry. Understanding that position and the growth of what became a major Norton line first requires a careful look at the development of the coated abrasives industry in the United States.

Coated Abrasives Evolution

Although coated abrasives were centuries old when the Baeder-Adamson Company of Philadelphia inaugurated production in the United States during the 1820s, the materials were simple and the manufacturing techniques primitive. Quartz flint had replaced sand to scour wood, and soon emery supplanted glass to sand metals. Subsequently in the 1880s, garnet replaced the softer flint for sanding wood products. Flexible backings included cloth as well as paper, and glues were made from animal hides. Paper backings were lightweight (95–105 pounds per ream) jute paper for fine pouncing work on felt hats and kraft paper from wood pulp. Both were manufactured by the Fourdrinier process from a single pulp layer.[24]

Early producers were actually small fabricators. They bought glue ingredients, paper, and grain and combined them into sandpaper. Manufacturing was simple, labor intensive, and controlled by a few skilled operators or makers, the counterpart of brewmasters in the beer industry. Hand production predominated until after midcentury and survived in isolated cases into the twentieth century.[25]

Mechanical makers or coaters dated from the 1850s and were simple machines made mostly of wood and rope.[26] A large roll of paper was unwound, received a coating of glue from wooden rollers, and caught grain sifted by gravity from a box. The coated "web," wet with glue and covered with grain, then had to be dried in loops on rope racks before receiving a final or sizing coat of glue. The dried web was either rolled and fed to a separate sizer for its final coat or went directly through the sizer to be looped onto another set of racks.

Proper making involved careful timing and very skilled judgment. Grain feed, glue temperature, and coating depth had to be constant and continuous throughout the paper roll's feed or "run," for variation spoiled the product. The key operator was the master coater, who made glues to the proper liquidity by his own secret formula and who set the rollers to assure proper depth of glue coating, adjusting both liquidity and coating depth according to temperature and humidity.

Master coater skills were essential to any firm's success. Each company carefully courted its coater, who in turn closely guarded his crucial skills and formulas, revealing them only to a son in the time-honored craft tradition. Donald Kelso, a half-century veteran of the industry, well remembered Bert Grimes, master coater of the American Glue Company,

> who had his glue mixture formulae in a little black notebook which he carried in the upper left hand pocket of his vest. His procedure was to instruct the crew to put into the glue vat so many bags of glue and so many pails of water. When this was reduced to the proper liquidity, he would examine the result by testing its adhesive properties between his thumb and forefinger and order an addition of so much more glue or water or both. He was very clever in these moves so that he left no consistent pattern to be learned by his assistants.[27]

Marketing was much simpler than manufacture. Most sales were left to distributors or dealers in the hardware, furniture, woodworking, shoe, and leather trades, which were the bulk of the coated abrasives market. As was the case in most nineteenth-century marketing, middlemen were the most economical means of breaking up larger lots of reams and rolls into the numerous small orders that characterized the trade. Coated firms employed only a few salesmen to contact distributors and a few direct accounts. The Behr Company, the industry's largest firm, had only seven salesmen, and in 1892 the entire industry employed only twenty-five.[28]

The product was relatively unspecialized; much of it went for hand sanding or simple drum sanders. Consequently, sandpaper could be sold in basic, standard shapes—in rolls or in sheet form by ream or quire, measurements adopted from the paper industry. Special shapes, such as belts, were generally made by consumers. Catalogs, then, were also small and simple; Behr printed its entire sales list on four sheets of 3-by-5-inch paper.[29]

Until about 1900 the sandpaper business was a small, derivative industry, as bonded abrasives had been in the 1880s. After more than seventy-five years' production, total sales were only $1.2 million in 1899.[30] The product owed as much to the paper-making industry as early bonded abrasives did to pottery manufacturing. Customary packaging and sizes were paper industry standards, and paper or linoleum companies furnished slitters, cutters, and some of the early making machinery. Other manufacturers designed and built their own making machines.

Few of the early firms entered the business directly; most followed some by-product into the tiny industry.[31] Baeder-Adamson sought an outlet for its fish glue. Glue sales also attracted the American Glue Company, a result of the 1890s horizontal combination movement, and Armour Company, the meatpacking firm, which had a surfeit of glue by-product. The Manning Sandpaper Company (predecessor of the Manning Abrasive Company) evolved from the Manning Paper Company's efforts to sell its cylinder rope paper for backings. For other enterprises the attraction was grain marketing. Carborundum sought to boost silicon carbide sales. The Minnesota Mining and Manufacturing Company (3M) originally mined emery, and the Wausau Company also evolved from mining operations. H. H. Barton of Philadelphia entered the business in 1876 after working in his father-in-law's sandpaper business for ten years, but his firm's real success depended on its development of garnet as an abrasive and the early acquisition of garnet mines near North Creek, New York.

Like the early bonded abrasives companies, coated firms were small, owner-operated, and often family businesses. Herman Behr, for example, started his operation in 1872 as a partnership with his brother Robert and his brother-in-law Gustav Heubach, and later brought a son into the business. At the Manning Sandpaper Company, the spin-off of a family paper firm, John Manning employed Lewis Greenleaf, his son-in-law and his partner's son. The Barton family ran their firm for more than half a century.

Unlike the bonded industry, however, there were few entrants and competition alternated between cooperation and cutthroat piracy. There were only seven firms in 1892 and the figure seldom exceeded twelve in the next thirty-five years.[32] The industry's small size and slow growth discouraged many competitors; even more crucial were limited supplies of grain and skilled personnel. Master coaters, so essential for success, were highly prized and usually associated with a single firm, like Bert Grimes at American Glue and Pete Kulzer at the Manning Company. In addition, while emery and flint were readily available, superior garnet grain was not. Much of it came from New York mines owned by Barton or by a Mr. Hooper who supplied many of the early, established firms like Behr and American Glue.[33]

While established firms may have cooperated to control grain supplies and restrict entry, they had less success in regulating prices. The tendency for companies to specialize in particular products or markets temporarily provided some stability. Baeder-Adamson's flint paper and emery cloth sold well in the hardware and general resale trades; American Glue did well in the shoe, tannery, and hat industries, as did the Behr Company.[34]

But the development of garnet products for new markets and the persistence of short-lived pirate firms frequently upset the market and retarded product standardization. Behr had a "knock-down and drag out battle" with the Union Company, an enterprise founded by former Behr employees, for the eastern shoe business.[35] Both companies evaded formal list prices by shipping larger quantities and better stock than they invoiced. Carborundum's entry also disrupted the shoe trade. When Behr found its garnet paper losing to silicon carbide in the shoe industry, it began battling Barton for garnet paper sales to the woodworking industry. Their efforts expanded wood-workers' use of garnet at the expense of established flint paper manufacturers like Baeder-Adamson and so precipitated still another battle. New entrants like 3M, which were denied domestic garnet, imported an inferior foreign grain and dyed it to imitate American supplies. The 3M Company survived as a fringe firm for more than a decade by price cutting and misrepresenting its own and its competitors products.[36]

Instability among tiny firms in a small industry characterized coated abrasives manufacture much longer than it did the bonded industry. Nevertheless, the evolution of bonded and coated abrasives had a number of parallels. Coated development, like the advance of the bonded business, depended primarily on changes in markets and technology, which also accounted for the differing pace of growth in the two industries.

Coated abrasives grew in three stages. The first era, which extended into the twentieth century, was dominated by handicraft production of simple, nonstandard products and resembled the state of bonded abrasives until the late nineteenth century. If anything, coated abrasives were even more primitive. Unlike grinding wheels, which went largely to metal-working industries from the outset, sandpaper markets were primarily in the furniture, woodworking, shoe, hat, tannery, and leather trades, whose production processes and machinery were relatively simple. Manufacturing by such customers remained labor intensive and there were few, if any, firms with mechanized, high-volume output. In the woodworking and leather industries and even in early automobile production, coated abrasives continued to be used for finishing or polishing operations performed by hand or by simple mechanical sanders on many wooden and some metal parts.

The second stage included rapid growth and increased application of sandpaper to high-volume, mechanized metal working. As a result, coated production became more technical and mechanized to assure standardization and predictability of behavior. Technological change and foreign expansion in turn shifted industry leadership, altered patterns of competition, and stressed interfirm cooperation, which terminated in combination and oligopoly. Finally, the third stage came in the two decades after 1939. New machinery and automation considerably expanded the application of coated abrasives, first in metal working and then in wood, leather, and plastics, and industry growth rates surpassed bonded abrasives.

Industry Development: Changing Markets and Technology

The second stage began between 1900 and 1910, and as in bonded abrasives, the automobile industry and World War I led the way by expanding metal-working markets. The coated abrasives industry responded with new products and processes as well as improved product standards and uniformity. As figure 4 indicates, coated output nearly quadrupled between 1899 and 1909, then almost tripled to $12.1 million by 1919 and jumped again to $20.3 million in 1929. Ironically, however, production by volume improved much more slowly since better grains, heavier backings, stronger glues, and improved coating techniques advanced coated abrasives' productivity to match the in-

Millions Of Dollars

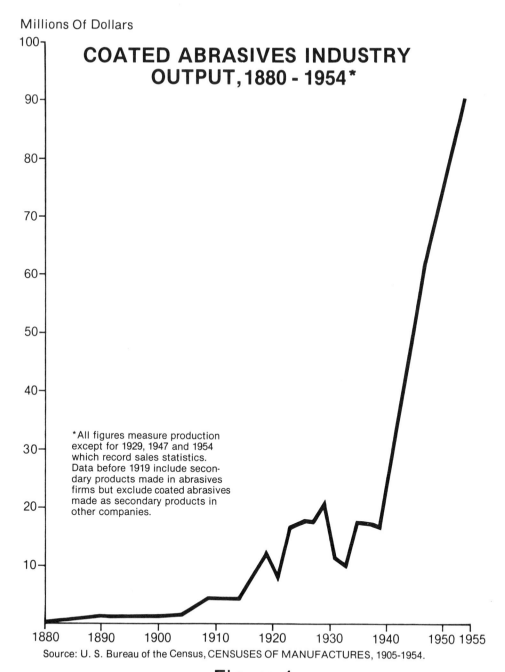

COATED ABRASIVES INDUSTRY
OUTPUT, 1880 - 1954*

*All figures measure production
except for 1929, 1947 and 1954
which record sales statistics.
Data before 1919 include secondary products made in abrasives
firms but exclude coated abrasives
made as secondary products in
other companies.

Source: U. S. Bureau of the Census, CENSUSES OF MANUFACTURES, 1905-1954.

Figure 4

creased demand.[37] Real growth in product volume came during the third stage in the 1940s and early 1950s with the rapid development of machinery for coated abrasive use.

The initial changes in coated products and production that so transformed the industry clustered in the second and third decades of the twentieth century. New electric furnace grains adapted from the bonded industry led the way. Carborundum's silicon carbide had only a limited impact in the metal trades but rapidly displaced garnet in the shoe business. Electric furnace corundum had an even greater effect. By 1920 firms like Carborundum, 3M, and Manning had readily adapted it to coated abrasives to replace emery in metal working. Carborundum developed tough, flexible cloth and paper disks for the portable sanders used to grind auto body welds. The Manning Company bought Alundum grain from Norton to produce its own Metalite brand of cloth-backed coated abrasives for the metal-working industries. The 3M Company developed flexible cloth sheets to be wrapped around files for grinding weld joints on automobiles, and by 1919 furnaced corundum on cloth accounted for 45 percent of sales. In addition, Norton Company's sharp, splintery E-17 grain was quickly adopted by Manning, Behr, and other firms to replace garnet in floor sanding in the late 1920s.[38]

As in the bonded industry, change often came from outsiders or new firms as new markets and technology upset established patterns. Carborundum, Manning, and the fledgling 3M Company, all of whom entered the industry after 1897, led the adoption of artificial grains, cloth backings, and disks. After Herman Behr refused to buy John Manning's rope paper, which was tougher, heavier, and 50-75 percent stronger than Fourdrinier paper, Manning pioneered its use as an industry standard.[39] The entrepreneur drew capital from his paper company and from Lewis Greenleaf, who had just sold his holdings in the telephone industry, and in 1912 established the Manning Sandpaper Company near his paper plant in Watervliet, New York. Along with Frank Gallagher, a Cornell-trained engineer who was working in the Manning Paper Company, John Manning learned the coated abrasives business the hard way. Breaking into an industry controlled by established firms and mastering the skills of coating, glue mixing, and making produced tons of waste product. After several years of costly learning, the superior rope paper, the adoption of Alundum grain, and increased demand set the company on its feet. By the 1920s Manning was one of the industry's leading firms.[40]

Better backings and better grains required improved adhesives. The most pressing problem was a waterproof paper and glue. Water-soluble, animal-hide glues performed poorly amid the moisture of stains and oils in the furniture industry's finishing operations. By the early 1920s the automotive industry posed an even greater challenge. Its new body lacquers, which replaced earlier varnish coatings, dried quickly to an "orange peel" skin that was dry sanded by aluminum oxide–coated paper, raising large quantities of dust. Water applied during the rubbing solved the dust problem, carried off the particles that clogged the paper, and helped control the depth of cut to ensure a smooth finish. It also dissolved paper backings and glue.[41]

The solution again came from one of the industry's newer, more vigorous firms, the 3M Company. Francis Oakie, a Philadelphia maker of printer's ink, independently developed a waterproof paper. When Oakie failed to interest such nearby established firms as Barton and Baeder-Adamson in his product and when they refused to supply grain for his own manufacturing efforts, he wrote other companies. The 3M Company investigated, bought Oakie's patents, and developed the product. The St. Paul, Minnesota, firm, like the Manning Company, was an upstart whose owners mastered the business the hard way. Undertaking sandpaper manufacture in 1902 after a disappointing emery-mining venture, the owners struggled through a decade of learning and losses, bankrolled by Lucius Ordway, a wealthy plumbing supplier, in much the same way that Greenleaf and Manning supported their firm.[42]

Alundum-coated cloth got the firm on its feet; waterproof paper and the bond that the company developed to go with it moved 3M, like Manning, to the industry's front ranks. A potential suit with Carborundum Company over the development of Alundum cloth taught 3M leader William McKnight the value of sound patent protection, and he added Paul Carpenter, a brilliant patent lawyer, to the firm. Carpenter established a 3M tradition by carefully tying up the new waterproof product in intricate patents. The firm then licensed the Manning and Carborundum Companies, which were independently working on the process, as well as the rest of the industry.[43] Like the patents, the licenses were tightly written to control manufacturing standards, packaging, prices, and further development of waterproof paper.

Process improvements, though less glamorous and less discussed, matched the outpouring of new products. Metal chains replaced rope racks to permit the curving or turning of webs when drying. Eventually, faster curing adhesives and better driers allowed the combination of coater and sizer into a giant making machine, or maker, for large-batch production. Glue, grain, and paper went in at one end and fully sized coated abrasives rolled out the other end ready for the drying rooms.

The substitution of sharper, harder electric furnace abrasives for natural grains permitted sparser coatings, which actually improved performance. The Behr Company discovered the process, which it called Openkote, when it accidentally shipped paper that had been sparsely coated with grain, covering only 50-75 percent of the paper. The paper proved surprisingly effective for sanding soft materials like wood and leather. Wider grain spaces reduced heat and clogging from oils, varnishes, and other soft particles and increased paper productivity two to five times.[44] Behr refused to patent the process and it quickly became an industrywide technique.

Electrocoating, a technique still used in all coated abrasives manufacture, was developed in a much more conscious, analytical manner, typical of the direction in which the industry was heading. Since the early days most coating had been done by gravity, although air blasting had been tried with the finer grains. Neither provided an even dispersal. Moisture tended to clump the grains, especially the finer grits, leaving uneven, wavy lines. Even a small stretch of streaky distribution could ruin an entire run.

Deposition by electrocoating to ensure proper dispersal was developed by Elmer Schacht of the Manning Company.[45] Schacht, a civil engineer from the University of Michigan, was a Manning salesman for five years before returning to head manufacturing operations at Watervliet in 1925. There he again encountered the grain dispersal problem about which his distributors and customers had long complained. From his engineering training, Schacht knew of electrostatic separation of particles in mining, and in 1926 he figured the process might give him the simple separation needed in coated manufacture.

When Schacht passed grain and glue-coated paper through an electrostatic field he got an unexpected bonus. The field not only gave each grain a like charge, thus repelling or separating it from the others; it also provided orientation. Previously, grains were coated in the haphazard positions in which they landed on the paper, some parallel, others perpendicular, and still others in all the intervening angles to the paper. A piece of sandpaper, then, was a mixture of varying sharp and blunt cutting edges. With the new process each particle's longitudinal axis lined up parallel to the force field so that the grains landed on the glued paper in a straight-up-and-down position with sharp cutting edges pointed outward toward the work.

Several years of testing and modification made electrocoating a standard manufacturing process by 1932. Abrasive was carried on an insulated belt, and glued paper with the coat facing downward toward the belt ran parallel to and just above the belt. (The position of paper and glue was a modification by Richard Carlton of the 3M Company.)

The paper and belt then ran between a set of electric terminals, a series of flat plates beneath the grain belt and above the paper. As the abrasive entered the electromagnetic field between the terminals, the grain was polarized by induction. The particles received a like polar charge, became vertical to parallel the lines of the force field, repelled one another to spread out, and were then attracted upward toward the negative terminal. Before reaching it they stuck straight up and down in the glued paper.

The process, which was incorporated into a making machine, ran continuously as the paper unrolled. After grain deposition, which was regulated by adjusting belt speed and voltage, the paper was lightly dried in the maker before receiving a second or sizing coat and being rolled up for final curing. Electrocoating created paper that cut faster, consumed less energy, and lasted longer. Productivity increased by 20-to-50 percent. By early 1934 electrocoated paper accounted for 40 percent of all company sales, and the process soon became and still remains the universal method of coating abrasives.[46]

Like controlled structure and B-bond in the bonded abrasives industry, electrocoating and product standardization to meet customers' more exacting specifications signaled the transition from judgmental, shop production under skilled foremen and mastercoaters to technically controlled manufacture with precise standards set by trained engineers and a factory staff. The change did not come easily, and once again new firms and new men led the way.

As the automotive industry and other customers sought more precise, predictable results from sanding, they complained bitterly about the variation in paper and grain specifications among firms and about the lack of uniformity among batches of a single company's product that resulted from sloppy production controls and from cutthroat competitors' efforts to capture one another's accounts. As part of the national standardization movement during and after World War I, John Manning and Frank Gallagher led the coated industry association's adoption of simplified, uniform paper weights and grain standards. No longer did customers have to experiment with each shipment to determine its suitability.

The toughest battles were fought within plants for production control. In the 1920s technical people had to overcome long-standing shop and craft traditions just as was done at Norton. In the 1880s scientific management began upsetting established patterns of work in the United States, but it was not accepted quickly and simply. Evolution and implementation required several decades, and the pace varied by industry according to technology and need.[47] Because the coated industry, like bonded abrasives, was slow in standardizing and mechanizing, the shift to scientific management was also late. The 3M Company needed two years and three laboratory chiefs before it wrestled glue-coating and liquidity standards from rule-of-thumb artisans. It established independent, uniform procedures and grades for glues, coatings, and rub tests only by the early 1920s.[48]

When Elmer Schacht took charge of Manning manufacturing in 1925, the lack of systematic production standards in even that progressive firm was appalling. Foremen kept drawers filled with samples from past runs. Whenever customers complained about performance, the foremen justified themselves with a quick rummage through the old pile, which always revealed a piece from a previous acceptable run that matched the batch in dispute.

Schacht quickly appointed Arthur Gerry, an engineering graduate of the Massachusetts Institute of Technology, to establish standards for grain and grit. Prior to each run he instructed the foremen to meet a standard sample and later checked to be sure they did. At American Glue, Harvard graduate Donald Kelso apprenticed himself to Bert Grimes and endured the old man's contempt until he had secretly gathered enough empirical data to establish standard formulas for glue mixture and coating depth.[49]

The new products and improved processes not only expanded the coated abrasives market; they helped restructure the industry as well. The new firms that pioneered the changes soon outstripped the established nineteenth-century companies. In addition to introducing better coated abrasives and manufacturing methods, 3M, Carborundum, and later the Manning Company established laboratories for manufacturing control, testing of output, and product development.

They also implemented more aggressive marketing techniques. At 3M, Sales Manager William McKnight inaugurated the practice of bypassing purchasing agents and getting into the shop for direct demonstrations with manufacturing superintendents and foremen. As the sales manager for Manning Company, Henry Elliot established an extensive network of branches and small distributorships to preempt or tie up markets.[50]

By the late 1920s Carborundum, 3M, and Manning had major market shares, while Baeder-Adamson and H. H. Barton, nineteenth-century industry leaders, were only fringe operations. The Herman Behr Company, the industry leader in the late nineteenth and early twentieth centuries, had slipped badly. When Manning consolidated with Behr in 1928, their combined market share was about 30 percent, the industry's largest, and Manning's sales were 50 percent greater than Behr's for the first half of that year. Behr-Manning was followed by 3M, which had about one quarter of the market in 1929, and by Carborundum.[51]

The new leaders, President Frank Tone and Sales Manager George Rayner at Carborundum, President William McKnight and Sales Manager Archibald Bush at 3M, and President John Manning, Vice-President Frank Gallagher, and Sales Manager Henry Elliot at the Manning Company, quickly turned to merger and interfirm cooperation to regulate prices and stabilize competition. Interfirm cooperation, which came through the coated abrasives association originally used to establish uniform product standards and through the collective efforts of industry leaders, took several mutually reinforcing forms, but the most effective was cross-licensing of patents.

Cross-licensing signaled the end of price competition and of the aggressive struggle for industry domination by controlling product development. By the early 1920s, 3M and Carborundum had added a new technique to industry competition: high license fees for crucial new products. The 3M Company and its boss William McKnight had suffered years of losses and mediocre performance before escaping from a hardscrabble, fringe position in the early 1920s. Aggressive battles and flinty competitive tactics left an indelible mark.

When 3M developed crucial waterproof patents in the early 1920s, it established a licensing policy calculated to squeeze out the highest possible profits during the patents' seventeen-year life without provoking other companies to patent infringement. The agreement compelled the licensee to share any future waterproof developments with 3M and established an upward sliding scale to protect the company's market position. Royalties remained 1 percent of sales if the licensee had less than one sixth of the market but climbed swiftly to 16 percent of sales for a licensee who dared to try for one third of the market.[52] Carborundum's disk patents were similar, requiring up to 12.5 percent of sales as license fees.

John Manning demonstrated a much broader vision when he licensed electrocoating in 1932 for a flat 1 percent of sales. Extortionate fees only invited retaliation and stimulated high prices, which in turn attracted additional competitors when patents expired.[53] Manning argued that profits were just as important to competitors as to his own firm. If rivals' profit margins were squeezed in one line, they retaliated in others. Cooperation promised greater stability and long-run profits. Manning may also have been influenced by the stagnant production figures that had characterized the industry in the fifteen prosperous years before 1930. Lower costs would increase volume and expand markets with greater profits to everyone.

William McKnight later suggested that the low-cost license resulted from a potential patent suit.[54] Minnesota's counterclaim to the electrocoating patent, based on work with dubious applicability by MIT professor James Smyser and triggered by information gained from an employee pirated from the Manning operation, explained its low license fee (.75 percent) from Manning but not the 1 percent Manning offered to other firms as well. Nor does it account for the industry's continued use of the procedure until an antitrust suit in 1950.[55]

John Manning's argument had attracted quick support from Henry Elliot and Archibald Bush, sales managers at Behr-Manning and 3M, and the success of low-cost cross-licensing perpetuated the practice.[56] In addition to disposing of wrangles over future products, it offered other forms of stability as well. At Behr-Manning directors confidently and accurately noted that their new contract for electrocoating would "give Behr-Manning Corporation, with 3M cooperating, control over prices and standards which will probably eventually extend to all products."[57] A 1926 test case involving General Electric allowed licensers to regulate conditions of sale for the licensed product, and the electrocoating and subsequent agreements specified product standards, packaging, and prices.

The contracts were also expanded to stabilize warehouse locations and distributorship representation. Former Behr-Manning Sales Manager Henry Merrill recalled that the licenses

> did everything but tell you what time to go to bed at night and get up in the morning . . . The branch system was set up under the license agreement identifying 15 or 16 spots where you could either have a stocking warehouse or you could have a distributor to whom you paid an additional 10 or 15%. For example, in Pittsburgh, we elected to have a distributor. We paid them an extra percentage for warehousing which then [our] general supply [division] did in a very substantial way. On the other hand, in Tacoma, Washington, we had a branch up there to service the plywood trades. Los Angeles, we had no branch; we had a distributor. But we had branches in Buffalo, Grand Rapids, Chicago, New York and so on. Relatively small inexpensive branches, all with a branch manager and maybe a couple of [salesmen]. This worked out fine. People adhered to this [until the late 1950s].[58]

With that kind of interfirm cooperation, coated abrasives manufacturers controlled entry into the industry and assured themselves of stable profit margins without ever having to discuss prices at association meetings.

While patent licensing legally helped stabilize domestic competition, a Webb-Pomerene corporation served a similar function for foreign sales.[59] Congress had originally passed the Webb-Pomerene Act in 1918 as an exemption from the Sherman Antitrust Act to encourage American firms to develop foreign markets.[60] The law permitted competing firms to form a joint enterprise to trade abroad. In the early

1920s, when George Link became counsel for the coated abrasives association, he created the American Surface Abrasives Export Corporation, a Webb-Pomerene enterprise that distributed literature and forwarded foreign shipments by U.S. coated manufacturers.[61]

In 1929 Link, who later also served as Behr-Manning's counsel, created two new Webb-Pomerene companies, the Durex Corporation and the Durex Abrasives Corporation, to tighten interfirm cooperation. Each U.S. coated company terminated its independent foreign sales subsidiaries, bought stock in Durex and Durex Abrasives in proportion to its export market share, and sent a representative to the two identical boards of directors. Durex Abrasives acted as an export company, buying products from domestic firms and selling them through its sales offices and distributors around the world. The Durex Corporation served as the industry's joint manufacturer abroad. Like cross-licensing, the Durex companies were quite successful and endured until a 1950 antitrust case.

Patent licensing and Webb-Pomerene companies were only two outstanding examples of the varied forms of interfirm cooperation established in the late 1920s. The coated abrasives association, through which Manning and Gallagher had implemented product standardization, also became a focus of interdependence. Its administrative arm was counsel and statistician George Link who gathered monthly data to compute industry totals, company market shares by product, comparative sales records, and license fees. Link and the association also held the Ruby garnet mine in upstate New York for industry benefit and published standard price lists and discount sheets.[62]

Outside the association, firms learned to depend on one another. They renewed an agreement not to pirate one another's key personnel after 3M had hired a Behr sales manager and engineer during the Behr-Manning consolidation. Behr-Manning supplied cloth backings to the entire industry because of its superior preparation methods. Companies also cooperated in equipment and process development. Behr-Manning and 3M, for example, worked together in 1937 to design and purchase large presses for belt manufacture for stainless steel polishing. By the late 1930s companies visited one another to exchange know-how on finishing processes so that they might share the cheapest costs after patent licenses had fixed prices.[63]

Consolidation soon proved the most effective means of cooperation and briefly preceded the industry's third stage. It eliminated cutthroat competitors and reduced the number of firms to be consulted and persuaded. In the late 1920s the coated abrasives association, apparently at John Manning's instigation, moved quickly to purchase the Standard Abrasive Company of Garfield, New Jersey, and the Federal Abrasives Company of Westfield, Massachusetts. The two new firms, established by former employees of Behr and American Glue, were disrupting the industry with price cutting and low-quality goods. Donald Kelso recalled that "the industry decided to buy them out, and I was asked to do this, using nominally the backing of U.S. Sandpaper Company where I was working at the time."[64] Generous settlements eased the departure.

The technique's success quickly led to the buyout and closing of others between 1929 and 1931. Such fringe operators as Wausau, U.S. Sandpaper, American Glue, Barton, and Baeder-Adamson had co-operated in stabilizing the industry, but they contributed little to its growth and they complicated the management of the Durex Companies and other joint efforts. Whether any coercion was used is not known; it seems doubtful. The breakup of American Glue and Baeder-Adamson, part of a horizontal combination originally assembled by the late King Upton, facilitated the process.[65] Carborundum bought the former and 3M the latter.

In other companies, owners and master coaters had died or were aging, and survivors were glad to receive cash for their assets. The advent of the Great Depression made offers still more attractive. Percy Sawyer at Wausau happily accepted 3M's bid in December 1929 to bail him out; he had no other market for his securities. The Barton family's second generation were indifferent businessmen and Frank Winter's U.S. Sandpaper struggled constantly to make ends meet. Both readily agreed to John Manning's price in 1930.[66]

Old age and declining performance also triggered the major combination—the consolidation of the Herman Behr Company with the Manning Abrasive Company in 1928. Herman Behr was in his 80s and top personnel in sales and production had died. One of Behr's sons was a stockbroker and the other had little enthusiasm for the business. The Behr Company had failed to penetrate the new metal-working markets and was rapidly losing ground to the younger, more aggressive firms.

The merger was a good fit; Behr's strength in the leather and wood-working trades nicely complemented the Manning Company's waterproof paper and metal-working markets. Frank Gallagher, who negotiated for the Manning Company, later explained that the primary purpose was savings through consolidation, and "our expectations as to savings were almost fully realized."[67] The Manning people, who dominated the new enterprise, closed the old Behr plant and combined sales facilities and sales and production personnel.

Combination finally and firmly rationalized the industry, although it did not give Behr-Manning, 3M, and Carborundum the entire market. Armour, the powerful meatpacker's sideline, insisted on staying in even though it had less than 5 percent of the market. In the 1930s and 1940s small makers of cheap, nontechnical goods reappeared, but the big three made no move to buy them out. The New Deal's advent had tightened antitrust procedures, and the depression tied up funds.[68]

The newcomers provided little real competition to the large firms. Their simple, cut-rate products held little attraction for major industrial purchasers whose cost departments readily appreciated the higher productivity of quality technical goods. Carborundum, Behr-Manning, and 3M were integrated firms with large sales and service departments. While they shared finishing techniques and did not compete on price, the three leaders jealously guarded their basic making procedures. These provided the quality variations on which depended the big three's dominance and the competition among them. Together they controlled more than 80 percent of the market for at least three decades; 3M and Behr-Manning each had one-third shares and Carborundum had about one sixth.[69]

The close cooperation and tight rationalization were not, however, either orderly or inevitable. A much more competitive industry with a few large dominant firms and a host of small companies like the bonded abrasives business was a distinct possibility. Even though the coated abrasives industry, like the grinding wheel business, had some traditions of association and cooperation prior to 1920, the history of periodic cutthroat competition was much stronger. And 3M, a former cut-rate competitor, remained a hardscrabble, litigious, and aggressive fighter after becoming an industry leader. Nor did the consolidation represent defensive measures by elderly firms in a mature business. In the three decades after rationalization, existing markets grew rapidly and machinery development opened many new markets for coated abrasives. Industry sales were $20.3 million in 1929 and exceeded $110 million by 1959.[70]

The shift in structure and character resulted from a simultaneous mix of circumstances. John Manning was able to implement his values and ideas of long-range stable competition, but he did not plan that implementation. Aging leadership, declining marginal companies, and the onset of depression encouraged rapid consolidation. The desire of 3M to establish European plants to protect its foreign waterproof patents and other firms' threatened retaliation triggered the cooperative Durex Companies.

In addition, 3M was beginning to turn its aggressive research, marketing, and patenting skills in other directions. In the late 1920s researcher Richard Drew developed masking tape as a supplementary product for the automotive market. He soon followed with the celebrated Scotch cellophane tape, for which 3M became so well known. The company already had one third of the coated abrasives market, whose product volume had been remarkably stable since 1914. Future growth in market share depended on rugged competition with able, powerful firms. Diversification through research and development into tapes, roofing materials, and other products in relatively open fields was much more attractive. Coated abrasives accounted for 94 percent of 3M sales in 1925 but less than 50 percent in 1935.[71]

Finally, cross-licensing proved more attractive to Carborundum and 3M by 1931 when Behr-Manning consolidated with the powerful Norton Company. For Norton, expansion into coated abrasives was a natural addition to its abrasive products line. The firm had considered sandpaper manufacture as early as 1907, but its own rapid growth and the disruptions of World War I and the 1921 depression delayed any action. As the Manning and 3M histories indicated, purchasing coated expertise was easier than internal development.

Behr-Manning: Autonomous Acquisition

By the late 1920s when Aldus Higgins began searching for a candidate, conditions were especially propitious. The coated industry had developed sales in the metal-working industries that paralleled Norton's markets. Rationalization was bringing stability to a prosperous industry where no firm was as large or powerful as Norton.

The choice of Behr-Manning was relatively simple. Carborundum was owned by the Mellon family and had long been a bonded abrasives competitor. William McKnight and Archibald Bush were happily running feisty 3M and contemplating diversification. Behr-Manning was the industry's largest firm. It was a progressive, growing, well-organized company, and John Manning, Frank Gallagher, Henry Elliot, and Elmer Schacht headed an excellent management team. The two companies had long been commercially associated; Behr-Manning was Norton's largest customer for abrasive grain.

Manning's reasons for selling are less clear. Contemporaries mentioned the grain contracts and pointed out that Manning had daughters to provide for but no sons to carry on the business.[72] Big Carborundum and growing 3M threatened powerful competition. Yet, the grain contracts were no reason to sell out, and in the absence of suitable kin to maintain the business, the familiar and excellent team already in place was as capable as any unknown management that Norton would provide. Carborundum was a large company but had never been an aggressive competitor, and 3M was still relatively small.

Behr-Manning leadership.
John Manning.

Finally, rationalization had brought more stability to coated abrasives manufacture than the industry had ever previously known.

The answer probably lies in the depression, which drastically cut Behr-Manning sales and resources. The automotive industry, a major Behr-Manning customer, slumped badly, and by 1931 the firm's sales

Frank Gallagher.

were only 52 percent of its 1928 total of $6 million. The Behr, Barton, and U.S. Sandpaper acquisitions had brought burdens but few realizable assets. All three plants were closed and practically unsalable. By 1931 Manning had spent over $900,000 in cash payments to Barton

Henry Elliot.

and U.S. Sandpaper, and was obligated for nearly $300,000 in annual dividends on the preferred stock that had helped finance the Behr acquisition. Inventories and accounts receivable were high; salaries and employment had been cut. In March 1931 comptroller Max Pes-

Elmer Schacht.

nel's special report indicated that the cash surplus was reduced to $108,000 with a $78,000 quarterly dividend due in July on the preferred stock.[73]

Behr-Manning was not bankrupt. Like so many firms in hard times it had a liquidity crisis, and there may well have been ready sources for additional cash, such as the Manning family paper company and bank loans. Elmer Schacht doubted that the company was in dire straits and argued persuasively that the depression awakened Manning to the vulnerability of his relatively small firm.[74] Norton's large cash reserves were a comfortable cushion for this or any future crisis. Its owners' conservative values and practices and the company's well-established position assured future stability and offered a powerful ally should 3M again become obstreperous.

Finally, negotiators Frank Gallagher for Behr-Manning and William L. Neilson and William Magee for Norton struck a bargain that protected both interests and involved no cash. In simple terms, Behr-Manning assets were exchanged for 446,303 shares of Norton stock (par value $10 per share), and the assets were vested in the Behr-Manning Corporation (of Massachusetts), a wholly owned Norton subsidiary. The Norton stock became the sole asset of Behr-Manning Holding Corporation (of Delaware), whose securities were held by Behr-Manning owners in proportion to their original shares.[75]

The financial crunch at Behr-Manning helped Neilson and Magee negotiate a very favorable deal. Norton acquired the leading coated abrasives manufacturer at no out-of-pocket cost. The $4,460,000 in Norton stock scarcely equaled the assets behind Behr-Manning's $4,500,000 preferred stock; nothing was paid for the common stock or for the Barton and U.S. Sandpaper assets.[76] The absence of large cash payments avoided the need for outside finance. The holding company further preserved Norton secrecy and internal control by assuring that Norton stock did not reach public markets.

Although they received no cash for their holdings, Manning and his people retained their positions and their control, a basic condition of the deal. Manning became president and Gallagher vice-president and general manager of Behr-Manning Massachusetts and of Behr-Manning Holding Corporation, and both joined the Norton Board of Directors. Tom Green, Aldus Higgins's brother-in-law, became treasurer of the new companies to act as Norton's representative in Watervliet, and George Jeppson and Aldus Higgins joined him on the new boards of directors. But the old operating organization remained intact and Green exerted no authority. Manning, Gallagher, Elliot, and Schacht continued to run the company under the Behr-Manning name and trademarks. With approval from directors Jeppson and Higgins, they conducted board meetings, declared dividends, and developed their own strategy. Behr-Manning became a fully autonomous operating arm of Norton Company.

The autonomy worked well. Throughout the 1930s Schacht and Gallagher continued to hire college-trained engineers such as Charles Lanyon, Randall Manchester, and Lee Hoogstoel to rationalize production techniques, speed output, cut costs, and generate new methods and materials. Chief Engineer John Amstuz's Experimental Department concentrated on process improvements, while the laboratory under Nicholas Oglesby emphasized product development. Charles Hubbinette redesigned machines with improved bearing protection for longer life. Frank Crupe devised better means to stretch and fill cloth backings so that Behr-Manning maintained its cloth-finishing monopoly for the industry. Charles Lanyon developed methods to dry and cure coated abrasives in roll form, thus replacing the cumbersome rack and loop system. Oglesby worked with Lawrence Redman of the Bakelite Company to produce phenolic resin adhesives, which cured faster and bonded tighter than the old animal hide glues. An even greater contribution was Oglesby's adaptation of inert materials like calcium carbide as extenders for the resins, an important economy still practiced and especially useful in conserving vital raw materials in World War II.[77]

Excess capacity generated by the 1930s depression encouraged Schacht and his team to try by-products and diversification. Expertise in paper making and handling led to cork fiber sheets, a spongy material with potential markets as press blankets, gaskets, and carpet pads. Schacht also supervised the application of his electrostatic process to textiles. Flock coating, the electrostatic deposition of short fibers onto cloth backings, produced artificial velvet for clothes, drapes, and auto interiors and artificial suede for the shoe industry.[78] During World War II Behr-Manning supplied wire harnesses for Bendix Aviation, and after the war, when 3M patents had expired, the factory followed its knowledge of adhesives and coatings into tape production.

Yet Behr-Manning never equaled its more illustrious competitor in diversification. Aggressive product development and strong patents gave 3M an insurmountable head start in tape development, the most profitable line of diversified products. Harness production, though ingenious, was a wartime measure only, and neither cork gaskets nor flock coating reached expectations. Rapid loss of compressibility limited the applications of the cork sheets. Electrocoated fabrics cost more than woven pile, and although the artificial suede was profitable, its market was limited. Furthermore, Behr-Manning lacked the full line of textile products necessary to support a large-scale marketing effort into broader fields.

Elmer Schacht and Henry Merrill later recalled ruefully that product know-how was not enough. Successful diversification required complete understanding and vigorous prosecution of new markets. In the absence of the resources and enthusiasm for selling textiles and other products, Behr-Manning eventually licensed its profitable but marginal by-products.[79]

The company proved far more successful, and in fact led the industry, in developing products that expanded coated abrasives markets. The key was the creation of new machinery using coated abrasive belts in place of older hand- and drum-sanding techniques.[80] Heavier cloth and cloth-and-paper combination backings along with stronger, more heat-resistant phenolic resins made superior belts possible. As in the case of diversification, excess capacity provoked Behr-Manning into machinery development in the 1930s and eventually led Frank Gallagher and Henry Elliot to establish a full-fledged Product Engineering Department first under Irving Burroughs and later under Dirck Olton.

Burroughs developed an idler backstand, the pioneer machine in the mid-1930s. It was a simple mechanism in which a coated abrasive belt moved over two wheels. The rear wheel or pulley was motorized while the front wheel was the contact point against which material was ground. The new technique ground more quickly, evenly, and completely than hand sanding or the old drum sanders. Drum sanders and set-up wheels required frequent, time-consuming replacements. For the drums, sheets of sandpaper had to be carefully trimmed, spiraled around the drum, and glued down. Polishing or set-up wheels of canvas, glue, and grain had to be remade. On the backstands, the simple flick of a lever released the pulley tension for easy belt replacement.

The stimulus to success, however, again lay in the markets themselves. The cutlery trade initially refused backstands because rebuilding set-up wheels with retirees or pensioners was even cheaper. The advent of New Deal minimum wage legislation and the growth of industrial unions soon began to raise labor costs, especially in steel, automotive, and other metal-working industries. World War II demand for rapid production and labor-saving mechanisms proved a big boost for coated abrasive machinery, and continually rising labor costs in the late 1940s and 1950s maintained the pressure.

The result was the rapid expansion of coated abrasive belt machinery. Idler backstands replaced polishing wheels for sanding electric motor rotors, auto bumpers, hub caps, small tools, and myriad other small metal parts. Eventually, Behr-Manning designed more complex machines that held and articulated automotive and other metal parts of complex shape for semiautomatic line and station polishing. A third wheel on the backstand deflected the belt to fit difficult contours on bumper guards and similar products. With the aid of the Production Machine Company of Greenfield, Massachusetts, Behr-Manning developed multiple-head belt machines, which replaced grinding wheels for centerless grinding of metal tubing at firms like Babcock and Wilcox and National Tube.

Almost simultaneously, the new techniques spread backward into basic steel as demand for stainless steel grew. Behr-Manning production engineers designed machines with belts 2, 3, or 4 feet wide to grind and polish steel sheets and later steel coils. Belt sanding permitted a new technique of prefinishing. Flat metal stock moved through a continuous line of machines with coated belts of varying grit to be smoothed, polished, and coated with a thick plastic film. The stock could then be stored until formed, and the film melted or stripped away, leaving a clean, unblemished surface ready for plating, lacquer, enamel, or paint. The technique eliminated expensive hand polishing, allowed faster routing, and encouraged the use of lower grades of steel. It polished rusty inventory cheaply and produced a better finish than older methods.[81]

In addition, coated metal-working techniques were rapidly transferred to the less mechanized leather and woodworking industries. Behr-Manning produced wide-belt machines for leather buffing and brought tanners to Watervliet for testing. At one plant three wide-belt, through-feed machines with thirty-one operators replaced twenty-six leather buffers and forty operators, at a savings of $300,000. The coated company's work with the Yates American Machine Company also supplied wide-belt machinery for the plywood and fiberboard industries.

Behr-Manning played a central role in the entire process. Electro-deposition gave improved orientation which permitted replacement of grinding wheels in some cases. New techniques produced superior belt joints, and resin-bonded belts lasted longer and cut better than animal glue–bonded products, for the resins did not soften from heat and clog with particles. Behr-Manning product engineers invented or worked closely with such machinery firms as the Sunstrand, Yates American, and Production Machine companies to create the necessary machinery.

The firm's decision to license all machinery developments and thus avoid competition with potential customers may have removed a lucrative opportunity for diversification. Nevertheless, the belts and the variety of specially shaped products—spirabands, spirapoints, and pencils—designed for machining small holes and tight corners comprised a major manufacturing department and were the key to rapid sales growth in the 1940s and 1950s when Behr-Manning produced a million belts annually.

Under Henry Elliot, Behr-Manning's Sales Department matched production growth with rapid market expansion. Elliot, however, was always careful to follow John Manning's dictum to compete "fairly" and preserve industry stability. He headed the coated abrasives association and met regularly with other licensers for pricing. One month prior to price changes, licensers assembled and exchanged prices listed on sheets by product. The sheets went back to each firm's sales organization, which simply transferred the data to price lists, and all were published simultaneously. Fair competition also meant holding back unusual new products, such as extra wide belts, until competitors were prepared to manufacture. Trust and confidence required that competitors rectify errors. When 3M mistakenly offered low quotes to Black and Decker, its representatives spent three days in Towson, Maryland, retrieving the quotes and setting things right. So successful were the stabilizing techniques that industry prices remained steady through the 1950s, even after the basic patents had expired.[82]

Elliot also protected Behr-Manning with an extensive sales organization. In the early 1930s he and his assistants carefully segmented the coated market into industrial mill supply, automotive, hardware, floor and other woodworking, and shoe and leather divisions. They established an elaborate network of salesmen, branches, and distributors to blanket each field. Unlike Norton, which relied on carefully trained, exclusive distributors, Behr-Manning used many small distributors to tie up an area. Often, its salesmen contacted customers directly and relayed orders to the distributors, assuring its control of the trade.[83] Though smaller, Behr-Manning had sixteen branches to Norton's six, with more than two hundred salesmen and over one hundred distributors in the 1950s.

At the same time the organization offered improved service and coordination as the trade became more complex. As the market grew after the 1930s, the proliferation of fibers, cloths, papers, and their combinations for backings; of glues, varnishes, and resins for bonding; of grains; and of shapes made selection of the proper coated abrasive almost as bewildering as in bonded abrasives. By 1951 Behr-Manning manufactured more than thirty thousand different items, and the 4-page sales catalog of the 1890s had become a 142-page book, listing sheets, rolls, belts, disks, and specialty items along with retail products and accessories.[84]

As at Norton the sales organization educated customers and distributors in product selection and application. In 1948 it cooperated with other manufacturers to replace antiquated quire and ream packing with simpler units and sizes, reflecting the coated industry's maturation and independence from its old dominance by the paper industry. Finally, like Norton's Sales Department, the Behr-Manning organization gathered data to forecast orders and coordinate production with demand, although the coated industry's slower growth naturally delayed the necessity of forecasting. Inventory costs during the 1930s first pointed to the problem, but as in bonded abrasives, real need came after the rapid growth of demand and explosion of product categories. In the late 1940s Walter Woodward in sales and Byron Keene in production set up a forecasting mechanism and began more careful scheduling of production runs.[85]

The success of Behr-Manning's management was reflected in sales and profits. The company retained its one-third market share through the 1930s, 1940s, and 1950s despite the market's expansion and the growth of rival 3M to gigantic size, surpassing even Norton Company in sales and assets. As figure 5 illustrates, by 1936 coated abrasives sales exceeded the predepression 1929 high of $4.5 million. They doubled to more than $10 million by 1941 and then tripled again to more than $35 million by 1953, reflecting mechanization and the market's rapid expansion. Separate profit figures for Behr-Manning have not survived, but dividends between 1936 and 1946 generally returned 20 percent per share, dipping to 14 percent during the war years because of excess profits taxes. The company also paid stock dividends of 50 percent in 1947 and 100 percent in 1954. By the late 1950s Behr-Manning's net monthly profits sometimes topped Worcester's total, and the firm was sending more than $2 million annually to its parent on $8 million invested capital.[86]

Although the policy of autonomous management produced generous growth and financial success, it also revealed the limitations of Norton's tightly centralized owner-management. Watervliet was never part of the Norton family. Despite the similar nature and functions of their products, the coated and bonded industries were quite different. Behr-Manning's markets were more diverse and its sales efforts more intense, while, ironically, its traditions of interfirm cooperation and cross-licensing were much stronger. Behr-Manning battled not only Carborundum, Norton's major rival, but also the aggressive, expanding 3M Company, a far more formidable competitor than any firm Norton ever faced.

Autonomous Behr-Manning leadership perpetuated the distinction between the enterprises. In the early 1930s disputes between Aldus Higgins and George Jeppson on the one hand and Manning and Gallagher on the other quickly strengthened the resolve to continue separate operation. Norton people may have feared the able Gallagher's rumored intention to assume leadership of the entire Norton Company; keeping him in Watervliet removed any threat (which was never serious) to the family firm.

Because Behr-Manning leaders had a significant minority holding of Norton stock and a well-established reputation, they also enjoyed the distance and freedom. With all the pride of a smaller company

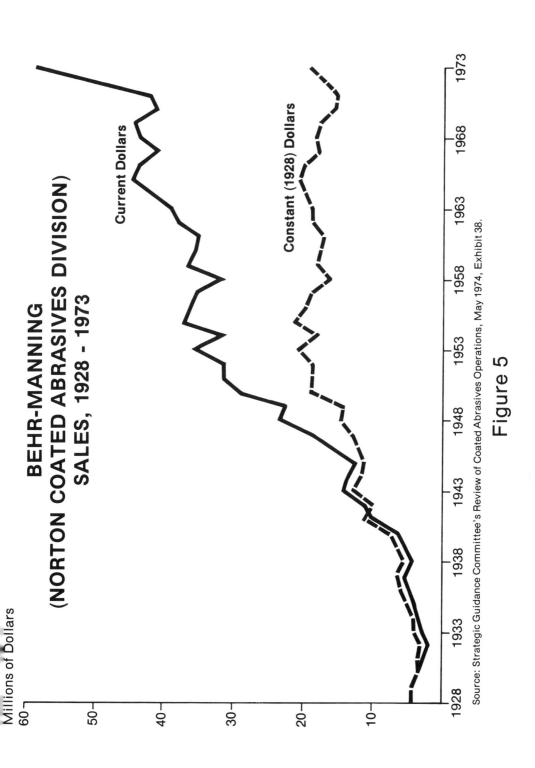

BEHR-MANNING
(NORTON COATED ABRASIVES DIVISION)
SALES, 1928 - 1973

Millions of Dollars

Current Dollars

Constant (1928) Dollars

Source: Strategic Guidance Committee's Review of Coated Abrasives Operations, May 1974, Exhibit 38.

Figure 5

beholden to a larger protector, they resented any efforts to remake them in the parent company's image. They vigorously defended their competitive practices and sales techniques and disagreed with Norton's decision to build rather than license machinery. As Elmer Schacht proudly put it, "We were not . . . a little Norton."[87]

The two companies were especially critical of each other's labor policies. The coated work force had been completely unionized from the outset, largely by the International Brotherhood of Papermakers along with separate American Federation of Labor craft unions for machinists, carpenters, millwrights, and tinsmiths. John Manning, who had invited unions in, believed them necessary for adequate worker representation, but he rejected Norton paternalism. Noblesse oblige required only that the working man be given a chance for fair bargaining; thenceforth company and union each looked after its own best interests.

Though flexible, the Manning approach was definitely more tight-fisted than Norton's. Behr-Manning in Watervliet, like Norton in Worcester, was a major employer, and through its Manning-Gallagher Foundation it contributed to local charities and civic improvement. Yet, during the 1930s, 1940s, and 1950s, company and union bargained hard. Wages remained near prevailing local rates and below Norton's pay scales, but there was never a serious labor dispute. Like Norton, Behr-Manning offered stock to employees, but only to a tiny, select group of top executives. Ad hoc pensions were available to long-time employees, but Schacht thought the plan "was like a charity division of the company" and recalled that Social Security "relieved us there."[88] Group health and retirement benefits for employees came only after Worcester made them company practice. Finally, the paternalism that characterized Norton management was far more limited at Behr-Manning.

What had begun out of necessity continued out of success, pride, and self-perpetuation. When the two firms consolidated in 1931, Aldus Higgins and George Jeppson could not have directly operated Behr-Manning even had they wished to do so. Expansion of centralized family management required direct control and a supply of adequate people. Neither George nor Aldus wished to move to Watervliet, and there were no experienced sons available to assume control as Aldus had done at Niagara in 1901. After the coated abrasives company's recovery and the mutual agreement to continue separate ways, Frank Gallagher succeeded John Manning in 1938 to guide Behr-Manning through the 1940s, and Elmer Schacht in turn succeeded Gallagher and headed the firm until 1961.

The perpetuation of veteran leadership and the company's success reinforced each other and deepened Behr-Manning pride and separateness. Even after Behr-Manning Corporation of Massachusetts, the legal operating organization, was abolished in 1954 for tax purposes and became a Norton division, its heads continued to elect a president and Board of Directors and vote dividends.

The immediate costs of thirty years' independence were small. Norton and Behr-Manning sales forces seldom cooperated, although Norton later found it advantageous to operate a joint marketing group. Researchers in Watervliet and Worcester rarely communicated, even though both were developing resin bonds with the aid of the same people. In the long run, however, Worcester's lack of management controls and knowledge left Norton vulnerable to a decline in Behr-Manning leadership and the resulting serious problems.

5.

Worcesterites Abroad:
Further Challenges to the Family Firm

EVEN BEFORE the Behr-Manning acquisition, Norton's expansion abroad had begun to test the capabilities of centralized family management. Norton Company moved first into foreign sales and then into production with the same values and techniques that had proved so successful in domestic enterprise. It ventured cautiously and successfully, but not without difficulty.

The owner-managers soon discovered that simultaneous pursuit of prudence and control conflicted. Prudent risk reduction in time-honored New England mercantile fashion suggested native partners who invested jointly with Norton in foreign plants to provide on-the-spot oversight and to share the vicissitudes of war, government regulation, and other uncertainties. Thrift meant recovery of investment as rapidly as possible through dividends, sales contracts, and raw materials supply. Control required careful financial accounting and tight regulation of bond formulas, production processes, and other manufacturing secrets. But sharing risks also exposed manufacturing techniques to outsiders who wished to reinvest profits for further expansion. And rigid controls ignored the realities of time and distance and denied the flexibility essential to advantageous on-the-spot enterprise.

The solutions reflected the New England firm. Expansion was taken at a leisurely, rather than an aggressive, pace. Between 1910 and 1950, Norton, like many early multinationals, built overseas when necessary to protect existing markets or when extremely profitable opportunities with little risk came its way. Caution helped reduce risk, and control, normally the most important value, dictated limited use of partnership.

The natural corollary was that Norton's foreign expansion, like its

190

management, was informal and idiosyncratic. Since the company reacted to external stimuli, it had no grand strategy for global coverage. Norton went overseas only when its exports were threatened, and plants appeared in established markets but not ahead of them. For several decades scant effort was made to coordinate plant operations; each location, headed by trained, loyal Norton people, was an autonomous enterprise monitored by careful financial controls.

Foreign Sales and Manufacture: Norton Joins the "American Invasion"

Norton's early and considerable interest in foreign markets and enterprise was not unusual among large American industrial firms. In the two decades before World War I, American direct investment abroad more than quadrupled from $635 million in 1897.[1] Although the 1890s depression encouraged some development of foreign markets, the major stimulus was the merger movement that accompanied the return to prosperity. The horizontal consolidations that swept U.S. industry between 1897 and 1903 created large-scale producing organizations that were soon rationalized and integrated forward into sales and backward into raw materials processing. Standard Oil, Anaconda Copper, Du Pont, and other firms in extractive industries or with raw material sources located outside the United States established mining operations—primarily in Canada, Mexico, and South America—to assure steady supplies.

Other companies moved abroad as part of a marketing strategy. Singer Sewing Machine, International Harvester, American Tobacco, Coca-Cola, and many firms in machinery, tobacco, food processing, and other high-volume or high-technology industries first built overseas sales organizations to exploit advantages of size, organization, and process. They located primarily in Canada, Britain, and western Europe—industrial nations where high per capita incomes produced the largest markets. Continued sales growth, the erection of tariff barriers, and the need to protect patents soon led these pioneers to buy or build processing or manufacturing facilities to hold onto existing markets.[2]

While Europeans at the century's turn watched "a veritable 'wave' " of American expansion and worried about "the Americanization of Europe," the leading historian of American multinational growth has noted that most U.S. companies did not have manufacturing or mining stakes outside the country and that foreign activities "did not make a substantial contribution to the profits" of most enterprises.[3] Nevertheless, American direct foreign investment was quite impressive. By 1907 Standard Oil was "a giant multinational concern"; it controlled fifty firms whose $37 million capitalization included marketing, refining, and producing facilities. American Tobacco's plants in Austria, Japan, Canada, and Germany produced over three hundred million cigarettes annually in 1901, and ten years later International Harvester had plants in Canada, Sweden, France, Germany, and Russia.[4]

Aggregate data are even more impressive than isolated examples. In 1914 American direct foreign investment was 7 percent of gross national product, a ratio that was still true in 1966. Total stakes were $2.6 billion, including $573 million in Europe alone. Norton Company was one of thirty-seven U.S. enterprises with manufacturing facilities in two or more foreign countries. At least twenty-two others had Canadian plants and an additional ten had single plants outside the U.S. and Canada.[5]

Like the majority of American multinationals, Norton Company moved abroad with marketing rather than extractive investments. As noted in previous chapters, clay and bauxite supplies were readily available in the United States, and while uncertain foreign emery sources might have eventually led the company into overseas mining operations, the substitution of manmade for natural abrasives resolved that difficulty before Norton grew large enough to consider a foreign mining venture.

Overseas sales, however, predated the firm's existence; John G. Sloan of Paris was a sales agent for F. B. Norton before 1885. Although fabricated grinding wheels only became commercially successful and significant in the 1870s and 1880s, American companies led by Norton soon developed superior vitrified emery wheels that captured the majority of the market. Subsequently, the pioneer commercial production of manmade abrasives by Carborundum and Norton Companies reinforced the initial advantage gained with superior bonds and higher product standards. By 1915 only German wheel manufacturers came close to rivaling Carborundum and Norton products, and they did not export to the United States as the American firms exported to Germany and the rest of Europe—a pattern that endured until the 1970s. Even as late as the 1950s, European distributors could sell higher priced Norton wheels with the slogan "We can duplicate a grinding wheel."[6]

Although Norton Emery Wheel Company's founders inherited a small European market from F. B. Norton, the firm establishment of overseas sales was one of the owner-operators' few aggressive actions in foreign enterprise. Organization followed Charles Allen's ascendancy as general manager over Sales Manager Walter Messer. Messer had continued what was apparently a commission arrangement with Sloan and had inaugurated a similar agreement with Strong and Trowbridge for Australian sales.

Based on the potential of the European industrial market and Norton's leadership in U.S. manufacturing, which already provided what he described to a local paper as "a large European trade," Allen quickly moved to provide more thorough coverage.[7] In 1891 he went abroad to establish two major European distributors. Buck and Hickman, hardware suppliers based in London, agreed to market Norton wheels through their outlets in England, Scotland, and Wales, while Schuchardt and Schutte, importers of machine tools in Germany, contracted for sales in Germany, Austria, Sweden, Belgium, and Russia.[8] Foreign sales, especially to the European market, rapidly became a significant part of Norton growth. During the 1890s depression in the United States, foreign purchases accounted for as much as one third of total sales, and in more normal times they generally ranged from 21 to 29 percent of wheel sales between 1903 and 1910.[9]

The same factors that stimulated Norton's growth at home also boosted foreign orders. Superior bonds, product uniformity, predictability of behavior, and the development of manmade abrasives persuaded European metal workers and other manufacturers, like their American counterparts, to pay higher prices for Norton wheels in exchange for better control and performance. Charles Norton's grinding machines helped develop production grinding, gave the company an additional popular product, and enhanced its reputation in the European market.

The company's foreign sales efforts expanded to service its growing markets. In the 1890s and early 1900s, Charles Allen appointed dealers in South America, South Africa, and the Far East and continued the pattern of direct contact with frequent European trips to confer with Bernhard Schuchardt, Alfred Schutte, and other major distributors and to add sales outlets in Switzerland and the Netherlands. Norton trademarks were carefully registered throughout Europe.

Powerful new distributors were recruited, frequently through the sales of Norton grinding machines. After Charles Norton's early European trips for demonstration and direct sales, Norton Grinding Company contracted with Ludwig and Loewe to manufacture and sell grinding machines in Germany and across the continent. In England Charles Churchill and Sons marketed first machines and then Norton wheels through branches in London, Birmingham, Manchester, Newcastle-upon-Tyne, and Glasgow. Founded in 1862 when Charles Churchill arrived from the United States to install machinery built by his father, the firm was a well-established importer of excellent American machine tools built by Morse Twist Drill, Brown and Sharpe, and Cincinnati Milling, among others.[10]

Churchill soon competed for Norton business with the vigorous Alfred Herbert Company. Herbert, which began manufacturing capstan and turret lathes in the 1890s, supplemented its product line by importing other machine tools, especially those of American manufacturers who were so popular in Europe. Herbert rapidly established branch offices throughout Britain and then expanded internationally with offices in Paris, Milan, Yokohama, Calcutta, and New York before World War I.[11]

Actual selling arrangements were subject to negotiation with individual firms, but the distributors generally assumed most of the responsibility. Occasionally, Norton's international distributors operated for a fee or commission. The powerful Schuchardt and Schutte compelled Norton Company to consign its original $20,000 shipment. In addition, in small, non-European markets, firms such as Holland and Reeves of Brazil acted as manufacturers' representatives, carrying little inventory and selling on a commission basis.[12]

Like most companies, however, Norton wished to sell outright rather than consign at its own cost. Just as he had with domestic distributors, Charles Allen quickly moved to put all sales on a cash basis—a pattern that endures to the present except in small markets. The Buck and Hickman contract of 1891 called for the outright sale of $2,000 in wheels for $1,000 cash and the balance in 180 days. Even Schuchardt and Schutte agreed to take title to shipments after two years. Early contracts negotiated by Allen that set the pattern for later years had the dstributor take title at Worcester and pay freight from the appropriate U.S. harbor. Freight forwarders handled the shipping itself.[13]

Distributors assumed most of the marketing obligations as well. A 1913 contract with Alfred Herbert specified discounts and made Herbert responsible for maintaining the resale price, supplying demonstrators and salesmen, and providing all advertising. Norton Company reserved review and approval of both prices and advertisements. Although the Herbert contract covered territory shared by Churchill, the agreements with major distributors usually defined exclusive territories while permitting Norton to solicit directly special large accounts and non-Norton users.[14]

Such firms as Schuchardt and Schutte, Churchill, and Herbert provided valuable services for Norton, Brown and Sharpe, Morse, and other American manufacturers of machine tools and industrial supplies whose products found ready European markets but who lacked the resources and experience for direct continental sales. The distributors had market knowledge, skills, and capital, and by combining a range of industrial products they achieved the volume necessary for an extensive selling organization far beyond the capacity of any single manufacturer.

In Norton's case the big distributors were an especially important means of resolving potential conflicts between the desire for rapid growth and the wish to maintain the values of prudence and control. Norton Company quickly penetrated large yet distant and little-known markets while passing most of the risk to the sellers. Simultaneously, carefully written contracts gave Norton at least some control over the independent selling organizations.

Norton's out-of-pocket costs were really quite small for a foreign business that probably exceeded a million dollars by 1914. They included a few salaried demonstrators who supplemented the efforts of European distributors and who later gathered accounts for manufacturers' representatives to develop small markets. To handle the domestic end Henry Sheehan became "export representative" when he joined the New York sales office in 1915. For over thirty years Sheehan dealt with freight forwarders for distributors' accounts and with outside commission agents like Henry W. Peabody who shipped to small dealers and manufacturers' representatives in Africa, South America, the Soviet Union, and the Far East. As export manager, Sheehan was Norton's entire department for foreign sales as well as its unofficial ambassador and greeter for all visiting dignitaries.[15]

The decision to establish foreign manufacturing facilities was a much riskier step, and typically, it grew out of market imperatives and external forces and not from any grand scheme for worldwide production. Building a plant considerably increased Norton's financial stake at risk in another land and raised a host of other problems. The company had to establish a management structure compatible with centralized owner-operation. The difficulty was not just oversight of a plant manager; foreign production also challenged Norton to maintain at a distance manufacturing standards that had previously depended on immediate, direct control. This in turn involved the export of heretofore secret bonds and equipment from Worcester.

The founders also faced the difficulties of doing business in a strange culture with a different language and another set of government regulations. And while Europe had been at peace for decades, militarism, alliances, and battles for empire at the century's turn reduced the chances for long-term stability. The classic solution—local partnership, a technique long used by New England merchants and their European forebears—raised its own problems. Partnership reduced the monetary stake and provided expertise and knowledge, but it also meant the sharing of control and of manufacturing know-how, which Norton's owners had so jealously guarded.

Prudent risk reduction won out over the tradition of complete control. Norton's first foreign plant was built at Wesseling near Cologne, Germany, in 1909 in partnership with Bernhard Schuchardt and Alfred Schutte precisely because the distributors urged German manufacture to preserve their considerable markets. Their arguments were clear and compelling. When Norton first began seriously considering German production in 1907, its second leading overseas market was in jeopardy: Carborundum Company was building a plant in Dusseldorf to serve German customers directly. Even Charles Allen admitted that using Norton demonstrators to support the German distributors was "quite effective," but "not as much can be accomplished by it as there would be by establishing a manufacturing and a selling force for pushing the goods over there in the same manner as we do at home."[16]

Furthermore, a change in German tariffs that had stimulated Carborundum's action also affected Norton. German wheels were solid emery and clay with no bushings, and American wheels were taxed as such. The discovery that American wheels were bushed put them in another category at double the rate.[17] As an additional factor for expansion, local manufacture not only protected an existing market; it ensured that Norton Company and its new German partners would continue to reap the sales growth resulting from American firms' leadership in the production of manmade abrasives.

If those arguments were not compelling, Schuchardt and Schutte's position was enough to tip the balance. Founded in 1880, the company had become, like Churchill and Herbert, a powerful distributor of machine tools and industrial supplies made by Cincinnati, Blanchard, Landis, and others. In 1902 when its two partners amicably split the business into eastern and western enterprises, the firm's $3 million in sales were five times Norton's revenues, and its share of Norton's orders accounted for 15 percent of total output.[18]

Suggestive of Schuchardt and Schutte's clout was the plant's Wesseling location, a site picked by Alfred Schutte from his Cologne offices. But if the Germans made Norton an offer it could not refuse, the New England firm was careful to hedge its bets. Norton's owners capitalized Deutsche Norton Gesellschaft (DNG), the German operating company, at only $200,000. The 30 percent sold to Bernhard Schuchardt and Alfred Schutte reduced Norton Company's cost while assuring its majority control of the new firm. The founders further protected themselves by writing a 5 percent management fee into the partnership agreement and by claiming 70 percent of all profits from its grain sales to DNG.[19]

Planning the German plant, 1908. Alfred Schutte is seated third from left between Milton Higgins and George Alden. Standing behind Milton Higgins is Aldus Higgins; to his left are Charles Allen, George Jeppson, John Jeppson, and Charles Norton.

Construction and operation reflected similar caution. Like seventeenth-century New England merchants, Norton owners relied on blood ties for management. Aldus Higgins carefully worked out the partnership agreement, which the Board of Directors approved, and George Jeppson oversaw construction and initial operation. Norton diligently educated a team of loyal Swedish workers in the German language and appointed Hugo Beth, a German-born foreman who had become a top assistant to George Jeppson at Worcester, as their head. Beth and the Swedes supervised construction, equipped the plant with machinery built in Worcester, started operations, and trained local personnel. Bonds were prepared and shipped from Worcester to protect their precious secrecy. After operations stabilized, George Jeppson surrendered management to William L. Neilson, a close friend of the Higgins family who had proved himself as assistant sales manager at Norton.[20] All major decisions continued to require approval by Charles Allen or the Board of Directors.

DNG was at least a modest success. List sales exceeded $1 million in 1913, which meant about $250,000 actual revenue. In addition to

5 percent management fees and profits to Norton on grain purchases, the German company paid 5 percent dividends in 1912 and 1913 and was making regular quarterly payments of earnings before World War I broke out. Bernhard Schuchardt and Alfred Schutte handled sales and by 1913 they were vending Wesseling wheels in Austria, Italy, and Belgium, as well as in the original German market.[21]

The Limits of Expansion: New England Enterprise Abroad

As it had in so many ways for the rest of the world, World War I marked a watershed in Norton Company's overseas enterprise. Along with many other U.S. firms, Norton considerably enlarged its foreign stakes, primarily in Europe and to a lesser extent in Asia and Australia. Once again, however, owner-operation determined that the character and pace of growth would suit the values of the New England enterprise.

The war itself had a dual effect. While the conflict temporarily eliminated Norton control, damaged the German market, and hindered the plant's growth, it also opened the doors for further Norton expansion overseas. After U.S. entry into the war in April 1917, Norton lost all direct contact with the plant and its five American personnel until after the armistice in November 1918.[22] Taxation, rising salaries, fixed prices, the German government's insistence that DNG pay half wages to all employees serving in the war (nearly 50 percent of the total), and wartime disruptions in trade and bauxite supplies that forced the plant to run half time soon converted a profitable operation into a losing one, although the plant had more orders than it could handle as late as February 1917. Subsequent Worcester estimates showed annual list sales at 4.3 and 4.0 million marks in 1917 and 1918 (a 33 percent decline in prewar dollar value), even though the wheel plant was eventually closed before the war's end.

The war's long-term effect severely constrained DNG's growth and profitability after Norton recovered the plant in 1919. Although the German government had considered seizing it and Alfred Schutte sought to control it in 1918, there was no actual disruption of title. But the conflict had badly hurt both market and operations. The German economy lay in ruins, racked by reparations, political instability, and inflation until 1923. The market for German products was understandably restricted by the trade barriers that accompanied the redrawn map of Europe and the sentiment and stigma that followed German defeat.

Furthermore, while the plant itself had suffered no direct war damage, Norton's cautious owner-managers were slow to replace worn equipment and outdated methods in a sickly market. The dollar value of list sales for 1920–1923 was 5 percent of 1911–1914 totals. DNG's considerable debt to Norton for fees and materials grew to more than $350,000 by 1924 and consumed more than 60 percent of its capital. Full recovery awaited Hitler's rearmament in the 1930s.[23]

Nevertheless, the war also stimulated overseas enterprise. Businessmen, like other Americans, gloried in their country's share in the victory. That victory and President Woodrow Wilson's foreign policy portended a growing American influence abroad. The historian of American multinationals notes that "when the fighting ended on November 11, 1918, most American businessmen could look to the promise of international investments." Their expectations quickly buoyed a wave of "U.S. business enthusiasm for foreign direct investment" in 1919 and 1920.[24]

Norton's leaders, especially Aldus Higgins, Foreign Manager William L. Neilson, and Sales Manager Carl Dietz, shared the enthusiasm. Dietz toured Europe, noting Germany's decline and Bernhard Schuchardt's and Alfred Schutte's waning power, and wrote Charles Allen that "we have to adjust our views to an entirely new set of conditions; former facts are in no way applicable."[25] War had quintupled total Norton sales and completed the rise of the large firm. Building on that success and continuing Norton's growth meant, in Aldus Higgins's words, that "the question of foreign trade is more and more commanding our thought and attention." To compete with numerous new European firms that had sprung up to meet wartime demand and to avoid growing tariffs, currency restrictions, and other international trade barriers, Higgins thought "it may be necessary to handle our European business eventually largely through our foreign plants."[26]

Norton's first and most aggressive step was reorganization of its distribution network. Dietz and Neilson quickly seized the opportunity to eliminate Norton's dependence on its formerly powerful German distributors. Neilson refused to punish Alfred Schutte for attempting a wartime takeover of DNG; Norton's top foreign man accepted Schutte's argument that he was merely protecting his own investment while trying to preserve the plant from government control. Nevertheless, Neilson and Dietz both argued that "other agency arrangements" were to Norton's advantage.[27]

Those arrangements restricted Alfred Schutte's sales to Germany itself and replaced his non-German branches with a series of independent national distributors, many of whom had originally worked in the German organization. Among others, Henri Benedictus in Belgium, Leonard Kellenberger in Switzerland, first Axel Ryden and then

Landelius and Bjorklund in Sweden, and O. Y. Machinery in Finland were established as exclusive Norton distributors for their own countries.[28]

The moves gave Norton greater control over its distributors and especially over resale prices. Norton sales people had long complained to no avail that Schuchardt and Schutte padded their profits with high prices at the expense of greater volume. In Germany itself, the German-speaking Dietz allied with Carborundum's general manager to force the wheel manufacturers and distributors to accept "complete adoption" of American specifications and a universal price list. Small national distributors were also a partial antidote to the proliferation of local firms and their mounting "buy native" campaigns.[29]

Norton's assertion of its new power over foreign distributors accompanied rapid extension of overseas manufacturing facilities. In 1919 and 1920 the firm added plants in Canada, France, and Japan while it deliberated on a site for an English factory and investigated a possible Italian location. But expansion did not reflect a wholesale abandonment of the New England firm and its traditions by any means. Even Aldus Higgins, a leading proponent of foreign manufacturing, wrote Neilson that he wished to continue seeking export business for Worcester.[30]

More to the point, no systematic plan for global expansion emerged. Each acquisition reflected an independent, carefully calculated Norton response to exogenous opportunity. Postwar optimism may well have facilitated decision making; it did not alter the values on which choices were based or the ad hoc, prudent approach by which they were implemented.

France was a case in point. Norton's directors had already commissioned Neilson to search for potential Italian and French plants or sites to combat rising local manufacture when their foreign manager found a Norton plant already built in La Courneuve outside Paris.[31] The factory, a duplicate of Worcester's plant number 6 and stocked with some Norton equipment, was owned by Compagnie Générale des Meules, an association including French steel and auto makers who sought to manufacture wheels for their own needs as well as for the growing French wartime market. To provide plant design and equipment, the French had contracted with the Springfield Grinding Company (later renamed the Max F Grinding Company) in Westfield, Massachusetts. Springfield Grinding then hired two Norton employees to copy or smuggle Norton plans, which served as the basis for the La Courneuve factory. George Jeppson and the Worcester people had independently discovered the leak and stopped it, but not before they faced the prospect of competing with themselves.

Norton's misfortune became opportunity when the French owners were unable to operate the business successfully. When the contraction of the postwar market and Max F's inability to supply and properly install all the necessary equipment soon resulted in losses, the French offered Norton a share in exchange for a bailout. Norton's owners characteristically researched carefully, debated the acquisition's fit with their own goals, and drove a hard bargain to protect their interests, reduce their risk, and ensure their control. Detailed examinations by Dietz, Neilson, and Worcester plant engineer Ed Van der Pyl confirmed the plant's value. To preserve Norton control, Neilson insisted on and got 51 percent ownership in exchange for Norton help. In lieu of payment for fees, the American firm took still more stock and by 1923 held 80 percent of Compagnie Générale des Meules Norton (CMN), which became Norton's largest and most profitable foreign operation at no out-of-pocket cost.

The Japanese acquisition, though less successful, also resulted from external circumstances.[32] F. W. Horne Company, Norton Company's distributor in the Far East, had agitated since 1913 for a Norton plant in Japan to speed service and avoid Japanese resistance to foreign products. When Norton refused to build, Horne bought control of a Japanese firm, the Hiroshima Grinding Wheel Manufacturing Company Ltd., in 1915. Like the would-be French manufacturers, Horne soon found itself unable to run the plant and invited Norton to be a partner. Norton's owners carefully investigated the site, took an option to buy a 52 percent controlling interest in 1917, and in 1919 acquired the entire 90 percent that Horne originally held.

Once again, Norton values, particularly reinforced by Allen's reluctance to share profits while shouldering the risks and burdens of operation, led to its predominant interest. One official in foreign operations aptly summarized Allen's trenchant philosophy that braked any tendency toward headlong expansion: "It is a mistake for us to try to start a manufacturing business with partners where we are expected to furnish all the experience, brains and improvements, and [then] divide the profits."[33]

The Canadian operation presented no problem of partnership and was strongly advocated by the Sales Department. General Sales Manager Carl Dietz and Robert Douglas, Norton's representative for eastern Canada, pushed for a plant to counter a 33.5 percent ad valorem tariff, the prospect of Carborundum's entry, and growing native competition. The 1920 construction of a small factory in Hamilton serviced the International Harvester and Westinghouse operations located there and was intended to expand Norton's 21 percent share of a growing Canadian market.[34]

But the real stimulus again lay in a set of external circumstances. The Canadian market was small ($851,000 total abrasives sales in 1917), and the Hamilton operation produced no profit for more than fifteen years. Nevertheless, a Canadian facility assured Norton's position in the British Empire after its failure to establish an English plant in 1919. An attempted partnership venture with Charles Churchill ended when one Norton official wrote Neilson that Aldus Higgins and Charles Allen rejected "arrangements resulting in considerable dilution of Norton interest and control when the Churchill and Norton interest would not be identical in other fields and countries."[35]

The decision was not just an overcautious insistence on complete control, for three of Norton's first four overseas plants (and five of the seven operations begun before World War II) did involve minority partners. In this case, however, a Churchill partnership threatened extensive Norton distribution handled by Alfred Herbert, Churchill's archrival in machinery and industrial supply. The Canadian plant, then, was a stopgap compromise to avoid entanglements with two powerful English distributors.[36]

The spurt of expansion immediately following World War I was unusual only for its speed. Norton's owner-managers had carefully tried to continue their cherished values of prudence, thrift, diligence, and control. Charles Allen, Aldus Higgins, William L. Neilson, and their experts had painstakingly inspected and approved each acquisition. As in the German case, the owners bargained hard to hold initial stakes and actual cash outlays to a minimum. The Canadian plant was to require $200,000, the Japanese stock cost $50,000, and French majority control came from equipment, expertise, and know-how.[37] Partnerships were reluctantly accepted as necessities as long as Norton had majority ownership. The balanced strategy helped defend or protect existing markets while assuring the firm's opportunity for future growth.

The uncharacteristic rapidity of the 1919–20 expansion ended almost as abruptly as Woodrow Wilson's hopes for world peace and order through American leadership. As Versailles negotiations soured and U.S. isolationism grew, the fervor of American businessmen for increased foreign stakes declined. Political instability in Russia and eastern Europe, continued economic chaos in Germany, and the halting recovery of the British and French economies blighted prospects.[38]

For Norton as for many other companies, the short but disastrous depression of 1921–22 was the turning point. For the first time foreign and domestic sales plummeted simultaneously. Since Norton found itself, in Aldus Higgins's words, "greatly overbuilt, overstocked, and generally inflated," the foreign plants proved an additional, serious drain.[39] Even though each acquisition was relatively small, together they consumed considerable sums for purchase, construction, equipment, and rebuilding. The French plant produced at only 5 percent of capacity, had a large debt, and required additional credit for working capital. Japanese and Canadian deficits continued to mount even though both were cut back until losses equaled shutdown costs. The German plant's small profits made no contribution to its Worcester debt; in fact Neilson sought further credits.[40]

The depression clearly emphasized the owners' priorities. Norton was an American, not an international, firm. Aldus Higgins advised "each foreign plant to work out its own salvation as far as possible" and to "get as near as possible to bed rock."[41] Modernization of the German plant was postponed and the abandonment of the French factory was considered, though not implemented, as Norton owners worked first to shore up the Worcester plants and domestic operations.

If the depression ended Norton's rapid expansion, it did not terminate overseas ventures. All four plants survived the crisis, and the subsequent sale of the Japanese plant in 1925 reflected the barriers of time, distance, and culture more than disillusionment with foreign enterprise.[42] The Japanese venture had been star-crossed from its inception, as Norton, Horne, and the Japanese partners bickered constantly. Norton Company fought Horne's pressure to enter the market while Horne bitterly resented Norton's insistence on buying out the distributor's interest. The delay in exercising a one-year option in 1918 increased the difficulties. The loss of skilled artisans to the war, Norton's reluctance to send modern equipment or reveal manufacturing secrets, impossibly high expectations based on Norton claims, and delays of equipment and decisions for as much as nine months because of distance and wartime restrictions further soured relations, while wheel quality actually declined.

Like most Westerners of the period, Norton people had little experience with or sensitivity to Japanese culture and pride. Ross Purdy wrote George Jeppson that "if Norton Company desires to train a yellow skinned man you could not pick a whiter souled one than Mr. Lin."[43] The Mr. Lin whom Purdy proposed as plant manager to boss Japanese workers was Chinese, even though the two nations had been bitter enemies for centuries. After Norton's purchase in 1919, Orello Buckner, the firm's representative in Hiroshima, recklessly advocated Norton methods and Norton equipment without regard to cost or to the embarrassing performance of 1918. When T. G. Nee questioned Buckner's prescriptions on behalf of his Japanese partners, Buckner arrogantly replied that "everything has already been worked out to a great nicety." Norton superiority was clear because "here in Japan conditions are very much worse than they are in the United States," and the number of bad wheels of 1918 "was not large enough to give this company a bad reputation if it had had a good one."[44]

A terrible start grew worse as U.S.–Japanese relations deteriorated and the Americans found themselves under surveillance. Losses in the 1921 depression consumed over half the company's capital. Despite a doubling of Norton's investment, the deficits continued until 1924, and then a defaulting bookkeeper absconded with the small profits. The weary Norton people happily sold out to their Japanese partners in 1925.

The depression and the Japanese failure only slowed the pace of Norton expansion. During the interwar years the company continued its course of reluctant acquisition on its own terms.[45] In 1931 Norton built a plant at Welwyn Garden City near London to protect its English market against buy-native campaigns and anticipated higher tariffs. Subsequently, when distributor William McPherson persuaded the Universal Grinding Wheel Company of England to build an Australian plant in 1939 and Norton and Carborundum threatened to build as well in the tiny market, Norton, which had the biggest market share, bought the largest share of and managed Australian Abrasives, the compromise firm established jointly by the four interests.

The Worcester company moved into Italy as well. When trade barriers threatened to reduce sales 75 percent in 1935, Norton acquired 60 percent of the Richard Ginori operation (Sapmarg) at Corsico near Milan in exchange for badly needed know-how and equipment. Prudence, thrift, and diligence were once again reflected by Norton's careful inspection with a team of financial and technical people and the tough bargaining that obtained control without cash outlay. Behr-Manning Secretary Lewis Greenleaf quoted Neilson that Norton "had much to gain and very little to lose, whatever happened in Italy."[46]

By 1939 Norton had six foreign plants on three continents. They contributed about one sixth of total sales and continued to help cushion sharp swings in the American market. During the major U.S. recession of 1937–38 when Norton's sales dropped as much as 45 percent, foreign sales remained steady.[47] But, while overseas expansion had contributed significantly to company revenues and growth, Norton's cautious, halting strategy did have liabilities. The delayed refurbishing of the German plant in the 1920s cost Norton the chance to establish a dominating position in that very competitive market. Postponed construction of an English plant for nearly two decades after Carborundum's location there left Norton permanently in third place in its largest foreign market.

The Japanese withdrawal, the English and German experiences, the francophilia of the Higgins and Neilson families, strong native management at La Courneuve, and the firm's virtually unopposed position among weak French manufacturers combined to put Norton in a peculiarly skewed position. The world's leading abrasives manufacturer, whose growth and major markets depended on metal working and other industrial producers was excluded from or weakly established in three of the world's most industrialized nations after the United States. Its strongest stake was in France whose international industrial reputation did not match that of Germany, England, or Japan. Despite its foreign success, the absence of any systematic international strategy may well have cost Norton an even greater position.

Like expansion itself, administration of international operations fitted the values and concerns of the New England family firm. Once again the owners' particular goals were reinforced by trends in American big business. At first Allen, Higgins, and Jeppson had to make few compromises to match the approach taken by most U.S. multinational manufacturers, which evolved in a three-stage process.[48] The original organization in most companies was a monocentric arrangement in which foreign operations were merely appendages, usually established along national boundaries, to the central American enterprise. Initially, establishment of foreign operations was novel enough to occupy top U.S. executives. Subsequently, the parent company created a division or department to administer separate foreign units with very little interdependence. The scheme was somewhat like spokes in a wheel.

More experienced multinationals passed into a second or polycentric stage in which the foreign enterprises developed increasing autonomy. They established a more independent history and character, with their own satellites, products, and research and development and were like moons circling a planet. Eventually, the polycentric stage gave way to an even more labyrinthine arrangement. In this case fully integrated, diversified, and autonomous foreign subsidiaries handled third markets (those areas where the parent company had no plants) and traded among themselves as well as with the American company. The enterprise was now an international business whose autonomous geographic or worldwide divisions enjoyed a much greater "element of choice" to organize and allocate resources.

While a few American firms in mining, public utilities, and agriculture had evolved into the second and even the third stage by the 1930s, Norton, like many U.S. manufacturing companies, remained in the monocentric stage until after World War II.[49] Foreign operations were long treated as a small but necessary outgrowth. Although Worcester controlled its Canadian subsidiary directly and the Japanese factory remained a remote outpost for its few years, European sales and plants fell to Norton's general sales manager, William L. Neilson. Actual administration at his London office went first to Frank Emery and after 1929 to Herbert (Bert) Stanton, Neilson's chief assistant and financial man.[50]

As in Worcester, however, the staff was kept sparse and most responsibility and personnel were assigned to line operations, in this case the plants themselves. Each foreign plant had its own resident manager who nominally reported to Neilson, but who actually administered daily operations.[51] The resident managers rapidly became the central representatives of the Worcester family firm as Norton moved to consolidate its control of foreign operations in the 1920s. In Germany, the company bought out its partners, revamped production, and established its own sales department reporting directly to the resident manager. In France, Norton bought the majority of its partners' shares and controlled sales and production; and in England, a sales department with branches in Leeds, Manchester, Newcastle, Birmingham, and Sheffield quickly replaced Alfred Herbert, which continued, however, to serve as chief distributor. Even the technical and research people sent to Europe from Worcester were assigned to particular plants and not to the London staff.

Recruitment was as informal as administration and involved little training.[52] Language expertise was preferred but not required. Higgins and Jeppson sent over some young men, including Ralph Gow and Andrew Holmstrom, to test and train them for eventual executive positions in Worcester. The foreign division also supplied jobs for relatives and friends. Neilson's early appointment as German resident manager served both purposes. Neilson in turn hired his son as traveling contact to third-world distributors, while Tom Green, Aldus Higgins's brother-in-law, was resident manager of the French plant throughout the 1920s.

Native administrators came from distributors, partners, or their offspring. Arnold Lee, head of English sales, was a former Alfred Herbert man. Pierre Baruzy, at first sales manager and later resident manager in France, was the nephew of Georges Bouillon, a pre–World War I Norton demonstrator. Otto Schutte, a nephew of Alfred Schutte, held similar positions in Germany. In Italy Luigi Marzoli and his successor Angelo D'Imporzano came from the Richard Ginori organization.

In addition, there also emerged a cadre of men originally trained in Worcester who served as a team to establish new plants, train workers, and head early operations.[53] Ed Van der Pyl first designed plants and equipment for Canada and France in 1919–1920 and was still working in foreign plant construction in the 1960s. Ted Meyer served as technical man in Germany and Australia, and John Bergman, the first Italian works manager, had previously been a foreman in France. The Norton team in Australia included the veteran three musketeers, Oscar Wahlgren, who had worked in France and England, Eric Olson, who had helped establish English, French, and Italian operations, and Carl Sorlie, veteran of Canada and France. The cadre was a logical extension of the team approach Norton had adopted for special projects, dating back to furnace operations in 1901. Experience and nepotism helped reduce risk and assure loyalty in distant ventures just as they had with seventeenth-century New England merchants.

The monocentric approach admirably fitted the requirements of the New England family company. Except for a normally placid Carborundum and possibly Universal, Norton faced no major international competitors and had little immediate impetus for an elaborate, systematic multinational structure. National plants and the tiny European headquarters admirably protected major market shares, held down bureaucracy and costs, and provided jobs for young talent, friends, and family. Central Worcester control was easily maintained, for in the absence of an elaborate structure and a large staff, the European division was not a major power center at Norton before the 1950s.

The selection of division heads reinforced the trend. Neilson, whom George Alden thought "pretty breezy," was a hard bargainer and talented executive but not a diligent administrator or an empire builder.[54] Always a Higgins man, he early earned the scorn and suspicion of George Jeppson, who accused him of laziness and inattention. While Aldus Higgins at first lectured Neilson to leave daily detail to resident managers and treat Worcester's missives as "recommendations" and not "instructions," Neilson never shared in top power. He deferred to "Mr. Allen's" final authority and always endured George Jeppson's scrutiny and criticism. Even his ally Aldus Higgins wrote in strident tones: "That is where we *want* to have the French plant . . . We *must* . . . let [the foreign plants] start business on the ground floor and build up" (italics added).[55] Neilson's successor, Bert Stanton, was largely a financial man whose unimaginative administration posed even less threat to Worcester.

Worcester control was most clearly reflected in the product itself. To maintain secrecy and product quality all bonds and grains were prepared and shipped from the United States.[56] The Worcester Swedes who served as early plant foremen jealously guarded bond formulas in little black books and taught native workers to follow instructions exactly and unquestioningly. Grading standards and research and product development flowed from Worcester; the overseas plants had only "technical men" to oversee product quality. Introduction of such new techniques as B-bond and controlled structure fell to Norton engineers Rennie Washburn, Elmer Taylor, and Ted Meyer, sent from Worcester to Europe expressly for that purpose. Any overseas product or process innovations such as B. E. bond, an improved B-bond first used in England, were accidents whose development the Worcester lab soon controlled.

Despite the apparently easy fit between the New England company and foreign enterprise, geographic expansion, like acquisitions for a full product line, tested the owner-operators' ideals. Furthermore, while the resulting compromises worked well at first, they created long-term weaknesses. Although the monocentric structure and the cautious, unsystematic strategy met Worcester needs for family control and frugality, any ideas of absolute centralization were eroded by time, distance, cultural differences, and political rivalries. Native managers gradually replaced Worcester men, at first in sales where Baruzy, Schutte, and Lee had superior knowledge of their cultures and markets. The policy soon spread to resident and works managers in the 1930s. Worcester appointees like Tom Green and Ralph Gow, who wished to return to the United States, insisted that talented natives like Baruzy, Armand Lefebvre, Michel Biscayart, Pierre Arnould, and Réné Didier in France and Schutte in Germany could direct operations efficiently and without the cultural barriers that hampered American executives in dealing with increasingly militant work forces and growing nationalism.[57]

Furthermore, in the 1930s new tariff barriers and other trade restrictions in Germany and Italy closed off bond and abrasives imports from Worcester, forcing the parent firm to share manufacturing secrets and rely on other sources for raw materials and processing. Simultaneously, the growing experience of men like French Works Manager Armand Lefebvre soon led to the sharing of those same secrets in other plants.[58] Even Worcester appointees had to assume a certain amount of contol in order to make daily decisions when mail to Worcester took more than two weeks to return and expensive, erratic telephone connections were used only in emergencies.

The frugality of staffing and oversight further contributed to de facto autonomy. Evaluation rested mainly on excellent financial reports developed by Duckworth's controllers and was administered by Bert Stanton. Mechanisms for broader appraisal of management, including long-range use of resources and training of successors, were absent. Personal inspections were necessarily infrequent and at times superficial. Annual European visits by Jeppson, Higgins, and Neilson, which naturally included family tours and vacations, generally alloted one day's intensive meetings with each plant manager. When Ralph Gow served as French works manager, he "soon learned [that] if you had the plant clean and well arranged, you were doing a great job. So, a month before they got there, we'd have everybody in the plant cleaning things . . . Then George Jeppson would say to me, 'Oh! Your plant's in great shape, Ralph! Your plant's in great shape!' And he didn't know how efficient it was at all."[59]

The division between authority and responsibility only widened with the advent of native management. Men like Schutte, Baruzy, Marzoli, and D'Imporzano, who served as top foreign executives for decades, eventually developed virtual fiefdoms as their markets expanded and profits grew in the 1930s, 1940s, and 1950s.[60] Local operating autonomy was contingent upon prosperous operation and was always formally circumscribed by Norton ownership and the de facto authority of the Worcester Board of Directors over major investment decisions. As at Behr-Manning, freedom contributed to the success of good people, but Norton lacked the general oversight to spot potentially serious long-run problems not reflected in operating statistics.

The key men in the relationship, of course, were the native resident managers. Insofar as possible they were trained and treated as members of the Worcester family firm. In addition to being descendants of Norton sales people, Baruzy and Schutte received at least two years' training in Worcester and a decade's experience as sales managers under Worcester-appointed plant managers before assuming the top spot. Both were charming men and developed warm personal relationships with the Allens, Jeppsons, Higginses, Greens, and Neilsons. Baruzy and Schutte were lavishly entertained and comfortably housed in the homes of Norton owners on visits to the United States and in turn acted as hosts and tour guides for visits by the Americans. Baruzy even called Tom Green's wife *ma grande soeur* ("my big sister").[61]

If continued financial success made their autonomy possible, Baruzy's and Schutte's charm and loyalty to Norton Company made the anomalous system of divided formal authority and responsibility work. Their contributions and importance were most clearly demonstrated as the heightened political tensions of the late 1930s exploded into World War II and stripped Worcester of all direct control of its European plants.

World War II: Testing New England Enterprise Abroad

Norton's owners never handled political issues with the astuteness characteristic of their business management. Like so many business-men in multinational enterprises, they coped rather than controlled. After the U.S. entry into World War I, they led patriotic support in Worcester but squirmed uneasily as their German factory and its new abrasives plant contributed directly (though inefficiently) to the enemy and five American employees were interned. When purchase of the Italian plant (renamed Mole Norton) was completed just as Musso-lini's invasion of Ethiopia provoked worldwide condemnation, Nor-ton owners pursued a World War I policy of "watchful waiting." Norton took control but delayed equipment, know-how, and addi-tional investment for two years.[62]

High U.S. unemployment rates and the growing threat of war did push the firm into a mildly defensive posture but caused little if any change in policy before Munich. Officials argued that foreign man-ufacture helped expand Norton sales and increase consumption of equipment and processed raw materials from Worcester, thereby sus-taining or enlarging instead of reducing domestic employment. In 1935 Aldus Higgins explained that foreign plants "spread Norton's reputation and good-will far and wide. They preserve business which would otherwise be lost to us. They furnish opportunity for foreign service to young men who are willing to follow careers abroad, and we believe that they aid in international understanding and friendli-ness."[63] By 1938 the erosion of international understanding and friendliness compelled even Higgins to admit "that our investments abroad are somewhat risky," but nevertheless "we believe the ad-vantages justify our policy and that the chances of a successful out-come in those plants are good."[64]

World War II's outbreak soon placed the outcome and the plants beyond the control of Norton's owners. The withdrawal of all Amer-ican personnel from Europe in 1939 and early 1940 removed any possibility of planned sabotage by Norton people in the event of U.S. entry into the war, as occurred at the Stanvac oil operations in the East Indies in 1941. The withdrawal apparently resulted from George Jeppson's and Aldus Higgins's determination to avoid a repetition of their World War I experience when Americans were interned or forced to work for the enemy. Control fell entirely into the hands of national resident managers—Baruzy in France, Schutte in Germany, and Mar-zoli in Italy, while Charles Wood headed Welwyn operations under the English government's authority. The astute maneuver helped re-duce the odds of nationalization. The resident managers, like ships' captains sailing long voyages for colonial New England merchants, were trusted for their experience and judgment in the absence of direct oversight.

Real leadership eventually fell to Otto Schutte because of Germany's early dominance of Europe and because the shrewd German began plotting his course for Norton before the war's outbreak. Although Alfred Schutte had sold his share of the Wesseling company to Norton in 1928, Otto developed strong ties to Norton Company and the German plant. His uncle was a primary Norton distributor for more than thirty years, and both Schuttes and the Norton owners had been guests in one another's homes during visits.[65]

Following the 1928 sale, Otto, more than any other individual, had directed the resuscitation of DNG. After two years' training in Worcester, he returned as a sales manager in 1928 to direct the transformation from hand crafting in a workshop to manufacturing in a modern factory. B-bond and controlled structure replaced the puddling process. Powerful presses, precise molds, and a tunnel kiln supplanted old bats, rings, and periodic kilns. Bakelite wheels expanded the product line. The work force quadrupled to 400 by the mid-1930s under the direction of trained engineers hired to demonstrate the product, introduce precise standards and quality control, and establish an engineering department. DNG created its own sales department under Tony Clark, whom Schutte soon succeeded. By the late 1930s more aggressive sales techniques and new products had given DNG about 10 percent of the German market, a strong second in a very competitive industry.[66]

At the same time the American-owned DNG and its personnel suffered increased scrutiny and suspicion from Hitler's Nazi government.[67] Ted Meyer, the Worcester research man assigned to DNG, and other non-Germans knew that they were being spied upon, although there was no outright harassment. In 1937, the year when President Franklin Roosevelt's quarantine speech drew bitter condemnation from the Nazi government, Norton quietly began replacing top non-German personnel with nationals. Walter Jaspers supplanted Works Manager Hugo Dahlquist, Karl Buchsieb followed Hubert Peake in the office, and Otto Schutte relieved the ailing Carl Griffin as resident manager. Simultaneously, Schutte, engineer Eric Becker, and other top people joined the Nazi party at Carl Griffin's request and with Norton Company's knowledge.

Party membership, leadership of DNG, Otto's expertise, and his determined loyalty to Norton Company placed Schutte in an excellent position after World War II began. In a remarkable series of actions he was able to protect and expand the American-owned German plant, provide aid to the Italian operation, reestablish and defend the French operation, and preserve Norton markets normally supplied by the European plants as well as those whose flow of wheels from Worcester was disrupted by the war.

At Wesseling Schutte had himself appointed trustee when war began in 1939 and custodian after America's entry in late 1941. He acquired the necessary work force and allocations of scarce abrasives, coal, gasoline, and other vital raw materials to keep the plant running at full capacity. He carefully husbanded profits by refusing to declare dividends, which would fall to the German government in a blocked mark account. Instead, he maintained a cash reserve ten times the prewar norm and reinvested heavily in another tunnel kiln and other equipment to expand capacity "on account [as he later wrote] of the questionable international value of the mark."[68]

Throughout the war he made semiannual visits to the Italian plant, nominally headed by a Fascist sequester, but in fact still operated by Luigi Marzoli, Angelo D'Imporzano, and other prewar Norton appointees.[69] DNG supplied crucial technical information for bond formulas as well as bond mixes and abrasive grain. Finally, Schutte intervened to help avoid a takeover by competitors that would have revealed secret formulas and proprietary equipment.

Protecting Norton by aiding the Italian plant was defensible as support for a German ally, but in France Otto's challenges were much greater.[70] The unexpected and rapid German victory in France had halted operations and scattered the plant's management and work force. Schutte quickly visited Paris and again had himself appointed first trustee and later custodian of the American-owned factory to prevent a threatened takeover by the Nazi government and shipment of the equipment to Germany. He had Pierre Baruzy made managing director by swearing responsibility for Baruzy's behavior. Next, Otto reassembled the operating force by acquiring travel permits and gasoline for some and by having others released from stockades where they were held as prisoners of war or as conscript labor. His influence as titular plant head and as a Nazi party member again obtained the necessary permits for transportation and for abrasives, coal, and other raw materials. The French firm (CMN) was even allowed to deliver goods and collect payment in unoccupied areas in France and the rest of Europe. Finally, DNG technicians, who had been mixing their own bonds since the mid-1930s, shared their bond formulas with the French who had depended on Worcester-mixed bonds until France's fall. As Otto saw it his "main task was to swing the French Norton plant in-[to] production in order to avoid that surplus machines would be shipped to Germany to relieve the pressure on machine tool factories."[71] This he accomplished by switching Wesseling orders to the French plant, which by 1941 had returned to full operation.

For Schutte, the protection of Norton's stake in Europe held undoubted primacy over patriotism, victory, and other considerations. Two month's after France's fall he wrote Bert Stanton that "we were greatly concerned about the fate of the French Norton branch and of its members of the management" and that he had reopened the plant at his own initiative "not least from a consideration to prevent others from getting inside information about our manufacturing methods."[72] At the war's end Baruzy confirmed that "O[tto] S[chutte] acted from the start as a friend and a Norton man, with the Norton interests constantly present in his mind," and Pierre's associate Réné Didier simply wrote Ralph Gow that Schutte "helped our task to a maximum."[73]

Despite the strong possibility, aid to France and Italy was not just a German's ploy to expand production for the Axis, for Otto repeatedly took positions that favored Norton's interests over Germany's. The preservation of CMN was of doubtful value to the German government. Although CMN was larger than DNG, during World War II it shipped wheels valued at 2.8 million marks to Germany, only 6-10 percent of DNG's output.[74] Relocation might well have been more effective. In addition, Otto's cash reserve and reinvestment decisions preserved Norton profits at the German government's expense.

As a Nazi Schutte had himself appointed head of the Sondering Schleifmittel, a government industrial association that originally included 164 German bonded and coated abrasives firms and later expanded to include companies in occupied territories. During his nine months' leadership he relied on his position to refuse government requests that Norton share its resources with other manufacturers. Subsequently, he used connections in the Air Ministry and Ministry of Armaments to resist government efforts to close the Wesseling plant and move its equipment to a safer location in central Germany. Such a shift would have protected German capacity but hurt Norton, for supervision of the move and control of the new operation would have fallen to the government and prying competitors.

Finally, Schutte connived to preserve Norton markets outside Germany at the expense of war production. He diligently supplied Norton distributors in Switzerland, Sweden, Finland, Czechoslovakia, Belgium, Hungary, and the Netherlands whose Worcester supplies had been cut off. During the war DNG exports grew from 2.5 percent to 20 percent of all German abrasives exports.[75] At the same time the

German government tacitly permitted DNG's increased exports since they could be exchanged for plywood, copper, and other necessary imports.[76]

Throughout the conflict, the enemy were Schutte's competitors instead of the United States and its allies. The accusations of treason and other war crimes and the SS investigations and interviews that Schutte endured were inspired largely, he felt, by influential competitors. He obtained the ring leadership to block their requests for Norton raw materials, bond formulas, and proprietary equipment, since a rival in that position could have successfully demanded that Schutte reveal Norton secrets. He resigned the job nine months later after it drew attacks that endangered his custody of DNG and CMN and after rendering the position powerless.

Despite Schutte's remarkable efforts on Norton's behalf, however, corporate loyalty was not the only factor influencing his behavior. He was, of course, subject to a variety of competing demands and emotions, and while Norton service remained the clearest and most compelling determinant, other factors did intervene. As the inevitability of German defeat grew in 1944 and 1945, Schutte clearly recognized that Norton Company represented his surest means to safety and recovery in the postwar era. He abandoned plans for flight to Switzerland to avoid threatened prosecution as a traitor to the Reich and stayed with the plant. When Allied forces reached Cologne, he left his home to looters and remained at Wesseling to protect the factory until troops arrived.

Eventually, the death of his 18-year-old son, the privations of postwar Germany, the loss of his home and property, the closing of the plant, and dismissal from his management position because of his Nazi ties wore down a proud and powerful man. In late 1945 Schutte wrote Baruzy: "I am very much depressed about all these developments. For many years I have put in my whole strength to bring DNG to the fore and I may say that in this I was successful."[77] Finally, he despaired of recovery. In 1946 he wrote Bert Stanton that "we have suffered too much" and asked that Norton relocate him in the United States or in South America.[78]

Schutte's behavior, however, was still more complex than a mixture of company loyalty and self-service that variously conflicted and reinforced each other. Simple humanity and friendship characterized other actions. He employed Jews, communists, and French, Polish, and Russian conscript laborers for wages equal to his German workers. He hid German workers who wished to avoid military service and relayed information between Pierre Baruzy and his son hiding in Switzerland.

Baruzy and the French forced the severest conflicts among Schutte's loyalties to country, company, and friends.[79] Baruzy and his French executives, like Schutte, were undoubtedly loyal to Norton Company, but as citizens of a conquered, occupied country they were more willing to jeopardize an abrasives plant to support national aims. Their responses to duty, emotion, and self-preservation were even more complex. As Réné Didier put it, "We found ourselves caught in the chain, having at the same time to satisfy the needs of the Germans, those of our customers and our desire not to produce too much which would be used against those whom we already considered as our future liberators."[80]

As common sense dictated, the French operated the plant to prevent a German takeover, diverted as much material and product as they could to help Norton at Germany's expense, and performed minor acts of resistance. They hid tons of abrasives in sandbags around the plant and consumed tons of precious steel and cement to build a second, unused tunnel kiln and an unassembled steel press. They deflected resources into production of sharpening stones, dental wheels, and other nonmilitary products, padded the work force to help young men avoid conscript labor, and shipped valuable cargoes into neutral territories. By sending defective wheels and diverting output, they shipped only 29 percent of total production to DNG instead of the ordered 50 percent, while maintaining workloads sufficient to avoid takeover.[81]

Schutte, who rented a Paris apartment and visited the La Courneuve plant at least once a month, was aware of the counteraction and chose to ignore it. What angered him and sorely tested his support were Baruzy's more overt, aggressive actions that endangered CMN, Schutte, and the entire fragile Norton structure. As a manager Baruzy was always more politically involved than Schutte. In prewar France he had been active in anticommunist movements. During the war his friendship with German collaborators and his service to the Vichy government as municipal counsellor of Paris and general counsellor of the Department of the Seine helped support his appointment as CMN manager, while at the same time he joined the French resistance movement. He relayed information, false identity papers, and ration cards to the French underground and helped downed Allied aviators to safety. The French plant employed escaped prisoners of war, including one who served as assistant personnel manager. Baruzy even hid fugitive prisoners and arms shipments destined for the resistance movement in Schutte's Paris apartment, which was protected by the DNG emblem.

Although Schutte suspected some of the activities, just how much he knew before the war's end is unclear. In any case his position as guarantor of Baruzy's behavior and his desire to protect Norton tied his hands. Otto's later bitter resentment and bewilderment underscored the two managers' conflicting views of duty. More than a decade later he still angrily insisted that "Pierre has poorly repaid for the confidence that had been placed in him."[82] Schutte thought the Frenchman had betrayed the German's trust, exposed him to punishment or death by the Gestapo, and jeopardized the entire Norton arrangement. Pierre, in contrast, thought the entire episode "dangerous" but "thrilling" and told Bert Stanton that Schutte, a " 'good old fellow,' has been a brick."[83]

Norton executives were not inclined to be judgmental. They felt that in extraordinary circumstances top management at the French, Italian, and German plants had acted well within the bounds of honor and duty, if not in harmony. Baruzy, Schutte, Marzoli, and their chief assistants were reappointed. Special efforts were made for Schutte, who became a company legend. Milton Higgins II, son of Aldus Higgins and George Jeppson's successor as Norton's president in 1946, still feels strongly that "all during the war [Schutte] was a Norton man primarily [who] had tremendous loyalty to the company, I know of no individual more loyal to the people in the United States and Worcester than Otto was."[84] With Higgins's approval, Norton Company helped Otto Schutte gather the data necessary to clear himself of the charge of being a Nazi official, a designation that disqualified him from any executive position. Following his acquittal, Schutte again became DNG's resident manager, a job he held until his retirement in 1959.

The extent to which Norton's European operations benefited from the war is unclear. German, French, and Italian plant assets nearly doubled in book value between 1939 and 1944; annual sales by 1943 and 1944 were running 60 percent or more above 1938 figures. Early in the war, net profits on sales running as high as 28 percent in Italy, 35 percent in France, and 25 percent in Germany helped produce healthy cash surpluses.

But the record was not one of unbroken prosperity and growth, for the Norton plants' well-being depended largely on the fate and conditions of their host countries. Rising taxes, materials shortages, and, after 1944, the growing ravages of war first slowed and then disrupted manufacture. The Italian plant operated in the red in 1943, as did the French plant in 1944 and both the Italian and German operations in 1945.[85] In Germany the tunnel kiln closed in November 1944 for lack of coal, and wheel output was ony fitful until 1947. While Allied bombing raids never stopped production, they destroyed several buildings, killed a few workers, and did over six hundred thousand marks damage.[86] Finally, the book value figures in Schutte's 1945 report exaggerated the prosperity. Milton Higgins recalls that plant and equipment were "pretty well worn out" when he visited in 1946, an estimate confirmed by a nearly 50 percent writedown of Wesseling assets between 1944 and 1948.[87]

Conditions were similar at the English, French, and Italian factories. Higgins thought the Norton European plants were "all pretty well run down" on his 1946 visit.[88] Although they had suffered little bomb damage, difficulties stemmed from equipment worn from heavy use and little maintenance. From 1944 until the early 1950s crippling shortages of bonds, abrasives, steel, and energy blocked production, and the ravaged condition of the European economy dried up sales. The postwar rise of tariff barriers, currency controls, and other restrictions further disrupted trade. Finally, the red tape of pacification and occupation severely hampered operations in Italy and Germany.

Nevertheless, its continued presence put Norton in an excellent position to take advantage of the European recovery stimulated by the Marshall Plan, Point Four, and other forms of U.S. foreign aid that began in the late 1940s. The limited amount of direct destruction was simply good fortune. The Wesseling plant outside Cologne suffered only light damage even though the city had been heavily bombed. Furthermore, the good luck came despite efforts by Norton and Carborundum executives and other U.S. abrasives manufacturers who offered data on plant locations and tried in vain to convince Washington authorities of abrasives' crucial importance to industrial and wartime production.[89]

The skill of Norton's resident managers—a residue of their careful selection and training in Norton methods and values—allowed the firm to build on the good luck and the economic recovery that it could not control. Baruzy, Schutte, Marzoli, and their associates kept the plants operating under Norton management throughout the war, maintained as best they could a strong staff and work force, and preserved Norton's distribution network and markets throughout Europe. In postwar Italy where the Corsico plant did not equal 1938 production until 1950, a 40 percent expansion of capacity was under way by 1952. The French plant matched prewar levels more quickly, grew to $5 million in sales by 1950, and then doubled output by 1958. English operations grew considerably in the 1950s, though German sales recovered slowly.[90]

Still, growth was largely in volume rather than profits, and much of the increase came at Worcester's expense. Annual net profits on all foreign sales averaged less than 1 percent between 1952 and 1954.[91]

And although European recovery and Norton's introduction of 32 Alundum, a superior new abrasive, stimulated sales, greater volume depended heavily on the ability of the European plants and their staffs to produce goods for third markets in Europe, Africa, and Asia that trade restrictions had closed to Worcester exports.

Growth and interdependence, however, little altered Norton's overseas strategy and structure. Authority and responsibility remained divided. The veteran plant managers became even more autonomous in daily administration and in their ability to wheedle funds by personal appeals to Milton Higgins and Ralph Gow. Yet, all were formally subject to Bert Stanton and his tight financial controls, and all overseas expenditures over $5,000 had to be approved by the Worcester Board of Directors. Worcester still directed foreign product engineering and insisted on exporting bonded abrasives, abrasive grain, and new equipment where possible.[92]

Durex: An Alternative Model

Although Norton's international bonded abrasives business lagged behind many U.S. manufacturing firms owing to the company's continued monocentric approach, the owners had an alternative model in their midst. The Behr-Manning coated operation was part of an organization that began foreign manufacture as a loose alliance of American firms two decades after Norton's Wesseling venture.[93] By 1950, however, the original combination had become an extensive enterprise, considerably more sophisticated than Norton's overseas operations.

As at Norton, the original stimuli for foreign growth were largely external needs to protect and expand market stakes. Coated operations departed from Norton's course as several factors pushed a timid, monocentric venture sponsored by a loose coalition into an autonomous, integrated multinational enterprise. Most notable was the absence of any single dominant authority among the American sponsors and owners. Because Norton owners had already conceded Behr-Manning's independence, the Jeppsons and Higginses did not intervene to maintain family control. In addition, the domestic coated abrasives industry's growth and changing structure, along with 3M's rise and diversification into tape and other products, altered the outlook of the U.S. manufacturers who owned the foreign enterprises. Finally, the shift grew out of a bureaucratic struggle among the three groups involved—the American manufacturers and owners, the Durex Abrasives Corporation whose president, Robert Young, directed industry exports, and Donald Kelso and his assistants who established and operated the foreign plants.

Foreign markets first became significant for American coated abrasives companies in the late 1920s, when a series of product and process innovations gave domestic producers technical superiority in sandpaper manufacture at the same time that leading makers sought to rationalize the industry to control price and production. Exports grew, principally to Canada and the European industrialized nations, but profits did not. The American Surface Abrasives Export Company, a Webb-Pomerene enterprise established by the ten leading manufacturers, was ineffective. Its four-man organization merely forwarded freight and published list prices, but competition for distributors increased the discounts. As one top executive put it, "We were all doing our best to see that no one else made a cent."[94]

The ten manufacturers reluctantly took the minimum action necessary to resolve the difficulty in 1929, since most were small companies with little overseas expertise and their major markets remained in the United States. Their solution was the reorganization of the American Surface Company as the Durex Abrasives Corporation, exclusive exporter for the ten owning firms whose shares corresponded to their portion of exports.

Purchases for export were allocated among domestic companies on the basis of their particular specialties. To prevent squabbles over allocations, profits were concentrated in the export operation and paid out as dividends to shareholders. Actual domestic manufacturers of goods received only cost plus a small fixed percentage.

Simultaneously, 3M's need to manufacture in England in order to protect its waterproof patents complicated the problem. Retaliation by Behr-Manning, Carborundum, and possibly others threatened overproduction and further chaos. As a result the manufacturers set up a second Webb-Pomerene firm, the Durex Corporation, to build plants in Canada and in Birmingham, England, and to act as the industry's exclusive foreign manufacturer. Robert Young, an executive from Baeder-Adamson and American Glue, and an identical top management team ran both companies from a single office in New York City. The corporations' symbol, a chain of ten links, aptly reflected the coalition.

Operation quickly exposed severe limitations. Young originally envisioned Durex Abrasives as the primary firm, simply shipping between producers and overseas distributors. Durex and English manufacture were to be a necessary but limited evil. Nevertheless, providing adequate service soon compelled him to establish a sales force of twenty-five (later one hundred) to contact distributors and customers and to construct warehouses in France and Germany to carry the necessary inventories.

Building and operating the English plant by committee was even more disappointing. Each American company sent two advisers, most of whom were, in Donald Kelso's judgment, untrained and "ineffective" and whose "absence would be welcomed" in their own firms.[95] The 32-year-old Kelso, already a ten-year veteran as manager at Baeder-Adamson, American Glue, and Barton, arrived as factory superintendent in 1930 and was greeted by chaos. The advisers had "got [to] fighting among themselves and some would work and some wouldn't work and some said they had secret information which they wouldn't disclose to others, and the place was rapidly going into a shambles."[96] Kelso fired most, hired a staff, and built the plant. He soon replaced its ineffective resident manager and operated with the day-to-day autonomy that characterized Norton's foreign plants at the time.

Rapid success expanded his powers. Aggressive marketing with a salaried sales force helped the firm outstrip John Oakey and Thomas Goldsworthy, its major English competitors. Built to produce $100,000 per month, the plant manufactured double that rate in fourteen months and eventually averaged $500,000 monthly production.[97] The success of Goodyear's Wolverhampton plant following the departure of American technicians led Kelso to replace Americans with Englishmen in 1932. He played off the American manufacturers against one another to get his own cloth-finishing operation and the freedom to select his grain sources. When currency controls restricted non-English markets in 1935, he aggressively supported the construction of a German factory at Dusseldorf and a French processing unit at Gennevilliers to cut up jumbo rolls and package the resulting products. Kelso supervised and coordinated all three plants while nationals managed daily business.

The real shift, however, from a monocentric into a multinational, polycentric strategy resulted from marketing rather than manufacturing issues. From his European power base Kelso collaborated with American manufacturers to challenge Young's leadership and U.S.-oriented approach. From the outset Young emphasized an export strategy designed to keep production in the American plants of his ten directors. The export business was the basis of his power, and to the fussy president overseas manufacture raised a host of problems, including foreign taxation, profit repatriation, currency fluctuations, and profit sharing with local minority partners. As he explained to Kelso in 1932, "The business in New York has been developed at great expense by the manufacturers here and to transfer it to England or to Canada, considering the greater taxes levied against profits in various countries as well as reduced earning power as represented in dollars, is not an easy matter to decide."[98]

As at Norton the initial forces for change were defensive—expanding overseas plants and their sales territories to protect existing markets. Young at first resisted even this simple maneuver. When fluctuating currency exchanges doubled the price of American goods over English exports to Australia, he fought the shift of Australian sales from U.S. factories to the English plant for two years. Kelso finally won the battle by appealing to Australian distributors and by writing 3M President William McKnight and Carborundum President Frank Tone about the imminent loss of the Australian market. Even then Durex Abrasives received a 20 percent commission on all Australian business as compensation.

The change in strategy was a modest one, and in 1932 Young determined that it only be repeated under dire circumstances, "transferring only to save markets, which cannot be sold from the United States."[99] In that same year he urged Kelso "to play cricket" and cease trying to build up South African business.[100] Subsequently, he persuaded the American directors of Durex Abrasives to agree unanimously "that wherever it is possible to maintain Durex Abrasives Corporation's position competitively in a foreign country that such business shall be retained by the American Companies."[101]

The Durex companies evolved from appendages to American manufacturing to become an international enterprise only when their owners shifted to an offensive marketing strategy. Protecting sales meant compensatory shifts. Developing and expanding markets required the location of manufacturing plants and the allocation of sales territories on the basis of comparative advantage, an approach Norton did not achieve until the 1950s when Kelso took over both its coated and bonded international business. In contrast, by the late 1930s American coated abrasives operators increasingly tended to think of world markets and stopped worrying about which pocket held their profits.

The earlier shift in coated abrasives resulted from the aggressive Kelso's efforts and the changing circumstances of American manufacturers. Kelso worked within Young's restraints to extend slowly the sales territories of foreign plants. The French and German plants built in 1935 immediately seized their national markets. The tendency of London-based, English colonial export houses to buy English-made goods diverted British Empire trade to the Birmingham plant. And price competition on cheaper goods for the shoe trade transferred sales for most of the continent to European plants in 1937. By 1938 foreign coated plants, which had not existed a decade earlier, accounted for more than 75 percent of all foreign sales.[102]

Kelso's success coincided with the American manufacturers' new point of view. Economic recovery by the late 1930s and the industry's successful rationalization by Carborundum, Behr-Manning, and 3M had eased competitive, defensive pressures. The reduction of Durex ownership from ten to four facilitated coordination of a more complex, aggressive strategy by larger, more prosperous firms. Growing foreign sales testified to the superior combination of American production and marketing methods. Finally, 3M aggressively sought to expand overseas markets for its very successful tape lines, which it marketed through the Durex companies and manufactured in Durex's European plants.

With the emergence of 3M the shift was rapid. In 1939 Durex directors created a merchandising committee to advise Young on how to reduce prices, expand volume, and market more aggressively in Canada, Australia, South Africa, and South America. In 1940 they voted a tape and rubber cement manufacturing plant for Australia (which World War II delayed until 1944), and in 1942 they approved tape plants with coated manufacturing or converting capacity in South Africa, Brazil, and Argentina.

By then even Young recognized that the export company's importance would "diminish as additional manufacturing units are established."[103] He wrote Frank Tone in 1943 that "the future of Durex . . . is to do precisely what our British friends will do, and that is, create subsidiary [manufacturing] companies in important markets throughout the world rather than depend upon being able to export under restrictive conditions and compete with locally manufactured goods . . . I am confident that Durex's position will be greatly benefited ten years from now if we have subsidiary plants in important countries . . . As time goes on some of our new subsidiary companies may better and more profitably serve territories in which the Durex Abrasives Corporation is now operating."[104]

As a result U.S. coated abrasives manufacturers were ready to expand aggressively at the war's end, well ahead of the general U.S. multinational growth of the 1950s. With Europe prostrate and with high hopes for new markets in Africa, Asia, and South America, they built tape and coated operations in Australia and tape plants with coated conversion potential in South Africa and Brazil. In 1948 Aubrey Sidford, Behr-Manning's representative on the Durex board commented matter of factly that "Durex is a world wide concern" whose goal was to "best monopolize the manufacture and market as far as we could do so before other interests moved in the same direction."[105]

Leadership of the autonomous international operation fell increasingly to Donald Kelso, executive vice-president and later Young's successor as president of both companies in 1948. Since 1936 Durex had ceased hiring personnel from the American firms and had recruited and trained its own people. The flexibility to set prices and discount rates which Durex had received as an emergency depression measure had become standard policy by 1940, when the directors also formally conceded Kelso's request to establish different products and standards to meet local market conditions. He had a small staff headed by Vice-President Wilfred Place and Sales Manager Jules Schaetzel to coordinate operations, build new plants, and oversee a worldwide sales organization. In the late 1940s when Louis Camarra traveled to Argentina to sell Norton grinding wheels in South America, he noted with envy and embarrassment the startling contrast between his shabby office and the well-appointed and well-established Durex organization under Paul Krumdieck.[106]

The Durex experience was significant for Norton in several ways. It expanded the market for U.S. and Behr-Manning coated abrasives products and contributed significantly to Behr-Manning profits. By 1936, total Durex dividends to Behr-Manning of $932,000 exceeded its actual investment in both firms, while its share of book value had grown to $927,000.[107] Durex provided the model and top personnel for an integrated, progressive Norton overseas division in the 1950s after an antitrust decision broke up the foreign coated venture. Finally, and most important, the antitrust decision created another, increasingly autonomous power center within the family firm. The growing size and complexity of Norton's international business quickly became important factors to help compel fundamental changes.

Expanded foreign enterprise and the development of a full product line had forced a major compromise on the owner-managed company. Preservation of owner-operation across national boundaries and product lines meant an anomalous organization characterized both by great centralization and remarkable autonomy. All final authority remained vested in an increasingly passive ownership at Worcester. Responsibility for areas and products that the top people could not handle directly fell to professional managers at Behr-Manning and in the foreign plants. In these cases, controls rested largely on financial and short-term operating data; such measures as profits on sales did not gauge market share, long-term capital appreciation, and the training of new talent. Shrewd judgment and careful indoctrination of Norton values at Worcester had originally supplied the able people necessary for such an arrangement. In the long run, however, age and retirement, shifting markets, new competition, and industry stagnation caused serious problems for the New England family firm.

6.

The Third Generation:
Continuity and Change

THE SECOND GENERATION had built successfully. Aldus Higgins and George Jeppson had guided Norton Company through a world war and a major depression and were to endure still another world war before surrendering control. The firm they left unmistakably reflected their efforts and the values they inherited from the founders.

In many ways the company resembled most large American manufacturing firms at midcentury. Norton Company was a multifunctional, multinational enterprise producing a full line of abrasive products. Excellent products and an extensive sales effort servicing a valuable international network of industrial distributors made Norton the biggest and most influential enterprise among the handful of companies that dominated the abrasives business. Like the other firms in *Fortune*'s 500 largest industrials, the functionally departmentalized organization was staffed with professional managers at its middle and lower levels and was operated by a few top executives in the central office.

But Jeppson's and Higgins's legacy still differed profoundly from most big U.S. companies. Norton remained a private company whose ownership was concentrated in relatively few hands. Owner-managers operated a deeply paternalistic organization whose main labor force remained unorganized. Furthermore, the two owner-managers had carefully recruited and trained still a third generation to continue Norton leadership and values.

In the quarter century after World War II, Milton Higgins II and John Jeppson II, sons of Aldus Higgins and George Jeppson, carried on many Norton traditions, including private ownership with prudent dividends, large cash surpluses and self-finance, a paternalistic labor relations program, product quality, price leadership, and direct management with characteristic New England values. Despite their efforts at continuity, however, the third generation inaugurated the most profound changes since the evolution of the big company. Largely external forces—government regulation, maturity of the abrasives industry, and the growth and complexity that were a necessary part of big enterprise—forced the founders' grandsons into a series of compromises that revealed the limits of family operation and undermined the firm's uniqueness. The alteration was a three-part process: taking the company public, diversifying away from the abrasives business, and then the advent of professional managers as the enterprise's top executives. Making Norton a public company was the first step and led almost unavoidably to the other two.

Continuity: Preserving the Family Firm

Such radical changes lay unplanned and unperceived when the third generation took control at the end of World War II. Since Norton Company and production grinding were both fully established, the war itself did not cause a major transformation as World War I had. World War II stimulated consumption but provoked little innovation except in the coated abrasives industry, as already noted. Wartime production ended the prolonged slump of the 1930s, and the emphasis on metal products and metal working for planes, tanks, guns, armaments, and ships stimulated Norton's quick recovery.

Once again prudence, diligence, and preparation helped cope with business that nearly swamped the firm. In the Machine Division alone 1940 production more than doubled 1937 figures, the division's previous high, and orders continued to increase until 1943.[1] Rapid growth quickly consumed the extra capacity resulting from Howard Dunbar's factory reorganization, which had culminated in the late 1930s with special U-bench subassembly areas to fabricate and feed parts to the basic flow of production.

The bonded abrasives business was just as busy, although the full impact lagged slightly behind the expanded production and application of metal-working and machine tools.[2] As in the Machine Division, retooling and reorganization during the 1930s provided essential capacity for the job. Nevertheless, a new tunnel kiln and truing plant were soon overloaded as the value of 1941 wheel orders more than doubled 1940's figure. Only the construction of two more tunnel kilns and round-the-clock, seven-day-a-week operation met the demand. As Milton Higgins aptly put it: "We were just running full out."[3]

Norton owners' prudence again paid dividends by helping to ensure adequate raw material supplies.[4] The growing threat of war in

the late 1930s had led them to stockpile bauxite for Alundum manufacture, and the carefully husbanded, bauxite-laden forty acres in
Arkansas were again mined to supplement Alcoa shipments from
South America. Milton Higgins II's and William L. Neilson's metic-
ulously tended ties to the De Beers syndicate assured an adequate
supply of bort or industrial-quality diamonds for diamond wheels. In
addition, synthetic rubber replaced natural resins for the firm's limited
rubber wheel manufacture.

As it had less than two decades before, war vastly accelerated industry sales. Wheel industry list orders nearly quadrupled from about
$90 million, the previous high in 1937, to more that $350 million in
1943. Preparedness helped Norton capture more than its expected
portion. In a growing market from 1938 to 1942 Norton's industry
share increased from 34 percent to 39 percent. While the total sales
of Carborundum Company, Norton's major competitor, grew from
$11 million in 1938 to about $57 million in 1943, the Worcester firm
expanded even more impressively. Sales of all domestic manufactured
products increased from $13.5 million to nearly $94 million, and total
consolidated sales leapt from $21.6 million to $131.3 million for the
same period. Profit data are unavailable, but despite high wartime
taxation, Norton owners were prudently able to amass a $22 million
cash reserve for future expansion and as a hedge against an expected
postwar slump.[5]

If war brought growth rather than change, it contributed positively
and significantly to Norton continuity. By World War II evidence
already reflected the first faint threats to carefully constructed family
control, as such largely external factors as the ravages of time, change
and growth in the economy, innovation in the strategy and structure
of large-scale American enterprise, and the growing demands of Norton Company itself undermined owner-operation.

The initial glimmer evolved from causes as basic as time, age, and
procreation. By 1938 George Jeppson and Aldus Higgins had both
turned 65. Fits of ill health had already disrupted Higgins's attention
to business, and even the hale and active Jeppson was ready to re-
linquish some of the daily cares of administration. New leadership at
this time had to come from outside the family despite recruiting of
sons for the business. Milton Higgins II, who had joined the firm a
decade earlier, was 35 years old and just undertaking his first major
managerial task, the operation of the Chippawa furnace plant. John
Jeppson II was entering Harvard Business School at 22. No other
owner's family had sons qualified for the job, but two able, veteran
managers were readily available—Tony Clark, general manager of
Norton sales, and Frank Gallagher, president and chief executive of
Behr-Manning.

War delayed resolution of the dilemma by compelling Norton's leaders to remain. The uncertain fate of overseas plants, unprecedented demand for expanded production, and increased government regulation of resources and business made wartime a poor choice for breaking in new top executives, especially when talented younger people went into military service. Aldus Higgins moved up to become chairman of the board, and George Jeppson assumed an even larger share of operating responsibility as president in 1941 with the aid of Andrew Holmstrom as vice-president and works manager.

By 1946, when Norton owners again faced the problem of succession, war and delay had eased the challenge. Milton Higgins now had more general training than perhaps anyone in the firm. Since 1938 he had completed three years of management at Chippawa and five years as treasurer. These positions, along with earlier time spent in the laboratory, in the plant, and in sales engineering and sales research, had trained him in all facets of the business—manufacturing, sales, reasearch, and finance. Few people knew the bonded abrasives business as thoroughly as Milton Higgins.

The younger Higgins was not yet 43 and worried that the presidency and the travel would separate him from his family, but Aldus and the board talked him into the job.[6] Milton was the logical choice to preserve family management, and George Jeppson's and Aldus Higgins's tight control of the functional organization left few nonfamily alternatives. Tony Clark, whose background was entirely in sales, departed during World War II and eventually became Carborundum's head. The talented Frank Gallagher was an outsider—a nonfamily and non-Worcester man who had already clashed with Jeppson and Higgins over how to run the business. Many of the top staff and functional people who had long worked with George and Aldus were too old.

Not only was Milton the best prepared family member and one of the few qualified young executives in the firm, he also embodied long-standing Norton values. He was wholeheartedly an abrasives man whose diligent attention to business gave him an amazingly detailed mastery.[7] He was firmly committed to the importance and continuation of private ownership and owner-operation and relied on his knowledge of and feel for the abrasives industry to grasp opportunity. Rigid organization and planning held little value, for, as he himself explained, "I never was a great systems man."[8]

Like his father and Charles Allen, Milton sought to avoid conflict by using persistence and knowledge to persuade or wear down opponents. As treasurer, he had carefully maintained and expanded the large cash surplus so characteristic of the firm, a policy that he continued as president. As he explained publicly in 1949, "As with our physical energy, we should maintain a reserve for the short periods of recession or the emergency that is bound to come."[9]

In addition, Milton's nearly two decades with the company had engendered considerable respect for Norton paternalism. He was quick to realize the policy's value in maintaining a stable, loyal, productive work force in Worcester and the positive effect of training foreign plant managers in Worcester, as Norton's recent war experience so amply demonstrated. Foreign managers were "proud of their individual plants and accomplishments but still more significant is that they are proud of being a part of the Worcester Norton Company."[10]

While Milton Higgins's appointment firmly established a third generation of family ownership and management that endured through the 1960s, the transition reflected several compromises that portended long-term change. There would be no team of owner-operators as in the previous generations since John Jeppson was too young and inexperienced for a top executive position.[11] In the Jeppson tradition, he quickly set to work in production, first as a plant superintendent and later as head of all abrasives operations, but he remained outside

The second and third generations (left to right): John Jeppson II, Aldus Higgins, George Jeppson, and Milton Higgins II, 1947.

the top two administrative and decision-making positions during the 1940s and 1950s.

Originally, John was committed to the continuation of the family firm, but his training at Harvard Business School and his experiences with automated production and professional management techniques in the 1950s weaned him from family operation. When his turn as chief executive came in the 1960s, Jeppson was fully committed to filling all positions with the best professional management available and to the policy of diversification so popular among managers in American business during the 1950s and 1960s.[12]

Despite the absence of a second family executive, Norton badly required a two-man team at the top. The burden of daily administrative control as well as the broader strategic and decision-making concerns of top management were too much for one man. While Milton replaced his father with a splendid, detailed knowledge of the business and with a comfortable, informal, and opportunistic philosophy of operation, a partner had to supply George Jeppson's direct, reasoned approach and ability to step back occasionally for the long view.

Ralph Gow admirably fitted the bill. Like George Jeppson before him, Gow was a trained engineer who had joined Norton after graduating from the Massachusetts Institute of Technology in 1925 and spent most of his two decades at Norton in production, eventually becoming works manager in 1941.[13] His strong personality and direct approach complemented a powerful, analytical mind. As Ralph himself put it: "I was primarily an administrator and organizer and that's what Milton needed. Aldus knew it because Milton is not an organizer."[14]

His excellent organizational and administrative abilities and his abrupt, no-nonsense style earned George Jeppson's grudging praise as "The Lord High Executioner of the Norton Company."[15] In 1948 Gow became executive vice-president and second in command at Norton. For nearly two decades he and Milton Higgins wielded supreme power, and in 1961 he became the firm's first nonfamily president. As the first outsider at the top, he was a central force in making Norton a publicly held firm.

Gow's promotion broke another company tradition. Even though his appointment preserved the team approach, Gow was recruited and boosted by Aldus Higgins.[16] For the first time top management lacked a Yankee-Swedish balance. George Jeppson had fought unsuccessfully to preserve the old symmetry by pushing Andrew B. Holmstrom as executive vice-president. Holmstrom was a Swedish-American with long experience in Norton production. His service as works manager and chief administrator during World War II carried on the firm's long Swedish factory tradition reflected in the management of John Jeppson I and George Jeppson. Yet, while Holmstrom was a popular leader, especially during the critical early period of the war, he lacked the overall vision and analytical mind of a top manager.

As an additional sign of change, the transition to the third generation was more abrupt than the previous shift. Charles Allen had continued to serve as chief executive and as a kind of avuncular guide during the first half of George Jeppson's and Aldus Higgins's tenure. Although George and Aldus had clearly planned a similar relationship after 1946, Higgins's death in 1948 removed the main link. George Jeppson served as chairman of the board and remained active in the business, especially in the process and product developments that had always intrigued him, but he was never close to Milton Higgins and Ralph Gow and had little positive impact on their management except for his advocacy of a major process innovation.[17]

George eventually exercised a kind of veto power. He often disapproved, but in Norton fashion he seldom, if ever, precipitated pitched battles. In some cases, such as the acquisition of South American plants, John or Milton undertook to persuade him; in others the chairman was content merely to express his doubt. The long-term effect was to separate further the Jeppsons from the top operating team as George became less active and John grew more convinced of the need for professional, systematic management and diversification.

Diversification, professional management, and public ownership, however, remained remote possibilities for fifteen years as the long-term consequences of the power transfer remained obscure. In the short run the policies and practices of the Higgins-Gow era successfully continued many long-standing traditions and suggested business as usual in the 1940s and 1950s. Norton continued as a privately held, owner-operated firm. Milton was always chief executive even after becoming chairman of the board in 1961, until John Jeppson succeeded him in 1967. Milton also consulted with George and John Jeppson and other major stockholders on any major decision. Ralph Gow recalled that he "felt very much the power of the family ownership" even as he and Milton exercised operating authority.[18]

The two men divided responsibility between themselves in less formal fashion than had Aldus Higgins and George Jeppson. Ralph was loosely responsible for manufacturing and Milton for sales. Both oversaw company finance, and in practice each made decisions in all areas of the firm, including major appointments. They replaced the aged administration, which had been held over during the war, with their own top team of functional executives, all of whom were Norton men of long experience. Ralph Johnson, former head of abrasives sales, became vice-president and general sales manager. Everett Hicks, a talented young financial man, replaced Howard Dunbar and Frank Smith to reorganize the limping Machine Division whose sales and profits had collapsed with the war's end. Wallace Howe, an experienced researcher in vitrified grinding wheels, became director of research. Edwin McConnell, William Magee, and later William Perks replaced their mentor Henry Duckworth as controller and treasurer. As already noted, John Jeppson eventually followed in his father's footsteps to become vice-president and head of production.

The team included only three outsiders. At Behr-Manning, long-time production chief Elmer Schacht succeeded his boss Frank Gallagher, and Donald Kelso from Durex was hired to head Norton Behr-Manning Overseas, a consolidation of Norton's foreign coated and bonded plants. And in the mid-1950s Ralph Gow recruited Fairman Cowan from Goodwin, Procter and Hoar, the prominent Boston legal

Top management about 1958: the inside board centered around Chairman George Jeppson. Clockwise: Lewis Greenleaf, Ralph Johnson, Wallace Howe, John Jeppson II, Edwin Evans, Ralph Gow, Milton Higgins II, George Jeppson, Edwin McConnell, William Perks, Donald Kelso, Andrew Holmstrom, Clarence Daniels, Howard Daly, and Everett Hicks.

firm, as corporate counsel. These top functional and operating men in time joined Higgins and Gow to continue Norton's long-standing tradition of an internal Board of Directors. With self-finance and only three major businesses to watch—coated abrasives, bonded abrasives, and grinding machinery—Higgins and Gow felt no need for expertise or guidance from outside directors.[19]

Owner-operation and the inside board meant that authority was clearly centralized in Higgins and Gow, who reviewed and approved all major decisions, and that centralized authority typically cut across bureaucratic lines. Milton and Ralph simply administered as much as they could. They tightly controlled Worcester abrasives operations as had George Jeppson and Aldus Higgins, whereas Behr-Manning and the overseas plants had nearly complete autonomy. The machine business fell somewhere in between. Everett Hicks ran it but Gow and Higgins approved all major decisions.

Like George Jeppson, Gow was an analytical thinker with a systematic approach to problems, but with their extensive experience in what was largely a single-industry business, neither Milton nor Ralph felt the need for an elaborate staff and a formal administrative network.[20] In 1962 top management was still twenty-five men, as it had been in 1941.[21] Ralph and Milton served jointly on committees for salary, personnel, capital allocation, charitable contributions, and plant engineering, and their decision, usually based on experience and common sense, was final. Contributions reflected personal and local interests. Salaries and promotions followed no plan; the two men simply dealt with requests or needs as they arose on a case-by-case basis.

Capital allocation was, in Gow's words, "very informal."[22] With a strong cash flow, Ralph and Milton simply scheduled major requests from top staff and operating people so that large expenditures did not conflict with one another. Revenue estimates, based on experience and managers' projections, were rough but adequate guides and were never rigorously and systematically compared with actual results for appraisal. Last-minute adjustments were handled by the Plants Engineering Committee. Composed of George Jeppson, Milton Higgins, Ralph Gow, and Plants Engineer Clarence Daniels, it approved every construction expenditure of $100 or more until the mid-1950s when Gow raised the minimum to $1000.

The centralized, personal approach extended to strategy as well as administration. As in most functionally organized firms, top Norton executives were responsible for both. Gow felt little need to separate the two: "After all we had pretty good growth of profits and sales in those years, and we did it our way."[23] As we shall see, overseas expansion in the 1950s continued to be an ad hoc, opportunistic process. Gow recalled that "we just drifted into these things. It was not a strategy."[24] The addition of a small wheel plant in Santa Clara, California, came only after West Coast Sales Manager Robert Cushman convinced headquarters that westerners were "irritated as hell" with poky rail shipments.[25]

Fairman Cowan, one of the few top people who came from the outside, summed it up best: "Final approval had to be Milton Higgins and if he and Ralph Gow approved of something, there was no question but that it would be approved by everyone else . . . You didn't have the kind of outside disinterested scrutiny that you now have, or the kind of detailed presentations of proposals that we now have. I don't think even anybody knew what R.O.I. [return on investment] meant in those days . . . It was much more a seat-of-the-pants kind of decision-making process."[26]

The Higgins-Gow management also perpetuated the long-standing traditions and values of the New England firm. In addition to owner-control, Norton operations continued to be characterized by diligence, thrift, and prudence, as well as profits. The company mothballed its Arkansas bauxite reserve and self-financed more than $85 million in modernization and expansion between 1946 and 1966 in Worcester alone while maintaining its large cash reserve.[27] It borrowed only at the Korean War's outbreak, as it had in World War I and World War II, as a hedge against expected inflation and short-term credit crunches. Careful daily oversight of Worcester operations by Gow and Higgins with the aid of a powerful Financial Department and strong statistical operating data assured their knowledge and control, while Ralph Johnson rebuilt and closely maintained an excellent network of industrial distributors and John Jeppson managed the implementation of advanced, automated production techniques in the abrasives division.

Top executives lavished careful attention on Norton's labor relations program. Milton, Ralph, John, and old George Jeppson especially worked to preserve the "Norton Spirit," the institutionalized program of corporate paternalism that Jeppson had established forty years earlier. All regularly toured the plant and knew hundreds of workers by name. Awards and banquets for ten, fifteen, twenty-five, and fifty years' service celebrated company loyalty, while the *Norton Spirit* newspaper continued to recount the doings of Norton workers and their families on a monthly or semimonthly basis.

The program of fringe benefits—including a gymnasium, an athletic program, a beach, concerts, a visiting nurse (who made more than 5,500 home and hospital visits to employees and retirees in 1957), and

annual outings (which still attracted more than 25,000 every year)—
went on unabated while Higgins and Gow carefully matched the
salary, health, and pension benefits of local American Steel and Wire
workers. By 1957 Norton stock had been sold at book value to several
hundred loyal employees at all levels. In 1953 the firm published *The
Norton Story*, celebrating Norton legends and heroes and dedicated
"to those men and women of our Norton family who have gone before
us."[28]

Perhaps the most outstanding example of Norton paternalism during the third generation resulted from a disastrous Worcester tornado
in June 1953 that killed 90, injured more than 1,200, left 10,000 home-
less, and did more than $60 million damage.[29] Although Norton Com-
pany suffered serious losses, including destruction of the roof of its
new Machine Division plant, the firm offered extensive private relief
to employees, their families, and the Worcester community. It contributed $25,000 to a relief fund and paid full wages to all employees
during plant closing and to 150 who volunteered for full-time relief
work. The Personnel Department operated a disaster headquarters
for employees and retirees that offered insurance advice, provided
referrals to relief agencies, coordinated workers, handled temporary
repairs, and supplied trucks, emergency funds, storage, and short-
term accommodations.

Without precise measurement, the benefits of Norton paternalism
can only be described qualitatively. Higgins, Gow, and other top
officials still feel that it repaid itself many times over through increased
productivity of a loyal and stable work force. By 1953 nearly two-
thirds of Norton's Worcester employees had ten or more years' service, and popular demand for *The Norton Story* forced a second print-
ing, unusual in company histories.[30] The program also helped maintain
the nonunion status of Norton's Worcester workers. When the United
Steelworkers sought to organize Machine Division workers in 1946
and the company successfully insisted on an election covering all its
Worcester employees, the organizers quickly conceded defeat and the
proposition never reached a vote. Since that time no serious unionization effort has ever been mounted.

Continuity: Plant 7 and the General Development Committee

Maintenance of company paternalism, values, and owner-operation
turned on an even more fundamental Norton tradition—industry
leadership based on superior products and manufacturing processes.
In this area the Higgins-Gow team benefited from George Jeppson's

special interest in bonded abrasives manufacturing and his almost fanatic concern with a possible postwar slump.

Aldus Higgins and George Jeppson never forgot the disastrous impact of the 1921 depression and Norton's failure to anticipate it. By 1943 Jeppson, along with many Americans in government and business, was anxiously trying to predict the economy's course when World War II's artificial stimulus disappeared. He hired Roland Erickson as a staff economist to help project the future, and in the Abrasives and Machine divisions, Holmstrom, Dunbar, and others desperately tried to piece together the postwar puzzle from data gathered by the federal government, business information sources, and their own sales forces. As Jeppson told the Grinding Wheel Manufacturers Association in 1943, "We must also predict the end of the war so that we do not all find ourselves full of inventories and debts, as many did at the end of the last war."[31]

Based on the 1921 collapse and the depressed economy of the 1930s, Aldus Higgins and Jeppson assumed that peace would slash orders and increase competition while the firm suffered reduced profit margins.[32] Since the Office of Price Administration regulated grinding wheel prices, Jeppson had little hope that price increases would keep pace with growing costs. In the five years since 1940, Norton average hourly wage rates had jumped 44 percent, weekly earnings were up 37 percent, and the growing power of AFL and CIO unions promised to push industrial wages even higher. Raw materials costs were up, higher freight rates were threatened, and Jeppson doubted that tax rates would return to prewar levels. Preserving market share in an increasingly competitive market would mean bigger discounts and larger distribution costs.[33] Already the success of deSanno and Son and other small firms manufacturing resinoid wheels for the foundry and steel industry was helping erode Norton's market share in grinding wheels from its 39 percent peak in 1942 to 32 percent in 1946.[34]

As it so often had in the past, Norton Company looked for help in the manufacturing end of the business. As Jeppson put it, because taxes, materials, and other costs were beyond Norton's control, the logical response was "an attack on our factory costs—ways and means of getting more production per individual worker."[35] Under Jeppson's leadership, the firm had been product- and process-oriented, and George Jeppson himself had been more interested in making grinding wheels better, faster, and cheaper than in selling them. His entire career, from founding the Norton Laboratory, through the application of Alundum and the development of 38 Alundum, to his long tenure as works manager and head of production, was committed to finding solutions in the factory. The answer in this case was continuous process manufacture. As George wrote Aldus Higgins, "The nub of the whole thing is that instead of making precision wheels like bricks, that we create making machines that mix, make, and burn in the same machine."[36]

The course of innovation was a familiar one. Jeppson was an idea man whose knowledge of grinding and bonded abrasives was sufficient to stimulate suggestions but inadequate to actually implement them. Thus in 1908 he wondered what would happen if pure alumina were fused. Ownership gave his curiosity authority and Lewis Saunders was assigned the development of what became 38 Alundum. Wallace Howe thought that Jeppson acted like a "sparkplug."[37] Owner-operation and the lack of bureaucratic control allowed him to bypass normal procedures, procure funds, and assign special personnel to investigate his ideas while he watched and encouraged.

In this case Jeppson turned to the familiar team approach.[38] He appropriated $50,000 and assigned the task to Howe, an experienced researcher in grinding wheels, and Edward Van der Pyl, the equipment expert. The two men typically reflected the mix of scientist and artisan in Norton history and manufacturing. Howe was a New England Yankee with an MIT engineering degree who had helped develop the Y-process and controlled structure. Van der Pyl was a largely self-taught mechanical genius whose inventions and improvements saved Norton hundreds of thousands of dollars.

With diligence and imagination they eventually developed a machine capable of continuously molding and firing small grinding wheels up to $\frac{3}{4}$ inch in diameter. After proudly exhibiting the machine to a pleased George Jeppson, they were stunned to discover that his conceptualization far exceeded theirs. "Now we will build a plant to make wheels fourteen inches and smaller." Howe recalled that "Van der Pyl and I nearly crawled under the table because we had never gone beyond $\frac{3}{4}$ of an inch. But he had optimism and he had vision and I didn't have."[39]

Jeppson's ambitious conceptualization resulted from his position and imagination. As a top executive he was most aware of competitive pressures to cut costs. As a prominent Worcester manufacturer he had visited a local firm whose encapsulating machinery for pharmaceutical companies had apparently given him the idea, although his original conceptualization was remarkably similar to a coated abrasives making machine. As a would-be technical man he knew something of past Norton work on controlled structure and high-speed firing that made the process feasible. And as owner-operator he commanded the resources to establish the operation.

Furthermore, as an experienced production man, Jeppson quickly grasped the importance of moving from a single new machine to a plant designed around an automated process. Increased capital investment in specially designed plant and equipment would convert batch manufacturing to continuous process production and concentrate responsibility and operation. What he envisioned would transform bonded abrasives manufacture into automated, line production. As he explained with some exaggeration to Aldus Higgins:

> The making of grinding wheels is pretty much an art. In the making of the millions of abrasive wheels and points, much is left to the judgment of individuals, and to the motions and sensitiveness of human hands. The steps of grain inspection, bond preparation, mixing, molding, burning, grading, are done under separate supervision. These Supervisors may report to different Superintendents.
>
> I believe that it is logical to conclude that we would do a better job if we could, as far as is practical, give a Superintendent one or two classifications and have him responsible for the complete operation. Make him a specialist and concentrate the responsibility for good product, and its economics in manufacture, in fewer and better individuals.[40]

Jeppson's ideas were not new in U.S. industry but they were a revolution in bonded abrasives manufacture. His plan promised finally to put job-shop wheel production in line with continuous process techniques long used in steel, food products, chemicals, automobiles, and other industries. Mechanized precision production, he thought, "will reduce our costs because we will save labor, rejections, handling and time."[41] Labor savings would result from substitution as well as from reduced labor content. World War II production demands had brought 1,900 women into Norton's Worcester plant, and Jeppson felt that the many who wished to remain after the war were well-suited to repetitive work as machine tenders.[42] Since that time women have been a significant part of Norton's wheel-manufacturing force.

His interest in automated manufacturing and his son's urging soon pushed Jeppson into an even larger task: a thorough examination and overhaul of the entire firm. Five years' concentration on production had delayed planned improvements, worn out equipment, and stifled consideration of new ideas. Once again, the review typified the owner-operated, private New England company. With traditional thrift the firm chose an internal audit of processes, while Carborundum paid outside consultants more than $100,000 for the same purpose with less success. George Jeppson congratulated himself that self-examination through the General Development Committee saved time, preserved secrecy, and profitably employed Norton's own expert talent.[43]

Chaired by Edward Van der Pyl and including Wallace Howe, Research Director Milton Beecher, and Plants Engineer Clarence Daniels, the committee was charged to cut costs with improved processes, reduced manufacturing cycle time, better layouts, more efficient material and product handling, and increased product quality and customer service. To preserve central control it reported to a management board of Aldus Higgins, George Jeppson, Milton Higgins, and A. B. Holmstom. To immerse his son in the business, George appointed John secretary. Finally, to gather information and ideas from down the line, George charged the committee to appoint some thirty subcommittees to make "process audits" at Worcester and in all branch and foreign plants, warehouses, and some administrative departments.[44]

The development of automated manufacturing, the original stimulus, proved the only major breakthrough, and implementation again emphasized the third generation's continuity with its predecessors.[45] Using its customary team approach for special projects, the company moved prudently and cautiously first into a small-scale experimental stage and then into a pilot plant before opting for a full-scale commercial production in a new plant. The researchers, headed by Howe and Van der Pyl and slowly augmented with David Reid and other technicians and engineers, developed three major innovations for continuous wheel manufacture. They designed a free-flowing mix based on volumetric proportions first developed in the controlled structure work of the 1920s. The new automatic presses dumped a precise, predetermined volume of mix into the mold (which was part of the press), leveled and capped the mold, stamped the wheel, and stripped away the mold. Automatic molding increased speed and reduced labor costs, producing a small, stamped green wheel every second.

High-speed firing made the continuous process possible. Electric kilns designed by Van der Pyl reduced burning time for vitrified wheels from one week to four hours and eliminated drying time. The key was firing through a wheel's thickness rather than through its periphery as was done in old bee hive and tunnel kilns. The new technique eased tensile and compression stresses that had previously accompanied quick heating and cooling.

After the difficulties were worked out in a pilot plant superintended by John Jeppson, the Higginses and Jeppsons committed the company to a $4.3 million plant that was a stark contrast to Norton's older multistoried operation.[46] Designed for straight line manufacture, the

Maintaining leadership: continuous firing of wheels.

single-level, 602-by-320-foot building reflected the open plant architecture characteristic of automobile and airplane assembly line production. A number of straight, parallel production lines ran the plant's
length, with the mix poured at one end and vitrified grinding wheels
flowing out the other.

The committee's other major developments consisted of implementation of projects begun before the war. At Chippawa Robert Ridgeway directed the commercial production of a new abrasive.[47] Based on pilot work done in the 1930s, 32 Alundum represented a new process. Electric furnaces fused high-purity alumina directly from bauxite, producing a nearly pure crystal without 38 Alundum's porosity and without the crushing necessary for regular Alundum. The result was a tough crystal with a bumpy or nubbly surface especially suited for metal grinding. Possibly because of the General Development Committee's influence, commercial production began in 1946 in a continuous process plant.

At the same time Chippawa began continuous casting of first 38 and then regular Alundum.[48] Ed Van der Pyl and Jack Upper designed furnaces to pour and cast the molten aluminum oxide to replace the old-style units that produced single, separate pigs. The poured mass moved in buckets along a track for twenty-four hours, cooling before it was cracked into lumps, broken into smaller pieces, and crushed. The entire operation was automated, replacing the labor that broke up the big, old-style pigs. The stimulus for commercial development was Chippawa Research Director Ridgeway's desire for greater wartime production and George Jeppson's willingness to risk $130,000 in laboratory and operating equipment for greater speed and lower cost.

In addition, self-examination significantly improved the grinding machine division's position.[49] Although Howard Dunbar had designs for a new building and line production dating from the 1930s, George Jeppson and Aldus Higgins had steadfastly refused extensive investment for a new plant. The improvements of the 1930s stopped the precipitous decline of the 1920s but failed to provide full recovery and growth. The steady-state policy's limitations were revealed when Norton had to refuse an offer to purchase the division because it was located amid abrasives operations. During the audit Dunbar's plans were dusted off and improved, and Everett Hicks, Dunbar's successor, soon convinced the Board of Directors to build a new plant.

Typically, the plant represented little risk; in fact, it was a cautious, prudent, and relatively inexpensive measure despite a nominal cost of $6 million. The analytical Hicks first persuaded the directors to stay in the machine business. All agreed that the division competed respectably with Cincinnati and Landis and that its machines were more visible and contributed more than grinding wheels to Norton's reputation. Ralph Gow recalled that General Motors President William Knudsen and other top executives instantly recognized the Norton name because Norton machines were among the major outlays they approved for capital equipment.[50]

The construction of a new plant followed logically from the first decision. Consolidation of production with rationalized line manufacturing in a large, open plant significantly cut costs and improved Norton's competitive position. Location adjacent to Norton's abrasives manufacture preserved Worcester control, and transportation expenses to midwestern automotive plants were judged insignificant since individual machines cost $25,000 or more. At the same time the plant made the division more attractive and its separate location made future sale feasible. Finally, construction during the Korean conflict allowed Norton 75 percent depreciation over five years against wartime excess profits taxes.

The General Development Committee's work was significant on several counts. Savings, greater efficiency, and new products increased Norton income and helped perpetuate its industry leadership. Its evolution also indicated the second generation's contribution to the emerging Higgins and Gow team. Furthermore, the project reflected the firm's strengths and weaknesses and portended future change.

Although direct statistics on the revenue generated by the various projects are lacking, the benefits were clear. The machine plant helped put that division back in the black. The new 32 Alundum helped secure the postwar wheel market both in the United States and abroad. New or improved processes helped cut costs significantly. On an earlier occasion George Jeppson referred to such processes as "little kinks in lubrication, dust proofing, all the thousand and one things that actually make these machines a success and that keep down repairs."[51]

Plant 7, the automated, continuous process plant for vitrified wheels, was of course the greatest breakthrough. Automation and precision manufacturing eliminated shaving, significantly reduced truing, and cut the rejection rate from 10 percent to 2 percent. The standardized, free-flowing bond could be mixed in large batches and stored. The technology eventually encouraged the further adoption of scientific management techniques: standardization of wheels for large batch runs, statistical quality controls, and grading and inspection by scientific sampling. Treasurer Ed McConnell later told Wallace Howe that the new process saved "a million dollars a year." Its success led Norton to spend $6.5 million in 1957–1959 to build and equip plant 8 on similar lines for resinoid wheel production.[52]

The most startling change was reduction of the manufacturing cycle from more than a week to less than one day. Top executives simply did not comprehend until shown the results. The skeptical Aldus Higgins did not believe until David Reid brought him a fully burned wheel that the chairman had carefully marked as a green wheel earlier that same day. Reid recalled that when Milton Higgins first saw the automatic press in action, the awestruck president stood there, chanting "fifty cents, fifty cents, fifty cents" to the rhythm of the press.[53] Automated, continuous process manufacture was so advanced that Carborundum did not duplicate it for a decade.

The technological improvement helped assure continuity between the second and third generations. Many of the improvements either originated in or evolved from technical breakthroughs made in the 1920s and 1930s and their internal development reflected the private firm. Norton people reviewed themselves and designed and built their own equipment. There was no tradition of sharing, as in the coated abrasives industry.

Of course, the firm was not self-sufficient. The stimulus and ideas for technical change often stemmed from related fields. The independent crystal structure of 32 Alundum evolved from several Italians' efforts to produce gem-quality stones. A magazine ad prompted Wallace Howe to try wax emulsion in the free-flowing mix, and he and Van der Pyl found molding processes in pill and spark plug manufacturing useful guides in building Norton's automatic molds.

More fundamentally, the technological innovations continued the product superiority and lower costs on which Norton profits and industry leadership depended. They in turn provided the buffer that permitted the extension of the single-industry, New England family firm well into the post–World War II period. Norton's sliding market share in bonded abrasives stabilized between 1946 and 1954 at about 33 percent.[54]

The General Development Committee's work also reflected Norton's weaknesses as well as its strengths. The committee's greatest impact came in Worcester wheel production where the influence of family management was strongest. Behr-Manning made no great breakthroughs, and the French and German plants initially rejected the open architecture and straight line production of plant 7. And although the new factory improved the Machine Division's profits, the division slowly fell behind Cincinnati Milling and return on investment never equaled the abrasives operation.

The bias was reflected in research and development as well. The greatest breakthroughs came in vitrified wheel production, long a Norton strong point and a market in which Norton held a 50 percent share. Plant 8 for resinoid wheels came almost a decade later and its impact fell far short of plant 7's. Norton research continued to concentrate best on those things "round with a hole in them." Pioneering work with Paul Bridgeman at Harvard in synthetic diamond production was never fully prosecuted.[55] In 1946 Norton broke off with General Electric, its partner in the venture, and pursued a slow and unsuccessful course, while GE soon designed a tetrahedral anvil for proper molding and discovered the nickel catalyst necessary for the reaction.

Like the transition of power to Higgins and Gow, the General Development Committee's work faintly portended long-term change. John Jeppson's prominence as secretary to the committee and superintendent of first the pilot plant and then plant 7 quickly immersed him in the adaptation of statistical sampling and other scientific management techniques to bonded abrasives manufacture.[56] The experience had a profound effect in helping him recognize the advantages of and Norton's need for increased professional management.

In one respect the plant 7 strategy ill-served Norton in the long run. Concentration on vitrified rather than resinoid production left the firm poorly positioned as resinoid products captured an increasing share of bonded abrasives sales. Furthermore, Norton chose to maintain prices and take increased profits rather than using its cost advantages to seek additional market share. Eventually, its high prices and weak resinoid positions would contribute to sales stagnation and declining market share.

Disruption: Coping with Antitrust

A much more immediate challenge to Norton sales leadership and the family firm, and indeed to the entire industry, evolved from a series of major antitrust cases that rocked the abrasive grain, bonded abrasives, and coated abrasives industries after World War II. Although industry officials complained that shifting policy made illegal the same behavior that had been proper or even encouraged during Hoover's tenure as secretary of commerce in the 1920s and during Franklin Roosevelt's National Recovery Administration, they had fair warning. Antitrust activity had considerably accelerated in the late 1930s and 1940s after Roosevelt's relationship with the business community soured.[57] Thurmond Arnold's appointment as head of the Antitrust Division of the U.S. Department of Justice and the investigations of the Temporary National Economic Committee led to close scrutiny of a number of industries.

Legislation and case law wiped out the fragile legal underpinnings of twenty years' price consultation, cooperation, and control throughout the abrasives industry. The courts had restricted the practice of price control by patent pools and licenses that stabilized prices in coated abrasives. At Worcester, Assistant Controller Everett Hicks's

1945 study of Norton's pricing system found that contrary to the law, there was "no basic pattern of discounts or differentials" for customers or distributors.[58] Neither cost nor quantity explained discounts on the same products that varied 12-40 percent for distributors, 5-17 percent for large consumers, and 18-20 percent for small consumers. Furthermore, case law that forbade fixing any part of a price struck directly at the Abrasive Grain and Grinding Wheel Associations' practice of publishing standard list prices.

Actually, control went further. The associations' merchandising committees set list prices based on cost data supplied by Carborundum and Norton, printed member firms' catalogs, and maintained a file of customer and distributor discounts as reported by the firms. The associations also established standard discounts informally in accordance with Norton's and Carborundum's practice. The use of string discounts and 10-15 percent variances allowed small firms some freedom and meant that prices remained close though not always identical.[59]

Ralph Gow put it flatly: "We were guilty as hell," and Norton counsel W. T. Kneisner thought that fighting the case on a legal basis "would be like leading the lambs to slaughter."[60] The delay in filing the cases until 1947, 1948, and 1949 resulted apparently from the Justice Department's choices. Early enforcement of the Robinson-Patman Act concentrated on the consumer trades that fostered it, and in industrial goods the complex and eye-catching Alcoa case was an early focus. After the war the department began looking more closely at a number of producers goods industries.

With one exception the three abrasives cases were settled quickly by consent decree.[61] Norton's leadership and excellent legal counsel helped overcome fragmented interests, and obvious guilt and fear of criminal penalties prodded the defendants toward resolution. In the precedent-setting bonded abrasives case, Carborundum counsel Bethuel M. Webster unilaterally sought a consent decree within three weeks because (an informed Washington lobbyist thought) Carborundum, like Alcoa, was largely owned by the Mellon family, "toward whom the attitude of the Antitrust Division has long been punitive rather than corrective."[62]

Despite a chaotic and unpromising start, Norton prudence and persistence moderated the damage. Interests fragmented along a number of lines: within firms, among firms, and between firms and the bonded association, which included twenty-six unindicted co-conspirators. At Carborundum Webster's offer of separate list prices, a discount policy based on volume, and changes in association by-laws apparently reflected the owners' rather than the managers preferences. Tony Clark, the company's chief executive, complained that unlike Norton his firm had not undertaken volume-pricing studies, which would require at least a year. Webster had not consulted him, and Clark argued that the chief executives should lead the settlement.

Norton's top people thought Webster's offer hasty and ill considered, but Milton Higgins was soon subjected to similar pressures. He received conflicting advice from his father and George Jeppson, from Prentice L. Coonley, his father-in-law and a Washington lobbyist, and from Norton's Legal Department. The addition of Joseph Welch, outside counsel from the prominent Boston firm of Hale and Dorr, added still another voice.

Welch's appointment signified a turning point. Owners at Norton and apparently at Carborundum prudently decided that lawyers, not executives, were best qualified for the task of strategy making and negotiation in this unknown field. As so often in the past, the association and the smaller firms acceded to Norton and Carborundum leadership. With occasional participation from Webster, Welch led the negotiations and set strategy while he consulted closely with Norton through its counsel. When a preliminary decree was agreed upon, Welch sent copies to other defendants with the pointed comment that "it is Mr. Webster's feeling and mine as well that this decree is quite satisfactory."[63]

A consent decree to an indictment based on civil law pleased both sides. For the defendants it avoided the stigma of a guilty plea and possible punishment from a criminal conviction. For the government it was the most effective means of assuring change from deeply rooted, long-standing practice. As Prentice Coonley explained, "It puts you into a harness."[64] Consent decrees had no time limit, and violations were immediately punishable by contempt of court citations against chief executives, which could include fines and jail sentences.

To avoid future collusion the Justice Department required and the defendants agreed to cease setting uniform list prices, to establish new prices on the basis of cost and quantity, and to abolish the old association and replace it with one that had no pricing functions. Norton fought hard to maintain its old list prices while changing its discount system, but in the clash between economic and legal requirements, the latter clearly won. Someone in the Accounting Department thought that creating a new price list "seems an impossible task," for the old list prices were used to measure order volume, sales, and inventory, to control inventory and production, to determine forecasts and budgets, and to compute incentives and efficiency, along with a variety of other internal functions.[65] Welch was skillful in exploiting splits among the antitrust people to secure Norton seven instead of two years for the change. He thought, and Milton Higgins agreed, that the settlement should make the defendants "not only satisfied but quite happy."[66]

Ironically, the agreement's immediate impact helped strengthen the firm and hence family control and Norton traditions; in the long run, however, the antitrust case contributed to major change at Norton Company. The seven years' grace period allowed it to delay price reform until it could incorporate the results of plant 7 and the new automated process. A three-year study forced a comprehensive overhaul that rationalized price and cost, often to Norton's advantage, and disclosed numerous instances, especially in grain manufacture, where rising costs had all but eroded profit margins.[67]

The old practice of basing discounts on total company purchases had been hurting both Norton and its customers. Stemming from the industry's early days when major customers like the steel, farm implement, and machinery companies were larger and more prestigious than the young, small wheel firms, the policy had little basis in actual costs. As Hicks pointed out to Milton Higgins, the plants of a large customer got the largest discounts, even if individual orders were small, varied, and scattered across several distributors. On the other hand, a single-plant firm in the steel industry, which continuously ordered carloads of standard snagging and cut-off wheels but whose total annual expenditures were small, got the smallest discount. By depending on annual sales rather than individual orders, the technique gave customers no incentives for large orders and forced Norton to carry inventory, maintain warehouses, and provide emergency service.

The new quantity plan rationalized discounts and costs by calculating discounts per item per shipment to a single destination. The new list prices accommodated postwar inflation and the plant 7 process while smoothing old inequities across product lines and special products. Along with plant 7 the plan reflected a steady, ongoing effort to standardize products and reduce inventory costs.

The work easily enabled the firm to maintain supremacy and industry stability. Norton quickly became a power in the newly organized Grinding Wheel Institute and retained its position in the old Abrasive Grain Association. When the new prices were introduced in 1953 after the government lifted Korean War controls, Norton soon reestablished itself as price leader. Market share remained relatively stable through the mid-1950s, annual profits on sales averaged better than 20 percent and total sales reached a high of $168,900,000 in 1957, 75 percent above the 1950 figure and more than double 1945 sales.[68] At first, quick responses to discount increases, zone changes, and other price-cutting efforts by smaller competitors slowed their attempts to buy market share.

In the long run, however, competitors began to pick away with selective price cuts, especially on standard items and during recessions. As the bonded abrasives sales curve flattened in the 1950s, Norton Company found it increasingly hard to maintain premium charges when it no longer regulated prices and when industry maturity decreased differences in product quality among firms.[69] Competition came not from Carborundum, which underwent a succession of managerial difficulties, but from smaller, aggressive companies like Bay State who skimmed or "cherry picked" larger, standard item accounts with selective discounts. Their cuts during the 1958 recession put them 12-15 percent below Norton prices. Sales Manager Robert Cushman wrote that "there is no question but what we have lost some business," for the reductions raised "rather serious price problems."[70] Norton's sluggish response portended serious market erosion.

The antitrust case also shifted power within the organization. Penalties for violation of the consent decree were always a threat, especially to Ralph Gow who worried that he was accountable for the behavior of numerous sales personnel long accustomed to discussing prices. Adequate compliance necessitated the overhaul of Norton's rather anemic Legal Department. The hiring of Fairman Cowan in 1955 added a shrewd and able newcomer. Memoranda and lectures carefully and clearly defined acceptable sales and pricing practices to Norton personnel. Cowan introduced the systematic discard of all nonessential records more than three years old (ironically titled the Record Retention Program) and skillfully handled compliance investigations. There has been no repetition of antitrust prosecution.

At first secretary to and later a member of the Board of Directors, Cowan soon became a powerful voice in the strategic deliberations. Whether the Legal Department's power made the organization more conservative, as one Norton lawyer has suggested, Cowan and the department played a leading role in the decisions to go public and to diversify.

The process of arriving at the bonded abrasives decision, as well as the abrasive grain settlement that closely followed it, very much reflected Norton Company. The firm led negotiations with the government as it had exercised industry leadership almost from its founding. Its calm approach, quiet compliance, and representation by a prominent, conservative Boston law firm typified the New England enterprise. Milton Higgins's ready acceptance of Welch's leadership repeated earlier owner-operators' willingness to surrender responsibility where they could not control.

The primary exception was again in Watervliet, where Behr-Manning executives joined the "otherwise minded" of the coated abrasives industry to fight antitrust proceedings. Behr-Manning, 3M, and Carborundum, the major targets of the suit, readily accepted a government consent decree for domestic operations that terminated exclusive patent pools, cross-licensing contracts, and price maintenance agreements, but they fought unsuccessfully the government's efforts to break up both Durex companies as conspiracies in restraint of trade.[71]

In Boston, U.S. District Court Judge Charles Wyzanski rejected the defendants' claims that the Durex companies were necessary responses to foreign countries' efforts to limit U.S. coated abrasives exports. Joint efforts for export and foreign manufacture by the four makers of 80 percent of domestic coated abrasives restricted the market for others, violating the Sherman Act's first clause. Wyzanski therefore ordered the dissolution of the Durex Corporation and the distribution of its plants among its owners. In the scramble for Durex properties that followed, Carborundum got the Dusseldorf operation, 3M acquired the excellent Birmingham plant and the tape-manufacturing units in South Africa and Brazil, and Behr-Manning took the French converting plant along with the Canadian and Australian factories.

Compromise: The Reorganization of Foreign Operations

The antitrust cases' final impact was to force a major reorganization of Norton's foreign holdings, which brought further shifts in power within the firm and challenged centralized owner-operation. Although 3M and Behr-Manning were preparing to buy out Carborundum's and Armour's interests in Durex before the antitrust case, neither was ready to manufacture abroad. The Behr-Manning name was virtually unknown outside the United States, and Judge Wyzanski decreed that the Durex trade name be abandoned. Furthermore, Behr-Manning had no overseas organization and personnel. Its need to reestablish itself abroad along with excellent opportunities for Norton expansion made consolidation logical. Typically, however, the decision to combine oversight of foreign operations in a new subsidiary, Norton Behr-Manning Overseas (NBMO), grew out of immediate personnel needs rather than system and logic.[72] Following the tradition of autonomy in coated abrasives manufacture, Gow and Higgins originally kept reorganization of the foreign coated business separate from other overseas business. In early 1951 they hired Donald Kelso to head a new organization, Behr-Manning Overseas.

Consolidation came later that year when Gow and Higgins decided to shore up oversight of foreign bonded plants. Bert Stanton, then head of the foreign bonded business, was ailing and nearing retirement. His perspective was European and his concerns were largely financial. Based on his postwar work in expanding Durex, Kelso's view was truly worldwide. He had negotiated for plants in South America and was already interested in the Asian market. He was a manager rather than a financial man, and he brought with him some of Durex's talented people, including Wilfred Place, his top operating man, Jules Schaetzel from the sales company, and Andrew Donaldson, recently involved in establishing an Australian plant.

Under Kelso, NBMO led Norton Company into the second or polycentric phase of multinational operation. Relationships among the foreign plants, between them and distributors in third markets, and between the plants and Worcester and Watervliet grew more complex. The dollar's increased value against European currencies and the spate of currency and trade restrictions that arose after World War II forced Worcester and Watervliet to surrender third-market business in Europe and in the British Commonwealth to more favorably placed plants. The English wheel operation, which began to supply South Africa and many European third markets, soon found itself competing with the French and German plants for the business of Landelius and Bjorklund in Sweden, Kellenberger in Switzerland, and Henri Benedictus in Belgium. South Africa acquired its own manufacturing operations as Norton joined forces with Lindsay Waller and William Campbell-Pitt, the experienced head of its long-time distributor there, C. H. Hirtzel.

Trade restrictions and exploitation of comparative advantages complicated raw material processing and manufacturing as well as marketing. Raw materials were no longer uniform since the European plants had ceased importing bonds from Worcester. The construction of an Alundum furnace at Hull, England, in 1958 and a silicon carbide plant at Lillesand, Norway, in 1965 provided independent grain supplies.

By the 1950s the overseas plants had acquired increased production autonomy as well. The Australian coated plant built its own making machine. The French bonded plant developed plastic bushings and new devices for cut-off wheel manufacture. German truing machines were widely adopted and a new balancing method was perfected jointly by the Italian, French, and German plants. By 1957 Donald Kelso proclaimed that Worcester's and Watervliet's manufacturing specifications were "guides rather than specific orders."[73] His executive vice-president, Wilfred Place, explained that "we believe in manufacturing abroad high quality products comparable to those made by Norton in the United States. This does not necessarily mean identical products because we try to supply foreign markets with goods adapted to their special needs."[74]

Growing complexity was even more obvious in marketing. NBMO now handled the full range of Norton products, including grain, bonded abrasives, coated abrasives, grinding machinery, refractories, pulpstones, floors, and tape. By the 1950s the foreign coated and bonded plants had begun to manufacture other lines as well. The Australian coated plant produced tape; the English plant had a thriving refractories business, especially for water and sewage treatment; and refractory manufacture in France led in the 1960s to a special contract with the French government to equip and help operate a plant for development of nuclear armaments.

To handle the variety of product lines, separate networks of distributors arose. Only Landelius and Bjorklund in Sweden distributed bonded abrasives, coated abrasives, and machinery. In most countries NBMO had several distributors, each handling a different product. (There were five in Switzerland, for example.) Subsidiaries followed Norton guidelines but set their own prices and determined their own merchandising plans. They bought textless American ads to get good color and makeup and supplied their own copy.

The creation of NBMO was the organizational counterpart of the shift in strategy in foreign marketing and manufacture. As noted in chapter 5, control of foreign operations was largely a matter of financial reports and personal visits in Neilson's and Stanton's time. As late as 1941 the staff for overseas operations was four men, and, of course, coated operations fell to Durex, two steps removed from Worcester. NBMO, which represented Norton's first joint enterprise for bonded and coated products, handled all exports, consolidated oversight of all sales and manufacturing operations outside the United States, permitted a clear-cut division of costs, and acted as a buffer between Norton and foreign tax authorities. The subsidiary was also a separate division of management, headquartered in New York City and New Rochelle, New York, and created to help free the overseas business from domination by domestic concerns.

Organized as a holding company, NBMO served as headquarters to monitor and appraise foreign susidiary operations and to coordinate strategy for a management fee and a percentage of foreign sales. Kelso separated its organization into export sales, foreign plant management, and corporate management, and subdivided both exports and plant management into bonded and coated categories.[75] His technical, sales, and financial people were a staff rather than a line operation. They fed continuously to each plant the research and development data produced at Worcester and Watervliet and advised on specific problems.

Eventually, Kelso realigned NBMO to fit Norton's two major products. Executive Vice-President Frank Ryan headed all bonded exports and foreign bonded plants while Vice-President Wilfred Place did the same for coated. Under them Ted Meyer and Eugene Uhler supervised product and technical development for bonded and coated operations respectively. Treasurer John Allison standardized accounting techniques and devised a series of statistical controls and reports to monitor costs, inform forecasts, and appraise performance.

NBMO reflected the increased complexity and autonomy in Norton's foreign operations as it rationalized and coordinated them, but it did not entirely supersede Worcester and Watervliet domination. More intricate market relationships, the maturation of foreign enterprise, and the antitrust decision had forced George Jeppson, Aldus Higgins, Ralph Gow, and Milton Higgins to recognize belatedly the need for more systematic overseas operation. With American roots and headquarters and with American-born leadership, Norton's managers, like their counterparts in many large U.S. firms, continued to view their business as a domestic enterprise with overseas extensions rather than as a multinational company. In addition, the strong traditions of centralized owner-operation and control at Norton deepened that view. Nevertheless, although continuity was as important as innovation during Kelso's tenure and systematic management was two decades away, NBMO's evolution and the ambiguous division of authority and responsibility that accompanied it portended fundamental long-term change.

In very basic ways the relationship of foreign operations to Worcester in the 1950s reflected the past. Change grew out of necessity rather than anticipation. Even Kelso, who had a worldwide marketing strategy, conceded that his policy was neither aggressive nor comprehensive. Expansion occurred on a case-by-case basis and each opportunity was measured on "its individual merits and disadvantages."[76] Kelso had the vision but not the power to implement a systematic, worldwide strategy that included establishing operations in South America, India, and Japan. Authority remained in Worcester carefully guarded by Higgins and Gow, neither of whom was interested in establishing a master plan. In Higgins's view, Norton was essentially an American company whose purpose was "to make dollars" for its stockholders.[77] Gow, like most top Norton people, was little concerned with foreign operations, and those limited concerns were largely European.

A strategy based on American manufacture and export when possible left the forces of overseas expansion to accident, personality, and heritage. While authority remained formally centralized, responsibility became even more dispersed with the entry of NBMO. In Europe powerful veteran managers like Baruzy, Schutte, and D'Importzano continued to run what were virtual fiefdoms. Kelso served as official head and "ambassador at large," and one executive explained that NBMO's functions were "to look after, not manage," the foreign plants.[78] As Kelso put it, "we do not attempt to maintain direct control of each plant's activities . . . nor do we try to mastermind its operations. We give each plant the tools and then demand reasonable results."[79]

The combination of foreign coated with bonded abrasives operations gave the Behr-Manning organization under its aggressive president Elmer Schacht still another share of accountability. The traditional autonomy accorded Watervliet was reflected in the split between coated and bonded abrasives operations within NBMO itself. NBMO built separate plants and maintained largely separate distributors for coated operations. Only slowly in the late 1950s and early 1960s were coated and bonded operations combined in South Africa, Italy, and Mexico.

The fragmentation of power and responsibility for international operations among plant managers, Kelso and his NBMO staff, Schacht and the Watervliet organization, the Worcester staff, and top management followed Norton tradition, and throughout the 1950s it became increasingly clear in foreign sales, product development, and plant location and expansion. NBMO's U.S. sales offices were divided. Oversight of bonded abrasives plants was handled from Worcester where the shadow of Ralph Johnson and the domestic sales organization influenced market allocation. Export sales originated in New York City, and coated abrasives sales were centered in New Rochelle.[80]

Furthermore, the tradition of autonomous foreign plant managers inhibited cooperation. When Louis Camarra took charge of NBMO bonded marketing in 1959 and began meeting regularly with foreign sales managers, they were astonished.[81] Previously, most discussion had taken place between Kelso and the plant managers to whom they reported.

In addition, although autonomy for pricing, production, and promotion gave each European factory maximum flexibility for its national market, such freedom produced chaos in European third-market areas. After Worcester's withdrawal from those markets because of trade and currency restrictions, the confusion was highlighted in the late 1950s when Donald Kelso visited an important European distributor and asked why none of its key people was available to greet him as was customary. An aide explained that they were entertaining four Norton European plant managers, who were vying against one another with competing discount offers to win the distributor's business. The incident compelled Kelso to appoint Camarra for more rational coordination.

Confusion was just as bad in product development. Although the overseas plants could buy their own raw materials and mix their own bonds, product development was controlled by Worcester and Watervliet for the U.S. market. Neither domestic division understood the need for new products to meet rising European competition from small native firms specializing in resin-bonded sandpaper and wheels. In one case the desperate French at Conflans secretly bootlegged the development of their own "S" paper, a resin-bonded coated abrasive, to battle SIA, a growing Swiss manufacturer.

Gene Uhler and Ted Meyer tried to funnel information and techniques to the European plants and rotated European technicians to Watervliet and Worcester for training, but ignorance and intransigence limited their efforts. Long traditions of secrecy inhibited the sharing of new techniques with foreign plants run by nationals, and sections of the Watervliet plant were closed to Uhler. Furthermore, the lengthy history of American product and process superiority made domestic manufacturers insensitive to European developments in equipment and products. Norton insisted on selling Worcester- and Watervliet-built machinery to equip foreign plants and overlooked cheaper European equipment of equal or better quality. In coated abrasives the clash between Uhler and the Watervliet people was a long, stubborn battle. In bonded abrasives Meyer thought Worcester research and development people had "too much to say about it for their own good" until he persuaded Research Director Wallace Howe to tour European plants and learn their problems firsthand.[82]

The fragmentation was clearest, however, in the case of plant location and expansion. Until NBMO Treasurer John Allison began instituting systematic capital controls in the late 1950s, European plant managers sought approval of major capital projects in conversations during Gow's and Higgins's visits. Responsibility for plant location nominally fell to Kelso, but in fact decision making directly involved Schacht, Gow, and Higgins, while old George Jeppson and Norton financial managers exerted some veto power. By heritage and experience Norton's top people were oriented toward Europe. Suspicion of South American and Asian nations whose cultures varied sharply with their own reinforced the owner-operators' conservatism and antipathy toward locations where currencies and governments fluctuated. Treasurer William Perks and George Jeppson were especially skeptical about Asian markets and fought Kelso's efforts for plants in India and Japan.[83] As Behr-Manning's president, Elmer Schacht battled Kelso to establish the location of new foreign coated abrasives plants. And in Worcester, Gow and Higgins made all binding decisions as part of their centralized top authority.

The upshot was piecemeal expansion based on opportunity and personal predilection. Norton Company established a South African wheel plant in 1950 because trade restrictions finally reinforced distributor Campbell-Pitt's pleas for local manufacture. Schacht negotiated the Belfast, Ireland, location of Behr-Manning's British coated plant as a by-product of another deal. The French location of Behr-Manning's major continental coated operation ignored the more industrialized German market and reflected at least in part traditional Norton francophilia, the strength of Baruzy's wheel operation, and the wishes of Wilfred Place and a strong French contingent in NBMO.

In still another area, although Kelso's arguments about the fast-growing markets in Latin America eventually overcame suspicions in Worcester, the process of expansion reflected old Norton traditions rather than systematic strategy. Despite their antipathy toward shared ownership, Norton executives entered into joint operations in Argentina and Brazil. Although their plants had limited technical value, the Meyer brothers in Brazil and a small native partnership in Argentina offered local brand names and knowledge of market conditions. In both cases Norton carefully assured itself of majority ownership, and as in the past it eventually bought out its minority partners in Argentina and Brazil as well as in South Africa and Italy.

Prudence and caution remained Norton characteristics. Extensive borrowing in the host nation and partnership helped reduce investment risk. The acquisitions were generally small—each costing a few hundred thousand dollars—and Higgins, Gow, George Jeppson, and Perks watched returns closely to see when Norton would "get the bait back."[84]

The fragmented, seat-of-the-pants approach allowed Norton Company to move into the polycentric stage of multinationalism and establish an international division while preserving traditions and values. Risks were small and carefully hedged, the informal approach left ultimate authority in the hands of Higgins and Gow, and the concentration of operating authority in plant managers kept staff small. As noted before, top executive staff in 1962 was no larger than in 1941.

Financial performance is more difficult to assess. Certainly the new plants in Argentina, Brazil, South Africa, and Mexico helped assure

Norton's presence in fast-growing markets. Along with European recovery, they expanded foreign sales to 33 percent of Norton's total by 1961 after depression and war had reduced international bonded revenues to 10 percent of Worcester's total sales in 1950. Profit data are fragmentary and less impressive. Although NBMO returned less than 1 percent on net sales between 1952 and 1954, accounting techniques probably understated foreign profits, for they ignored management and research fees ranging from 5 to 10 percent of sales and income from grain and equipment sales.[85]

In light of Milton Higgins's determination to make dollars, Norton's continued foreign expansion doubtless signified some profit. Even during the poor performances of the early 1950s, NBMO figured (probably optimistically) that its coated share ranged from 35 to 38 percent and its bonded share was 39 to 43 percent of the noncommunist market outside the United States. Furthermore, as was typical of Norton's conservative approach, foreign profits were usually determined not by the accountant's measure of return on total investment, but on dollars produced against actual Norton outlays. Profits on sales and on scanty Norton cash investment looked quite good.

Nevertheless, problems had begun to appear by the late 1950s that signified the need for fundamental change and a more systematic approach to foreign management. The slapdash approach to acquisitions burned Norton Company on at least one occasion. When Elmer Schacht accidentally met Florencio Casale in Worcester, he struck what he thought was an excellent deal to acquire a silicon carbide plant in Mendoza, Argentina, to supply Behr-Manning's South American coated abrasives operations.[86] Norton would acquire 60 percent of the plant in exchange for know-how and $100,000 cash. Kelso, normally Schacht's rival, quickly examined the project and supported it as a cheap aid to Latin American expansion. Both men agreed on the need for haste, and together they persuaded Gow and Higgins, who had despaired of any arrangement after earlier talks with Casale.

The two top executives then pushed through the Board of Directors' ex post facto approval, but everyone soon began to regret the "bargain." Casale's capital shortage forced Norton to supply $225,000 and guarantee a $146,000 loan. More critical was the failure to ensure an adequate power supply, a major cost in silicon carbide production. Power costs more than doubled, promised tariff protection disappeared when a friendly government fell, and the Argentine market proved too small to absorb plant output. The ignominious venture (losses on loans alone were $197,000) ended with the sale of Norton interests to Casale.

Difficulties were also beginning to appear in Europe where Norton's position was threatened with long-term erosion because high profits on sales were obtained at the expense of market share.[87] The growth of aggressive local competitors further eroded that position, and the establishment of the European Common Market, or EEC, portended their expansion beyond national boundaries. Furthermore, as described in chapter 7, the opportunities offered by the EEC required more careful planning and coordination of production and sales in Norton's European plants than NBMO's autonomy policy offered.

The advent of EEC, Norton's expansion into Africa and South America, and its imminent entry into Asia made foreign management a much more complex problem. Planning and implementing proper strategy required a more careful matching of authority and responsibility, which in turn necessitated delegation of power from the president and executive vice-president. The rivalry between Schacht and Kelso and the jealousy and conflict between Worcester and NBMO were symptoms of the organizational strain. In addition, the expanded size of NBMO and the eventual decentralization of authority required more careful and systematic attention to managerial recruitment and training to ensure management in depth all along the line.

Going Public: The Limits to Private Control

By the late 1950s the needs of the large enterprise extended beyond NBMO to the entire organization. The slower growth of the firm and the abrasives industry, along with the size and scope of Norton's activities, rapidly raised the cost of private ownership and owner-operation. Preservation had necessitated awkward compromises, increasingly generated internal difficulties, and restricted opportunities. Resolution of its problems forced Norton into four major changes between 1960 and 1980. It became a publicly held company listed on the New York Stock Exchange and regulated by the Securities and Exchange Commission, it diversified into new industries including safety products and petroleum and mining tools, it replaced owner-operation with professional management at the top, and it decentralized authority and responsibility.

The challenges were fundamental and interrelated. The varied nature of the firm's businesses—coated abrasives, bonded abrasives, abrasive grain, grinding machinery, industrial and consumer tape, and refractories—in worldwide markets exceeded the capability of any small, tightly centralized management. Piecemeal separation of authority and responsibility since the 1930s had coped with the difficulty. But by the early 1960s increased competition at home and abroad, especially in the mature machinery, coated, and bonded industries that provided the bulk of Norton's income, demanded more concerted action.

Decentralization of authority and responsibility was the logical and popular response of the period. Following the pioneer efforts of Du Pont, General Motors, Standard Oil of New Jersey, and others, large American industrial firms were rapidly creating autonomous product divisions.[88] The head of each division could then concentrate knowledge and attention on a major business. Norton created product divisions in the late 1950s, but Higgins, Gow, and Treasurer Bill Perks balked at real decentralization, which threatened their traditional tight control.

Furthermore, the prospect of decentralization along with Norton's growth created management problems. With a very limited supply of talented, trained owner-operators, Norton Company increasingly relied on professional salaried managers at all levels, including Ralph Gow as president after 1961. Owner-control, private ownership with limited stock opportunities for management, and Norton's conservative, stodgy position were hardly enticing to top prospects from colleges and business schools in the 1950s, although Norton did recruit some of today's top managers in that period. *Fortune* described "a horse-and-buggy atmosphere" at Norton. Estabrook and Company, stockbrokers, argued that Norton was "not a particularly well-known name" and was "associated with such cyclical industries as steel and machine tools."[89]

Growth was as important to prospective managers as to investors, and diversification was the logical strategy. It offered opportunities and challenges to managers, fitted easily into a decentralized structure with product divisions, and promised to spread risks and alleviate the slow expansion of the sluggish, cyclical abrasives industry. But top executives saw scant opportunity for internal development of new businesses based on their technology and expertise. Norton had little to offer. Machine tools were just the kind of mature, cyclical business the company wished to escape, and refractories markets seemed small. Growth by acquisition was limited to small cash deals unless Norton could offer publicly held stock.

Going public seemed to solve a lot of problems. Stock in a publicly held company listed on the New York Stock Exchange traded easily and, if properly managed, at multiples of a firm's actual book value. Such public securities were a ready and often cheap currency for acquisitions. In a systematic bonus and option plan they were also attractive incentives for professional managers and promised future expansion and opportunity.

Although going public, diversification, decentralization, and professional management at Norton were intertwined, the changes were typically little planned and not carefully concerted. The piecemeal approach to problem solving that had characterized owner-operation from the outset continued to shape decisions and the decision-making process. Gow, Higgins, John Jeppson, and other top people certainly anticipated that the first departure, turning Norton into a public company, would have important long-range consequences for family control and the direction and operation of the business. What they could not foresee was the rapidity and fundamental nature of the shift. By 1980 the traditions that had long characterized the firm and made it so unusual among large American industrial enterprises—secrecy, tight private ownership, financial independence, and owner-operation—were gone.

Although the impetus to take Norton public did not originate with the owners, this first, radical step came relatively quickly. The opportunities were most apparent to outsiders, professional managers and top officers like Ralph Gow, Fairman Cowan, and Richard Nichols, the first outside member of the Board of Directors. Milton Higgins was perfectly content to continue running Norton Company as it was. The aging George Jeppson and Clarence Daniels enjoyed sitting on the board of the private company they had known so long. John Jeppson, despite his increased respect for professional management and a budding interest in diversification, remained comfortable with private ownership.[90]

The remaining shareholders did not push for change. Descendants of Allen, Higgins, Daniels, and Alden were perfectly content to enjoy their lucrative dividends. Cash flow was far more important than return on investment and careful scrutiny of management. Employees were only temporary holders of 13 percent of the stock and had no voice. Ralph Gow explained that "there were relatively few people, even among the stockholders, who knew the actual earnings . . . Each one of the original families knew the earnings, but there seemed no need that the descendants should have access to all the details of the company as long as profits continued to increase and the figures were properly audited. It would only have been a disclosure of privacy to many people in the community and the industry."[91] Norton paternalism and privatism endured to the end.

The change's relative speed resulted in part from its obvious need and its promoters' positions, but the pace depended fundamentally on persuading Milton Higgins. As chief executive and a veteran operating man, his advice quickly swung the other owners into line. By 1962 Milton faced a formidable array of advocates, the most prominent and important of whom was Ralph Gow.

Gow had spent thirty-five years at Norton and had been Milton Higgins's partner in running the business for nearly fifteen years. In his reorganization of the administration he had encouraged the creation of product divisions in 1956 and delegated a number of lesser financial and administrative decisions to division heads and plant managers. Rationalization of structure and decentralization were less important to him, however, than the recruitment of good managers, and he was much disturbed by the difficulty in getting talented young men from graduate business schools.[92]

The importance of diversification bothered Gow most, but not Norton's need for additional businesses. His New England conscience worried about shareholders whose very considerable wealth and income remained concentrated in one security that had no market.[93] In the previous generation the problem had been less pressing. The firm's value was smaller and its owners were either operators or close kin. By the late 1950s, however, founder stock was dispersed among 151 trusts and individuals, some of whom were fourth generation and far removed from the business. If pressed, they could only sell back to Norton at a book value that far understated their securities' real worth. Simple prudence suggested diversification of holdings to reduce holders' risk and increase their flexibility.

Gow found a ready ally in Fairman Cowan, corporation counsel and the first top officer who had not come through the ranks. Cowan thought the levels of secrecy and informality were "unbelievable" when he arrived. "The stockholders were never given anything except a copy of something called a Certificate of Condition. It was filed in the State House in Boston and the annual meeting was a nice social occasion where Bill Perks got up and showed some charts which really didn't reveal anything." The radical change of going public, he told *Fortune* magazine, was "like walking down the street with no clothes on."[94]

Cowan shared Gow's concern for stockholders with securities locked up in an enterprise about which they were abysmally ignorant. In addition, although much of the founder stock was deposited in family trusts, estate problems loomed. Major holders from the second generation, including Mary Norton Allen, John Woodman Higgins, Olive Higgins Prouty, George Jeppson, and Clarence and Harold Daniels, were in their 70s and 80s. In the absence of suitable market tests, their securities would be valued for taxation by the U.S. Internal Revenue Service, which could not be expected to accept the book values on which all previous transactions had been based.[95]

Employee stock created a second and more pressing problem. Its wide dispersal among as many as five hundred owners required registration with the Securities and Exchange Commission. Previous exemption by private offer had been premised on sale to top officers who well understood the business. Norton's unsystematic distribution scattered stock throughout the company, and by the 1950s holders included foremen, secretaries, retirees, and their wives and children. Since Norton Company had to register the stock and sacrifice secrecy, Cowan argued that the firm might just as well go public.[96]

To help resolve the problems, he persuaded Gow and Higgins to add to the board an experienced outside director. Richard Nichols, a partner in Cowan's old Boston firm, Goodwin, Procter and Hoar, admirably suited. Nichols, who was as much a promoter as a lawyer, had sat on nearly fifty boards, encouraged and overseen mergers, and participated in initial public offerings by several old, private New England firms including the Houghton Mifflin, Dennison Manufacturing, and Foxboro companies. Nichols felt strongly that Norton had to go public to anticipate its future needs. It needed to diversify by acquisition and that required "market cognizance, confidence and distribution" of Norton stock.[97] He quickly teamed with John Jeppson to urge a program of diversification and acquisition predicated on Norton's listing on the New York Stock Exchange.

Nichols's outspoken independence as an outsider and his vast experience much impressed Milton Higgins. Though not especially enthusiastic about diversification, the thrifty New Englander was intrigued by the ability of firms like 3M to acquire companies cheaply with their highly valued stock.[98] More significant for him was the legal need for registration of employee stock, which would put Norton in the over-the-counter market anyway. At the same time, the popular acceptance of Behr-Manning Holding Corporation stock (which held Norton securities as its sole asset) in local, private sales bred optimism for Norton's prospects.

Milton persuaded the major holders with Nichols's arguments. Given the necessity of registration (which occurred in August 1962), listing on the New York Stock Exchange followed logically. The crucial challenge was meeting the exchange's dispersal rules for listing, which required that Norton have 1,500 holders and 500,000 shares on the market.[99] At Nichols's suggestion Behr-Manning Holding was terminated and its Norton stock distributed among the Behr-Manning owners. The remaining quota would be met by a secondary offering of 10 percent of the major holders' securities in the fall of 1962.

The relatively smooth process broke, however, on the rock of Norton values and reputation, and ironically, the collapse accelerated fundamental change in the company. The underwriters, Paine, Webber and Goldman, Sachs, insisted on a conservative valuation. They offered to guarantee the founders' securities at $28 a share and place them on the market at $32 a share, arguing that the firm's stodgy image and its highly cyclical businesses would depress the market.

The proud and thrifty Norton owners refused to sell for less than $32. Most were unwillingly parting with a portion of their heritage only because Milton advised it, and they were not about to sell cheaply.[100] When the secondary offering failed to materialize in late 1962, Norton's managers were in a quandary. They could not turn back; registration and over-the-counter trading were accomplished facts. Meeting New York Stock Exchange standards for listing would soon turn the company toward merger and diversification.

In the face of increased competition at home and abroad, government regulation, international expansion, and more complex production and marketing arrangements, Norton Company's third generation had struggled to preserve its inheritance. Like their predecessors, Milton Higgins, John Jeppson, and Ralph Gow had sought solutions in the abrasives industry and within long-standing Norton traditions. Owner-operation maintained centralized control through a lean line organization. Firmly committed to Norton's reliance on abrasives, Higgins and Gow worked hard to continue its primacy through product and process innovation and price leadership. Tight financial controls and cautious investment protected cash reserves and independence, while paternalism encouraged employee stability, loyalty, and productivity.

But growth and complexity in large-scale enterprise were self-reinforcing and produced challenges that eventually ended the New England family firm. Attempts to retain it led to patchwork solutions and exposed serious limitations. Milton Higgins's appointment as president extended owner-management but necessitated Ralph Gow and an increased reliance on nonowners at the top. International expansion and plant 7 helped assure industry leadership but required scientific management, bureaucracy, and delegation of power for coordination and efficient operation. Concentration on a single industry and centralized administration eased owner-control, but stagnation in the abrasives business encouraged diversification, while Norton's increased size promoted autonomy and fragmented authority and responsibility. Premium pricing helped swell revenues and continue self-funding, but it also eroded market share in an increasingly competitive industry.

Finally, private, carefully controlled issues of Norton stock provided incentives and preserved paternalism but also confronted the firm with increased government regulation. Complying with those regulations forced exposure of the private company in the over-the-counter market, which in turn encouraged more public exposure on the New York Stock Exchange and even more radical change.

7.

"Buying the Unknown with Confidence": Diversification and the Time of Troubles

THE 1960s WERE A PROSPEROUS TIME for the national economy. The celebrated "go-go sixties" saw steady economic growth, full employment, and a booming stock market fueled by a wave of conglomerate mergers. For a while Norton seemed to share in the heady atmosphere. Its conversion to a public company catapulted the New England abrasives firm into an image-conscious enterprise looking to exchange abundant cash for diverse and more exciting products.

Success was fleeting, however, for at Norton, unlike most large American industrial enterprises, the 1960s brought upheaval, uncertainty, and declining returns on sales and investment. Diversification, decentralization, and shifting markets rapidly exposed the centralized family firm's inability to cope with change. Diversification and fundamental reorganization were major challenges for large, single-industry American industrial firms.[1] After World War I when Du Pont moved from explosives into other chemical products, it was beset by confusion and losses. At the same time near-bankruptcy at General Motors pushed out its entrepreneur-operator and encouraged the transformation of what had been a holding company into a rationalized operating organization. Norton Company's problems, though not so extreme, often reflected other firms' experiences.

At Norton, going public stripped away its privacy, deliberate approach, and virtual independence. It accentuated the worst and negated the best of Norton business traditions and values. Stock market pressures for image and performance were especially great in the 1960s when companies expected to boost stock prices well above book value, thus gaining leverage or cheap currency for acquisition and expansion. Jimmy Ling, Royal Little, and other financial entrepreneurs set the pace with their ability to build large conglomerate en-

262

terprises by acquiring essentially unrelated businesses and then inflating their stock for still other mergers.[2]

Norton's diversification to match 3M's and Carborundum's stock multiples and product array rapidly moved the firm into high-technology and consumer products. Its typically ad hoc, piecemeal approach produced disappointing results. Norton Company had neither the experience nor the expertise for direct management of its new lines, and the centralized abrasives company's inability to monitor and guide decentralized operation proved disastrous when combined with acquisitions that were variously hasty, ill-managed, and poorly organized.

Serious problems in established lines exacerbated difficulties and further stretched managerial resources. By the 1960s growth in the mature grinding machine, coated abrasives, and grinding wheel markets scarcely kept pace with the economy. Overcapacity sharpened price competition in the United States, while in Europe companies with new products, better processes, and lower costs aggressively fought Norton in Britain and the Common Market. Profits and market share eroded seriously as the firm reluctantly recognized the problem and struggled slowly to adjust its traditional strategy of premium pricing and costly service to new conditions. After three generations of owner-management, price leadership in a stable industry, financial independence, and other entrenched traditions, the decade-long search for order amid rapid change was as painful as it was unexpected.

Desultory Diversification and Decentralization

Prior to its 1963 merger with the National Research Corporation, Norton had little useful experience with diversification and decentralization. As we have seen, Norton Company's management of businesses other than bonded abrasives was as informal as the rest of its approach. Proximity and heritage shaped control. The Behr-Manning acquisition of the 1930s filled out Norton's product line but did not generate significant moves into unrelated industries. Furthermore, while Behr-Manning autonomy presaged the decentralization of authority so popular in the 1950s and 1960s, Worcester provided no systematic oversight and controls to monitor its coated operation. Until the 1960s Watervliet's profitability and determined independence discouraged close regulation. Top Worcester executives who sat on Behr-Manning's board provided very little operating oversight but assured formal Worcester approval of major capital requests, a pattern common to many highly centralized firms.

Because refractory and grinding machine production were situated in Worcester and grew historically from the founders' days, they were under closer control. In the Machine Division a mixture of close investment scrutiny and otherwise undirected operation continued throughout Everett Hicks's tenure in the 1950s and 1960s.[3] Although Hicks made several small acquisitions—including an encapsulating firm and a gear-hobbing machine manufacturer—and encouraged the internal development of centerless grinding machinery in the late 1950s, none of the projects significantly diversified production or expanded sales. By the 1960s management was largely a caretaker operation to maintain existing modest profit levels and the possibility of sale.

Refractory manufacture was always a stepchild of abrasives operations.[4] Marketing people reported to the vice-president for bonded sales, and Norton maintained production largely to supply its own needs. Higgins and Gow made some modest efforts to encourage further development. Norton built a new plant in Worcester for more rationalized manufacture and freed prices from restrictions imposed by the Abrasives Division's purchases.

In the mid- and late 1950s, refractories became the center for a stillborn program of diversification by internal development. Ralph Gow explained in 1955 that "while we believe . . . that unlimited diversification is unwise, we are anxious to expand into new products where they fit in with either our marketing or manufacturing facilities."[5] Refractories research built on Norton's expertise with high temperatures, aluminum oxide, and silicon carbide to add a number of new products, including "hot rod" heating elements, fused stabilized zirconia that withstood 4,500° F. temperatures, aluminum oxide catalyst carriers, and "Rokide," a line of pure oxide refractory coatings.

New products and an expanded market stimulated sales. The advent of jet engines, the emerging electronic industry's need for coatings in capacitors and insulators, and application of higher temperatures in atomic power plants, electric-fired steel furnaces, and improved steam turbines quintupled industrial demand between 1940 and 1953. Norton's 1947 sales had doubled by 1951, and 1954 output was ten times the 1941 level. Yet, despite its growth, refractory manufacture was only about 5 percent of Norton's business. Profit margins were small, research and development continued to concentrate on abrasives, and Carborundum maintained its lead over Norton in the refractories industry.

Structural reorganization occurred separately from any efforts to develop nonabrasives businesses. In 1956 Gow and Higgins, at John Jeppson's urging, announced that Norton would follow a popular trend in American industry and shift from functional departments to five product divisions: abrasives, refractories, coated abrasives, grinding machines, and electrochemicals (the grain plants and Chippawa research).[6] NBMO was also treated as a division though on a geographical rather than a product basis. Each division had its own production, sales, and engineering staffs and an operating board composed of younger, middle-level executives who met regularly with the division manager to discuss appropriations, forecasts, prices, schedules, and inventory policy.

Ostensibly, the change was to decentralize authority from the president and executive vice-president to autonomous division heads. Each manager ran a separate business, and the company announced that "each will be more self-sufficient and responsible for results."[7] The operating boards offered young executives general experience for future promotions. Higgins and Gow gradually surrendered some of the decisions made by them or the Board of Directors, including pricing, salaries, and appropriations. In 1956 the board approved all appropriations over $1,000; in 1963 it considered only items over $100,000. To monitor operations, the controller's office developed techniques for annual division sales forecasts, budgets, financial plans, and profit and loss accounting.

Despite the fanfare, product divisions changed very little and merely ratified existing practice. NBMO, Behr-Manning, bonded abrasives, and the machine department had acted as separate businesses for years. When Norton's subsequent controller, John Dingle, joined the firm in 1947, he found a "holding company atmosphere" where operating heads of the foreign, coated, and machinery departments sent in dividends, retained earnings by rule of thumb and negotiated with Gow and Higgins for formal approval of major capital projects.[8] After 1956, division financial reports recorded sales and income but provided no asset accounting and capital budgeting. There was still little management of assets, nor were the operating boards new. Kelso, Schacht, and Hicks had already initiated the practice in the early 1950s.

Finally, autonomy was as uneven as before. Behr-Manning and the foreign operations continued to go their own ways, but in Worcester the division of authority and responsibility was unclear. John Jeppson served as both vice-president of the Abrasive Division and director of manufacturing to offer functional guidance to the general managers. Jeppson and Robert Cushman, his successor, found that their division's controller and purchaser reported to the Financial Department instead of the vice-president for abrasives. They did not see their own balance sheets or control their own inventories, and they obtained cost data with great difficulty.[9] As Ralph Gow put it, "Still, Milton and I held the strings."[10]

As a result Norton did not really achieve the modern decentralized structure before diversification in the mid-1960s. Worcester operations remained tightly controlled by Higgins and Gow. The corporate staff, except for financial functions, remained quite small, lacking the techniques and mechanisms to monitor, appraise, and coordinate the separate divisions. Coated abrasives, for example, installed a computer incompatible with bonded abrasives' system and launched an expensive, unsuccessful venture into consumer tape production after a largely financial review from Higgins, Gow, and their staff.

Nor did the creation of product divisions signify more serious efforts at diversification. The refractory sales curve remained flat in the 1960s, plagued by "increasing volumes of relatively low profit items."[11] The Electrochemicals Division was terminated for lack of product development, and its operations were absorbed by the Abrasive Division as resources continued to funnel into abrasives research.[12] Work on fusion cast refractories and other sidelines languished while George Jeppson ordered top laboratory people to concentrate on a crash program to develop a new abrasive grain.

Furthermore, diversification by acquisition failed to replace the faltering internal development program before 1963. Norton Company had a staff man scout potential candidates in the late 1950s and early 1960s, but lack of public securities for mergers deterred deals. More important, as Ralph Gow recalled, "We really weren't interested in acquisitions."[13] Milton Higgins was even more emphatic: "I wish one could make progress without growing . . . but I don't know how you do it."[14]

The National Research Merger: Means and Ends

Diversification came only as a by-product of going public, after failure to agree on a secondary offering increased the pressure to put the company on the New York Stock Exchange (NYSE) by another means. Even Milton Higgins thought that over-the-counter sales offered the costs but not the benefits of public scrutiny.[15] Merger with another firm provided an alternate route to the dispersal of stock required by the NYSE, and when the ever-active Richard Nichols found what he thought was a good match for Norton, the momentum became nearly irresistible.

The National Research Corporation (NRC) of Cambridge, Massachusetts, had been founded in 1940 by Richard Morse, a flamboyant entrepreneur (who coined the chapter title), and by William Appleton

Coolidge, wealthy descendant of a long-prominent New England textile family.[16] At first Morse developed new businesses in exotic high-technology fields and spun them off to more established firms. NRC products included frozen orange juice concentrate, blood plasma preparation, vacuum lens coating for binoculars and periscopes, and thin film metalizing for television tubes.

Because the erratic development business meant wildly fluctuating earnings and cash flow, Coolidge and Nichols, who had been associated with NRC since the 1940s, replaced Morse with Hugh Ferguson and encouraged NRC to develop stable lines from its work in electronics and its contract research for the U.S. space program. Long experience in vacuum research led to a vacuum equipment division that produced complex, sophisticated instruments to create and measure vacuums used in laboratories and in the manufacture of transistors, tubes, capacitors, semiconductors, and jet engine parts. The coating of wire and tubes generated a tantalum powder business for heat- and acid-resistant coatings and shapes in solid electrolyte capacitors, heat exchangers, and condensers for the electronics, chemical, nuclear, and aerospace industries as well as for research laboratories. Just developing in 1962 was the manufacture of superconducting niobium-zirconium and niobium-tin wire (Supercon) to carry high currents with no resistance at low temperatures for coils and magnets used in research laboratories at the National Aeronautics and Space Administration, the Atomic Energy Commission, and elsewhere. Finally, the firm maintained a contract research division, occupied mostly with aerospace and other federal government assignments. Sales in 1962 were over $12.5 million.

With Richard Nichols's smooth promotion, what *Fortune* called "as unlikely a [match] as Norton could have found" appeared quite attractive.[17] There was no hesitation at NRC since a stock exchange offered shareholders listing on the big board and gave NRC managers and researchers access to Norton cash for developing Supercon and other new ventures.[18] Ferguson would receive 8,200 Norton shares, stock options, and a position, along with Coolidge, on Norton's Board of Directors.

At Norton, the merger provided Gow, Cowan, Nichols, and other advocates of going public a quick, cheap means to achieve NYSE listing. Stock exchange with NRC's 2,350 holders would disperse an additional 361,000 shares, and the exchange rate, based on over-the-counter values, would dilute Norton earnings only 2 percent.[19] For major holders like the Alden trust, the combination promised both liquidity and new growth.

Glamour and diversification attracted even more attention and reinforced the argument for merger; otherwise, the secondary offering could have been renewed in a stronger market. Staid Norton would not only be public, it would be in the center of the space race and the development of exciting high-technology products. For John Jeppson and other young managers who felt that "the world had been passing us by," NRC meant "research capability for turning out new products" after the disappointing results of internal development.[20]

Newer Norton leaders from the outside eagerly rationalized the prospective marriage. Fairman Cowan recalled that it was generally thought that the fit of "their brains and our money" seemed perfect.[21] Nichols, who sat on both boards, was confident the match was excellent. Hugh Ferguson and James Gardner, his projected successor, would manage an autonomous division that complemented Norton's metal industry market and supplemented it with sales in the electrical, aerospace, chemicals, and plastics industries. The younger firm's dependence on government-sponsored research and markets opened new vistas to the older company whose government business accounted for less than 2 percent of sales. Revenues from contract research and Norton's excellent cash flow were to fund NRC exploratory work under Research Director Robert Stauffer to put Norton into "interesting areas" for the future.[22]

To Richard Nichols and other promoters the merger promised additional opportunity for external as well as internal growth. Following the pioneering efforts of Du Pont, General Electric, and others in the 1920s and 1930s, large American industrial firms began diversifying extensively after World War II. To tap steadily growing markets in the 1950s, most successful companies expanded by internal development of related product and process technologies. The process was open, however, only to the limited number of enterprises big enough to support their own research and development departments and familiar with a technology that had wide application. Chemical, petroleum, and electrical machinery companies were well suited, but small businesses and large enterprises such as railroads, shipping lines, textile, and tobacco companies that concentrated on a single or narrow product line with little potential transfer of technology were excluded from such rapid internal growth.

Attracted by the bull market of the 1960s and a booming economy stimulated by the 1964 tax cut and the Vietnam War, the latter group turned to growth by acquisition. Since antitrust law forbade the purchase of competitors, latecomers like Textron, Ling-Temco-Vought, and Litton Industries pioneered conglomerate mergers of companies in unrelated fields. The acquisitions were largely financial and often predicated on the availability of some company undervalued by the stock market rather than on any strategic product or market fit.[23] Startling profits from the securities transactions promoted widespread imitation, fueling the surging stock market of the 1960s. One market observer aptly titled the period the "go-go years," meaning "free, fast, and lively, and certainly in some cases attended by joy, merriment, and hubbub."[24]

Nichols hoped to push Norton Company squarely into the booming conglomerate movement. Painstaking internal development in such stodgy fields as machinery and refractories would do little for the market value of Norton stock, and in any event the firm had long ago forfeited its opportunities in those areas. Since Norton's staid image and prosaic products left the stock market unexcited, the financial promoter hoped to marry the company's healthy cash reserves and the revenues from its mature lines to more alluring firms whose promise of rapid growth would inflate stock values. The acquisition of NRC meant eye-catching products to glamorize Norton securities for an investing public already excited by the Kennedy space program and the rise and performance of electronics firms. Accelerating demand for Norton stock would increase its price/earnings (P/E) ratio and thereby cheapen the cost of future acquisitions. Furthermore, in the growth and merger minded market of the 1960s, the promise of additional expansion added glitter to a stock.

Nichols, Gow, Cowan, and Jeppson worked hard on a reluctant Milton Higgins, who finally had what Nichols called a "conversion" experience. The thrifty New Englander thought the purchase price too high but admitted that NRC "had some glamour to it."[25] Its research people, experience, and vacuum equipment business were strong selling points. When the company's stock values dropped in the late fall of 1962 so that the exchange ratio was $\frac{5}{8}$ Norton share to one NRC share, Higgins approved the deal and the merger was completed in May 1963. Norton's initial listing on the NYSE at $40\frac{3}{8}$ for stock previously valued as 32 by the underwriters was instant gratification.

The rapid transition from private abrasives company to public diversified enterprise in less than a year was a major watershed. The change dragged Norton Company into new businesses and a new world where the experience and values of the old New England firm seemed to have little application. Robert Stauffer recalled that the staid, cautious approach soon gave way to "wild enthusiasm . . . Everybody was caught up!"[26]

In short order Stauffer's research people in Cambridge spewed out a variety of wondrous new products. Norton moved into consumer goods and began marketing "space blankets" from fabric developed for space suits by NRC. The acquisition of the Houston-based Supercon Company quickly elevated the superconductor business to full division status equal to vacuum equipment and metalized products. The laboratory also produced "Flubber," properly called energy-absorbing resin or EAR and named after the Walt Disney movie that jokingly conjured up a similar product. The soft, rubberlike material absorbed energy, which suggested applications in vibration and shock-absorbing fields. Electroluminescent diodes of silicon carbide provided sound tracks for cameras and promised home movies with sound.

NRC contributed directly to older Norton businesses as well. John Hansen helped Norton people get government agency contacts and contracts, especially for the molded boron carbide shapes that soon became a million-dollar body armor program during the Vietnam War. Milton Higgins conceded reluctantly: "I may be old fashioned . . . but I like to be independent of the government. However, I suppose when you're doing research you can get money from the government and get some benefit too."[27]

NRC also helped reorganize Norton's research operations. Robert Stauffer began a major rationalization and integration of all laboratory work to eliminate the isolation, secrecy, and bootleg development that had variously characterized the foreign plants' relationship to Worcester and Watervliet. Building on work begun earlier by Meyer and Uhler, Stauffer arranged for regular exchange of research reports and visits by overseas technical people to Worcester and inaugurated annual meetings of key laboratory people from Canada, Europe, and the United States.

Besides putting Norton into new businesses and adding vim to research and development, the merger exposed owners and managers to unaccustomed public scrutiny. Gow, Higgins, and Jeppson were called upon to soothe security analysts with honeyed words about Norton products and prospects. For the first time *Fortune* magazine devoted a major article to Norton Company, which it described as a money maker, "a technical innovator, an aggressive competitor" with "a horse-and-buggy atmosphere."[28] Although attendance at annual meetings grew very little, the company was embarrassed when an astonished Lester Smith of the *Wall Street Journal* complained that the press was not allowed to ask questions.[29] Outside directors such as Nichols, Coolidge, Raymond Corey of the Harvard Business School, and Jerome Ottmar from Textron, a darling of the conglomerate movement, began to weaken the owners' hitherto undisputed control of directors' meetings. Most startling of all, the NYSE briefly suspended trading in Norton stock when a poorly worded press release seriously overstating success with the silicon carbide diode stimulated wild rumors and boosted Norton stock 13 points in one day. Although they had acted in good faith, Norton officials had also naively released the news during trading hours without informing the exchange.[30]

As an additional change, a company that looked to one of its salesmen "more like an institution than a thriving, driving business" and whose products and services had generally spoken for themselves with simple advertising in esoteric trade journals now became self-conscious about its image.[31] A corporate identity program began in late 1962, and in the following fall Norton adopted the parallelogram logo still in use. Harry Seifert, Norton's new director of advertising and sales promotion, began the slow, arduous task of convincing Behr-Manning, NRC, and other divisions to include their Norton affiliation and the logo in trade advertising.

Diversification and Disillusionment

By the mid-1960s change began to perpetuate itself. The need to go public had generated diversification as a by-product, and outside scrutiny of the public company and the popular interest in new NRC products encouraged further diversification. In fact the chain was circular. Growth was necessary to protect and expand stockholder equity and maintain high P/E ratios, especially since the conglomerate mania, the limits of Norton's technology, and the stock market's demand for rapid expansion pointed to acquisition rather than internal development. But favorable acquisitions (growth) in turn depended on P/E ratios. One consultant advised Norton that it was necessary to diversify in order to maintain the opportunity to diversify: "The risk in this delay [to acquire a new firm] is loss of opportunity. The present favorable public image and market evaluation may deteriorate and substantially increase the problem of diversification."[32]

At Norton the major pressure for further acquisition, diversification, and change came from promoter Richard Nichols and (to a lesser extent) from the firm's outside directors and Fairman Cowan, its first top officer recruited from the outside. Conversely, the need to satisfy external constituencies—analysts, stockholders, and directors—weakened the owner-managers' hold.

The change was not complete and instantaneous, however, for the habits of three generations died slowly. Although Norton made two additional significant acquisitions in 1964 and 1966, the selection of candidates and the process of merger followed previous patterns. Both were ad hoc responses to particular opportunities rather than the outgrowth of a systematic search. Even though they involved some exchanges of stock, Norton cash was a crucial factor in both mergers; and although both additions moved Norton into new markets and products, there was at least some matching of technology.

The 1964 acquisition of Clipper Company of Kansas City, Missouri, not only had Milton Higgins's consent; he was a leading promoter as well.[33] Neligh Coates founded Clipper as a basement operation in 1937 to manufacture and sell by mail masonry saws and blades to cut brick, tile, and concrete block. As business grew he added the Eveready Bricksaw Company to sell the same line through dealers. In response to increased highway and airport construction he chartered Pavement Specialists Inc. in 1957 as a contract operation for concrete cutting, slicing pavement joints, core drilling, and sealing. In the early 1960s he expanded his line with the Air Placement Equipment Company, which produced concrete pumps, conveyors, placing equipment, tie rod guns, and other machinery for concrete construction. By 1964 he employed nearly six hundred people, maintained branch offices in Australia, Belgium, and Holland as well as in the United States, and had total sales approaching $12 million.

Because Coates needed funds to establish his overseas offices, expand his equipment line, and complete a huge plant at Grandview, Missouri, to house his entire manufacturing operation, he approached Norton in 1964 for a merger. Despite the impressive array of products, more than half his sales were blades—silicon carbide and diamond grinding wheels purchased from Norton and sold under the Clipper name. Coates purchased up to $2 million in wheels annually and was Norton's largest wheel account. His threat to sell out to Bay State, Norton's most aggressive competitor, could not be ignored. Even though financial analysis suggested there would be little additional profit in Norton's sale of wheels, Milton Higgins felt merger was necessary to protect the volume alone. In early 1964 Norton bought all Coates's companies for $8.5 million and left him in charge of what soon became an autonomous construction products division.

While the Clipper acquisition moved Norton into the construction industry, the 1966 merger with the U.S. Stoneware Company (USS) of Akron, Ohio, put the Worcester firm into more exotic and eye-catching fields—chemical process products and plastics—though Stoneware, like Norton, had originated in the ceramics industry.[34] Frank Knapp founded the business in 1859 to produce crocks, jugs, and other stoneware. In an 1888 reorganization J. M. Wills replaced the ailing Knapp as superintendent and, like Norton, USS soon became a family operation as first Wills's son-in-law, John Chamberlain, and then John's son, James Chamberlain, headed the firm. When metal cans and glass bottles replaced stoneware, the Ohio company moved into chemical stoneware—containers for mixing, handling, and storing acids and other volatile, corrosive chemicals—in 1907. When World War I disrupted trade with the German chemical industry, USS expanded its ceramics container line to include nitrating vessels for explosives manufacture, filters, acid eggs, towers, and acid elevators.

The renewal of postwar competition and the slump of 1921 forced Stoneware to search for additional products. When Howard Farkas arrived in 1922 to head ceramics sales in New York, his contacts with eastern chemical companies moved USS into tower packings and distillation trays, devices to speed chemical reactions by increasing the flow, expanding the surface for reaction, and reducing the volume drop. The original tower packings were simply stones placed in the container housing the reaction. Subsequently, Rashig rings, Pall rings, and other packings were specifically designed for the chemical industry. In the 1920s they were ceramic bodies, although steel and plastic rings appeared later. U.S. Stoneware had entered the field in the 1920s and 1930s, but its dominance (it held about two thirds of the tower packings market in 1965) dated from 1950 when designer Max Leva licensed USS to produce the Intalox Saddle, a vastly improved design.

Stoneware moved outside its ceramics lines after James Chamberlain took over the firm in the late 1930s. An entrepreneur and an engineer with U.S. Rubber for several years, Chamberlain dragged Stoneware into numerous ventures provoked by his curiosity and talents. Excess capacity during the 1930s depression led him to manufacture rubber tank linings. When rubber linings proved inadequate, he drew on research experience at Goodyear and substituted polyvinyl chloride (PVC). Subsequently, Chamberlain successfully extruded PVC to produce plastic tubing. The tubing, which Chamberlain brandnamed Tygon, soon became Stoneware's other major line. A tough, flexible product, the inert and easily sanitized tubing was ideal for food processing, milking machines, blood transfusions, and other medical fluid transfer operations. By 1965 Chamberlain had nearly two thirds of the premium plastic tubing market where the emphasis on quality and sanitation provided high profit margins.

In addition, the impetuous, intuitive Chamberlain, whom an associate called "a junior Howard Hughes," tried a variety of other lines, though none so successfully as Tygon.[35] By the mid-1960s the entrepreneurial organization included fifteen plants and at least ten different companies scattered across Ohio and Tennessee. Organized around U.S. Stoneware and the Chamberlain Engineering Company, in both of which Chamberlain owned two thirds and Farkas one third, Chamberlain's miniempire manufactured products from ceramics, plastics, rubber, and stone, including vinyl tile and paints, vinyl shoe soles, tombstones, hula hoops, quarry tile, rubber gaskets, bathroom and kitchen fixtures, rubber crutch pads, and airplane radomes. In 1965 before-tax profits were $3.8 million on total sales of $16.4 million.[36]

As in the National Research and Clipper cases, Norton's purchase was not part of a general strategy of expansion. Farkas's age, Chamberlain's ill health, their strained relationship, and the lack of kin to carry on the business made both men willing sellers. After a sale to Electric Bond and Share collapsed because of USS's chaotic legal structure, Robert Hunter, Chamberlain's able second in command and the real administrator of the business, partially rationalized the corporate organization. A college classmate praised the opportunity to Ralph Gow, and, following lengthy negotiation, Norton purchased the operation for $10 million cash and 135,000 shares. Gow recalled that the opportunity was "plain luck. We deserved no credit for it whatsoever. But it turned out to be great."[37]

USS was the last and most successful of Norton's important mergers in the 1960s. Ironically, after John Jeppson, a major proponent of diversification, became president and chief executive officer in 1967, he was unable to make even a single major acquisition. Although disappointing performance and the economy's downturn did not stem the conglomerate merger movement until 1969, piecemeal acquisition and poor management within NRC and Clipper forced the day of reckoning much earlier at Norton.

When Jeppson and his executive vice-president, Robert Cushman, took office, Norton Company's crucial need was rationalization and divestment, not expansion. The evidence of diversification's failure was clear and would grow even stronger during Jeppson's four-year tenure. Between 1963 and 1967 abrasives had declined from three quarters to just under three fifths of Norton's total sales, and the company had added a variety of catchy product lines including plastic tubing, contract space research, vacuum equipment, superconductors, space blankets, rare metal coating, vacuum cleaners, and concrete construction equipment.[38]

But the financial strategy failed. As table 3 indicates, return on assets, which had averaged over 7 percent between 1961 and 1966, fell to 4.5 percent for the next six years. Norton stock ranged between the mid-30s and mid-40s, dropping occasionally into the 20s. Its P/E ratio lolled in a rather mediocre (for the 1960s) 10-15 range and remained lower than Carborundum's ratio. After all the trouble of the NRC merger and the NYSE listing, Norton cash was still crucial to acquisitions. More than $18 million was needed for the Clipper and

Table 3. Norton Financial Data, 1940–1982.

Year	Consolidated Net Sales ($ millions)	Net Income ($ millions)	Consolidated Assets ($ millions)	Return on Assets (%)
1940	37.6			
1941	69.0			
1942	100.9			
1943	131.3			
1944	102.7			
1945	77.0			
1946	60.2			
1947	73.8			
1948	81.5			
1949	71.7			
1950	95.2			
1951	140.8			
1952	143.9			
1953	156.5			
1954	131.0			
1955	152.8			
1956	165.2			
1957	168.9	14.7		
1958	146.0	9.1		
1959	171.2	11.1		
1960	176.6	12.0		
1961	178.6	10.9	180.7	6.0
1962	200.8	14.2	191.8	7.4
1963	216.0	14.1	208.2	6.8
1964	250.6	18.2	219.8	8.3
1965	272.7	18.4	234.5	7.8
1966	310.4	18.8	276.3	6.8
1967	305.0	12.1	272.1	4.4
1968	324.0	17.0	284.2	6.0
1969	353.1	16.1	292.6	5.5
1970	359.3	11.3	321.9	3.5
1971	346.6	11.4	325.5	3.5
1972	374.4	14.5	332.4	4.4
1973	475.4	21.3	368.7	5.8
1974	558.3	25.1	428.9	5.9
1975	548.3	20.9	447.9	4.7
1976	629.9	27.5	483.3	5.7

Table 3. (Continued)

Year	Consolidated Net Sales ($ millions)	Net Income ($ millions)	Consolidated Assets ($ millions)	Return on Assets (%)
1977	847.9	41.3	615.7	6.7
1978	959.9	62.0	707.8	8.8
1979	1,132.9	80.2	811.5	9.9
1980	1,281.8	86.7	953.4	9.1
1981	1,334.6	95.0	1,019.0	9.3
1982	1,264.1	19.3	1,007.9	1.9

Sources: Assistant Controller Guy Williams to the author, December 29, 1982 (for 1940–1957); Norton Company, *Annual Reports*, 1962–1982 (for 1958–1982).

Note: Figures for 1940–1945 do not include the Italian, French, and German plants; German figures are also missing for 1946–1950. Fragmentary data suggest that missing sales were usually less that 10 percent of total reported company sales. Data on net income and consolidated assets were not available between 1919 and the time Norton went public.

Stoneware mergers.[39] In 1966–67 and again in 1969–70, the normally cash-rich firm scrambled for loans to assure adequate working capital.

Behind the failure lay poor performance. None of the diversified lines contributed 10 percent of sales, and by 1971 90 percent of the profit from diversified products came from Tygon tubing alone.[40] Serious problems plagued all three acquisitions in the late 1960s. USS faced a major price battle that wiped out profit margins. Koch Engineering entered the tower packings field after the expiration of the Intalox Saddle patent. Furthermore, Abbott Laboratories, the biggest customer for Tygon tubing that accounted for nearly 25 percent of tubing sales, decided to manufacture its own products.[41]

The situation was worse at Clipper and NRC. The tantalum powder market shriveled when the biggest buyer, Sprague Company, licensed capacitor production to Union Carbide, which already produced its own tantalum. Inventory fluctuations resulted in further large losses. Contract research dried up, the diode never became practical for home movies, space blanket sales remained tiny, and the vacuum equipment line faced rapid obsolescence. NRC businesses consumed cash and produced little profit almost from the outset. In 1963 after-tax profits were only $43,000 on $11 million sales. Net profits on sales remained less than 10 percent through 1965, jumped briefly in 1966 and 1967 because of tantalum inventory fluctuations, and then nosedived again for the next three years.[42]

At Clipper a 1966 investigation of the Grandview plant disclosed utter chaos, "the result of many compounding factors accumulated over a period of years."[43] Sloppy accounting, poor product design, an inadequate sales force, and weak quality control forced Allan Hardy, Norton's new group vice-president for machinery and electronics, to conclude in early 1967 that Clipper was in "serious trouble" with "shrinking profits and skyrocketing inventories."[44] After a $178,000 loss in 1966, the division returned 0.7 percent on sales and 1 percent on net assets in 1967.

Business Week's "seasoned observer," who labeled Norton's diversified lines of 1971 "a big portfolio of junk," was only partially correct.[45] Products such as vacuum equipment, space blankets, and metalized coatings, which were "junk" in Norton's hands, generated profits when spun off to others in the 1970s. Part of the problem lay with the original firms. Although National Research, Stoneware, and Clipper had turned profits prior to their mergers with Norton, all were poorly organized, cash-starved, entrepreneurial operations. Each had diversified into several fields, simply adding plants, corporations, and sales organizations for new products. NRC had plants in Palo Alto, California, Columbus, Ohio, and Newton, Massachusetts, in addition to its Cambridge facilities. USS had fifteen separate plants, while Clipper had consolidated chaotic manufacturing operations into its gigantic, elaborate white elephant in Grandview.

Rapid expansion under original management prior to and just after Norton acquisition burdened the firm with costly development problems for lines with uncertain futures. At NRC Stauffer never found a successful application for EAR (which ironically was best suited for ear plugs), and the electroluminescent diode could not be adapted for home movie cameras. Efforts to launch the Supercon Division with Niostan, a niobium-tin wire, were superseded by technical developments at RCA, forcing a write-off of the entire project in 1964.[46] Clipper's new line of concrete pumping equipment proved a disastrous failure. Poor design, patent infringement, obsolescence, and duplication necessitated elimination or consolidation of thirty-one of thirty-six products.[47] Clipper's Billy Goat vacuum cleaner, designed to clean up construction sites, was unable to suck up concrete particles, and the firm's concrete pumps were too weak. Finally, sales volume failed to justify Clipper's new overseas sales offices.

Management was weak at both Clipper and NRC. Hugh Ferguson had only mediocre results before falling ill, and by then the talented James Gardner, his projected successor, had left the company. Neither Neligh Coates, who was in his 60s, nor his organization was equal to Clipper's rapid expansion.

Only at USS was the problem avoided. Robert Hunter, who became Chamberlain's chief operating man by 1965, and Ralph Gross, who left his advertising agency to head USS sales, provided the Ohio firm with a crack team. Not only had the bluff, shrewd Hunter already begun rationalizing Stoneware's operations before its sale to Norton Company; his tenacious negotiating wrung from Norton more concessions and funds than either Farkas or Chamberlain expected. With Hunter heading an autonomous division, the USS acquisition became and remains a mainstay among Norton's diversified products.

The Hunter case was atypical, however, and points out the real problem with the 1960s acquisitions. Recognizing the need for and supplying adequate management were Worcester's responsibility. Norton variously paid too much for what it bought, picked the wrong companies, and left inadequate people in control. And although some of the difficulties were inherent in the process of diversifying any single-industry company, Norton's heritage as a tightly centralized, owner-operated abrasives firm and the timing of diversification were at the heart of its troubles.

The emphasis on growth as an end in itself and the popularity of conglomerate mergers caused problems for many companies in the 1960s.[48] Pure conglomerates like Ling-Temco-Vought ultimately discovered that mere size did not expand earnings sufficiently to meet increased financial and other overhead charges. Without coordination of marketing, research, and production resources to reduce costs and increase output, simple expansion offered largely temporary financial advantages that ended with the stock market downturn after 1969.

Norton was never a true conglomerate. In the midst of the 1960s diversification it remained a dominant-industry firm, with abrasives always accounting for at least 60 percent of sales. But it suffered from inadequate coordination and cost reduction similar to the conglomerates. The firm had always performed best either in domestic bonded abrasives, which fitted the owners' expertise and interest, or in coated abrasives and foreign operations under strong, able managers.

As the experience with grinding machines after 1920 indicated, the owner-operators had little success in weakly run areas outside their interests. Neither Gow nor Higgins sought diversification for the businesses themselves. Gow and John Jeppson ardently supported the NRC merger, and a reluctant Higgins acceded, as a means of going public, and in their haste to get on the NYSE, all three ignored warnings from Wallace Howe, Allan Hardy, and other investigators. Although Higgins urged the Clipper acquisition because of its impact on bonded abrasives, neither he nor Gow was enthusiastic about USS.

Diversification: early successes.
Tower packings.

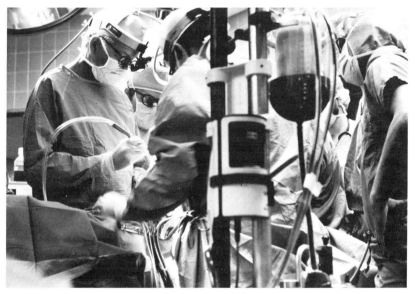

Tygon tubing on a heart-lung machine.

Even though he remained as president until 1967, Gow later felt that after taking Norton public he had made his major contribution. "We handled that [NRC investigation] very, very poorly . . . We didn't know how to go about it and we took Dick Nichols' word for it." Higgins agreed that "we were babes in the woods . . . We didn't know enough about that racket."[49]

But even though Gow and Higgins were little interested, their assent to acquisitions was sufficient in the centralized company. In a firm that had generally operated by consensus, there was little opposition. Nichols, Ottmar, Jeppson, Coolidge, and Cowan were vocal supporters of diversification. Those directors who ran operating divisions often had more immediate concerns. Everett Hicks, director and head of machine tool operations, recalled that he voted for the NRC merger "because I saw no reason not to."[50]

Norton's heritage and structure left little to fall back on in the absence of real interest and close scrutiny by top executives. The technique of granting autonomy to presumably able managers, beginning in Watervliet and the overseas plants in the 1930s and extending to NRC, Clipper, and USS in the 1960s, was certainly sound business practice. But Norton, like many centralized firms, had insufficient means to appraise that management. As a long-time, single-industry firm with a strong line organization, the company lacked an elaborate staff capable of guiding, coordinating, and appraising a variety of businesses. Research, sales, and marketing people in Worcester were trained for the abrasives business and were in fact largely a divisional rather than a general staff.

Finance, always Norton's strongest functional department, covered only a limited range. Since its founding, the owner-managed enterprise had always been more concerned with actual revenue than with more abstract return on investment. Nonmanaging stockholders were largely interested in the steady income Norton supplied. Managing stockholders like George Jeppson, Charles Allen, Aldus Higgins, and Milton Higgins had always measured efficiency in terms of operating costs, like the nineteenth-century railroads. Return on sales had long been a useful index; return on investment was less important in a company with ready cash and no serious investment alternatives to abrasives before 1960. Major capital projects like the World War I expansion, plant 7, and plant 8 occurred only sporadically, and John Dingle and the controllers' staff developed divisional capital budgeting controls only in the 1960s.[51]

As a result there was no authority independent of the divisions themselves to monitor performance in its broadest sense, including return on investment, technical capability, market share, and development of management in depth along the line, as well as operating efficiency. Norton could not, for example, spot Neligh Coates's inability to move from simple concrete saws to more complex concrete pumping and construction equipment.

In addition, selection and encouragement of some poorly fitting businesses aggravated Norton's managerial limitations. As we have seen, the poor fit partially resulted from inexperience and competing goals, but a significant portion of the problem reflected the newly public firm amid the promotional, go-go spirit of the 1960s. At first Norton encouraged Neligh Coates to continue his ill-fated expansion as part of the eye-catching, think-big spirit of diversification.[52] Clipper was to be a construction business, not just a concrete equipment business.

National Research proved the clearest example of lack of planning. Richard Nichols may have overstated NRC's case, but he did not sell Norton an utter failure. One small, typical example was the space blanket, a profitable item but a consumer product for which Norton had no experience and no complementary lines. Limited volume forced the firm to sell its single item through manufacturers' representatives with low profits and little future for the resources expended.

NRC's flashy lines represented a scale of risk and return radically different from Norton's steady abrasives business. Except for industrial diamonds (which the De Beers syndicate regulated), Norton had no experience with high-cost raw materials. Tantalum supplies were expensive, and careful hedging with futures contracts was necessary to protect against frequent fluctuations. During recessions, the proper strategy was to buy at low prices, but Norton's abrasives experience had always encouraged it to shrink raw materials inventories in hard times. New, sophisticated products like vacuum chambers and superconducting wire were often monopsonistic, that is, they depended on a few large customers. Rapid technological change, licensing, or merger could quickly decimate a market, as in the Niostan wire case.[53]

The poor fit between Norton's tradition of cautious risk aversion and its new divisions was clearest in new product development. As a result of its discomfort with its existing acquisitions, Norton refused to acquire the Wa Chang Corporation, which might have stabilized and filled out both the rare metals and the Supercon lines, and James Gardner quit in disgust. Top Norton executives had difficulty appraising the ebullient Stauffer's promises regarding NRC. Early enthusiasm from John Jeppson, Nichols, and others for the diode, EAR, and other hopeful developments soon soured as costs rose faster than success. Research Director Newman Thibault, a forty-year Norton

Diversification: early failures.
NRC space blanket.

veteran, thought the projects were simply "too risky [and] too long range for Norton."[54] The disenchantment was mutual. Stauffer eventually left for greener pastures after owner-management ended in 1971, and Norton sold the Cambridge operation for exploratory development and turned to directed research in the 1970s.

Abrasives Operations: Stagnation and Challenge

Diversification was not Norton's sole problem in the 1960s; important changes in the bonded, coated, and grain industries exposed limitations even more serious for the company's long-term well-being. Steady maturation was the most significant challenge. Technological change slowed in both the bonded and grain businesses. Although the application of diamond grinding and the use of resinoid bonds continued to expand through the 1950s and into the 1960s, the introduction of 32 Alundum in 1946 had been the last great breakthrough.

Maturation was most clear in industry sales growth.[55] As figure 6

Clipper "Billy Goat" vacuum cleaner.

indicates, bonded sales nearly doubled in real terms during World War II and the first postwar decade. But without major technological innovation and new applications, annual growth rates began declining as the switch to plastics and cost-cutting techniques, such as closer forging in the metal-working industry, restricted the market for grinding. Between 1957 and 1964 the list sales curve for the bonded abrasives industry (excluding diamond products) remained flat, while physical volume actually declined. (Figure 6 includes diamond products and therefore shows an erratic increase.) Limited growth in the next five years did not match the Federal Reserve Board's products index for durable manufactures. Within the industry the shift to resinoid wheels for steel conditioning retarded demand for vitrified wheels, traditionally Norton's strongest product. The story in abrasive grain was similar. William Fallon, head of Norton's Abrasive Materials Division, reported "substantial over-capacity, low growth, and low return on heavy capital equipment."[56]

Industry structure remained fairly constant. The biggest potential change—3M's attempt to acquire Carborundum in 1951—was averted

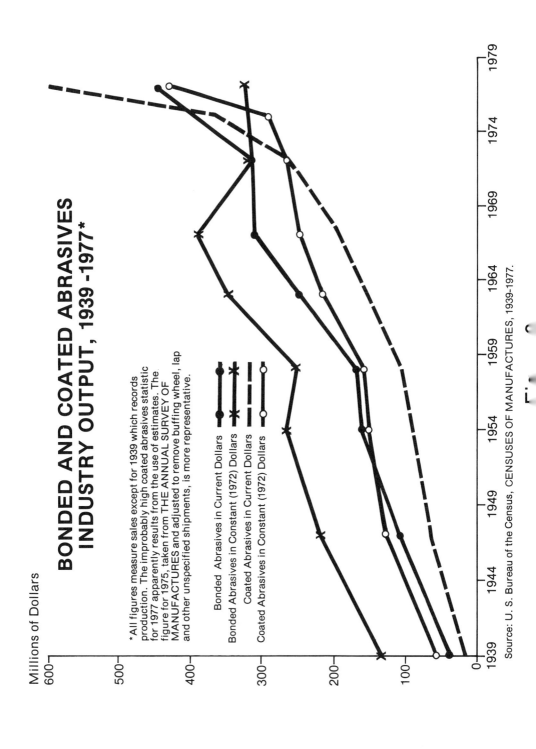

BONDED AND COATED ABRASIVES
INDUSTRY OUTPUT, 1939 -1977*

Millions of Dollars

600

500

400

300

200

100

0

1939   1944   1949   1954   1959   1964   1969   1974   1979

* All figures measure sales except for 1939 which records production. The improbably high coated abrasives statistic for 1977 apparently results from the use of estimates. The figure for 1975, taken from THE ANNUAL SURVEY OF MANUFACTURES and adjusted to remove buffing wheel, lap and other unspecified shipments, is more representative.

Bonded Abrasives in Current Dollars
Bonded Abrasives in Constant (1972) Dollars
Coated Abrasives in Current Dollars
Coated Abrasives in Constant (1972) Dollars

Source: U. S. Bureau of the Census, CENSUSES OF MANUFACTURES, 1939-1977.

by the passage of the Kefauver-Cellar Act to strengthen the Sherman Antitrust law. The failed acquisition was 3M's last big push in coated abrasives; growth rates in other fields such as recording tape diverted its interests elsewhere. Carborundum performed indifferently in the 1950s while undergoing several reorganizations. Recovery in the 1960s under William Wendel depended heavily on diversification.[57]

Oligopoly continued. In 1960 Norton, Carborundum, and the next two largest grinding wheel manufacturers controlled 62 percent of the $197 million market.[58] The major change resulted from the expansion of aggressive smaller firms in an increasingly competitive market. With growth through market expansion closed off, the little companies increased price cutting and skimming or "cherry picking" high-volume, standard items. Bay State, the most successful of the also-rans, had reached third place in the industry. In 1967 it captured a guaranteed 30 percent of Chrysler's business in exchange for an across-the-board maximum discount and negotiated seriously for a similar deal with Ford.[59] Furthermore, low entry costs for resinoid production (which did not use the expensive kilns required in vitrification), encouraged many new entrants, swelling the number of wheel manufacturers to more than one hundred in the 1960s.

Norton was no longer impervious to the little guys. By 1966 their competition helped push the grinding wheel price level 8 percent below the recession level of 1958.[60] At the same time the smaller companies had acquired powerful financial support as a result of the conglomerate merger movement. Federal Mogul acquired National Abrasives, Bendix took over Macklin, and even Bay State became part first of AVCO and then of Dresser Industries. By 1967 Carborundum and Norton were the only independents among the bonded abrasives industry's ten largest firms.[61]

The impact of maturity on Norton Company was considerable and serious, although the perception of it was slowed by complacency and a complex pattern of slow, irregular erosion. Slower technological change narrowed the differences in quality between traditionally superior and premium priced Norton products and competitors' cheaper output. Norton aggravated the problem in the 1950s by creating and maintaining a price umbrella. Following a policy that manufacturing people thought "ridiculous," but which aptly reflected the company's lengthy heritage of price maintenance and premium pricing, Norton did not lower prices to take advantage of cost savings from continuous process production.[62]

As the number of competitors and their manufacturing efficiency increased, the firm gradually lost first its cost advantages and then market share, especially after the 1958 recession sharpened competition. In the mid-1950s Norton accounted for about 33 percent of all sales reported to the Grinding Wheel Institute; by 1965 its share was 28.6 percent.[63] In what had become almost a $300 million market, the nearly 5 points surrendered represented $15 million lost business. In fact the problem was worse. The growth of small firms independent of the association during that period meant increased underreporting of industry sales.[64]

The impact on return on investment was even greater. Skimming robbed Norton Company of its most profitable standard-item, high-volume accounts. Norton's extensive burden of fixed costs reduced flexibility in slumps like the 1958 recession, and the company had magnified that burden by poorly timed increases to capacity based on rapid postwar recovery. In the late 1940s and 1950s Norton had built grain plants at Huntsville, Alabama, and Cap de la Madeleine, Quebec, and huge plant 8 at Worcester for continuous process manufacturing of resinoid wheels.

In the same period the firm became increasingly dependent on Vice-President of Sales Ralph Johnson's network of powerful industrial distributors that accounted for 70 percent of total domestic bonded volume.[65] In the hodgepodge practices that accompanied quantity pricing and the antitrust decree, the distributors captured a number of large-volume accounts that the company could have profitably serviced, and Norton continued to sell directly smaller accounts that should have gone to distributors. Norton traditions of service and high inventory levels also meant additional fixed costs that were especially burdensome in recessions. When sales fell 15 percent in 1958, profits fell 44 percent, a pattern repeated in downturns in the 1960s and early 1970s.[66]

The company's response was confused, sluggish, and inadequate. The tradition of price maintenance that helped create the problem in the 1950s militated against aggressive price cutting in the early 1960s. Harry Duane, chief accountant in the Refractories Division in 1962, expressed the organization's philosophy most clearly: "1. We should not pursue a policy of under-cutting competitive prices. 2. Pricing should be the last Sales management tool to be used to influence a market—after product quality, extended utilization, service, delivery, engineering, salesmanship, advertising, etc."[67]

Furthermore, the job-shop nature of wheel production, the haphazard dispersal of accounts between Norton and its powerful distributors, and the apparently random skimming of competitors left unclear the connection between price and market share and just which, if any, prices should be cut. Inflation and slow industry growth did expand the company's abrasives revenues; in 1968 they were up 56 percent from 1960.[68] Continued high profit margins and the emphasis on return on sales obscured the seriousness of the market share slide.

Finally, Norton's gut response, as always, was to look to production, not sales. In 1958, old George Jeppson called in his top researchers and ordered a major emergency effort to develop a new abrasive grain. The project eventually led to zirconia-alumina abrasive, the greatest breakthrough since World War II, but lengthy research and development delayed its impact until the 1970s. At the same time, Norton, along with other abrasives and grinding machine manufacturers, supported "abrasive machining," an extensive research and promotional program begun in 1961 to better understand, improve, and promote grinding. Stronger bonds, greater pressures, and higher speeds only moderately expanded grinding's metal removal market at the expense of lathes, milling machines, and other metal cutters.[69]

Similar problems—slow growth, overcapacity, competitive price cutting, and declining profit margins—plagued the international abrasives business as well, especially in the mature European markets. The English bonded operation, which had always held an also-ran position, deteriorated badly in the 1950s and 1960s as indifferent management struggled to counteract the collapse of Alfred Herbert, its major distributor.[70] In Germany there was a similar decline. Norton's German company never recovered fully from World War II, and the "yes-men" who surrounded Otto Schutte could not cope in the most competitive bonded market in Europe.[71] Even in France, where Pierre Baruzy had led the strongest Norton team abroad, market share dipped from 40 percent to 30 percent.

European coated operations grew profitably in the 1950s. Then local competition, encouraged in part by World War II and in part by the breakup of Durex, began offering improved new products and lower prices on high-volume items to capture larger chunks of the slowly growing market. In the words of Harry Duane, one-time manager of the Italian plant and later head of all Norton overseas operations, the company was "a sleeping giant," too confident of its "technological mystique."[72] It responded complacently and sluggishly as Rappold, Tyrolit, and other local firms in bonded abrasives, along with VSA, Hermes, and SIA in coated abrasives, analyzed, duplicated, and improved Norton products and successfully pursued special, profitable market segments.

Norton's heritage of autonomous, informal management of overseas operations, combined with its heavy reliance on return on sales, continued to obscure its problems, fragment authority, and slow its response. In addition, market shifts, nationalism, and the increasing importance of overseas sales and power in the organization complicated that response.

Market changes involved both size and location. Markets with potential for major growth were no longer European, as in the pre–World War II era. By the 1950s and 1960s Latin American and southeast Asian economies underwent rapid industrial development. The expansion of steel, metal working, and automobile manufacture there quickly inflated abrasives demand, which conflicted with Norton's European-oriented heritage. While Donald Kelso's urging pushed Norton into Latin America, indifference or opposition from George Jeppson, Milton Higgins, Ralph Gow, and Treasurer William Perks delayed entry into India and Japan until 1967, in part to preserve a policy of Norton majority ownership.[73]

At the same time, accelerated world trade after World War II encouraged and was encouraged by the reduction of trade barriers. These included the Latin American Free Trade Association, the European Free Trade Association (EFTA), and the European Economic Community (EEC) or Common Market. For Norton, the EEC was the most significant challenge, involving the Italian, French, and German operations as well as major third markets in Belgium, Holland, and Switzerland. Rapidly expanding and successful local competitors like Hermes of Germany soon began challenging Norton all across Europe. To compete with the smaller aggressive firms, Norton had to turn its heavy fixed costs from a liability to an asset, which meant careful segmentation of markets and production among its various plants along regional rather than national lines.[74]

Coordination of operation, however, not only challenged the holding company approach that Kelso had so successfully practiced; it also conflicted sharply with strong traditions of national autonomy. Long-time managers like Schutte, Baruzy, and D'Imporzano had proudly run their own fiefdoms. Asking nationals to surrender authority was difficult enough; the rise of a French clique under Belgian Wilfred Place in Norton International Incorporated (NII), successor to NBMO, to coordinate Italian, German, and British producers as well as Swiss, Scandinavian, Belgian, Dutch, and other third-market distributors complicated an already serious problem.

The French imbalance was as natural as it was accidental. The French coated and bonded operations were by far the strongest in Europe, and Wilfred Place had risen to become Kelso's second in command and projected successor by 1960. In 1963 Place established a Parisian organization to head European operations, which included Elio Bennamias for finance, Georges Bykhovetz for coated manufacture, Réné Didier for bonded manufacture, and Marcel Teissedre for marketing. The retirement of Schutte and Baruzy removed two long-time barons, but the opposition to coordination remained strong. French bonded people resented submission to an organization composed largely of coated abrasives people. Proud Angelo D'Imporzano, Italian head for more than fifteen years, battled Place bitterly before resigning.[75]

Centralization and coordination of international business moved fitfully and indifferently through the mid-1960s. Despite growth and profits in the South African, Brazilian, and Australian operations and the increase of foreign sales from 33 percent in 1961 to 43 percent of all sales in 1970, Europe remained a problem.[76] Troubles extended beyond the allocation of research and development resources to predominantly U.S. needs, the European orientation of Worcester's outlook, and the inertia of the "sleeping giant" to confusion about the international division's place in the business. Worcester jealously clung to authority as Norton increasingly became a world enterprise. The appointment of William Fallon, a Worcester man and former head of the South African plant, instead of Wilfred Place, as president of NII left leadership in Worcester. It also fragmented authority between Place and the Paris organization and the Worcester-based Fallon, aided by a team including Louis Camarra in sales, Harry Duane in finance, and Stan Berman in manufacturing.[77] To Georges Bykhovetz, it was the "era of technocrats" as conflicting systems and red tape grew in a three-way struggle for authority among Worcester, Paris, and the plant managers.[78]

Coated Abrasives: Decay and Decline

As troublesome as were developments in domestic bonded and international abrasives operations, domestic coated manufacture suffered a much greater collapse. As figure 5 in chapter 4 indicates, annual coated sales growth in current dollars slowed from 19.6 percent for the 1945–1955 period to 5.1 percent in 1963–1973. In constant dollars sales actually declined slightly between 1955 and 1973. Profit margins dwindled badly so that what had been a major cash source in the 1950s returned 7-9 percent on sales annually between 1960 and 1965 and 4-6 percent between 1966 and 1971. Market share plummeted from 32 percent in 1960 to 24 percent in 1969.[79]

Behr-Manning, like Norton, found itself in a stagnating market by 1960. The decline came later and more sharply than in bonded abrasives because of the buoying effect of the belt business in the 1950s. As figure 6 shows, annual industry growth rates decreased, but stagnation hardly accounts for Behr-Manning's far worse fall.[80] The 3M Company, which shared leadership with Behr-Manning in the 1950s, actually expanded its portion as Behr-Manning surrendered its hold.

Some of the problems had begun to appear in the late 1950s. Elmer

Schacht's regime, like Worcester's, was slow to recognize industry maturity. Cash flow and return on sales masked a slight decline in market share as smaller firms began skimming volume accounts with price cuts. Faced with growing competition, Behr-Manning failed to mechanize to reduce costs, especially in the labor-intensive finishing and converting areas of production.

Gallagher and Schacht built an excellent management team during their very successful tenures, but Schacht left no general leaders capable of succeeding him and battling 3M in the stagnating and increasingly competitive market. He selected Edwin Evans as his successor in 1961 because he saw no other able Behr-Manning candidate, and he thought a Norton man would be disruptive.[81] Evans, whose background was largely in purchasing, unfortunately lacked both technical and labor experience just when the Watervliet laboratory had begun to slip, especially in process improvement, and when rising labor benefits and rigid work rules were fast becoming a crucial element in Behr-Manning costs. Major investments went into an elaborate office building and a $2 million laboratory that increased overhead but did little to mechanize finishing processes and tighten cost controls.

The challenge of aggressive competition in a changing industry was simply too much. Adjustment to price rivalries after the antitrust decree proved difficult. Like Norton, Behr-Manning set high prices and profit margins in the 1950s, creating a shield from which small competitors could snipe. Henry Elliot, the retired sales manager who headed the Coated Abrasives Manufacturers Institute and helped stabilize prices by persuasion during the halcyon 1950s, exerted little control by the decade's end when first the little firms and then Carborundum began cutting prices.

Elliot's successor, Henry Merrill, recalled that "it was very sad for me because I spent my lifetime in a controlled industry. And it was a very difficult thing to handle . . . God, the thing just becomes a horrible mess . . . when the Carborundum Company begins to move in the wrong direction . . . they are a big company. Then you've got problems."[82] Mid-West Abrasive Company took Behr-Manning's Allegheny-Ludlum account and Carborundum took the big NAPA auto parts business. Merrill admitted that "they still accuse me of having lost it because I wouldn't let them cut the price. I guess maybe I did hold off too long."[83]

Part of Behr-Manning's difficulty was competition with a powerful, able rival unlike any Norton ever faced. By this time 3M was larger than Norton and preoccupied with more lucrative, higher growth fields. It was not an aggressive force for change, but it was an efficient organization that kept its costs down and cut prices defensively and selectively. It outperformed both Behr-Manning and Carborundum under shifting conditions to become the domestic industry's undisputed leader.[84]

As an additional problem, Behr-Manning's ill-advised venture into tape manufacture diluted vital managerial and technical resources for a will-o'-the-wisp.[85] In the late 1940s John Cook and Henry Elliot of sales persuaded Frank Gallagher and Elmer Schacht to enter the tape field as 3M patents expired. Tapes were to give Behr-Manning badly needed additional volume in the automotive, paint, and hardware trades to maintain a sales force competitive with the huge 3M effort. Since the Norton subsidiary was already an expert in adhesives, coatings, and backings, the technology was not expected to be challenging.

For more than twenty years Behr-Manning poured thousands of hours and millions of dollars into what Schacht later called "a tragic mistake."[86] The technology proved difficult and an expert hired from Johnson and Johnson was little help. In the mid-1950s Lee Hoogstoel, Randall Manchester, and other talented production people were shifted from coated to tape operations. The 3M Company refused to license its water-saturating process, forcing the Watervliet company to pioneer a more costly solvent-saturation technique. After resolving numerous problems with "many setbacks and much realignment of equipment," the firm expanded slowly from automotive into industrial and technical tapes until finally, Schacht, with the backing of his Tape Division, committed it to an even more ill-fated venture in cellophane tape in 1957.[87] "We never got so bloody in all our lives," his sales manager later admitted.[88]

Behr-Manning lacked product quality, market recognition, and sales experience. The 3M product Scotch Tape was by this time a household word, and the Norton subsidiary, which had only limited sales resources and contacts through its hardware trade, found it difficult to handle volatile consumer marketing and distribution patterns in drugstore and supermarket chains. After two decades' wrestling with what a knowledgeable consultant called "a major financial drain," Behr-Manning had less than 10 percent of the market and was scarcely breaking even.[89]

The company's only major strike, a six-week shutdown in 1966, transformed a steady decline into a major collapse. Evans had watched the firm's market share fall from 32 percent in 1961 to 26 percent in 1966, which undercut its price leadership position.[90] At the same time rising costs, especially labor outlays, were squeezing profits. He explained to Worcester that 1965 earnings fell below forecast "largely because of the 5/1/65 wage/salary adjustment" and some higher material costs.[91]

Personality clashes, poor handling, and bad timing triggered the disastrous strike.[92] Behr-Manning's unions, led by the United Paper-workers and Papermakers, had become increasingly militant after World War II, bringing in an outside negotiator, winning larger pensions and other fringe benefits, and forcing increased concessions in work rules. Elmer Schacht had directed labor negotiations since the 1930s and had maintained peace in the generally prosperous postwar period. Evans not only lacked Schacht's experience and prosperity but he had lost Henry Gentile, his predecessor's labor troubleshooter and advisor, as well. The struggle between Evans and union head Edward Olszowy became a personal one as the company president was unable to convince the unions of the need for cost controls. Shop rules with indulgent seniority entitlements and easy piece work schedules blocked operating reorganization, and fringe benefits were fixed. The battle turned on wage rates with the firm offering a 30¢ per hour raise and the union insisting on 32¢.

For 2¢ per hour both sides suffered heavily. The strike stopped production for six weeks in May and June, and the bitterness and disorganization that followed slowed output for a year. The company's inadequate stockpiles frightened off exclusive accounts and left long order backlogs. Delays were still running one to four weeks the following January.[93]

Much of the difficulty lay in poor preparation and inexperience. A ten-week strike at 3M in 1967 had little long-run effect on that company. At Behr-Manning profits were almost nil in 1966, and the disruption, combined with the company's already weakened position, precipitated a 6-point slide in market share between 1966 and 1971. Lost revenue and poor performance (earnings were down 50 percent) stopped wage increases, forced hundreds of layoffs, and eventually led Norton to move a large share of the business to Texas.[94] Within ten years the Watervliet company was a shell of its former self.

Once again, the Behr-Manning collapse pointed to weaknesses at Worcester. In thirty years the owner-operators had made little effort to learn the business or bring the coated abrasives people into the "Norton Family." Harry Seifert, a twenty-five-year veteran at Watervliet by 1962 and head of its advertising, felt that "most of us didn't even recognize that we were part of Norton Company." When asked to include the Norton name in Behr-Manning ads, "we printed it white on white."[95] Twenty years later former Behr-Manning managers still show pride in their own operation and scorn for Norton's role in their success. Norton Company, they argue, was best known in the ferrous metals industries; the sandpaper company was recognized in the metals field as well as in leather, woodworking, and other industries.

The autonomous approach, which had treated Behr-Manning like a product division for three decades, was quite advanced for the 1930s. Yet, Worcester's top management remained committed to administering the bonded abrasives business and did not develop the organization and techniques to oversee coated abrasives performance and coordinate it with the full enterprise. Even Milton Higgins conceded that "they didn't want to be understood and we had nobody that had grown up enough with them."[96] Higgins, Gow, and other Worcester people gave a largely financial examination and easy approval to the tape investments and the building program. They monitored operating results for revenues but failed to see growing managerial problems in the 1960s. Furthermore, they were not informed about the factory labor situation and provided little useful guidance in the strike.

As Milton Higgins and Ralph Gow approached retirement in the mid-1960s, Norton was definitely due for reorganization. The rapid changes they had overseen had exposed the weaknesses of and outmoded the Worcester-oriented, centralized, owner-managed firm. Going public had shoved the company into a new arena that did not prize the old New England values. External directors, market analysts, financial people, and potential buyers of Norton stock valued growth and image over thrift and prudence. Diversification to establish a more exciting aura committed significant resources to businesses in which Higgins, Gow, and their Worcester abrasives team had little knowledge or interest. Stagnation in the abrasives industry undermined price stability and sales leadership based heavily on product supremacy. The increased importance of worldwide markets challenged the firm's strong domestic and European outlook. Finally, the proliferation of product lines, the collapse of Behr-Manning, and the growing need to operate a coordinated international business simply outstripped the ability of a highly centralized Worcester management devoted mainly to administering the domestic bonded abrasives industry.

In 1964 an outside evaluation, quite reflective of the period, aptly summarized Norton Company's position. After going public, Norton had employed Bruce Henderson of the Management Consulting Division of the Boston Safe Deposit and Trust Company to study the firm and help outline its strategy. Henderson, who would soon establish his pioneering Boston Consulting Group to consult in corporate strategic planning, strongly recommended that Norton "move from a defensive posture to an aggressive one" of diversification by acquisition.[97] For the stodgy firm "to grow old gracefully and to stick to its familiar basic business . . . would be a low-risk and predictable course," but would not be "an appealing policy for either the stockholders or the employees." Henderson argued that Norton's management must "be continually concerned with the corporate image and its effect on Norton's common stock prices." The firm was "at a stage in its history where major changes in the company character will be forced upon it if it does not take major actions to preserve this character," which was based on a "long tradition of growth, pioneering and leadership." Among Norton employees and operators Henderson found "a clear-cut and widely-spread feeling" that management and company had lost momentum.

Only diversification from the mature abrasives industry offered long-run recovery of momentum, and Henderson argued that acquisition was essential because Norton's previous limited attempts at internal development had produced "technological curios rather than major market opportunities." Rational selection was also essential to avoid dilution of talent. Although Henderson had some hope for National Research as "an excellent vehicle" for locating profitable areas, he thought the Cambridge business would be "an extreme test of Norton's ability to manage a diversified operation." The Worcester company's history restricted its opportunities. It could not take a sick firm or one whose employees had to be whipped into line. The most successful acquisitions would be of enterprises with similar traditions of leadership and stability.

As an additional change, reorientation of management was essential for success. Worcester executives would have to abandon abrasives administration and assume broad, policymaking responsibility. Norton needed to integrate its domestic and overseas operations to establish worldwide product divisions. Henderson urged that both Behr-Manning and NRC be tied more tightly to Norton. (The Clipper merger had occurred too recently to evaluate.) NRC "in no way identifies itself with the Norton corporate character of leadership, stability or corporate power," while coated abrasives leadership was "highly defensive" and in "sharp" conflict with headquarters' attitudes.

Along with the failures at NRC, Behr-Manning, and Clipper and Norton's declining position in the abrasives business, the company's overall performance in the mid-1960s rapidly bore out Henderson's fears. Despite recovery by 1962 from the recessions of 1958 and 1960–1961, overall return on sales had dropped to 7.3 percent from a 10 percent return in 1956, and earnings per share were down 13 percent in the same period. Between 1964 and 1966 in spite of what *Forbes* called "the greatest capital goods boom in history," Norton's earnings rose only 3 percent, in sharp contrast to rival Carborundum's 36 percent improvement. Norton Company's annual growth rate, which averaged 10 percent between 1890 and 1960, fell to 7.5 percent in the late 1940s and to 6 percent in the 1950s, and it continued to decline in the 1960s.[98]

Henderson's report received only token consideration. His evaluation was perceptive but hardly startling. In 1962 Alfred Chandler's widely acclaimed *Strategy and Structure* had analyzed the post–World War II trend toward diversification by large American industrial firms. Such an enterprise typically decentralized into autonomous product divisions overseen by a general office comprised of both policymaking executives without administrative responsibility and large functional staffs to supply information and aid.[99] And as noted earlier, the subsequent shift to diversification by merger was central to the conglomerate merger wave so popular in the 1960s.

Norton's owner-managers rejected Henderson's specific recommendation that the company acquire mill supply firms in the $10-25 million range because they were often Norton customers and because poor stock performance militated against any mergers.[100] Broader consideration awaited the retirement of Gow and Higgins in favor of a more receptive management.

The Transition to Managerial Enterprise

John Jeppson's appointment as president and chief executive officer in 1967 signified just such a shift. Jeppson's term lasted only four years, but it was a crucial bridge between the old family firm and the modern managerial enterprise that evolved in the 1970s. He maintained Norton's long tradition of owner-operation: although Ralph Gow had served five years as president until becoming vice-chairman of the board in 1967, Milton Higgins remained chief executive officer until Jeppson's promotion.

At the same time Jeppson's sensitivity to Norton's need for diversification, rationalization, and analytical, professional management moved the firm away from old values and traditions. Norton Company had already abandoned its financial independence in 1966 and incurred long-term debt exceeding $11 million. Under Jeppson's leadership it accepted the need for systematic planning, sold the deposits of Arkansas bauxite that had long been its prudent reserve, and invested the funds for a better return. With Higgins's and Gow's concurrence Norton overcame its Asian phobia and established operations in Japan and India.

Furthermore, although Jeppson formally preserved owner-leadership, he decentralized authority to division managers while shifting the general office in Worcester from abrasives administration to policymaking, coordination, and support for all Norton's businesses, as reflected in figure 7.[101] Free-wheeling autonomy ended as serious problems were recognized. National Research, Clipper, and U.S. Stoneware were reorganized into divisions for vacuum equipment, metalized products, Supercon, construction products, chemical process products, and plastics and synthetics. (On figure 7 the new divisions are grouped by corporate origin.) Behr-Manning was split into two Norton divisions for tape and coated abrasives, while the huge abrasives operation became the grinding wheel and abrasive materials divisions. These ten plus the previous industrial ceramics (refractories), grinding machine, and overseas operations gave Norton thirteen autonomous divisions with some seventy-five product lines.

Each division manager headed an entire business with his own sales, production, research, and financial people. The managers were fully accountable for profit and loss and were charged "with the responsibility of pursuing opportunities closely related to their established products."[102] To coordinate divisions and free the president and executive vice-president for more general strategic and policy-making duties, Norton Company added group vice-presidents for abrasives (the grinding wheel, coated abrasives, tape, and abrasive materials divisions), machinery and engineering (machine tool, construction products, and engineering services), advanced materials (chemical process products, plastics and synthetics, industrial ceramics, metalized products, Supercon, and vacuum equipment), and overseas operations. In addition to the president and the executive and group vice-presidents, headquarters included a corporate Finance Department, headed by Vice-President and Treasurer William Perks and Controller John Dingle, a Legal Department headed by Vice-President and General Counsel Fairman Cowan, a marketing vice-president (not shown on the chart), a small planning staff under Richard Harris, a corporate Personnel Department under Vice-President Tom Green, and a research staff located in Cambridge under Robert Stauffer, vice-president for research.

Norton Company's organization now matched the decentralized structure so pervasive among U.S. diversified industrial firms after the 1950s. The shift had meant a tightening of some controls and loosening of others. The hodgepodge of centralized owner-operation of domestic bonded abrasives and autonomy for other areas, which had evolved over sixty years, was now rationalized. All divisions carried the Norton name and uniform Norton logo.

In keeping with the transition theme, Jeppson's appointments reflected both the old and new.[103] Harry Brustlin and Allan Hardy, group vice-presidents for abrasives and machinery, were Norton veterans who had risen through the ranks. Hardy had been with the

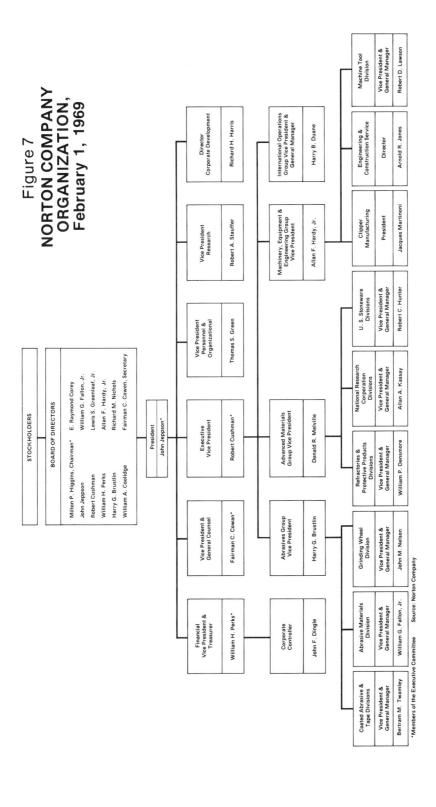

Figure 7
NORTON COMPANY
ORGANIZATION,
February 1, 1969

STOCKHOLDERS

BOARD OF DIRECTORS

Milton P. Higgins, Chairman*   E. Raymond Corey
John Jeppson   William G. Fallon, Jr.
Robert Cushman   Lewis S. Greenleaf, Jr.
William H. Perks   Allan F. Hardy, Jr.
Harry G. Brustlin   Richard M. Nichols
William A. Coolidge   Fairman C. Cowen, Secretary

President
John Jeppson*

Financial
Vice President &
Treasurer
William H. Perks*

Vice President &
General Counsel
Fairman C. Cowan*

Executive
Vice President
Robert Cushman*

Vice President
Personnel &
Organizational
Thomas S. Green

Vice President
Research
Robert A. Stauffer

Director
Corporate Development
Richard H. Harris

Corporate
Controller
John F. Dingle

Abrasives Group
Vice President
Harry G. Brustlin

Advanced Materials
Group Vice President
Donald R. Melville

Machinery, Equipment &
Engineering Group
Vice President
Allan F. Hardy, Jr.

International Operations
Group Vice President &
General Manager
Harry B. Duane

Coated Abrasive &
Tape Divisions
Vice President &
General Manager
Bertram M. Twamley

Abrasive Materials
Division
Vice President &
General Manager
William G. Fallon, Jr.

Grinding Wheel
Division
Vice President &
General Manager
John M. Nelson

Refractories &
Protective Products
Divisions
Vice President &
General Manager
William P. Densmore

National Research
Corporation
Divisions
Vice President &
General Manager
Allan A. Kassay

U. S. Stoneware
Divisions
Vice President &
General Manager
Robert C. Hunter

Clipper
Manufacturing
President
Jacques Martinoni

Engineering &
Construction Service
Director
Arnold R. Jones

Machine Tool
Division
Vice President &
General Manager
Robert D. Lawson

*Members of the Executive Committee   Source: Norton Company

company since 1935 and served as plants engineer and general manager of refractories, while Brustlin had worked in bonded abrasives sales for nearly two decades. Other veterans included Abrasive Materials Manager William Fallon, who had headed the South African plant and industrial ceramics during more than two decades with Norton; Thomas Green, who followed his father's thirty-five years with twenty of his own; and Machine Tool Manager Robert Lawson, who had spent fifty years in that division.

Balancing the experience were more recent recruits, products of modern managerial training, many of whom John Jeppson had encouraged as he became more committed to analytical, professional management. Grinding Wheel Manager John Nelson and the vice-president for vacuum equipment and metals, Allan Kassay, were business school graduates who had been with Norton for less than ten years. Another MBA, English-born Donald Melville, had been recruited from Continental Can to head corporate marketing before becoming group vice-president for advanced materials. Robert Stauffer came from National Research and Robert Hunter from U.S. Stoneware. Harry Duane, vice-president for international operations, and Bernard Meyer, manager of industrial ceramics, had received engineering degrees from the Massachusetts Institute of Technology and Rensselaer Polytechnic Institute in the mid-1950s.

Jeppson's key appointment was Executive Vice-President Robert Cushman, who combined Norton experience and analytical professional management. The Dartmouth graduate had known Jeppson socially, and at his suggestion had left the Gulf Oil Company to become a Norton salesman in 1944.[104] His success as West Coast district manager in the early 1950s brought Cushman to Worcester as assistant general sales manager and manager of marketing services in Jeppson's Abrasive Division. With both Jeppson's and Ralph Gow's support for an obviously able executive, Cushman became general sales manager for abrasives in 1959 and succeeded John Jeppson as vice-president and general manager of the Abrasive Division in 1961.

His successful revitalization of that sliding business underscored his executive ability and analytical approach. Following Norton Company's earlier decision to maintain prices on vitrified, organic, and diamond wheels and to look for competitive relief in product breakthroughs, market share continued to erode badly in all three segments. Cushman was skeptical of quick technological solutions; the abrasive machining campaign was geared for the entire industry, and zirconia-alumina and other product innovations were slow and uncertain. Based on his own experience, he looked for help in marketing.[105]

Implementing change meant several battles, but by 1965, Cushman recalled, "we were desperate; we had to do something."[106] He first had to overcome traditional Norton aversion to price competition, and he had to wrest cost data and price-setting authority from the financial people. Simple analysis was impossible amid the confusing hodgepodge of Norton abrasives marketing, which included direct accounts and industrial distributors who handled 70 percent of the business, hundreds of thousands of different items, millions of orders, and a welter of quantity and distributor discounts, along with separate prices for special products. Cushman quickly created a team of experts, including Harry Duane for his controller's background, David Reid from abrasives production, and Harry Brustlin from abrasives sales. To perform the actual study linking price and market share he hired Robert Casselman from the Boston Consulting Group after discussions with Bruce Henderson underscored the consultant's ability to define the problem.

Casselman's six months' computer analysis of abrasives orders disclosed a pattern of losses on large-volume items sold to smaller firms. In the early 1950s Ralph Johnson's strong distributor organization and quantity pricing had been imposed on marketing procedures that had evolved piecemeal over three generations. To attract distributors Johnson had built a distributors' margin into Norton's best price, leaving a 40 percent margin between cost and price. At the same time allocation of orders remained confused. Norton continued to service small sales for big customers while distributors handled many big orders to small customers.

Armed with Casselman's data, the ad hoc committee developed the Norton Plan, which Cushman implemented in 1965 with approval from Higgins, Gow, and Jeppson. All customers who bought a minimum annual quantity (which varied by item) qualified for a lower price. Norton Company shipped directly and invoiced but did not collect until the customer reordered to replenish his stock. The customer took title and lowered his purchase and inventory costs while assuming the burden of taxes, insurance, storage, and record keeping. Direct sales and volume items cut the firm's shipping and packing costs from Worcester to the warehouse and to the distributor. In fact Norton closed six warehouses and consolidated three others with coated abrasives.[107] To compensate distributors for lost volume, the company gave them all the small orders that it had previously handled directly. The plan could have alienated a crucial and powerful network of distributors and generated even bigger sales losses, but Cushman never saw it as a great risk. He confidently felt the careful analysis had made the need "so clear" that no alternative remained.[108]

The plan, which stunned competitors, was a major success. It gave Norton greater control over its own distribution and prices while reducing costs. Distributors initially grumbled at the reorganization, but most were mollified with offsetting volume from small orders. Only one large firm defected and then only temporarily. Within six weeks, Cushman announced that the plan had generated 238 agreements for $1,650,000, one quarter of which was new business. After six months, agreements totaled $5.6 million, of which $2 million was new business. As a result of careful analysis and three years' rational marketing, John Nelson, Cushman's successor as head of the division, told the Board of Directors that "the decline experienced in the early 60s has been halted."[109] In the interim the Norton Plan assured Cushman's promotion in 1967 as executive vice-president.

Cushman's performance rapidly marked him as John Jeppson's successor. A quiet, determined man, he had (in his own words) a real strength for people, "recognizing talent and trying to motivate them and make them grow and putting a team together."[110] He played a central role in the structural reorganization and in recruiting the new management team. A confident believer in systematic analysis, he strongly supported planning for rational allocation of precious capital and managerial resources. Almost immediately he instituted the Product Line Study Committee to identify Norton's businesses, measure their place in the firm's future, and determine a strategy of divestments and acquisitions to restore balance and growth to the enterprise.

Implementation, however, was delayed until his own presidency. Part of the opposition stemmed from simple inertia, for Norton Company had never previously made significant divestments. Other obstacles developed from continued financial difficulty and the slow transfer of power from the third generation.

The family firm had two types of power transfer at the top. Formal authority passed quickly with appointment to office. Real control came more slowly as previous owner-operators gradually surrendered the leadership they had exercised for years. Charles Allen had served as chief executive for fourteen years after George Jeppson and Aldus Higgins were ready to run Norton Company. Aldus Higgins and George Jeppson had expected to guide Milton Higgins and Ralph Gow, and George Jeppson exercised a significant veto power well into the 1950s.

Higgins and Gow originally planned similar guidance for John Jeppson and Robert Cushman, but neither man was ever comfortable with "theoretical," business school, planning types, who, in Gow's words, depended on "a bunch of flip charts . . . a carefully prepared speech . . . [and] all these projections."[111] Like their predecessors in 1947, Cushman and Jeppson quickly sought to run the firm themselves, and Gow, who felt useless as vice-chairman of the board, retired within a year.

As chairman of the board and a major stockholder, Higgins's position was different. Just as George Jeppson had done in the 1950s, Milton continued to preside at board meetings, advise, and exercise a veto power while John Jeppson served once again as mediator, this time between the older owner-operator and the rising managerial group.[112] Milton Higgins disapproved of but tolerated the heavy reliance on Henderson's Boston Consulting Group and the sale of the Arkansas property. Although he accepted in principle the Product Line Study Committee's recommendation to sell the Machine Tool Division, he questioned the specifics of two attempts to divest it.

In addition, Norton Company's worsening performance after 1966, which was aggravated by the economic downturn after 1969, delayed further rationalization. In a falling market and a recession that disgraced many conglomerate companies, there were fewer buyers for Norton divestments. Norton's own decline, which included a slight sales drop and a 29 percent decrease in net income between 1969 and 1971, dried up cash flow and depressed its stock, blocking significant acquisitions. As its poor performance indicated, the company still lacked a clear-cut general strategy to direct the resuscitation of its established businesses and the flow of resources into research and diversification. Jeppson and Cushman were busy raising funds, economizing, and shoring up shaky operations.

Despite Norton's unpromising condition, Cushman's performance amply demonstrated his ability to revitalize the enterprise. Jeppson, who had intended to serve as a bridge to professional management, was ready to step aside after thirty-one years with the firm, and Milton Higgins, who had reached his late 60s, acceded to the change after a decade's troubles. In 1971 Higgins stepped down to become chairman of the Finance Committee, Jeppson became chairman of the board, and Robert Cushman became president and chief executive officer, formally marking the shift from family to managerial enterprise.

8.

Farewell to the Family Firm: The Rise of the Modern Managerial Enterprise

IN JUNE 1971 shortly after his promotion as president and chief executive officer of Norton Company, Robert Cushman announced a series of corporate objectives. Norton would remain independent and would be a balanced, diversified company manufacturing consumable industrial supplies. Balance required a mix of businesses, some to generate cash and others to stimulate growth. Annual corporate growth would be at least 10 percent, with return on stockholders' equity at 15 percent. Since the focus was on growth, at least 70 percent of earnings would be reinvested. Diversification meant that 40 percent of 1980 profits would come from nonabrasive products; the ultimate target was at least 50 percent.

New businesses would be selected for high growth potential and their ability to counter the metal-working cycle. Norton looked to internal development for a "major part" of its expansion, but would use acquisitions when appropriate. Much of this responsibility was to fall on the product divisions themselves. To maintain and strengthen its leadership in abrasives markets, the company would pursue a global strategy. Norton expected to become or remain a leader in all its "basic product lines" with technical product development, cost reduction, and new emphasis on marketing effectiveness. Finally, Norton would be a "good citizen," emphasizing integrity and social responsibility as well as obedience to law.[1]

As Cushman's statement suggested, the late 1960s and 1970s were the biggest watershed in Norton's history since the rise of the large firm early in the century. Going public, diversification, and John Jeppson's recognition of the need for reorganization and rationalization opened the door for Robert Cushman and a cadre of young, talented,

302

professional managers to alter radically Norton strategy, structure, and administration.

System and analysis replaced intuition and personal operation. The managers shifted the emphasis at the company from revenue gathering and short-term risk minimization to assurance of long-term, steady growth. They transformed a predominantly abrasives company into a much more complex enterprise of many businesses. They abandoned informal centralized control for decentralized operation with systematic oversight and substituted salaried management at the top for owner-operation.

The once privatized, internalized, and independent firm assumed the peculiar mix of other modern American industrial corporations. Private ownership and operation remained, yet a very public dimension was added. Managers assumed a responsibility and accountability to numerous audiences—descendants of founders and their family trusts that still owned more than half the stock, other shareholders from the general public, security analysts and the New York Stock Exchange, employees, government regulatory agencies, and the communities where Norton did business.

The transformation meant a series of complex challenges. For the immediate future Cushman and his associates had to prune, rationalize, and economize to restore prosperity, cash flow, and credibility and to assure their freedom for continued action. At the same time they had to determine objectives, outline strategies, and develop a means of application for the long-term health of large fixed investment.

Implementation proceeded in several fields. Managers integrated Watervliet, Worcester, and overseas abrasives operations into an efficient, prosperous worldwide abrasives business that remained the core and cash generator of the enterprise. They also developed industrial ceramics, safety products, and other diversified lines selected to run counter to the abrasives and capital goods cycle and to provide steady income and smoother growth to the overall enterprise, while at the same time fitting Norton's resources and abilities. In addition, one major acquisition moved the company into petroleum and mining exploration equipment, which had a high-growth, long-term potential. Finally, top executives implemented long-range planning and institutionalized procedures to assure continuity of opportunity, growth, talent, and funding. By 1980 they completed the permanent transformation from a Worcester-centered, owner-run, abrasive business to an international, diversified, decentralized, professionally managed enterprise.

Robert Cushman and the Evolution of Systematic Management

Robert Cushman's promotion to president in 1971 validated a leadership he had begun to assume in 1967. As executive vice-president he had in reality been John Jeppson's chief operating officer, while staff operations reported to the president. He and Jeppson fully agreed on the need for analytical professional management, rationalization of Norton holdings, and clarification of the firm's goals and direction. In fact Cushman's 1971 corporate objectives restated more precisely goals first announced by John Jeppson in 1968.[2] By 1969 Jeppson admitted publicly the urgent need for rationalization. New lines had "siphoned off too large a share of company funds and management time and effort, and none . . . was of sufficient size or had sufficient growth impact to markedly change the company as a whole."[3] With their basic agreement and with all line operators reporting directly to Cushman, he remarked confidently that "there were very few things I wanted to do that I didn't get done."[4]

Underlying his changes was a fundamental shift in values and emphasis. Central to the process were techniques and concepts widely taught in business schools and practiced by professional managers in the 1970s—rationalization and systematic administration, articulation of goals, strategic thinking, and business planning. The American business community's emphasis on such procedures followed logically from the popularity of internal diversification and delegation of authority during the 1950s and from the extreme decentralization that characterized the conglomerate mergers of the 1960s. In the 1970s management stressed coordination and overall control of their new or rapidly expanded enterprises.

Cushman was in the vanguard of the movement and outlined much of the change for Norton when he became executive vice-president in 1967, after watching Norton Company double its product lines to more than sixty and jump from four to thirteen divisions in less than five years. He was firmly committed to continued diversification but did not want a conglomerate. In a multidivisional firm, each division was to be a profit center and yet be integrated enough to take advantage of mutual cooperation. The logical corollaries were strategic planning and decentralization. After watching the chaotic and disappointing acquisition program of 1963–1967, Cushman was certain that planning was crucial for mutual cooperation and integration. It assured the firm's direction, and if kept flexible, its responsiveness. He pushed strategic planning "on the premise that plans will have to be altered to meet changing conditions, but that some plan is better than no plan at all."[5]

As head of the Abrasive Division Cushman's earlier battles with Worcester's top executives and powerful financial staff and the disappointing performance of Robert Stauffer's research department made him stress decentralization of authority into line operations to the point of involving line people in planning. "If we wait for this small group of individuals [the Executive Committee] to act, we will be forever in solving the problems we know exist. Every division and department of the Company must have its own set of objectives and communicate them to its people." It followed that corporate staff must be trim. "Overuse or misuse of corporate staffs . . . adds to the confusion in assigned responsibilities." Research, too, was to be focused on operating needs. "While freedom to explore in completely unchartered fields may be rewarding for some, we believe our long range plans are broad enough to provide sufficient opportunities."

The eventual thrust was to center entrepreneurship in the divisions, which were to be Norton's profit centers. "We want more decision makers than administrators," and "we want a strong line decision making organization" so that "committees will exist more to keep people informed than to make decisions." Coming from a veteran operating man, the call for delegation of freedom and authority could hardly have been more explicit. At the same time accountability and appraisal had to be systematic and established within corporatewide goals. Cushman called his program "management by results," reflecting the analytical, management-by-objectives philosophy so popular in American enterprise in the 1970s. The phrase meant "the management of people by measuring their results and performance against a set of agreed upon objectives; which themselves are designed to further the company's aspirations . . . Once the objectives are agreed upon, an individual is given freedom within which to act."

The first challenge, then, was the identification of the appropriate strategy, followed by the creation of a planning system and mechanism to implement that strategy. Strategic thinking and planning, Cushman thought, "had more to do with turning around the company than any other single thing."[6]

Strategic thinking and business planning had begun with Cushman's mentor, John Jeppson; Ralph Gow and Milton Higgins had made only desultory efforts.[7] A 1955 review had projected Norton growth and profits against expectations of other major industrials. W. C. Wickenden's 1961 study included some disquieting projections for Norton's future and Jack Ewer was appointed at the corporate level to study acquisitions, but nothing resulted. Both Gow and Higgins remained apathetic at best. In his last year as president, Gow warned that "we are still more bureaucratic than we should be. We still tend to spend too much time studying and analyzing. Our people down the line must be taught and allowed to make decisions and get results. We must avoid too many approvals, too many studies, too many committees, and too much caution."[8] Milton Higgins was even more forthright: "We had nice five-year plans. And they were for the birds in my opinion . . . The more businesses you get into, the more difficult it is. You can plan one business, but planning five businesses is five times as difficult."[9]

When John Jeppson became Gow's executive vice-president in 1961, he began encouraging more systematic strategic planning—long-range (five or more years) determinations of what Norton's businesses should be and resource allocations to meet those needs. At first the plans were extended sales projections like the five-year forecasts Jeppson had sponsored in the Abrasive Division. But he also encouraged broader analysis such as Allan Kassay's 1962 diversification studies for the Refractories (Industrial Ceramics) Division. Jeppson first institution-alized business planning in 1965 to devise strategies for Norton's increasingly diverse product lines. Richard Harris, controller and a graduate of the Massachusetts Institute of Technology, became cor-porate planner, assisted by Harvard Business School graduate Marlin Zimmerman. Along with Jeppson, Research Vice-President Robert Stauffer, Corporate Controller John Dingle, and Corporate Economist J. E. Cotter (who had made five-year projections for Behr-Manning in the 1950s), Harris formed the Corporate Planning Committee.

Instituting the new procedure was a slow and awkward innovation for the inexperienced organization. Between 1965 and 1967 the small planning staff wrestled unsuccessfully to educate line operators and to organize isolated planning exercises into a useful tool for resource allocation. Most managers substituted sales projections for strategic planning and loaded reports with elaborate statistical and financial forecasts. Others looked upon planning as a kind of review or house-cleaning, a time to confront or solve lingering problems, rather than a continuous analysis. Many managers resisted the process to save time and energy and to protect precious line authority from staff control. Finally, the most crucial part—the method, timing, focus, and content of corporate and divisional goal setting—remained in-complete. Financial projections, sales forecasts, and predictions of resource allocation had little meaning until Norton evolved a broad strategic framework to fit the new diversified, public company.

The evolution of Norton's present strategy and planning techniques began in 1967 as Executive Vice-President Cushman supplanted Har-ris. The company's poor performance in abrasives and diversified operations, the promotion of Jeppson and Cushman and the appointment of seven new men to corporate executive positions disrupted Harris's implementation of corporate planning. To bring order from the chaos accompanying rapid diversification, Cushman proposed a careful study of just what Norton had. He established and chaired the Product Line Study Committee, which included Group Vice-Presidents Harry Brustlin and Allan Hardy, Marketing Vice-President Donald Melville, Corporate Controller John Dingle, and Research Vice-President Stauffer. For several months until its report in early 1968, the top-level committee scrutinized Norton's seventy-five product lines and fifteen major research projects for their condition, prospects, and fit with the firm in order to rationalize the diversified firm by re-grouping, divestments, and acquisitions. With a heavy debt to pop-ular business theorist Peter Drucker, committee members asked themselves whether they would enter each of their businesses if they were not already in it.

For Cushman, there were three keys to successful planning. First, he was convinced that disaggregation was necessary to understand just what Norton had and to plan for it. Charles Ames's 1963 article on product and market management had helped develop his ideas on segmentation.[10] The Norton Plan of 1965 was his first successful exercise in analysis by segmentation, while his work to implement the Corporate Planning Committee's guidelines had convinced him that "planning must become a way of life."[11] The Product Line Study Committee then followed naturally. As he put it later, the committee was "the first effort to really segment the company and say 'what the hell have we got in this company today?' . . . We had conglomerated the company by mistake. We had added all these businesses, and we knew we didn't understand them."[12]

The study committee recommended both a financial benchmark and a strategic policy. It agreed that Norton businesses should average 10-20 percent return on assets and 10 percent annual growth, and it argued that the company should concentrate on consumable indus-trial supplies where its marketing and production expertise lay. Such products were technical but with a low- to medium-range technology. They needed engineering and research and could not be efficiently produced in a garage or simple fabrication operation. They were gen-erally sold through distributors but required an internal sales orga-nization for marketing, demonstration, and service. Capital goods such as machine tools and construction equipment, consumer goods such as space blankets, and services such as contract paving and job coatings all fell outside that area, and the committee called for their sale or termination as unprofitable or low-return lines with little future at Norton Company.[13]

At the same time the study committee raised a more fundamental issue. Financial standards of growth and return provided a convenient rule-of-thumb measure for isolated product lines but were no substitute for an overall strategy. The abrasive materials and Chipper blades businesses did not meet the committee's financial guidelines, but all members agreed that both were necessary for the overall health of Norton's abrasives lines. The blades provided crucial steady volume to absorb overhead in a business plagued with overcapacity, and the materials division assured grain supply and ready access to the latest improvements.

Moreover, the study committee recognized that abrasives would not supply the long-run rates of growth and return essential to maintain Norton's position in American industry and attract investment. Diversification was necessary to counter cyclicality and assure long-term prosperity, but how should limited financial and managerial resources be allocated? Segmentation was an excellent analytical device, but what would provide direction and coherence? Cushman recalled troublesome capital allocation battles as a member of the Executive Committee in the early and mid-1960s. "The thing that bothered me about the executive committee . . . was that it was a conscientious group of people who were making decisions, but we looked at each appropriation in isolation from everything else." Cushman wished he "could see all of these requests on the walls as I sit here so I could look at this one . . . and make a comparison."[14]

In the cash-rich abrasives company such choices had been a lesser matter, but in the diversified enterprise with severe competition for investment, rational choice was crucial for long-term success. By the late 1960s such issues were immediate problems. At the Conflans coated abrasives plant, for example, orders were running 50 percent over forecast. When Norton International head Harry Duane proposed to protect the growing business with a $2 million investment to expand Conflans's capacity and to specialize production among the Canadian, Belfast, and French plants, Controller John Dingle pointed to Behr-Manning's slide and the discouraging projections for its long-term growth. Duane quickly responded that "the Executive Committee must answer . . . whether we are going to remain in the coated abrasive business on an international basis or whether we should withdraw from this business."[15]

Establishing a general corporate strategy and framework, then, was the second key to successful planning. Cushman drew on his operating experience, just as he had with the Product Line Study Committee, and turned to Bruce Henderson and the Boston Consulting Group, which had proved so helpful with the Norton Plan.[16] Promoting a policy that naturally followed Cushman's segmentation and that would become a very popular planning concept in the 1970s, Henderson argued that Norton Company should think of itself as a portfolio of businesses that fell in the field of consumable industrial supplies. What Norton required was a strategy to manage its portfolio, much as an investor balances his holdings with a mixture of mature cash generators, long-range growth securities, and risky ventures with rapid growth potential.

The businesses could be best understood if placed on a grid whose axes were growth and market share. The emphasis on growth has been a constant theme in American business and was especially strong in the 1960s. The choice of market share rested on the Boston Consulting Group's assumptions that evolved from modified learning curve theory. The consultant argued that costs decreased with experience in predictable fashion. For businesses experience meant volume, and market share was the best determinant of volume. Since market leadership represented the greatest experience, it also meant the lowest cost and greatest profit margin in an industry. By knowing a product's market share and its life cycle to determine potential growth, Norton could readily assess that line's chances for success.

As figure 8 indicates, the technique provided just the kind of simple graphic representation that Cushman sought to demonstrate balance and help guide resource allocation. The horizontal axis is relative market share; the zero (center) point is the share of Norton's largest competitor. The vertical axis is real market growth; its intersection with the horizontal axis was the point of average real growth sought by the firm. Businesses in the upper left quadrant were profit makers who needed cash to maintain high growth and leadership. Using a terminology that became common in the 1970s, Henderson's people called them "stars." Those products in the lower left quadrant were more mature cash generators requiring little investment. They were labeled "cash cows." Businesses in the lower right quadrant were the worst combination. They had inferior market share and slow growth potential. Since they consumed cash, had high costs, and offered little prospect, the "dogs" were candidates for divestment. Finally, in the upper right quadrant fell the "question marks," which called for cash to develop leadership but which offered potential growth.

The portfolio was not static and charts chosen at different times could measure change and improvement. Ideally, a firm wished to get rid of its dogs and move question marks left toward market leadership or sell them off. A company's chart should also reflect a mix of mature, lower growth, cash generators and younger, higher growth cash users. The balloons representing each business segment varied

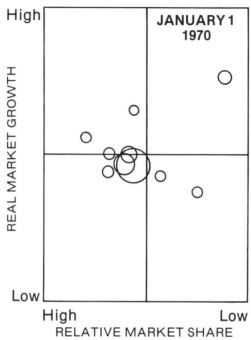

STRATEGIC PLANNING ANALYSIS

Source: Norton Spirit (Spring 1977), p. 4.

Figure 8

in size by total sales. Segments representing a product group were expected to expand to a minimum size (Norton specified $100 million) to justify the time, money, and talent lavished on them.

For each category the Boston Consulting Group described an appropriate strategy. Stars should be "built" to seize growth opportunities. Their heavy cash investments were to be derived in part from cash cows whose market leadership and profitability were to be "maintained" with minimum investment. Cows with rapidly declining market share and growth and some dogs were to be "harvested" of all possible income without further investment until liquidation or sale. The "real" dogs were to be divested, as were question marks that failed to respond to "build" strategies.

Furthermore, the strategy and technique lent itself to further segmentation and scrutiny. The business represented by any balloon could itself be split into product or geographic market segments for a similar analysis and application of strategy. For increased flexibility there were also mixed strategies such as build/maintain and maintain/harvest in addition to the simpler strategic designations.

The portfolio and segmentation approach meant that Milton Higgins had understated the complexity of planning. A diversified multinational enterprise like Norton Company required dozens of charts and plans to represent the appropriate strategy for each of its many product lines and markets. Financial Vice-President Richard Flynn estimated that the segmented approach made Norton as complex to run as a business three times its size.[17]

Strategic Planning: Innovating Decentralized Planning

The Henderson model helped Norton identify the businesses it wished to be in and the appropriate strategies for those lines after the Product Line Study Committee had inventoried the businesses Norton held. Establishing a mechanism and the appropriate tools for planning was the final part of the procedure. Under Cushman's leadership Norton developed an innovative approach in the 1970s that has continued to evolve even as it has proven successful.

In most large American industrial enterprises, corporate planning was a staff function. When pioneer firms like Du Pont diversified and decentralized, their leaders created a general office that separated daily administration from broader strategic considerations.[18] Line authority passed from the president and the executive committee through group vice-presidents to managers responsible for profit and loss in the product divisions they headed. Divorced from them in the larger general office were corporate staffs for planning, research, finance, marketing, and other functions. Corporate vice-presidents, who headed the staff operations, and the president were to plan, coordinate, and appraise. To assure their freedom and to protect the operating people, the corporate executives could advise but were specifically excluded from any line authority and responsibility. John Jeppson had adopted this approach when he created the Corporate Planning Committee and appointed Richard Harris head of planning.

Cushman was never happy with the technique. As operating head of the Abrasive Division he felt left out. He and others diligently gathered information and shaped plans before presenting the data, but ultimately all material went to Harris's staff committee, which presented each division manager with his final plan. Cushman argued that without final determination by those responsible for implementation and results, planning was merely an empty exercise for division heads, producing voluminous documentation and discontent with imposed plans.

Like Charles Allen, George Jeppson, Ralph Gow, and Milton Higgins before him, Cushman was strongly committed to subordinating staff to line authority. He argued vehemently that Norton's planning process was too specialized and isolated. "The wrong people were doing the job . . . The top line and staff managers must be personally involved in developing the corporate strategy and plans. They cannot delegate to a group of individuals in a department called Corporate Planning . . . answering those three key questions: (1) Where and what are we now? (2) Where and what do we want to become? (3) How can we best get there? They cannot or should not delegate the second and ongoing job of determining the character and content of the corporation's portfolio of business investments."[19]

Cushman's solution shifted planning responsibility from Harris and his staff to a committee of top executives.[20] At first the Product Line Study Committee served this purpose until the Strategic Guidance Committee replaced it in 1972. The Guidance Committee included the major line and staff executives from the general office, including Cushman, the group vice-presidents, the regional vice-presidents of the Abrasives Group, the financial vice-president, the controller, the vice-president of corporate development, and the director of planning and control from Diversified Products. Harris's Corporate Planning Office, which soon became Corporate Development, was confined to acquisitions, and planning people were added as staff at the divisional level. Division managers were encouraged to substitute a briefer, more flexible approach that emphasized strategic instead of financial planning and uniform, detailed presentations.

By 1972 Norton had combined its lines into some thirty strategic business units defined by product and market. Each unit appeared biennially before the Strategic Guidance Committee (which met about twenty-five times annually) unless expansion or other extraordinary circumstances dictated a more frequent review. The unit manager submitted his plan beforehand for careful study by committee members. The review itself was a two-to-five-hour meeting to critique the manager's assumptions and plan, their fit with corporate objectives, and the effectiveness of previous implementation, while committee members watched for specific opportunities and assured themselves that adequate resources were being applied. No vote was taken, but the committee's consensus was later communicated to the manager by the proper line authority. The manager then adjusted his plan in light of recommendations, and formal approval rested with the line management.

Like so much of bureaucratic management, the process depended on cooperation and compromise rather than confrontation. Each manager was responsible for his own plan, but the Guidance Committee, using Henderson's planning model, had determined the broader corporate strategic framework for the unit plans and could rank the portfolio by return on net assets (RONA) and long-range objectives. As Cushman explained, "It really has to be a top-down direction of where the company wants to be and what it is trying to become. But there also has to be involvement from the bottom up." In short, the manager determined his plan based on "his unit's place in the portfolio or his ability to move into a 'winning position,' " and the committee reviewed the appropriateness of his strategy based on that position.[21]

In addition to its guidance meetings, the committee also met twice a year to review Norton Company's financial budget and five-year plan. Five-year plans from the units were consolidated into a five-year master plan for the enterprise. Computer modeling allowed the corporate staff to discount the fourth and fifth years and offer a range of alteratives based on changing assumptions. The Financial Department also established an annual financial budget, the preliminary cash flow data of which was sent to unit managers to aid in their planning.

The shift from staff to a line committee system placed a considerable burden on the reviewers to supply the knowledge and expertise necessary to evaluate each presentation. In part, of course, this ability was based on careful scrutiny of the presentation, the broad interrelatedness of divisions as producers of industrial consumables, and each committee member's considerable experience with the business. In addition, by the late 1960s, the problem of knowledge about planning for diversified industrial enterprise had become extensive enough to support independent firms for that purpose.

Norton's reliance on the Cambridge-based Strategic Planning Institute resulted from Robert Cushman's contacts with Dr. Sidney Schoeffler and his work.[22] In 1960 General Electric had asked Schoeffler to determine why some of their many lines succeeded and others did not. Ten years' study of 800 strategic decisions in 150 General Electric product lines isolated key variables such as market share, rate of growth, investment intensity, and percentage of capacity used. Schoeffler's regression analysis indicated that thirty-seven variables accounted for more than 80 percent of the difference in profitability results.

Cushman was impressed with the researcher's work and invited him to address Norton executives at Watervliet in 1967. He had Norton Company participate in the analyst's Marketing Science Institute at Harvard Business School, a research project that evolved into the Strategic Planning Institute in the 1970s. Norton and more than fifty other corporations representing over six hundred diverse businesses joined under Schoeffler's direction to establish a strategy data bank. The program, called Profit Impact of Market Studies, or PIMS, offered a series of models based on experience that predicted the appropriate profit levels and the impact of alternative strategies on profits and cash flows for Norton businesses. These models, supplemented by additional formulations for return on net assets developed by Graham Wren, secretary for the Strategic Guidance Committee, provided independent criteria against which committee members could test proposed unit strategies. The entire program, called PIMS PAR RONA, was added to Guidance Committee deliberations between 1973 and 1975 to supply standards and a statistical basis for what had previously been only broad discussions of strategy. Specifically, projected return on net assets helped members to compare plans and allocate resources most effectively within long-range goals.

Along with the Product Line Study Committee's analysis and the Boston Consulting Group's model of corporate strategy, the Strategic Guidance Committee's development by the mid-1970s completed the evolution of Norton Company's planning process. Norton's line planning very much reflected the values of Robert Cushman, its prime mover. It extended the segmentation techniques that he had found so helpful for analyzing the firm and provided an overall framework and a continuous focus for review and adjustment of corporate strategy. It preserved the authority of line operators on which Cushman and his predecessors had long insisted. The involvement of division managers reinforced the decentralization for which he and others fought so hard in the 1960s, while the committee supplied a general plan and direction for the enterprise. Finally, as a by-product, Guidance Committee membership offered valuable experience and a vital corporatewide view for line and staff people who were logical successors to Cushman and the executve vice-presidents. The evolution of strategic planning at Norton Company indicated clearly the shift from traditional emphasis on centralized power, intuitive operation, and risk reduction to systematic, aggressive management of a decentralized enterprise.

Implementation of strategic planning was a challenge in bureaucratic management. Despite Cushman's determination, his basic agreement with John Jeppson, his rapid promotion to chief executive officer, and the clarity of his goals, enactment of his policies required more than ten years. In fact, a decade was rapid for the radical departure he contemplated in an organization steeped in three generations of centralized, intuitive owner-management of an abrasives business. The pace of complex strategic and bureaucratic change depended on overcoming both internal opposition and external obstacles as well as on developing the necessary ancillary tools.

Internal restrictions were most evident during Robert Cushman's tenure as executive vice-president. Despite his general accord with John Jeppson, Cushman firmly opposed the owner-operator's commitment to centralized line planning under Richard Harris. Jeppson, too, was always more enthusiastic about Robert Stauffer's eye-catching and exotic corporate research projects than was his vice-president, and since Jeppson controlled staff operations, major cut-backs awaited Cushman's final promotion.

Corporate politics and power groups also played a role. In deference to the efforts of members Hardy and Stauffer, the Product Line Study Committee urged that Norton cease investment in metalized products and superconducting wire but stopped short of calling for outright divestment. It also noted extensive obsolescence in the Vacuum Products Division but took no action. Furthermore, since its recommendation to sell the grinding machine business lacked Milton Higgins's and John Jeppson's full support, there was no immediate sale.

Milton Higgins, who served on Norton's Executive Committee first as chairman of the board and then briefly as chairman of the Finance Committee, disagreed with Cushman as he had with Jeppson. He clashed with Cushman over stock options, acquisitions, divestments, and managerial incentive plans, which portended basic departure from the family-run abrasives business of three generations. But Higgins could no longer preserve old values and traditions. The firm's public character and its poor performance in the late 1960s and early 1970s underscored his formal surrender of power in 1967. Norton could no longer endure intuitive centralized management, and even the old owner-operator could not long buck the outside directors, market analysts, and other critics who advocated change especially after Robert Cushman became president in 1971.[23]

While poor performance helped remove internal restrictions, it remained a serious hindrance in its own right. As Cushman admitted, "We weren't anxious to see security analysts . . . until we got ourselves straightened out."[24] His first actions as president were mainly short-term efforts to shore up the firm's financial position. A lengthy strike at General Motors in 1970 deepened an already serious cyclical downturn and aggravated Norton's financial position that had previously been weakened by its bad years in the late 1960s. The company paid out 60 percent of net earnings between 1967 and 1969 to maintain its dividend level.

In addition, Cushman, in what he later described as "a cold-blooded thing," wielded a heavy axe to cut costs and free up cash flow.[25] He reduced salaries 10 percent, laid off 1,200, curtailed inventories $37 million in two years, and decimated the corporate staff, terminating corporate statistical, marketing, business planning, and research operations. Robert Stauffer's exciting, free-wheeling research and development operation ended as Norton's research facility in Cambridge was sold to Cabot Corporation. Cushman's Focused Growth Program redirected research "on projects which can have a material effect on those markets and businesses where growth prospects for Norton are greatest."[26] A number of the highly touted lines of the 1960s, including the Billy Goat vacuum cleaner and the concrete pumping equipment, were sold or dropped.

Restoration of $3 per share earnings became Norton's first goal, and by 1973 internal savings and general economic recovery had more than achieved that aim. Per share earnings were $3.94, up from $2.09 in 1970 and $2.12 in 1971. Computerized control of inventories alone had freed up a net $13 million.[27]

At the same time the new president's short-term efforts had a distressingly negative character. They focused on the bottom line, cost cutting, and divestment. Norton became smaller, falling forty positions to 317 in the *Fortune* 500 industrial ranking between 1969 and 1972, and the economizing underscored even more deeply the firm's conservative, stodgy image. In the long run, however, recovery meant stability, credibility, and freedom for Cushman and his team to reshape fundamentally the old New England family business.

Besides the impact of corporate politics and hard times, the pace of implementation of strategic planning reflected the process of innovating new procedures. In addition to the planning exercise itself, major needs included financial tools and programs for managerial standards, incentives, and education.

Controller John Dingle, Graham Wren, and others offered several new techniques to help managers appraise and be appraised. They established capital budgets and net-asset-based accounting for divisions and introduced a standard and more analytical form for capital investments, which identified the project, its objectives, the nature and size of risks, key assumptions, the precise amounts required, and the dates of expenditure and operation. Each sponsor also had to project annual net benefits in sales, profits, income, and cash flow; key financial data, including rate of return calculated on the basis of discounted cash flow; and impact on his capital budget. Following the project's completion and implementation, a "post audit" measured actual cost, time, return, and impact against the original projections. In each case the operator submitted the form for review and comment by the corporate controller, who indicated if additional monitoring was necessary. Corporate and operating executives could now evaluate proposed investments on a common basis while knowing investment impact more precisely.[28]

The financial people also offered division heads analysis and tools for risk reduction in foreign operations. These aids included heavy local borrowing to cover exposed assets in politically or economically unstable areas as well as careful monitoring of a host nation's inflation rates, trade balances, wage levels, and other factors influencing the native currency against the dollar. Continuous attention allowed managers to make short-term adjustments in inventory and accounts receivable to cover dividends and other foreign payments.[29]

In corporate purchasing, George Bernardin extended similar help to divisions with systems contracting for bulk, low-value items, long-range planning for major materials purchases, and guidance to division purchasers for maximum decentralization and flexibility.[30] Furthermore, by 1975 the corporation had added its own domestic transport fleet covering at least twenty high-volume routes to assure more certainty, increased flexibility, greater speed, and lower costs for product divisions.

Like corporate planning, management of executive resources was too important to be isolated in a staff department.[31] Norton's corporate Personnel Department remained largely concerned with hiring and firing. Cushman and Tom Green, vice-president for human resources, created an Executive Resources Committee of top line and staff people to identify, track, and rate 200 top managers from the entire enterprise. They rejected the more elaborate plans of Shell, General Electric, and others, which carefully scheduled careers for outstanding personnel; much of actual managerial development fell to key line people.

To match the flexibility provided by segmentation, Cushman and his executives encouraged top line people to pair appointments and personalities. Thus, they sought entrepreneurs for units with "build" missions, administrators for "maintain" positions, and economizers for "harvest" jobs. For analytical measurement of management compensation, the salary committee adopted the Hay Point Evaluation System in 1967 to identify job opportunity to contribute to corporate results. In 1971 more than fifty different incentive plans were tailored for the eighty-odd people eligible, and within a decade plans covered more than five hundred managers worldwide. For Cushman the establishment of precise objectives for appraisal and reward were crucial to his program's success. "I want [appraisal] to be a way of life at Norton, all the way down to the first line supervisors . . . Planning isn't much use unless something is done to follow up on the strategies and action progams that have been developed."[32]

Besides the contributions from corporate staff and committees of top line and staff people, there was an active program for general education. Preparation and presentation of strategic plans directly involved eighty managers and indirectly included nearly five hundred others. With annual planning and a biennual presentation for each business unit, education was a constant, continuing process. In addition, first Jeppson and then Cushman carefully articulated Norton's goals in a series of broad, scrupulously worded statements outlining the firm's major strategic purposes, financial objectives, and ethical positions. Jeppson, Cushman, and other top executives broadcast the goals, the new strategic planning techniques, and even the Boston Consulting Group jargon in memoranda, discussions, speeches, and articles in the *Norton Spirit*. The most effective education was handled through speeches and seminars at a series of management conferences. These began with the Bermuda and Taormina Conferences of the late 1960s and in 1971 were institutionalized as five-year world management meetings for the company's top two hundred to three hundred managers.[33]

Ultimately, education, like strategic planning itself, had to be implemented through the line. In the Cushman era, as in previous Norton generations, top operation depended not on a single individual but on a small team of managers with complementary talents. When he became president in 1971, Cushman carried Jeppson's original reorganization one step further. Norton Company's commitment to diversified enterprise in consumable industrial supplies was reflected in its reorganization into two major product groups. As figure 9 illustrates, Abrasives Products and Norton International were combined to form the Abrasives Product Group, a worldwide organization including all bonded abrasives, coated abrasives, and abrasives materials operations. Representing Norton's heritage and more than 75 percent of its total sales and profits, the new group under Executive Vice-President Harry Duane was the firm's "cash cow." All remaining product lines were assembled under Executive Vice-President Donald Melville as the Diversified Products Group. They included "dogs" and "question marks" like pressure sensitive tape and the machine division, which were to be harvested and divested. But fundamentally, Diversified Products was intended as Norton's future high-growth or "star" area, as reflected in figure 9. This chart dates from 1978 and includes new diversified lines added in the 1970s as well as the Christensen Group, all of which will be discussed later.

NORTON COMPANY
ORGANIZATION, 1978

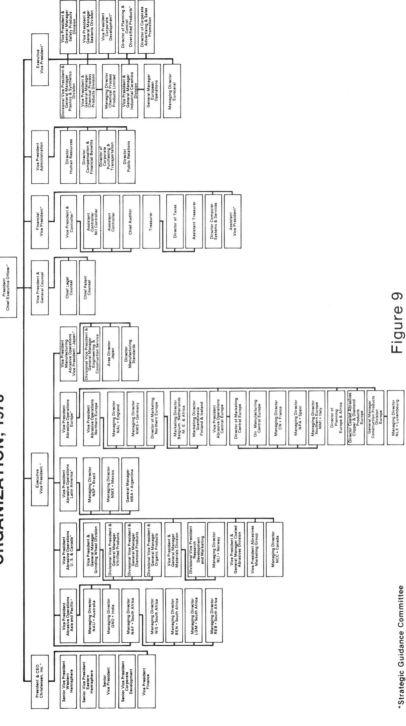

Figure 9

*Strategic Guidance Committee

The Cushman team (left to right): Robert Cushman, Donald Melville, and Harry Duane. (Photo: *Business Week*, August 7, 1971, p. 80. © 1971 Steve Hansen.)

Application: Harry Duane and the Abrasives Group

Just as Cushman's efforts in the 1970s were natural extensions of concepts and plans developed during his executive vice-presidency,

Harry Duane's commitment to analytical, systematic management and decentralization had already evolved during his leadership of Norton International after 1967. Segmentation for analysis came naturally to Duane. As a controller of Industrial Ceramics, he and John Dingle in Abrasives had developed profit variance analysis to test profit forecasts systematically against variations in volume, product mix, price, and cost, a technique he had later installed as NII controller and then as group vice-president. Intrigued by his work with Cushman and the Boston Consulting Group on the Norton Plan, Duane followed closely the development of strategic planning and passed along informally the new concepts and techniques to his managers.[34]

As head of NII, Duane moved quickly to centralize ultimate control and provide overall guidelines for his line managers. He terminated Wilfred Place's Paris-based European organization and restored the international division's headquarters in Worcester. Working with a strong functional staff, which included Louis Camarra in marketing, Stanley Berman in manufacturing, and Graham Wren in finance, Duane swiftly rationalized NII operations with a Profit Opportunities Program (POP). POP first necessitated a comprehensive survey of all profit improvement opportunities and of NII human resources.

Duane then focused his people on thirty-three projects ranked according to potential profit improvement (there was a $100,000 minimum) and probability of success. POP no. 1 was the creation of a Basic Information System, covering all markets and source locations and categorized by manufacturing process and industry code. For the first time in its history, Norton could integrate all marketing, accounting, and production information for cost/source analysis and ultimately for more rational scheduling and sourcing. A second POP established a uniform, worldwide inventory control policy based on economical lot size to extend the potential for integration and to reduce annual inventories by $1.9 million.[35]

After making clear what he wanted line operators to do, Duane decentralized authority in what he called a delegation of power from "authority of position" to "authority of knowledge." Product scheduling and pricing were left to production and sales managers.[36] Duane appointed "the achiever type of person" for management and gave him "freedom [to act] within [defined] bounds," while he and his associates acted as peers and coaches and consulted continuously for consensus.[37] Eventually more than two hundred fifty top managers had individual incentive programs, while conferences and seminars formally taught strategic planning concepts and techniques to more than five hundred people in fifty-five plants around the world. At the same time pushing down daily administrative tasks allowed headquarters to concentrate on "co-ordination, planning, and major strategy development."[38] By 1980 Duane's line people were developing medium-range plans for the 1990s.

Duane's promotion and the creation of a worldwide abrasives division in 1971 completed the formal integration of Norton's abrasives operations. Following the example of Coca-Cola and other dominant-product multinational enterprises, Duane created geographic divisions: Asia and the Pacific under John Adams, Europe and Africa under Allan Kassay, South America under Alfredo Povadano, and North America under John Nelson. Stanley Berman soon headed Japanese operations as a separate division, while the large European market was subdivided into northern, central, and southern regions.

Regional organization was the natural outgrowth of the merger of domestic operations with an international business already geographically segmented. Subdivision by product rather than geography, the trend in multinational organizations, was not seriously considered.[39] In 1971 Norton Company had no major international product lines besides abrasives. International operations from the National Research and Clipper lines were sold or consolidated with Abrasives, and Cushman and Melville were selling the machine tool business which had a small English plant. Within the Abrasives Group the historically separate coated abrasives segment was in serious trouble, while diamond and other bonded products had always been treated as a unit.

Reorganization into worldwide abrasive product divisions came gradually and depended on Duane's success in reestablishing the "cash cow" and on the growth of markets. In 1977 bonded and coated product divisions replaced the original three subregions in Europe, and in 1981 Bernard Meyer, Duane's successor, created worldwide divisions for the coated, bonded, abrasive materials (grain), and construction products (blades) lines. In smaller markets like South Africa and South America the regional approach continued.

To outsiders and perhaps even to some within the company, Duane's assignment in 1971 was hardly enticing. He was to rationalize, cut costs, and restore the prosperity of Norton's "cash cow," but his overall mission was to maintain or hold. Norton projected continued slow growth for the mature abrasives industry and existing excess capacity in the grain, bonded, and coated fields was expected to keep profit margins down. There was little incentive for expensive market share battles with entrenched competitors. Abrasives profits were to fuel expansion and investment in more exciting high-growth areas under Melville in Diversified Products.

In fact abrasives operations remained rather lively. Under Duane's shrewd guidance the segmented approach provided flexibility for rapid expansion in some regions, aggressive new development in others, and careful cost cutting and rationalization in still others. Planning, preparation, and systematic analysis not only restored profts; they also expanded market share by helping Norton Company seize un-expected opportunities.

Moving into new areas required Norton to abandon past shibbo-leths about total control. The logic was clear: without licensing, mi-nority positions, and sale of know-how, Norton would surrender to its competitors revenue to be gained for small cash investments. In a mature industry the firm had to forget old assumptions about pro-tective secrecy, for by the late 1960s the exclusiveness of many Norton products and processes was largely a mystique.[40] Duane and Berman persuaded the Board of Directors to permit the sale of know-how and the construction of turnkey plants making pulpstones, bonded ab-rasives, and coated abrasives in the USSR, Poland, and Romania. Accepting a minority partnership with the Sidhva family in the Grind-well Company of India assured market participation, a source to sup-ply industrializing Asian countries, and royalties for technology and know-how.

Japan offered the clearest case for compromise with past traditions. Maintenance of its reputation and position as the leading manufac-turer of abrasives compelled Norton to enter the world's third largest abrasives market where it had less than 1 percent participation in 1967.[41] Not only were there potentially excellent Japanese industrial domestic sales; Duane also feared that exports by Japanese abrasives manufacturers (some of whom had already formed partnerships with Carborundum and 3M) might erode other Norton markets in Asia and the Pacific. As he explained to the Board of Directors, "If the Japanese cost position were to become overly domineering, Norton could participate in the domination rather than be defeated by it."[42]

The key was a flexible approach through segmentation. To assure a steady, quality grain supply, Norton licensed Japan Carlit, Pacific Metals, and NKG Insulators to produce silicon carbide, Alundum, and Rokide coatings and thus avoided heavy investment in a low-profit area. To enter the Japanese market and meet government reg-ulations on outside investment, Norton formed partnerships that gave it operating equality and a minority holding with the Mitsubishi Metal Mining Company for diamond abrasives, Riken Corundum Company for coated abrasives (later altered to a license), and Kure Grinding Wheel Manufacturing Company for nondiamond bonded abrasives. After chartering a trading company to facilitate imports, exports, and exchange in 1974, Norton Company found itself very well placed.

The carefully selected Kure and Mitsubishi partnerships assured Norton at least second place in the bonded markets and two excellent, powerful partners. And while reinvestment for expansion limited dividends, license fees and royalties assured Norton more than $1 million cash flow annually.[43]

In other areas Duane moved aggressively to expand operations where industrial and economic development promised rapid growth. To take advantage of Brazil's "Economic Miracle" of the 1960s and 1970s, he authorized manager Alfredo Povadano to double plant capacity and cut profit margins as a means to expand Norton's existing 50 percent market share.[44] Decentralized authority assured the talented Povadano the freedom he needed to meet the competition. In one notable case his recognition of Brazil's need for lower cost, less technical products led Povadano to introduce an oil-bonded waterproof paper, nearly obsolete in the United States, in competition with Carborundum's and 3M's very successful latex product. The oil bond, though technically inferior to latex, met Brazilian requirements at much lower cost and soon captured that market while becoming a major export for Latin America, the Far East, and parts of Europe. By 1979 economic growth and expanded market share had absorbed all the new capacity.

Norton enjoyed similar success under John Adams in Australia, Ian Hetherington in South Africa, and Charles Lahaussois in Spain.[45] Adams reequipped the Australian operation after Norton bought out its partners in the early 1970s and expanded branch production into New Zealand and Singapore. In South Africa Hetherington's lucrative operation held over half the domestic market and exported heavily to neighboring nations, while Lahaussois expanded market share and capacity from a small plant begun in the mid-1960s.

Additional expansion occurred as Norton growth approached diminishing returns in such areas and their managers were encouraged to diversify for more efficient use of resources, especially when currency restrictions made profit repatriation to the United States difficult. Following Norton's consumable industrial supplies strategy, Hetherington moved quickly and successfully into the manufacture of shovels, hoes, and other simple tools popular in a labor-intensive mining economy. The Brazilian and Spanish operations began refractory production as the Industrial Ceramics Division became a worldwide operation, and the Australian plant continued to dominate that nation's pressure-sensitive tape market.

In more mature industrial economies such as the United States and Western Europe, the Abrasive Division cut costs with more careful integration of production and marketing and increased profits by developing proprietary products to justify premium pricing. Consolidation of coated and bonded sales into the Abrasives Marketing Group (AMG) with joint sales training required eighty fewer people and seven fewer warehouses in the United States. With the addition of Norton's own trucking fleet, computerization, and standardization of inventory, all domestic coated and bonded sales in 1976 were handled by a force smaller than the coated sales group in 1971.[46]

Even more complex efforts were required to specialize and coordinate European production and marketing. Again the pressures were rising costs in a relatively stagnant market. Norton's old European plants were poorly located in high labor cost areas and badly needed revamping. Relocation and investment in new plants ran counter to Duane's mission, and rising indemnification charges for workers left behind eventually made the cost of rebuilding prohibitive. As the Italian plant manager in the early 1960s, Duane had realized that bonded plants had already achieved sporadic, limited specialization; some were net importers and others net exporters.

Sourcing, the specialization of European manufacturing and marketing by plant, became one of the major POP projects.[47] The Common Market, Norton's basic information system, and its product standardization helped make possible what costs and competition made necessary. The procedure was incredibly complex and is still evolving. It necessitated careful negotiations with labor unions, government officials, and distributors and meticulous calculation of labor and transportation costs, currency fluctuations, trade barriers, market preference, and reserve capacity for possible disruption.

At first individual coated and bonded plants in Germany, France, and Britain became prime manufacturers of particular products in the late 1960s; then in the mid-1970s Duane assigned each plant exclusive product lines. In coated abrasives the Belfast plant manufactured light products while Conflans produced the heavy-backed materials. By 1980 European coated plants were even cross-sourcing with the United States on a limited basis. In bonded abrasives, English, French, and German operations divided vitrified and organic products. Spain was omitted, since it was a new plant that stood outside the Common Market, and the Italian plant remained a general producer and reserve source in case of an overflow of orders or disruption. Distribution was coordinated by Vero Biondi, marketing vice-president for all Europe.

Success is difficult to measure. European return on investment remained below Norton targets, but the erosion of its market share slowed or halted. The substitution of plant specialization for the flexibility of multiple product sources along with more careful engineering in manufacturing processes cut costs and allowed Norton to compete more successfully with the specialized European firms that grew so aggressively with the Common Market.

Supplementing coordination and specialization have been research efforts to cut costs with process improvements, to increase product performance, and to introduce new products giving Norton Company a proprietary edge, especially in its traditional areas of expertise where cost/performance evaluation was critical. Such improvements have included bond maturation at lower temperatures to save kiln capacity and fuel, more precise wheel molding to reduce finishing costs and material wastes, two-station, multicavity presses, automation of jumbo roll conversion, and polyester backings for coated abrasives.

Easily the most impressive innovation has been the development of zirconia-alumina abrasives, "a once in a generation opportunity."[48] A mixture of zirconium oxide and alumina, the new product's high strength and impact-resistance properties help retain cutting abilities under severe conditions. Fast cutting at high temperatures and pressures make it ideal for coated abrasive metal finishing and for foundry and steel conditioning as a bonded abrasive.

The product had a long heritage. Norton had experimented with zirconia abrasives as early as World War I, and both the Worcester firm and its competitors had developed zirconia-alumina for stainless steel grinding in the late 1950s and early 1960s. Its widespread adoption in the 1970s resulted from a more economical impact-crushing process of manufacture, wider application, and the determination to focus on development of products for the foundry and steel-conditioning markets where Norton Company was traditionally weak. Norton's careful development work gave it a proprietary advantage with as much as 70 percent market share in 1975 when sales exceeded $2.4 million.[49]

Strategic planning and segmentation not only restored the abrasives group's prosperity; it increased profits and market share. Cost cutting, exploitation of key markets, and positioning for recovery from periodic recessions allowed Norton to grow while Carborundum and Bay State, its two closest competitors that were under new management, both slipped. International expansion permitted Norton to take advantage of higher growth rates outside the United States. In 1967 foreign sales were 45 percent of all abrasives revenue; in 1980 they were 53 percent of sales. Japanese penetration and European recovery helped the company to maintain sales to the auomotive industry despite the slump in production by American manufacturers. Worldwide market share has increased from 21 percent in 1971 to 25 percent in 1980, while profits have grown at a 20 percent annual compound rate to more than $60 million per year.[50]

Application: Donald Melville and the Diversified Products Group

Despite the recovery and success of abrasives, diversification advanced even more rapidly. Donald Melville, Cushman's vice-president for diversified products, became Norton Company's "Mr. Growth." His assignment was to provide 40 percent of the firm's profits by 1980, and strategic planning established a framework to avoid the chaotic diversification of the 1960s. As Cushman explained, he only wanted new lines "that would make sense for Norton Company to be involved in."[51] Nonabrasive products were to resemble Norton's core business: consumable industrial supplies without elaborate technology and capital intensity in industries without heavy government regulation or purchase.

Melville's first job was implementation of the Product Line Study Committee's recommendations. Wasting additional managerial resources on businesses that had no future at Norton was pointless, and the earnings slump in 1970 and 1971 made additional cash welcome. Melville moved quickly, and between 1969 and 1971 the Cambridge Research Laboratory, Pavement Specialists, the gear hobbing, the Billy Goat vacuum cleaner, the concrete pumping equipment, Supercon, and the quarry tile lines were all sold, while many others were simply discontinued.

For the prudent company, however, speed did not mean a fire sale.[52] Melville's careful targeting of customers paralleled Norton's new, analytical, segmented approach. Except for the sale of pressure sensitive tape, all divestments returned at least book value. Sale of the tantalum metals operation was even delayed until a proper buyer was found in 1976. The $5.3 million loss on tape in 1974 reflected large fixed capacity, which limited flexibility, and the decision to curtail all Watervliet operations.

Divestment of the Machine Tool Division was the most radical and difficult severance. Despite the reluctance of Milton Higgins and John Jeppson, its necessity was clear. The division was mired in the capital goods cycle, and despite Everett Hicks's efforts in the 1950s and 1960s, its return on investment always lagged behind the company average. Higgins and Gow knew this intuitively even though a controller had written in 1961 that "it is impossible to compare Norton's [machinery division's] return on investment over the last decade to other companies' returns, in that Norton Company does not have records adequately segregating its investments by divisions."[53]

They simply had no better use for the cash at the time, and sale would violate the traditions of Norton paternalism. Experienced descendants of Swedish and other early Norton workers were spread across the abrasives and machinery divisions. Robert Lawson, a fifty-year veteran and division head, explained that "they had so many people in the Machine Tool Division that were brothers and sisters and fathers of the grinding wheel division, both in the blue collar class and in the executive group, not necessarily top executives, but in the department heads, and they just didn't feel that they wanted to cut it off."[54]

By the late 1960s the costs of retention were even greater. Obsolescence threatened the entire line, and Norton Company lagged in the development of numerical controls for machine tools. Labor was 45 percent of the selling price, and Norton could maintain sales and its small profit margin only by holding down wages. A 60¢ average hourly differential in piece rates (24 percent of the machinery rate) between the abrasives and machine divisions caused real morale problems.[55] Furthermore, the Machine Tool Division no longer offered marketing advantages in the mature wheel market as it had in the industry's fledgling period. In fact, competitors like Cincinnati Milling offered their own wheels or carefully specified a non-Norton product. Finally, going public had removed flexibility. Outside directors and market analysts fretted over the low return and stodgy image of capital goods manufacture.

Melville did his best selling job and carefully selected Warner and Swasey, a long-time manufacturer of lathes and other machine tools for metal removal.[56] By 1970 more grinding machines than lathes were used for metal removal in the United States, but unlike Cincinnati Milling, its major competitor, Warner and Swasey had no grinding line. Melville persuaded the buyer to pay book value by pointing out that direct sales by its new owner would reduce costs and that adoption of numerical controls could be spread across Warner and Swasey's entire output. John Jeppson drew on his mantle as embodiment of Norton paternalism to reassure employees of their security and future and helped ensure a smooth transition in early 1972.

By 1974 Melville had efficiently completed the first step of his strategy. Norton had sold sixteen businesses and terminated forty-four small product lines. Divestments of businesses, land, and buildings generated $42 million cash (including the 1976 sale of tantalum operations) and scarcely dented income per share. And despite the loss of $64 million in sales, growth from new diversified products represented a net sales gain of $66 million.[57]

Rational diversification, the second step, evolved in two ways. Like Harry Duane in abrasives, Melville first encouraged and educated managers of Norton's remaining nonabrasive products to adopt the new strategic planning concepts and methodology. Careful segmentation in each division identified products with growth and profit potential and pointed up gaps to be filled by small acquisitions. He supported an "entrepreneurial atmosphere" among managers, emphasizing compensation for sales growth over cash return.[58]

At the same time the Diversified Products Group became a microcosm of Norton. Melville treated it as a portfolio of businesses. After divesting the "dogs" and encouraging internal development, he worked closely with the directors of corporate development and business planning (who reported directly to Melville) to monitor cash flow, capital allocation, and acquisitions for new lines.

Internal development focused largely on industrial ceramics, the U.S. Stoneware products, and sealants. Industrial ceramics continued to be a natural fit for Norton. The division produced a consumable product marketed by distributors to industrial users and employed kilns and a high-heat technology similar to abrasives. As in abrasives, special orders bulked large; a 1974 review disclosed twenty-five product lines with only one exceeding $4 million sales. The reviewer commented aptly, "We are, in fact, a job shop for customized industrial ceramics."[59]

Following the planning model, division managers William Densmore and Bernard Meyer carefully segmented products and markets and focused efforts for profits and growth. They dropped unprofitable heavy refractories, virtually a commodity item, for which Norton could develop no proprietary advantage. They concentrated on ceramic shields, coatings and cements, industrial furnace components, metal-melting and casting systems, engine components, and waste water treatment systems. And they decentralized operations by placing a manager responsible for profit and loss at the head of each integrated product or segment.

The Vietnam War led Norton Company to manufacture armor comprised of the Norbide (boron carbide) it had developed three decades earlier. A new hot-press technique perfected at Chippawa allowed the production of large, curved shapes to protect bodies and machines with weight reductions up to 40 percent of conventional armor. In four years sales jumped sixteen times to more than $8 million. Eventually the hot-press technique, which pressed material at one ton per square inch at 2,000° C., was adapted to a large line of pressed or sintered ceramics with excellent heat, wear, and corrosion resistance. Norton's later entry into the petroleum field helped encourage the development of proppants, tiny ceramic balls used to expand and maintain deep fissures in rock and thus speed oil flow. By 1976 industrial ceramics sales had doubled and profits had quadrupled since 1970, and in 1980 the division was fast approaching its $100 million sales target.[60]

At the old U.S. Stoneware operations in Ohio, Robert Hunter used Norton cash and planning techniques to reorganize, fight off domestic challenges, and expand abroad.[61] USS continued to focus on its two major profit and growth items—catalyst carriers and biomedical tubing. Following Norton models, Hunter established his own operating and financial plans and decentralized operations into two divisions: Chemical Process Products and Biomedical Products (later Plastics and Synthetics). The Chemical Products Division absorbed Worcester's catalyst carrier production and fought off a determined challenge from Koch Engineering to maintain market leadership while selling a full line of metal, plastic, and ceramic carriers. Biomedical Products' new customers at Colt Industries and Technicon were developed to replace Abbott Laboratories, a major customer that had begun manufacturing its own tubing. The Norton name was phased in gracefully over a twelve-year period, and by 1980 the two divisions were models of autonomous, successful operation.

As an additional internal development, Norton Company established a Sealants Division after careful segmentation of its tape business. Analysis indicated that 3M's dominance and Norton's inexperience with consumer marketing offered a dim future in pressure sensitive tapes, but that vinyl foam tapes were a consumable industrial supply item that could grow into an effective sealants line. Norton purchased Sandon Incorporated of Granville, New York, expanded operations there, and concentrated on the manufacture of sealing and insulating tapes for the automotive, truck, mobile home, and general industrial markets. The acquisition of Novagard Company in 1978 added liquid sealants for window insulation, glazing, and other construction trades. By 1976 return on net assets was 14 percent.[62]

More startling and successful was diversification by acquisition. Success in ceramics, plastic tubing, and catalyst carriers depended largely on reorganization to maximize returns on products Norton already had. Rapid growth of new diversified products came primarily through buying businesses. Despite Norton's public commitment to internal development, Robert Stauffer's record in the 1960s, the strong abrasives orientation of existing Norton research resources, Robert

Cushman's emphasis on directed research, and the time needed to develop new product lines discouraged reliance on internal generation of new businesses.

In the early 1970s, Cushman and Melville moved quickly to institutionalize acquisitions as part of Norton Company's new strategic planning network. Richard Griffin, director of corporate development, Ray Shonfeld, his assistant, and Norman Johnson, director of business planning, devoted full time to acquisitions as part of Melville's staff while Melville worked half time and Cushman spent one third of his efforts.[63]

Griffin, who had headed his own consulting firm and specialized in acquisitions before being hired by Melville, played the key role.[64] In an office contiguous to both Melville's and Johnson's, he established the mechanism for selecting and analyzing candidates and spent the majority of his time in actual analysis, while Johnson did market surveys before moving to line management. Following Cushman's earlier objections to Richard Harris's scatter-shot techniques, Griffin established specific criteria for candidates. They were to manufacture consumable industrial supplies with demand cycles different from and growth rates higher than abrasives. Norton looked for unconcentrated fields or one of the three largest market shares in order to assure leadership potential. Finally, rates of return were to exceed Norton's 5.5 percent average and businesses were not to be so highly capital intensive as to restrict future mobility.

Success depended on fit and timing. Richard Harris, Griffin's predecessor, had gathered much data but a lack of clear corporate objectives, distraction by poor corporate performance, and the need to divest and raise cash negated his work. Griffin followed a segmented, systematic, and analytical approach, which reflected strategic planning and Cushman management. He divided the search into three categories. Type I was small cash mergers such as Sandon to fill out existing nonabrasive lines. Griffin announced Norton's interests to more than three hundred intermediaries, gathered information, and made initial contacts. Consistency with Norton's emphasis on decentralized line management, however, meant that any further action rested with the appropriate division manager.

Type II mergers were large acquisitions of new lines. Griffin expected growth rates of 5-10 percent, competent management in place for autonomous operation, and a price range of $30–120 million, payable in Norton stock. In addition to depending on intermediaries, Griffin carefully conducted his own search. Working from Standard Industrial Classification codes, he listed all nonconsumer and non–capital goods industries at the three-digit level. A computer program screened out any that would heavily dilute earnings. A further screening based on ten-year financial performance and personal knowledge reduced the list to 200, for which Griffin established files, opened negotiations, and maintained continuous contact. By 1973 he had turned up more than 30 serious possibilities, including catalysts, nylon tubing, bearings, batteries, thermostats, and glass containers. For a variety of reasons, including the poor performance of Norton stock, the company's refusal to pursue unfriendly mergers that would poison relations with crucially needed management, and Cushman's insistence on a careful fit, none worked out.

Griffin was more successful with type III, the acquisition of small related firms to establish a major new division. Beginning in 1973, he instituted a series of mergers to build a Safety Products Division. He had identified safety products from an Arthur D. Little report in 1973, and careful scrutiny disclosed a near-perfect technological, managerial, and financial fit.[65] They were consumable goods sold largely through distributors to industrial users. The field was fragmented among dozens of tiny firms, many privately held or trading over the counter at low price/earnings ratios. Technology was relatively simple, but the need to ensure quality offered a proprietary edge and eliminated the commodity stigma. As a corporate review explained, "Norton's diversification move to Safety Products is diversification in terms of *products* but *not* diversification in terms of *markets*" (italics added).[66] Finally, while the safety products industry was not heavily regulated, expanded government regulation of potential customers as expressed in the Occupational Safety and Health Act of 1970 promised rapid future growth. The real growth rate was projected to nearly triple to 9 percent annually. Although sales of industrial safety products and abrasives fluctuated in similar patterns, the opportunity was too good to miss.

Melville and Griffin moved swiftly to create a successful division. Within two years they had acquired twelve firms and twenty-two plants manufacturing such diverse items as ear plugs, ladder safety devices, industrial gloves, hard hats, safety clothing, and first aid supplies. An integrated sales force was established with twenty-two salaried Norton salespeople and a network of fifty distributors, all working under a standard discount policy. In 1976 Norton reached second place in the industry with a work force of 2,000, sales exceeding $50 million, and an excellent return on assets.[67]

By 1976 rational diversification had much improved Norton Company's performance and moved it toward the target set by Cushman in 1971. In six years sales of all nonabrasive lines had increased from $5 million to $160 million. They now accounted for 28 percent of

Norton's total and were well on the way to the firm's goal of 40 percent by 1980. Return on net assets for nonabrasives had jumped even more spectacularly from 2 percent to 12 percent, the goal set in 1971. Divestments and operations had netted $28 million cash for reinvestment after deducting the cost of acquisitions. Norton was also beginning to enjoy some freedom from the abrasives cycle as diversified products cushioned downturns. During the 1975 recession as sales slipped 2 percent, profits slid only 3 percent, a considerable improvement over the 29 percent profit drop that accompanied the 2 percent sales decline of 1969–1971.[68]

Furthermore, what had started largely as a domestic operation was fast becoming a series of international businesses. Industrial ceramics had five European plants, and Euroceral was in full production as a French joint venture using alumina ceramic products in the process of uranium enrichment. Based on production begun in the 1960s for the French military, the new operation was expanded for nuclear reactors and other civilian uses and quickly became a big cash generator. As noted earlier, industrial ceramic production had also spread to Latin America and southeast Asia under subcontract to the abrasives group. The acquisition of a former U.S. Stoneware licensee, the Arrowsmith group, had moved chemical process products into England and Australia, while in Luxembourg the plastics and synthetics division had also built a plant.

The Limits of Planning

Neither Melville nor Duane enjoyed unqualified success, and the limits of both the abrasives and the diversified operations pointed the way toward changes that are still being implemented. Problems resulted from a variety of causes: unexpected external change, the adaptation of planning theory to actual operation, the heritage of earlier operation, and normal adjustments in the course of innovation.

Based on a Boston Consulting Group study, Melville had high hopes for Norton expansion into plastics, but that never worked out.[69] The idea was logical enough. Norton Company had experience with plastics dating back to resin bonds in the 1920s, and USS added considerable expertise and application, especially in proprietary products. Yet, neither the sealants line nor a foray into injection-molded plastic machine components developed as expected. The sealants business suffered seriously after a decline among its customers. Mobile home sales dropped as energy costs rose, the U.S. automotive industry slumped as prices rose and foreign manufacturers moved aggressively into developing small car markets, and home construction slowed with escalating interest rates in the late 1970s and early 1980s. In addition, the Novagard merger was, in Melville's words, "a bum acquisition."[70] The attempt to build a line of engineered plastic parts around a small acquisition (Lakeville Precision Molding Company) foundered as rising petroleum prices drove up raw materials costs, and Norton simply never developed a good marketing organization. Both lines were eventually added to biomedical products to become the Plastics and Synthetics Division.

Nor did Diversified Products grow as fast as was hoped. As of 1976 abrasives still accounted for 72 percent of total sales, in part because of Harry Duane's unexpected success in increasing abrasives sales. Norton Company found internal development of new products slow and disappointing; focused efforts on improving existing products and processes absorbed research resources. Furthermore, the Safety Products Division was almost impossible to duplicate. Melville thought the mixture of preparation and opportunity was "luck."[71] He and Griffin found it nearly impossible to meet Cushman's stringent standards, and Griffin eventually quit in frustration with Norton's conservative approach to mergers. A firm that insisted on product and market compatibility, majority ownership, and a willing candidate had few opportunities. In short, Cushman's insistence on control, which grew from the chaos of the 1960s, was sometimes at odds with the push for entrepreneurship and rapid growth.

Duane's Abrasive Group endured similar difficulties. It failed to anticipate the rapid recovery of 1973 and a serious capacity shortage restricted a golden opportunity to expand share. The crunch was especially critical in abrasive materials, whose mission was simply to supply Norton's needs. To meet unexpectedly heavy demand, Norton hurriedly depolluted all its old Higgins furnaces in 1974 to meet new clean air standards. By 1976 forecasts were revised downward and price differentials for proprietary grains shrank, causing excess capacity and lower returns.[72]

As in the Diversified Products Group, administration of abrasives lines also disclosed conflicts between theory and application. The Boston Consulting Group's criteria suggested the sale of furnace operations since overcapacity and heavy capital costs forecast extended low returns on a commodity item. Norton executives demurred because the furnaces assured the firm a scheduled supply of grain of necessary quality and character. The Chippawa laboratories remained an important source of process and product improvements, and in addition Norton leaders correctly expected that zirconia-alumina would become a proprietary product with premium pricing. Nevertheless, the exception to investment strategy lowered corporate returns and raised morale problems. For abrasives managers and workers to be told they labored for a "cash cow" was hardly attractive, but the constant reminder that furnace people worked for a "dog" stirred protests and led to modest efforts to tone down language.[73]

The problem was not just terminology; it extended to the missions themselves. Despite attempts to match personalities and assignments, few worthwhile managers were content to be maintainers or harvesters; most had some entrepreneurial spirit and wanted to build. Some, like Stanley Berman in Japan, protested strongly that while research directed toward cost cutting and incremental improvement admirably suited sluggish domestic and European markets, the cautious approach was totally inadequate for an expanding market with aggressive competitors.[74] Others, like Joseph Palermo, who helped resuscitate Watervliet operations but who could not invest to build on that recovery, left in frustration. Duane himself repeatedly acted counter to his general maintain mission: he reinvested returns, and he approved aggressive, low-return strategies to build in promising markets like Brazil, South Africa, and Australia and to increase Norton capacity and service in order to capture extra market share in cyclical upturns.

The most serious challenge and the area of least success in the Cushman era was domestic coated abrasives operations in Watervliet.[75] While Behr-Manning's difficulties had originated during the late 1950s and 1960s, Norton Company's hesitant, poorly timed, and sometimes inconsistent reactions in the years after the 1966 strike deepened the problem. Return and market share plummeted between 1966 and 1971 when reorganization in Worcester occupied center stage.

At first Worcester delayed instituting new production and marketing strategies for the once powerful, autonomous division. John Jeppson explained that Norton took too long "simply because they [the Watervliet people] wouldn't hear of it."[76] Then headquarters jumped in forcefully without a clear sense of direction. After Edwin Evans left in 1968, Worcester appointed three different managers in six years with little success. It dropped the Behr-Manning trade name, which was much better known than Norton outside the metal trades, in the midst of Watervliet's decline. It first stopped and then reinstituted sales efforts in the automotive and general trades fields. Sale of tape operations in 1974 forced additional overhead costs onto coated abrasives. The hasty movement of labor-intensive operations to Brownsville, Texas, suffered from "cultural difficulties," low productivity, and wretched service in the late 1970s. As late as 1978 the division had still failed to achieve its target of 12 percent return on net assets and was consuming instead of producing cash.

There has been some improvement. The disastrous slide of 1966–1971 halted in the mid-1970s during Palermo's tenure as Watervliet's head. Careful management, mechanization, and revamped operations helped restore morale and productivity, and at Brownsville officials feel they have overcome the high costs of accelerated start-up.

As in the case of abrasive materials, continued manufacture of coated abrasives has meant major compromises with strategic planning theory. The Boston Consulting Group's guidelines and financial projections dictated divestment, but with entrepreneurial spirit Paul Midghall and John Nelson argued successfully in 1974 that Norton could maintain a viable, cash-producing second place in the domestic coated abrasives industry. Furthermore, research and U.S. production were a central part of Norton's international coated operation, and coated abrasives were judged essential to a full-line strategy for a firm determined to maintain its place as the world's leading abrasives manufacturer. The Brownsville move and the careful coordination of coated and bonded markets reflected the determination to stay.

Norton Company has paid a high price for the long decades of ignorance about Behr-Manning. Fifteen years passed while Worcester learned the coated business and recognized that no miraculous Norton Plan was going to wrest market share easily from 3M, the domestic industry's rugged, established leader, and from VSM, Hermes, and SIA, the rapidly encroaching European firms. In the parlance of the Boston Consulting Group, Norton has spent that time learning a business that it has owned for half a century. Based on its recent experience, the firm now expects modest recovery after having finally achieved stability.

The Watervliet debacle and the other compromises challenged and probed but certainly did not discredit the strategic planning approach. Planning could only help predict and prepare for, but not control, the future. Constant data gathering, analysis, and monitoring kept Norton informed and ready to respond quickly and appropriately to opportunity and change. As Robert Cushman explained to the business press, "We're being far more specific than we ever were about our goals and about how we want the company managed . . . This way we can keep on top of trends and start our action before something hits us."[77]

In fact Cushman's success in using business planning and analytical management to restore abrasives operations and initiate profitable diversification opened the door to Norton's major and most successful strategic move of the 1970s. If the safety products opportunity was luck, preparation and focus made Norton the firm that seized the chance. Building the Safety Products Division deepened confidence in the acquisition approach and allowed Kenneth Zeitz, Richard Griffin's successor as director of corporate development, to pursue more flexible strategies such as minority purchase.

Limited profitable diversification also encouraged a larger step. Norton's returns were high; in 1976 return on equity was 10 percent. The company's new challenge was to find profitable outlets for its cash. As late as 1975, 76 percent of all assets were in industries with less than 5 percent annual growth.[78] The firm now sought a third "leg" or product area, which entailed a major acquisition in a new, high-growth field.

The Acquisition of Christensen Company

As in the case of safety products, Norton planning and preparation enabled it to recognize and grasp the lucky opportunity to acquire the Christensen Company of Salt Lake City, Utah. Christensen was an owner-operated firm that produced diamond drill bits and core barrels (hollow bits that store samples) for the petroleum and mining industries and that did some contract drilling through its Boyles Brothers subsidiary. In 1976 it employed 3,000 employees in eighteen plants and one hundred service centers in eleven nations scattered around the globe.[79]

The core of the firm's success was its diamond drill bits. Three-cone rock bits were standard for drilling in 85 percent of oil and mining operations. Diamond bits were much more expensive but amply repaid their costs with longer life and less disruption in deep, awkward, and rocky drilling. Replacing a bit in a two-mile hole involved pulling up and unscrewing more than three hundred fifty sections of thirty-foot pipe and consumed precious hours while high fixed costs mounted.[80] As with Norton's abrasives products, the price/performance ratio outweighed initial costs for industrial users.

Christensen Company dominated the industry as a result of its early position, pioneering technological and service advances, and carefully cultivated raw material supply. When they founded the firm in 1944, Frank and George Christensen, who were unrelated, had known each other as professional football players with the Detroit Lions in the 1930s.[81] Each had considerable experience with diamonds and mining. George had worked as a salesman for the Koebel Diamond Tool Company and in the late 1930s had established the Christensen Diamond Tool Company of Detroit, which had manufactured a few diamond bits for the Tennessee Copper Company. Frank joined his family's firm, the Christensen Machine Company of Salt Lake City, which manufactured stokers and mining and milling equipment and which cast a few diamond bits for Boyles Brothers, mining contractors based in Salt Lake City. When George invited Frank to form a partnership for diamond bit manufacture in 1944, their friendship and experience fitted together naturally.

Although they had three other partners in the $24,000 Christensen Diamond Products Company, Frank and George were its operators. Using the machine company's facilities Frank manufactured diamond bits with a powdered metal bond, while George supplied the diamonds from his New York contacts and marketed products to Boyles Brothers, Tennessee Copper, and others. The firm's technological breakthrough came in the late 1940s when Frank Christensen and Charles Cutler perfected a tungsten carbide matrix for diamond bits at the Rangely, Colorado, oil field. Tungsten carbide's superior erosion resistance to mud and fluids held diamonds in place and lasted much longer than the old powdered metal bits. At the same time the Christensen firm developed core jars, core barrels, and other products to provide a full line of diamond drilling equipment. By 1950 the diamond bit company had absorbed the machinery firm.

Frank pioneered service as well as better products. Since diamond bits were too expensive to inventory, Christensen manufactured on call. The company provided twenty-four-hour, on-call operation at drill sites to meet drillers' demands for rapid service to hold down their costs. Frank Christensen recalled: "You work until you get the product done. You have to design it, put it together and deliver it out there. Many times we would make the diamond bit and then eleven o'clock at night [when] it's finished, put it on an automobile and drive to Rangely. Put it on the drill rig and stay there and drink whisky with the tool pusher until daylight until they had penetrated the Weber formation and come on back."[82] Because air service was unreliable, Christensen Company soon established five branches in the Southwest that took blanks from the Salt Lake plant and fabricated bits for on-site service to the Texas, Louisiana, and Oklahoma fields.

George concentrated on diamond supply, at first from New York City diamond dealers. However, as volume grew a visit to Otto Oppenheimer in London garnered a direct import allocation from the De Beers diamond syndicate of South Africa. As at Norton, trust and a careful personal rapport cemented the relationship and expanded the allocation as volume expanded still more. As the Christensens kept promises to use diamonds only for industrial purposes and not for resale, E. T. S. Brown, head of De Beers's industrial diamond business, scheduled annual allocations with uniform distribution of sizes.

The relationship soon prospered into partnership. As the best material, called congo, grew scarce and prices rose from 80¢ to $8 per carat in two years, Christensen Company pioneered the adaptation of processed stones—large, round diamonds that were previously little used—for petroleum and mining drilling. The development of the processed market helped sustain De Beers's industrial sales after General Electric introduced synthetic diamonds in the mid-1950s. At the same time De Beers became a business partner with its valuable end user. Its subsidiary, Boart Metal Products, contributed diamond inventory and became co-owner when Christensen Company set up its first foreign plant in France in 1953 to service the Middle Eastern oil fields.

In the next decade diamond inventory supplied by De Beers helped finance rapid foreign expansion with plants in Japan, Canada, Mexico, Germany, Italy, Algeria, Venezuela, Ireland (for distribution), India, and Lybia, and Boart became half owner of Christensen. Christensen acquired Boyles Brothers as a laboratory and revenue producer, contracted with the Longyears Company for distribution of mining products, and joined De Beers in mining companies in Costa Rica, Canada, and the Philippines.

In addition to establishing a raw materials supply and developing new products, Christensen assured its leadership by maintaining service and continuing research and development during industry recessions. Careful positioning gave it the lion's share of new business during recovery. When the firm went public in 1975, it had 56 percent of the world's petroleum diamond bit business and 10 percent of the mining market with sales of $118 million and a return on net assets of 16.8 percent.[83]

Norton's successful acquisition was a matter of timing, preparation, and personality. Christensen Company was ripe for sale.[84] George's death in 1968 had saddled Frank with sole leadership, and as he reached 65 in 1975, the surviving partner wished to ease his full-time burden. As at Norton, going public had added the responsibility of cultivating outside analysts and investors, a task Frank Christensen did not enjoy.

Furthermore, the firm needed cash. Settling George Christensen's estate and buying out Boart when De Beers sold its U.S. holdings to avoid antitrust prosecution had forced Christensen Company to go public and contract a $6.5 million short-term debt. At the same time the enterprise needed millions to launch a new line of downhole drilling tools to supplement its bits. The depressed conditions of the oil service industry and of Christensen's securities precluded new issues and limited borrowing capacity.

Norton's top management, however, was unaware of those factors when its careful monitoring for a major acquisition first focused on Christensen. In fact, Norton analysis was so systematic that the proposal surfaced independently on two occasions at corporate headquarters. Financial Vice-President Richard Flynn, who had recently joined Norton from Riley Stoker, read Christensen's prospectus for its first public issue among personal investment data and was struck by its apt fit with the eight criteria Norton Company had articulated for mergers, including high growth rate and proven market image, production of an industrial consumable, emphasis on customer service, strong past performance, freedom from the abrasives cycle, and potential for market leadership.[85] He notified Cushman, who, although he liked the firm, was skeptical because of potential antitrust problems. Christensen was already involved in Justice Department investigations of De Beers's activities in the United States, and although no indictments were made, De Beers did withdraw from U.S. operations. Norton and Christensen were major syndicate customers, and there was a small overlap since both produced diamond blades for concrete construction machines.

Cushman and Flynn had sent the issue to the company's Legal Department for study when Kenneth Zeitz, Norton's new director of corporate planning, independently included Christensen in a pool of candidates for a new program of minority acquisitions.[86] Zeitz reasoned, and the Board of Directors agreed, that because depressed stock values and high costs precluded immediate outright purchase, Norton should consider 20-50 percent investments in targets for likely future mergers. The investments were to be public tenders acceptable to the management of the target company. The investments' size qualified Norton for accounting advantages and insured the candidates against unfriendly takeover. As Zeitz's proposal surfaced, chance again intervened. Norton stock rose and Christensen stock dropped, making outright purchase feasible.

The systematic, analytical approach to eventual merger was a striking contrast to the hurried National Research Corporation purchase, the comparable acquisition in the third generation. Counsel Goodwin, Procter and Hoar's careful scrutiny eroded fears of antitrust violations. Detailed study of reports on the oil service industry, investigation by Arthur D. Little, consultation with Salomon Brothers, a leading investment banking house, and thorough internal examination confirmed Christensen's fit, value, industry leadership, rapid growth, and excellent prospects in a fast expanding industry. In four years sales and profits were up 139 percent and 239 percent, respectively, and ADL confidently projected continued 8-10 percent real growth annually in a world market estimated at more than $200 million.[87]

Norton Company made a formal proposal in February 1976 and completed the merger a year later. Negotiations determined a stock exchange of one Christensen share per .56 Norton share, which made Christensen a wholly owned subsidiary of the Worcester company. Both sides later agreed that however good the fit, personal chemistry sealed the bargain. Despite the apparent contrasts between the western-born former football lineman and the slender, conservative New Englander, Frank Christensen and Robert Cushman quickly generated deep mutual respect and trust.

Christensen's recent experience had soured his hopes for merger.[88] In less than a year he had ridden a roller coaster from the high promise and praise of financial analysts, which accompanied listing on the New York Stock Exchange, to critical analyses that depressed his stock's values and invited a takeover proposal that he contemptuously rejected as ridiculously low. A genial, forthright, but very shrewd man, Christensen was skeptical of merger possibilities at equitable terms. Norton's long reputation as a conservative, fair firm and Cushman's candor eased his resistance.

The course of negotiations bore out both sides' faith. When Christensen Company's performance and stock values slipped after preliminary agreement, Norton made no move to renegotiate more favorable terms. Its plans were long range, and squeeze plays would only sour future operating relationships and could have terminated the deal. Frank Christensen for his part did not try to use counteroffers generated by his financial agents to jack up the .56 ratio even though he might well have gotten a higher price.[89]

Strategic planning and careful management not only ensured an excellent acquisition; they also helped facilitate fine performance and fulfillment of Norton's growth and profit projections. Christensen Company naturally remained an autonomous operation equivalent to the Abrasives and Diversified Product groups; it was called Norton's third leg. As in the Behr-Manning merger in the 1930s, an excellent operating organization was at first left intact; in this case, however, Norton moved much more rapidly to learn and control the business as it gradually became more integrated with Worcester. John Nelson, previously in abrasives operations, was appointed operating head. He and Frank Christensen worked well together, and the former owner-operator used his strong paternal relationship with the Salt Lake City firm to help smooth Nelson's entry.[90]

Nelson for his part introduced tools and techniques to help the firm maximize its opportunities and to allow Norton to monitor operations. Segmentation decentralized the company into three worldwide product divisions: petroleum bits, mining equipment, and downhole tools.

Nelson's seminars taught Norton's strategic planning concepts, and he introduced systematic financial controls and management analysis. In addition, Norton Company also provided the savvy to handle security analysts.[91]

Norton's major contribution, however, was capital and guidance to implement an aggressive build strategy for Christensen's new line of downhole petroleum tools after careful analysis of the market and competition.[92] The Salt Lake City company's German branch had pushed it into downhole tool manufacture in the mid-1970s to help capture the burgeoning North Sea oil market. The tools were attached to the lower part of the drill string and included four major items: a drilling jar, which helped free the string while still in the hole; a shock absorber to cushion rig vibration; a downhole motor, which drove the bit with mud flow; and a coring or fishing jar to take samples and free the string. Like the diamond bits, they represented increased costs to reduce time and risk and were especially applicable for deep or awkward drilling, a market expected to increase rapidly since higher petroleum prices had pushed exploration and drilling into more remote areas and difficult formations.

The product expansion's success, like the merger itself, soon exceeded Norton's expectations. By 1979 Christensen had invested more than $24 million and quickly captured an 18 percent market share as the only enterprise with fully integrated manufacture and service for the drill string. Drilling market potential quadrupled original expectations, and the company added several new products to its line, including Safeflow (a device to avoid downhole blowouts), twist kick (a mechanism to direct drilling sideways), and a measurement-while-drilling (a licensed tool that monitors direction and location without withdrawing the string).[93]

All fitted the Norton product profiles as consumable industrial supplies and proprietary items whose additional cost was merited by time saved and superior performance. In addition, Christensen began expanding its bit market by using synthetic diamond bits to replace rock bits in formations of medium difficulty. By 1980 Christensen sales had increased 107 percent and business income before taxes was up 153 percent since 1977. As Norton's most rapidly growing product group, which contributed 17 percent of sales and 30 percent of business income before taxes in 1980, the acquisition provided the high-growth diversification so long sought.[94]

Systematic Management and the Public Firm

The Cushman administration also paralleled its successful efforts to rationalize and diversify operations with the application of professional, systematic management to Norton's relationship with its various publics. Outsiders received a clearer view. In the 1970s the majority of the Board of Directors became non-Norton people and included Richard Chapin, the president of Emerson College, Edwin Etherington, former president of the American Stock Exchange and of Wesleyan College, and Thomas Wyman, senior vice-president and general manager of Polaroid Corporation.

By 1977 Norton inaugurated continuous courting of market and financial people. Cushman, Melville, Duane, Flynn, and other top executives conducted more that forty meetings with brokers and analysts in sixteen cities. The company strove to present its message and image in colorful, catchy annual reports that clearly articulated company goals and positions. In 1973 the staid, old Worcester firm began sponsoring The Norton Spirit, a racing car, in the Indianapolis 500, Michigan 500, and other major automobile races. In the next decade the car, which was "to put more excitement in our advertising and sales promotion program" and "reinforce" the "new management style" and "aggressive stance," entertained thousands of customers, distributors, suppliers, and employees in dozens of races, and in 1981 it won the prestigious Indianapolis 500-mile race.[95]

Cushman also directed a determined effort to systematize Norton Company's public role in local, national, and world affairs.[96] An ethics code, originally drafted in 1961, was revamped to define ethics as "a philosophy of human conduct" and distinguish them from absolute moral standards as "a matter of spirit and intent as well as a matter of law."[97] The code pledged Norton to operate within the spirit and letter of the law, prohibited political contributions and payoffs, required proper recording of all expenses, and carefully listed as an exception small gratuities to minor public officials to facilitate, but not to complete, transactions. It also provided for annual review of compliance and established a Corporate Ethics Committee of directors and top executives to specify procedures and act as a final authority.

In addition, the systematic public policy program included a Corporate Action Manual, which spelled out policies for loaned executives and for public service by employees. Norton also broadened and decentralized corporate contributions. Employee advisory committees at division and plant levels were empowered to review and determine local contributions. Besides its traditional charitable donations, the firm undertook a number of voluntary programs, providing employment for the handicapped, ex-offenders, and early-released convicts and offering treatment or counseling for drug addiction, alcoholism, smoking, job placement, and stress.

Like strategic planning, the new public activities were part of the application of professional management to Norton Company. They included the definition of responsibility, establishment of goals, systematic application and appraisal of effort, and, where possible, a flexible decentralized approach. Beginning in 1973, Norton published a ten-page statement, variously titled *Accountability*, *Response*, or *Social Investments*, with each annual report and carefully reviewed each year's activities and measured them against publicly stated corporate goals.

The motivations were, of course, varied. In part the new program signaled the decline of the Norton Spirit and Norton family. The old, paternal labor relationship had weakened in the face of expansion, diversification, and the passing of owner-management. By the 1950s the original Swedish immigrant workers had given way to American-born and Americanized second and third generations. Increased income, the automobile, and television provided alternate, diversified recreation and social activities.

Increasing numbers of employees worked outside Worcester and outside the United States (44 percent by 1959), where the traditions of patriarchal owner-management meant very little. By 1973 half the work force was unionized, and in the United States alone 12 percent were in unions.[98] The professional managers who followed Gow and Higgins made little effort to know personally even the workers in Worcester. In 1974 Norton corporate offices were separated from the Greendale plant area and moved to a downtown office building. The passing of the annual outing and Norton Beach as well as the advent of identification badges, gate checks, and counseling programs vividly proclaimed the substitution of a more formal employee relations program for the old Norton paternalism.

The new activity also reflected modern professional managers' vague sense of the large corporation's public responsibility. While the enterprise's first responsibility was to generate returns for investors, the large agglomerate of people and resources was willy-nilly a social force. For Norton, that tradition in Worcester was a long-standing one, typically expressed through its contributions and the civic services of owner-managers and their families. Under Cushman the emphasis fell on the enterprise itself "to help the society in which it lives" by offering facilities for local action or by training public officials in financial accounting, management techniques, and other areas of Norton expertise.[99]

As another motivation, corporate accountability was designed to preserve the environment within which the enterprise acted. Tom Green, the vice-president of human resources who directed the program in the 1970s, saw "it as a necessary involvement if business is going to survive at all."[100] Cushman echoed that "social responsibility is just good business."[101] In familiar language they and other corporate

The three legs of Norton Company, 1980.
Abrasives.

managers argued that if corporations did not move to regulate their behavior and meet broader social needs, government would act.

The timing of Norton's activities reflected their defensive nature. The first ethics program was written after the price-fixing scandals in the electrical industry in the early 1960s and was revamped in the mid-1970s amid sensational exposés of American firms' illegal corporate political contributions in the United States and bribery of foreign officials to facilitate overseas business. Concern over environmental quality, safety, and equality of employment by race and sex followed implementation of the Environmental Protection Agency, the Occupational Safety and Health Administration, and the Equal Employment Opportunity Commission in the 1960s and 1970s. Norton was not involved in the bribery, pricing fixing, and illegal contributions; a careful internal review disclosed only isolated, insignificant violations. Nor was it a special target of government regulation. Yet, prudent management simply could not ignore the rising tide of enmity to big business and multinational enterprise that had evolved during the upheavals of the 1960s and early 1970s.

Diversified products.

Determination of success was difficult. Expectations and standards varied with the measurer's values, and limits were easier to total up than accomplishments. Cultural differences and legal requirements seriously hindered efforts to expand the company's social responsibility worldwide. As the seat of Norton's headquarters, Worcester still garnered the largest share of social action and contributions within the United States. Defining and innovating appropriate responses was difficult since the public role of large enterprises remained obscure in our society. Despite Cushman's best intentions, Norton's work became a largely ritualized, statistical review measuring contributions and employment quotas.

At times, too, the firm's economic and social responsibilities conflicted. Norton Company continued to maintain and expand profitable operations in South Africa despite its repugnant apartheid policy. It signed the Sullivan Principles and tried to improve wages, working conditions, and job opportunities for blacks, but at the same time it decentralized operations to meet government racial quotas.[102]

While exploiting profitable opportunities on behalf of its investors remained the primary function for Norton and the rest of American

Petroleum drilling and mining products.

private enterprise, the company's accountability program was unusual. Few firms so carefully set open standards and consistently and publicly measured themselves. A 1977 survey of 501 large enterprises revealed that few had institutionalized ethics policies and fewer than 6 percent had ethics committees.[103] Systematic analysis increased awareness and chances of improvement. The number of blacks and women in managerial positions, for example, was small, but there was "real growth" as Norton's accountability statement mercilessly announced the annual statistics. Cushman readily conceded the limits but also pointed up the effort. "We stood up and said what we thought business should be."[104]

Whatever the judgment may be of professional management's success in social policy and public responsibility, its economic performance was indisputably excellent. By 1980, when Cushman surrendered the post of chief executive to Donald Melville, Norton Company had met or exceeded the stringent goals set in 1971. A firm that had stumbled badly in the booming 1960s became a prosperous, trim operation amid the inflation, recession, and increased unemployment that characterized the 1970s. Norton was a true multinational with half its income and work force outside the United States. It had increased its leading share in the American and world abrasives industries while generating higher return on investment. It had become a balanced producer of consumable industrial supplies. An economic slump in 1980 indicated a considerable reduction of cyclicality: a 9 percent reduction in abrasives income was offset by a 16 percent increase in revenues from Christensen and other diversified operations. Nonabrasives lines contributed 41 percent of total earnings in 1979, against the 40 percent target established a decade earlier; by 1980 more than half of all profits came from nonabrasives businesses for the first time in Norton's history.[105]

Financial growth was just as spectacular. While the Commodity Price Index and the Consumer Price Index doubled between 1971 and 1979, Norton sales jumped 327 percent to more than $1 billion, and profits shot up 705 percent. As table 3 in chapter 7 indicates, return on assets increased from 3.5 percent to almost 10 percent, and earnings were growing 15 percent annually against a 10 percent goal. Between 1974 and 1979 Norton stock nearly quadrupled in value while the Standard and Poor's Index rose 58 percent and the NYSE Corporate Price Index climbed 72 percent.[106]

Conclusion

THE PRECEDING CHAPTER concludes the coverage of Norton's history. Incidents in the 1980s occurred too close to writing and publication to permit an analytical perspective. A brief outline of major events clearly indicates, however, the continuation and deepening of the changes made during the 1970s. Donald Melville's promotion to president and chief executive officer confirmed Norton Company's abandonment of the owner-operated abrasives firm for a professionally run diversified enterprise. Melville's appointment was an even sharper departure from past practice than Robert Cushman's rise. Like Cushman he had a sales and marketing background, and an MBA from the Harvard Business School added another dimension to his professional training. He was the first Norton chief executive who spent a significant portion of his career outside the company and who had never served in abrasives operations. His experience in divestment, acquisitions, and the Diversified Products Group underscored Norton's commitment to continued diversification. Coincident with Melville's promotion, John Jeppson's resignation as chairman of the board ended the last founder connection with Norton management.

A further sign of diversification's permanence was the expansion and reorganization of the Diversified Products Group in 1982. Melville and Emile Francois, the new vice-president for diversified products, first sharpened its focus by concentrating on the development of high-performance ceramic and plastic materials. Renamed the Engineering Materials Group, it included industrial ceramics, chemical process products, and the Materials Division, which was formerly part of the Abrasive Group. Norton also added three new divisions. The Performance Plastics Division brought together the old sealants and industrial plastics lines with recent acquisitions in fluoropolymers. High-Performance Ceramics centralized advanced ceramics operations such as proppants, and Health Care Products combined Tygon tubing with a newly purchased line of health care devices. At the same time Melville established the Corporate Technology Committee with a corporate vice-president to cut across divisional and product group lines. Building on Norton's expertise in ceramics, plastics, grains, and other shared know-how, it searched for new products for high-growth markets and new uses for existing lines.

Safety products, which were less technical industrial consumables, remained outside the Engineering Materials Group, and after a decade Norton had realized much of the potential growth in that market. Competitors were strongly entrenched in foreign markets, and growth of domestic users was expected to slow. Further expansion of what was a very profitable business would have carried the company into manufacturing and servicing burglar and fire alarm systems, and it did not wish to enter the service field. In addition, sales of industrial safety products fluctuated in a pattern similar to the abrasives cycle, as had been anticipated. Like Cushman, Melville and Francois reasoned that portfolio management and strategic planning were a dynamic process, and they soon seized a profitable opportunity to sell the business and free resources for use in new fields with greater potential growth. In late 1982 Norton sold controlling interest in its Safety Products Division to Siebe Gorman Holdings PLC, an English manufacturer of industrial safety devices.

Norton Company: Family Enterprise and Big Business

Prior to its diversification, Norton's long experience as a private, owner-managed company made it an increasingly rare and difficult-to-sustain alternative model to the publicly held, professionally run firm that eventually characterized much of large-scale American enterprise in the twentieth century.[1] Nevertheless, despite very favorable conditions for family operation in Norton's early days, its integrated strategy and centralized structure based on functional departments was far more reflective of American enterprise than the amorphous, holding company approach that typified most large combinations in Britain or the Zaibatsu in Japan.[2]

The timing and causes of the big company's rise also reflected a general pattern among large U.S. industrial enterprises. Like most of them, Norton was an early entrant in an industry spawned by increased emphasis on the economies of speed and volume during the later stages of America's industrial revolution. Use of bonded abrasives to remove quantities of metal rapidly and precisely for high-volume, standardized production rose quickly between 1880 and 1920, especially after the automobile's advent and the development of specialized, heavy precision grinding machinery. Application of a new energy source—the electric furnace—made grain production more capital intensive and pushed the enterprise into the acquisition and preparation of its major raw material—bauxite. The need to service the new product—especially to guide wheel selection and to demonstrate proper application—forced Norton forward into marketing to supplement the efforts of the industrial distributors who were its major sales outlets.

Bonded abrasives' rapid growth precluded powerful, established competition, and Norton Company's early leadership and association with Charles H. Norton, a pioneer of precision production grinding machinery, offered an excellent opportunity to dominate the new, big industry in the early twentieth century. Execution was assured by entrepreneurial enterprise. The firm's founding partners pooled capital, talent, and deeply held values. Commitment to thrift, diligence, and prudent risk taking encouraged independence as well as maximum use of expertise in production, marketing, administration, and technological development. By World War I the founding generation had financed, built, and maintained control of a large, integrated, industrial company. Norton was America's, and probably the world's, largest manufacturer of grinding wheels and other bonded abrasives, and its sales ranked it among the 400 largest industrial enterprises in the United States.

Timing, success, and values also allowed Norton's owners to preserve the private, owner-managed firm, and thus deviate from the general trend toward professionally managed and publicly held enterprise. Self-finance assured independence, and success and thrift assured self-finance. The company's high returns from premium products and careful marketing generated ample cash flow, while moderate dividend policies kept those funds available for reinvestment. The firm's powerful financial position also permitted use of short-term loans for additional capital without surrender of any authority to the investment community.

At the same time the company's status in the rapidly maturing abrasives industry helped ensure its continued dominance. Development of a marketing network, integration of raw materials operations, and increased capital intensity owing to the application of electric furnaces and tunnel kilns to production erected financial barriers to the entry of new large firms. Furthermore, increased experience with product and process development and with the distribution system added a knowledge barrier that required time as well as money to breach. Within the industry, Norton Company's only integrated major competitor was Carborundum Company, whose bonded market share was probably half of Norton's. The Mellon firm's owners and managers were more committed to maintenance of position and revenue than to growth of market share with costly price wars and extensive investment.

Financial independence and industry dominance permitted the extension of private ownership and administration. As heirs to the heritage of family operation common among New England merchants in the seventeenth and eighteenth centuries and among small-scale manufacturing enterprises in Worcester and the rest of New England during the nineteenth century, the founders shared a deep commitment to direct control, and the timely arrival of talented, interested sons assured continuity. George Jeppson and Aldus Higgins had grown up with the firm during its transition from small- to large-scale enterprise. They not only had experience with the big business; they had helped create it.

With the tutelage of Charles Allen, Jeppson and Higgins institutionalized founder values and firmly established the pattern of continued owner-operation. The acquisition of the Behr-Manning and Pike companies and the expansion of overseas operations to Australia and across Europe completed a strategy of full product line and preservation of leadership. The Norton Spirit substituted a corporate labor relations program for John Jeppson's earlier personal, paternal relationship with the predominantly Swedish work force. Along with the leaders of many other industrial firms, Jeppson, Allen, and Higgins created a functionally departmentalized structure for integrated operation and then maintained owner-control as top executives in a central office to whom department heads reported. Expansion of the laboratory from quality control to research and development helped assure continued innovation and industry leadership. A strong financial department ensured careful cost controls and centralized oversight of operations. Otherwise, corporate staff remained spare, a sign of New England thrift and the desire to retain control from the top down through a powerful line organization.

To further preserve owner-operation Jeppson and Higgins recruited and trained descendants for top positions. Norton Company remained a multifamily enterprise that provided a broad field of candidates essential for continuity and quality. The employment of various sons, nephews, brothers-in-law, cousins, and other male offspring from four of seven founders made nepotism obvious, but advancement to the top was not reserved to any family or individual. Those with less talent were held to lower or middle management jobs until they quit or retired; those with aptitude were moved and promoted. Many applied but few were chosen.

At the same time, extension of centralized owner-management introduced anomalies and forced significant compromises. While a small top team's lifetime experience readily let it handle the bonded abrasives industry, George Jeppson and Aldus Higgins had little time for, knowledge of, or interest in other lines. At Norton Company, refractory manufacture remained a small business supplying the firm's own needs during the time that Carborundum carved a significant place in that market. An outstanding position in grinding machine manufacture eroded in the 1920s and 1930s, partially because of a conscious policy to restrict investment.

Even in the abrasives business, central control depended largely on direct oversight. Personal management encouraged the continued concentration of manufacture in Worcester even though the rise of the automotive industry and production grinding had shifted major markets to the Middle Atlantic and North Central states. The growing West Coast market that resulted from aircraft manufacture was even more remote. Where geographic expansion was absolutely necessary, Jeppson and Higgins and the Worcester organization played little role in the management. Norton's relationship to Behr-Manning was that of a holding company to an autonomous subsidiary.

Oversight of foreign plants was no tighter. Time and distance meant that responsibility, but not real authority, for overseas abrasives operations fell to the gallivanting William L. Neilson and the limited financial controls of Herbert Stanton. In fact strategic initiative as well as administration was left to on-site managers, and in foreign coated plants, Jeppson and Higgins exercised no control at all.

To be sure, success reinforced the autonomous strategy, but Worcester was only partially responsible for the prosperity. Norton trained Otto Schutte and Pierre Baruzy, and Jeppson and Higgins approved their appointments as managers in Germany and France. At Watervliet, Norton's contribution to prosperity was essentially passive; Jeppson and Higgins recognized a strong team and left it alone. However, they tolerated mediocrity in Germany during the 1920s and subsequently in England, and they never found an effective head of the international business.

Continued family control also slowed the introduction of aggressive new people with the perception and authority to push fresh opportunities. Fresh or external perspectives had long been a key at Norton Company. Charles Allen and the first John Jeppson recognized a potential for the abrasive business that F. B. Norton never saw. Charles H. Norton came from Brown and Sharpe to pioneer production grinding. The first Milton Higgins, an academician, pushed the company into furnaced abrasives, and in their youth, Aldus Higgins moved the firm rapidly into bauxite processing and mining and George Jeppson oversaw the development of the Norton Spirit and an administrative structure.

Creativity slowed as the industry matured, and the emphasis shifted from growth and prudent venture to revenue and to risk reduction as the founders died and the sons aged. Foreign expansion was almost entirely defensive. Norton went into Germany after Carborundum's entry and the entreaties of its most powerful distributor. It went into England to avoid a tariff barrier after Carborundum had nearly twenty years' head start. The French and Italian plants were virtual gifts from local partners desperate for Norton expertise and equipment, and Australian manufacture was a joint venture to match competitors' growth. Expansion in coated abrasives was left outside the partners' control.

Caution and inertia were also reflected in domestic production. Within bonded abrasives, product development was strongest in the vitrified line, the area Norton knew best. The company lagged consistently behind Carborundum and smaller competitors in resin-bonded production, which grew rapidly after 1930, and although Baalis Sanford first developed a diamond wheel in 1930, Norton did not move into commercial production and eventual world leadership until 1934 when Carborundum began marketing its own diamond wheel. The most rapid expansion after 1940 came in coated abrasives under Gallagher and Schacht and outside Worcester's control.

Nevertheless, a strong market position and a powerful organization helped maintain leadership and revenues even though growth rates and industry share declined between the 1920s and 1940s. Profits paid handsome dividends to an increasing number of nonmanagement descendants who did not care about and were not told return on investment to measure maximum use of resources. In addition, the appointments of Milton Higgins and Ralph Gow were carefully planned to continue Norton values and traditions.

By the 1950s, however, internal and external forces raised the cost of compromises necessary to maintain the private, owner-operated abrasives company. Industry maturity eroded Norton's superiority in product and process that had been so crucial to its premium pricing and high profits. Industry growth curves flattened, and the removal of price control by antitrust decrees opened the door to price competition as firms sought to expand by taking business from one another. Declining growth also threatened Norton's long-term future and encouraged John Jeppson, Fairman Cowan, Robert Cushman, and young, middle-level professional managers to look toward diversification.

Meanwhile, Norton Company's continued expansion raised its own problems. With the merger of foreign coated and bonded abrasives operations in 1951 and the gradual shift to such overseas markets as South Africa, South America, and Southeast Asia, which were expanding faster than U.S. sales, Norton became a worldwide firm. Under Donald Kelso the international division evolved as another power center beyond tight owner-control in the 1950s. In the 1960s it required delegation of final or real authority to reorganize and coordinate coverage, production, and marketing in the face of rising local competition and the Common Market's advent. The formal commitment to internal diversification through a refractories division created still another line beyond direct owner-manager oversight.

In the late 1950s the firm adopted a formally decentralized, divisional structure, but much authority remained concentrated in a top team that simply could not cover Norton's product and geographic range. Under Gow and Higgins Worcester's central office continued to function largely as a domestic bonded abrasives business. The coated and international divisions were run like subsidiaries of a holding company, and the Worcester-based machine tool and refractories divisions were subject to a top management that did not know those businesses as thoroughly as it did abrasives.

Furthermore, increased size created personnel, legal, and financial problems as well. Norton needed additional able middle and lower level managers, but top management worried about the firm's ability to continue to attract talented college and business school graduates to a privately held, single-industry firm tightly controlled by owner-management. Company lawyers argued that wide dispersal of Norton stock among employees, retirees, and spouses compelled registration with the Securities and Exchange Commission, and Ralph Gow was concerned that the now sizeable fortunes of descendants were tied up in a single, unsaleable asset.

Urged largely by nonowners, especially Gow, Fairman Cowan, and Richard Nichols, Milton Hughes inaugurated change that soon swept beyond owner-control. Going public opened a Pandora's box of challenge, transformation, and trouble. It exposed Norton Company to the scrutiny of important external groups, including shareholders, analysts, brokers, and outside directors. It raised questions about the rate of return, the unpromising future of abrasives, and conservative Norton values that emphasized risk reduction and perpetuation of owner-operation. It compelled diversification, which increased size and complexity even further beyond the ability of a small centralized owner-manager team.

Following disappointing acquisitions and declining performance in the 1960s, the modern firm appeared as Norton abandoned the alternative model of three generations. Like most large U.S. industrial enterprises, Norton Company was now publicly held and made itself continually accountable to outside directors, owners, traders, and analysts. The remarkably swift transition was inspired by John Jeppson and largely engineered by men who had originally served as middle-level managers under Milton Higgins and Ralph Gow. Led by Robert Cushman and a talented team including Harry Duane and Donald Melville, company management was professional, analytical, and systematic. Goals and strategy were carefully defined and continuous strategic planning implemented. A program of balanced diversification created a portfolio of businesses to reduce cyclicality, assure income and provide growth while fitting Norton's expertise in consumable industrial supplies. Within the framework of precisely articulated objectives and techniques, Cushman, Duane, and Melville decentralized authority and responsibility to encourage entrepreneurship in what eventually became worldwide product divisions.

Continuity and Compromise

While Norton became more like General Motors, General Electric, Du Pont, and other large industrial firms that have long been professionally managed, diversified, and decentralized, it also remained somewhat different. The older industrial firms followed a careful strategy of controlled diversification by internal development of product lines related by technology and market to their existing expertise. Each separated administration of its decentralized product divisions from the general office where top management, aided by a large corporate staff for research, finance, and marketing, was charged with planning, coordinating, and appraising for the entire enterprise.[3]

Conglomerates, on the other hand, grew rapidly in the 1960s by acquisition of largely unrelated businesses. In a structure reminiscent of the holding companies of the 1890s, the acquired lines received virtually complete autonomy.[4] The general office was much smaller, and staff work concentrated largely on finance to audit income and prepare securities issues and further acquisitions.

Cushman's emphasis on line planning, entrepreneurship in the ranks, and small corporate staff put Norton between the older industrial firms and the newer conglomerates. It sought to combine the rational diversification of Du Pont with the operating autonomy of the conglomerates. Management has historically pushed growth by both internal development and acquisition, with mixed results in both cases. Tape was a failure, sealants a modest accomplishment, and industrial ceramics a genuine success. Safety products and Christensen prospered and expanded, while molded plastics disappointed. Norton emphasized acquisition in the 1970s because existing technology and research resources offered limited opportunity, and inflation made purchase less costly than development. Yet products developed internally and carried to the commercial stage since 1977 accounted for more than 12 percent of business income in 1980.[5] The fundamental point is that both techniques were focused on areas that fitted Norton production and marketing experience and expertise.

Like its strategy, the company's structure was also a hybrid. The portfolio technique suggested the autonomy and financial orientation of conglomerates, while the new Corporate Technology Committee and line planning through the Strategic Guidance Committee reflected the coordination characteristic of Du Pont and the older diversified firms. Norton's corporate staff was fairly small and largely financial. There were no corporate executives and departments for planning and marketing and only one corporate executive for research. Line planning directed by top corporate and line people in the Guidance Committee provided both top-down direction based on a corporate-wide view and entrepreneurial opportunity for middle managers who drew up and were responsible for their own plans.

While Norton moved to its position from its single-industry heritage, a number of the successful conglomerates approached the same state with rationalization and divestment in the 1970s.[6] The sharper differences between older firms and conglomerates in the 1960s seemed to be moderating. Established industrials like Mobil and U.S. Steel began expanding by acquisition of lines often only remotely related to their existing technology and markets. Conglomerates developed logical product groups and tighter central control. The strategic business unit technique was pioneered at General Electric, an early internally diversified company, and by 1976 was employed by perhaps 20 percent of the *Fortune* 500.[7]

Despite the striking differences between the modern enterprise and the old Norton family firm, the company's heritage of values and traditions offered impressive continuity. Cushman's diversified approach with its emphasis on increased freedom and opportunity at middle management levels actually restored the entrepreneurial characteristics of the early enterprise. Although they worked within articulated, general guidelines, dozens of people now contributed directly to the allocation of Norton resources among its portfolio of businesses. Like the early seven-member partnership, they offered a much wider variety of perspectives than the two-man top teams of the second and third generations.

Collectively, modern Norton management recalled the first Milton Higgins, who was a portfolio of businesses himself. Like the old New England merchants who engaged in a variety of enterprises including production, distribution, retailing, transportation, finance, and warehousing of many commodities, Higgins was active in a number of different lines, although the economy's growth encouraged him to specialize in production by the late nineteenth century. Between 1885 and 1912 he helped organize, finance, and run firms to produce hydraulic elevators, bonded abrasives, pressed steel, and underfeed stokers. His scientific training and active mind led Higgins to push Norton into furnaced abrasives and to urge the expansion of the laboratory into research and development of new processes and products. Modern management, like the first Milton Higgins and his New England merchant predecessors, viewed themselves as flexible managers of capital. Strategic planning freed them from rigid ties to any one business and encouraged them to deepen or restrict investment according to expertise and opportunity.

In addition to restoring entrepreneurship, modern management also reflected the old Norton character and values. Segmented line planning helped insure flexibility, focus, and maximum return, but its effectiveness depended on continuous, diligent application reminiscent of Charles Allen and his colleagues. As Robert Cushman himself put it, "The degree of success in the execution of a corporate strategic plan will be in direct proportion to the degree of dedication to it."[8]

The modern insistence on precise articulation of goals, line planning, and careful fit of new businesses to existing expertise and needs echoed the virtues of prudent risk reduction and maximization of direct control espoused by the founders. The small corporate staff with its low overhead, the traditionally high percentage of reinvested earnings (dividends averaged 32 percent of net earnings between 1975 and 1979), and the modest debt-to-equity ratio (which averaged 39 percent between 1975 and 1979) reflected Norton's long tradition of thrift and independence.[9] Finally, the recent policy of social accountability mirrored the founders' long-standing Yankee confidence that there were right and wrong ways to do business and that Norton could and would do it "the right way."[10]

Continuity of values and traditions suggests a different focus for the long-standing debate over entrepreneurship in business history.[11] Alfred Chandler has persuasively demonstrated that a firm's technology and markets rather than any individual's personality and ability determine a company's evolution in the long run.[12] Yet in some cases the influences of particular people have extended far beyond their tenures. Alfred Sloan at General Motors, William McKnight at 3M, and Pierre du Pont and Donaldson Brown at Du Pont have left an enduring legacy.[13]

To such firms are attributed a particular character or culture. A recent examination by experts in organizational behavior found a surprising number (over 20 percent from a sample of eighty) of strong cultures in large American enterprises.[14] Norton's experience makes clear that its heritage was not due to personality but to deeply held values institutionalized in its structure and strategy and perpetuated in the selection and training of its top people. Although the analysts of corporate culture describe it as "a cohesion of values, myths, heroes, and symbols," they agree that "shared values define the fundamental character of the organization."

As a tool, company "character" must have modest uses. It is too vague and often too weak to provide any systematic classification. Yet the heritage of traditions and values is a useful device to delineate the history of a particular enterprise. It may even help to distinguish between contrasting decisions made simultaneously by firms in the same industry. One example was the difference in the mid-1970s between the rapid redirection of investment into small car production at General Motors where Sloan's long-term analytical outlook has always dominated and the strategy of delayed investment to boost short-run revenue at Ford where owner-managers have generally ruled.

Entrepreneurial contributions depend on numbers as well as time. Unlike most modern professional managers, a Henry Ford or an Alfred Sloan reached the top early and literally had decades to establish a legacy, and frequently, lasting success and dominance depended on a team. Popular historians and textbooks have often exalted colorful individuals while ignoring vital contributions by less spectacular partners. Alfred Sloan, Pierre du Pont, and Donaldson Brown worked closely in the reorganization of General Motors in the 1920s. At the Ford Company Henry Ford depended on Charles Sorensen and William Knudsen in production and James Couzzens in marketing, among others. At 3M the successful firm was led by Richard Carlton in research and development and Archibald Bush in marketing in addition to President William McKnight.[15]

Since the days of general merchants, cooperation or partnership among a small group of businessmen has historically provided a pool of energy, talents, and contacts as well as funds. Focus on a small team has helped illuminate successful business development in areas as diverse as steel and urban transit.[16] Furthermore, the Norton case suggests that the sharing of values and traditions as well as capital and talents in a team deepens and extends an entrepreneurial legacy.

Value Judgments and Challenges

Two questions remain: Was the change from the long-time family abrasives firm to the diversified professionally-managed enterprise good or bad, beneficial or harmful? And, where does Norton go from here? Neither question is properly part of a company history. Judgments about the quality of change ultimately depend on the values and experience of the viewer. At Norton Company, present-day professional managers, veteran retirees in Worcester and in Water-vliet, shareholders and founders' descendants have their answers. This book should allow readers to make their judgments.

One point is indisputable, however. Recent criticism of poor per-formance of large American enterprises has focused on managers who are alleged to be too dependent on short-run expectations geared to financial markets.[17] Certainly the Norton case contradicts such a the-ory. Going public increased accountability and shifted emphasis from revenue getting to growth and maximum use of resources.

Although Robert Cushman's approach relied heavily on financial techniques, including the portfolio concept and return-on-investment benchmarks, they did not condemn Norton to short-term manage-ment. The portfolio concept emphasized growth as well as risk re-duction. As have so many American professional managers before him, Cushman sought to balance investors' wishes for quick revenue with steady, long-term expansion for an enterprise in which he and his colleagues have built and will continue to develop their careers. While financial measurement was more rigorous, strategic planning through the Strategic Guidance Committee emphasized the fit of re-source allocation with the expertise and experience of Norton man-agement and with the needs of existing Norton businesses. It also elevated more nonfinancial people into major decision-making roles than in the second and third generations when Henry Duckworth and his successors had management's ear.

Nor did the evidence of the 1970s indicate that the increased turn-over in top personnel, so characteristic of professional management, led to lack of commitment and poor performance. Indeed, perform-ance standards were now much more analytical and systematic than ever before, and they were geared to increased entrepreneurialship. Based on the economist's standard of efficiency, the maximization of return on resources, the change from family to managerial firm was a real improvement, and its success made reversal virtually impos-sible.

Prediction of Norton's future belongs to its analysts and top ex-ecutives, not to its historian. Certainly, however, Melville and his associates face a series of challenges in the 1980s, which they have already begun to articulate. Strategic planning is becoming more dif-ficult. The long-range growth anticipated for Christensen will force top management to make hard choices in capital allocation for the first time. The Strategic Guidance Committee will have to discipline more firmly its "maintain" segments to reduce their capital con-sumption.

At the same time Norton will be giving a long-range test to such concepts as decentralized planning, the "maintain" strategy for abrasives leadership, and the portfolio balance for countercyclicality. The planning mechanism itself may need modification as the number of business units expands beyond the top management's capacity for direct review, and the maintain strategy is yet to be fully implemented. In the 1970s, abrasives prospered heavily from zirconia-alumina, a product developed in the 1960s, and consumed more investment than anticipated. In the next decade, however, the policy should pay unexpected dividends because Carborundum Company, one of Norton's major world competitors and a division of Kennecott Copper Corporation since 1978, has announced its discontinuation of coated and bonded abrasives manufacture.

Top executives have also realized that diversification is not a foolproof method of escaping economic slumps. The markets for abrasives, diversified products, and drilling tools in the petroleum and mining industries do not usually fluctuate in unison, but they are not necessarily countercyclical as the harsh recession of 1981–82 demonstrated. In 1982 sales fell 5 percent and income plummeted 80 percent from their 1981 levels as all three product groups suffered declines. The income drop was exacerbated because weaknesses in the Mexican economy shut down an abrasives operation in Puebla and a slowdown in Europe forced the closing of Norton's Welwyn and Belfast plants, giving the company its first quarter in the red in twenty years as a public firm. Nevertheless, since both Christensen and Diversified Products declined less sharply than Abrasives, the diversification strategy continued to help cushion apparently inevitable cyclical slumps.

Norton Company's increased international character raises problems as well. Already some managers have criticized the dichotomy between formal and real multinationalism. Even though more than half of profits, employment, and assets are outside the United States, ownership is almost exclusively domestic. The firm is not listed on any overseas exchanges, and its top management has been largely of American origin. Until Emile Francois's promotion, no foreign-born manager had risen directly from non-U.S. operations to the general office.

Multinationalism also compels Norton to examine its investment and product development assumptions. In the past abrasives products designed for the American market were expected to assure Norton's international leadership. By the 1970s the rise of major rivals— notably Japan and West Germany—to the United States' position as the world's leading industrial nation seriously challenged that assumption. Already European coated abrasives manufacturers are penetrating the American market. And as Japanese and European automobile firms continue to outstrip American producers, Norton will have to look elsewhere to replace lost domestic business. Mitsubishi-Norton Company Ltd. is beginning to develop diamond-bonded products in advance of Worcester.

With such diversity the established policy of focused research becomes more difficult to maintain, especially in view of discredited past beliefs that domestic needs come first. Melville is already discussing a flexible, decentralized policy that would free line managers to pursue basic, nondirected research. Such a policy seems necessary if Norton is to generate more products internally, as its president hopes.

Furthermore, expansion and diversification continue to raise the issue of corporate responsibility. Not only is it difficult to implement a policy across political and cultural boundaries; multinational operation and increased decentralization of authority also raise issues of national policy and sovereignty. When the U.S. embargoed goods to Iran during the 1979–80 hostage crisis, Worcester employees grumbled because Norton subsidiaries and distributors in Europe were free to continue supply. At the same time, Christensen's expansion into downhole tools brings Norton into increased contact with state-owned petroleum operations and promises to test its business ethics code.

In addition, if Norton is to push its social role much further than donations of cash, time, and resources and public measurement of legally mandated activities, it will have to determine more carefully the precise role of large corporations in modern society. Such an examination could well be part of a broader "identity crisis." As noted in the introduction, Worcester employees have long asked jokingly, "What's a Norton?" With continued diversification and the planned shrinkage of abrasives' contribution, the question becomes more serious. Describing Norton Company as a manufacturer of consumable industrial supplies is bland and vague.

Whatever the solutions to such issues, the problems of corporate identity, social responsibility, multinational operation, and continued growth and profitability are not unique to Norton. It no longer sees the world with the peculiar view of a privately held, owner-operated business. Its long experience as an alternative model has ended. Like most other large American firms, Norton Company will face future challenges as a modern, diversified, professionally managed, multinational enterprise.

NOTES

INDEX

Notes

Introduction

1. Robert Averitt, *The Dual Economy: The Dynamics of American Industry Structure* (New York: W. W. Norton, 1968); Alfred Chandler, "Global Enterprise: Economic and National Characteristics—A Comparative Analysis," unpublished paper, pp. 2–2a, 17–21, and table 1.

2. Bernard Bailyn, *The New England Merchants in the Seventeenth Century* (New York: Harper and Row, 1955), pp. 76–86.

3. Frances W. Gregory, *Nathan Appleton: Merchant and Entrepreneur, 1779–1861* (Charlottesville: University Press of Virginia, 1975), pp. 43, 114–116, 122–124, 136.

4. Thomas Cochran, *Business in American Life: A History* (New York: McGraw-Hill, 1972); Stuart Bruchey, "Success and Failure Factors: American Merchants in Foreign Trade in the Eighteenth and Early Nineteenth Centuries," *Business History Review*, 32 (Autumn 1958), 272–292; Bruchey, *The Roots of American Economic Growth, 1607–1861* (New York: Harper and Row, 1965), pp. 42–54.

5. Bailyn, *New England Merchants;* Gregory, *Appleton;* James P. Hanlan, *The Working Population of Manchester, New Hampshire, 1840–1886* (Ann Arbor: UMI Research Press, 1981), pp. 30–45; Paul Faler, *Mechanics and Manufacturers in the Early Industrial Revolution: Lynn, Massachusetts, 1780–1860* (Albany: State University of New York Press, 1981), pp. 109–139. For the shift in Yankee imagery from sharp practice and crass commercialism in the nineteenth century to being a fundamental contributor to national character, see William R. Taylor, *Cavalier and Yankee: The Old South and American National Character* (New York: George Braziller, 1961), p. 48; Daniel Chauncey Brewer, *The Conquest of New England by the Immigrant* (New York: G. P. Putnam's Sons, 1926), pp. 4, 24–36; Barbara Miller Solomon, *Ancestors and Immigrants: A Changing New England Tradition* (Cambridge, Mass.: Harvard University Press, 1956), pp. 31, 66–67, 74–76, 92–93.

6. Faler, *Mechanics and Early Manufacturers*, chaps. 6–7.

7. Thomas R. Navin, *The Whitin Machine Works since 1831: A Textile Machinery Company in an Industrial Village* (Cambridge, Mass.: Harvard University Press, 1950), pp. 166–168, 174; Edward T. Fairbanks, *The Town of St. Johnsbury, Vermont* (St. Johnsbury: Cowles Press, 1914), pp. 416–418; George S. Gibb, *The Whitesmiths of Taunton: A History of Reed and Barton, 1824–1943* (Cambridge, Mass.: Harvard University Press, 1943), pp. 146–149. See also Hanlan, *Working Population*, pp. 30–45; Gregory, *Appleton*, pp. 160–162, 187–188, 191; Tamara K. Hareven, *Family Time and Industrial Time: The Relationships between the Family and Work in a New England Industrial Community* (Cambridge: Cambridge University Press, 1982), pp. 53–57; Thomas Dublin, *Women at Work: The Transformation of Work and Community in Lowell, Massachusetts, 1826–1860* (New York: Columbia University Press, 1979), pp. 59–60, 77, 142–143.

8. Research has been led and dominated by Alfred Chandler. See *The Visible Hand* (Cambridge, Mass.: Harvard University Press, 1977); *Strategy and Structure* (Cambridge, Mass.: MIT Press, 1962); "The Beginnings of 'Big Business' in American Industry," *Business History Review*, 33 (Spring 1959), 1–31.

1 From a Bet on a Bucket of Beer

1. For the evolution of pre-nineteenth-century grinding, I have relied heavily on Robert S. Woodbury, *History of the Grinding Machine*, in his *Studies in the History of Machine Tools* (Cambridge, Mass.: MIT Press, 1972), pp. 1–6, 13–28. See also William G. Pinkstone, *The Abrasives Ages* (Lititz, Pa.: Sutter House, 1974), chaps. 1–5; Muriel G. Collie, *The Saga of the Abrasives Industry* (Greendale, Mass.: The Grinding Wheel Institute and the Abrasive Grain Association, 1951), pp. 1–3.

2. Woodbury, *Grinding Machine*, pp. 16–22.

3. Ibid., pp. 38–44. For the evolution of grinding machinery in the nineteenth and twentieth centuries, I have relied heavily on Woodbury's monograph. Nathan Rosenberg, "Technological Change in the Machine Tool Industry," *Journal of Economic History*, 23 (December 1963), 414–443, and David Allen Hounshell, "From the American System to Mass Production: The Development of Manufacturing Technology in the United States, 1850–1920" (Ph.D. diss., University of Delaware, 1978), provide an excellent framework for placing grinding in the development of machine tools and metal working in the nineteenth-century United States.

4. B. E. D. Stafford, "Tool Steels, 2," an undated and unidentified article in a Norton Company scrapbook of 1890s clippings; H. R. Schubert, "The Steel Industry," in Charles Singer, E. J. Holmyard, A. R. Hall, and Trevor I. Williams, eds., *A History of Technology*, 6 vols. (New York: Oxford University Press, 1954–1978), V, 53–71; Leslie Aitchison, *A History of Metals*, 2 vols. (London: Macdonald and Evans, 1960), II, 570–577.

5. Woodbury, *Grinding Machine*, p. 48.

6. Rosenberg, "Technological Change."

7. Woodbury, *Grinding Machine*, pp. 51–62.

8. Ibid., pp. 66–67.

9. Ibid., pp. 68–69.

10. Joseph Horner, "Grinding Machine and Process, No. 1," *Engineering*, 74 (July 4, 1902), 1.

11. Ibid.

12. Hounshell, "American System," esp. chaps. 2–3.

13. *Worcester Daily Telegram*, August 5, 1886, p. 2.

14. James F. Hobart, "Emery Grinding," *American Machinist*, 8 (January 24, 1885), 1.

15. Hal Bryant to A. B. Fritts, March 30, 1939. Unless otherwise noted, all correspondence is in the Norton Company Archives, Worcester, Mass.

16. Hobart, "Emery," p. 2.

17. U.S. Department of the Interior, U.S. Geological Survey, *Mineral Resources of the United States*, 1883–84, p. 713; 1901, p. 791.

18. Ibid., 1901, p. 788; Pike Manufacturing Company, *Sharpening Stones: History and Development* (Pike, N.H., 1915); Behr-Manning Corporation, *History of Norton-Pike in the Sharpening Stone Industry* (Troy, N.Y., 1954); Behr-Manning Corporation, "Sharpening Stones and Their Development," typescript, Mildred Tymeson Papers, library of the Worcester Polytechnic Institute.

19. U.S. Bureau of the Census, *Fifteenth Census of the United States: 1930, Manufactures: 1929*, II, 1354.

20. "Reminiscences of Mr. Charles H. Norton," December 12, 1929, typescript history for the Ford Museum in Detroit, p. 10; Charles H. Norton, "A Brief Autobiography," p. 7. Both documents are part of a collection of Charles H. Norton papers in the Norton Company Archives.

21. U.S. Bureau of the Census, *Eleventh Census of the United States: 1890, Report on Manufacturing Industries of the United States*, pt. 1, p. 76; *Fifteenth Census, Manufactures*, II, 866.

22. U.S. Bureau of the Census, *Eleventh Census, Manufacturing*, pt. 1, p. 76; *Fifteenth Census, Manufactures*, II, 866.

23. Collie, *Saga*, pp. 91, 95, 103, 176.

24. For the industry's early days, see ibid., chaps. 3, 5.

25. Ibid., pp. 90–91.

26. Woodbury, *Grinding Machine*, p. 78.

27. Collie, *Saga*, p. 34; *Journal of the Franklin Institute*, 3rd ser., 45 (1863), 93–94; 55 (1868), 82–83.

28. T. Dunkin Paret, "Emery and Other Abrasives," *Journal of the Franklin Institute*, 137 (May 1894), 354, 359; Collie, *Saga*, p. 7.

29. Department of the Interior, *Mineral Resources*, 1901, pp. 803–804.

30. Charles N. Jenks to Mr. Pratt, February 10, 1928; George N. Jeppson speech, October 1, 1946, in a collection of Jeppson papers held by John Jeppson; Norton Emery Wheel Company, *Catalogue*, 1901, p. 6; U.S. Department of the Interior, *Mineral Resources*, 1893, p. 677; 1900, p. 800.

31. Henry Richardson, "Recalls Early Days of Industry," *Abrasive Industry*, 1 (October 1920), 22–23; Collie, *Saga*, pp. 28–41.

32. Walter C. Gold, "Grinding Wheels," *The Metal Industry*, 13 (November 1915), 451.

33. Mildred M. Tymeson, *The Norton Story* (Worcester, Mass.: Norton Company, 1953), pp. 2–8; Worcester Historical Museum, *The F. B. Norton Pottery* (Worcester, Mass., 1980).

34. The Pulson experiment has been recounted many times with varying details. The most direct account is George Jeppson's notes from an interview with Pulson on November 26, 1926. Company legend dates the experiment as autumn 1873 but Pulson remembered it as 1874. The notes and all subsequent unpublished sources, unless otherwise noted, are in the Norton Company Archives in Worcester.

35. Ibid., and contract between Swen Pulson and the Vitrified Wheel and Emery Company, December 7, 1875.

36. Ibid., U.S. Patent no. 187, 167, February 6, 1877.

37. For pottery manufacture, see Cornelius Osgood, *The Jug and Related Stoneware of Bennington* (Rutland, Vt.: Charles E. Tuttle, 1971), esp. p. 48. For published material on early grinding wheel manufacture, see Tymeson, *Norton*, pp. 48–51, and Collie, *Saga*, pp. 31–34.

38. For John Jeppson's career, see clippings from Worcester newspapers, March 27–29 and April 8, 1920, in Norton Company scrapbooks of published materials, vol. 7, unpaged; *Norton Spirit*, April 1920, pp. 1, 3; "Career of John Jeppson," undated typescript, and clippings from *Worcester Daily Telegram*, May 2, 1915, and August 26, 1916, in Jeppson Papers; John Jeppson [II] interviews, March 11, 1980; March 20, 1981. All interviews were conducted by the author unless otherwise noted.

39. George Jeppson interviews, June 28, July 28, 1950, and typescript of a Jeppson article for the *Norton Spirit*, April 1935, Tymeson Papers. See also notes from an interview with Nils Nymberg, April 8, 1926, in Norton Archives.

40. American Machinist, *Metalworking: Yesterday and Tomorrow* (New York: McGraw-Hill, 1977), p. 29.

41. Ibid., pp. 29–32; Harry G. Stoddard, "Romance of Worcester Industry," *Worcester Historical Society Publications*, n.s., 3 (September 1945), 10–32; Charles G. Washburn, *Industrial Worcester* (Worcester: Davis Printers, 1917); Robert W. Doherty, *Society and Power: Five New England Towns, 1800–1860* (Amherst: University of Massachusetts Press, 1977).

42. Mildred M. Tymeson, *Two Towers: The Story of Worcester Tech, 1865–1965* (Worcester: Worcester Polytechnic Institute, 1965).

43. For the clustering of U.S. machine tool manufacture, see Joseph Wickham Roe, *English and American Tool Builders* (New Haven: Yale University Press, 1916), chaps. 12–17.

44. *Worcester Daily Telegram*, August 5, 1886, p. 2. For the distributors, see Norton Emery Wheel Company's first (and only surviving) letterbook for summer 1885.

45. Loring S. Richardson to M. P. Higgins, May 25, 1885.

46. Ibid.

47. Ibid.

48. Advertisement in *Worcester BiCentennial*, October 15, 1884.

49. Richardson to Higgins, May 25, 1885.

50. Nils Nymberg interview notes, April 8, 1926; untitled and undated book published in the early 1920s which contains short biographies of the founders and all twenty-five-year men.

51. Charles Allen, "Mr. Allen Recalls Early Norton Days," *Norton Spirit*, January 1935, p. 1; notes of Allen's reminiscences, undated but probably late 1934, in Norton Archives.

52. Richardson to Higgins, May 25, 1885. The 10 percent figure is based on Norton's wheel sales for 1882 ($42,420.65) and the Census report on industry output for 1880. U.S. Bureau of the Census, *Eleventh Census, Manufactures*, I, 76.

53. Nils Nymberg interview notes; Charles Allen notes; Charles Allen, "Allen Recalls," p. 1; Allen, "Another Chapter of Half Century Ago," *Norton Spirit*, February 1935, p. 2; George Jeppson interviews, June 28, July 28, 1950, and one undated interview, Tymeson Papers.

54. Charles Allen, "Another Chapter," p. 2.

55. George Jeppson interview, undated, Tymeson Papers.

56. George Jeppson speech, June 7, 1943, in Jeppson Papers; Charles Allen, "Allen Recalls," p. 1; George Jeppson to Harry Stoddard, January 17, 1945, in Jeppson Papers.

57. Jeppson to Stoddard, January 17, 1945; George Jeppson, speech to the Worcester County Club, May 10, 1960, in Jeppson Papers.

58. "Massachusetts," vol. 99, p. 101, and vol. 102, p. 42, R. G. Dun & Company Collection, Baker Library, Harvard Business School, Boston, Mass.

59. George Jeppson, "Fifty Years of Norton," *Norton Spirit*, April 1935, p. 3; John Jeppson interview, March 11, 1980.

60. The story of the partnership's evolution has been told many times with varying detail. I have relied on George Jeppson to Harry Stoddard, January 17, 1945; George Jeppson's speech, June 17, 1943, in Jeppson Papers; Charles Allen, "Another Chapter," p. 2; and Allen's notes.

61. Milton P. Higgins, quoted in Olive Higgins Prouty, *Pencil Shavings* (Cambridge, Mass.: Riverside Press, 1961), p. 138.

62. Norton Emery Wheel Company charter; George Jeppson to Harry Stoddard, January 17, 1945; Ellery B. Crane, *Historic Houses and Institutes and Genealogical and Personal Memoirs of Worcester City, Massachusetts* (New York: Lewis, 1907), II, 137.

63. *Abrasive Industry*, 12 (October 1931), 23–24.

64. Josepha M. Perry, "Sketch of the Life and Work of Milton Prince Higgins, 1842–1912," *Bulletin of the Business Historical Society*, 18 (June 1944), 33–53; Aldus C. and John W. Higgins, *Milton Prince Higgins (1842–1912): Father of the Public Trade School Movement in America* (New York: Newcomen Society of North America, 1947).

65. Tymeson, *Two Towers*, pp. 32–33, 49–50; *Abrasive Industry*, 7 (October 1926), 119; *Worcester Gazette*, September 14, 1926, p. 12. The organization chart is in W. E. Freeland, "Two Years' Growth of an Abrasive Industry," *Iron Age*, 99 (January 25, 1917), 248–251.

66. Alfred Chandler, *The Visible Hand* (Cambridge, Mass.: Harvard University Press, 1977), pp. 67–72.

67. Richardson to Higgins, May 25, 1885.

68. John Jeppson interview, March 11, 1980.

69. George Jeppson interview, June 28, 1950, in Tymeson Papers.

70. Perry, "Sketch," *Worcester Gazette*, September 20, 1926, p. 12.

71. "Milton Prince Higgins," undated typescript belonging to Milton P. Higgins II.

72. George I. Alden to Milton P. Higgins, August 31, 1885; Norton Emery Wheel Company, "Minutes of the Board of Directors," December 24, 1887 (hereafter cited as Minutes, date).

73. George Jeppson speech, June 7, 1943, in Jeppson Papers.

74. For examples, see delayed decision on Norton's first catalog and chart of wheel speeds, Norton Company, Minutes, April 9, 1888; and the delay in authorizing purchase of machinery, Norton Company, Minutes, April 23, 1888.

75. Prouty, *Shavings*, pp. 1–2.

76. Thure Hanson, *Swedish-American Souvenir* (Worcester, 1910).

77. For Swedish-Americans, see Allan Kastrup, *The Swedish Heritage in America* (St. Paul, Minn.: Swedish Council of America, 1975), esp. pp. 522–544; Lars Ljungmark, *Swedish Exodus*, trans. Kermit B. Westerberg (Carbondale and Edwardsville, Ill.: Southern Illinois University Press, 1979), chaps. 8–9; Leonard Dinnerstein, Roger Nichols, and David Reimers, *Natives and Strangers: Ethnic Groups and the Building of America* (New York: Oxford University Press, 1979), pp. 176, 179; Dinnerstein and David Reimers, *Ethnic Americans: A History of Immigration and Assimilation* (New York: Dodd, Mead, 1975), p. 123. For Swedes in Worcester, see Esther Mary Wahlstrom, "A History of the Swedish People of Worcester, Massachusetts" (Master's thesis, Clark University, 1947); Charles W. Estus, "A Swedish Working-Class Church: The Methodists of Quinsigamond Village, 1878–1900"; Kenneth J. Moynihan, "Swedes and Yankees in Worcester Politics: A Protestant Partnership"; Kevin L. Hickey, "Geography and Leadership: An Interdisciplinary Evaluation of Worcester's Industrial Development." The last three papers were presented at the Joint Conference of the Victorian Society of America and the National Archives, Washington, D.C., March 1979.

78. For New England merchants, see Bernard Bailyn, *The New England Merchants in the Seventeenth Century* (New York: Harper and Row, 1955).

79. Norton Company, Minutes, September 21, 1886; *Norton Spirit*, November 17, 1926, p. 3; George Jeppson speech, May 15, 1962, in Jeppson Papers.

80. "Massachusetts," vol. 99, p. 101, Dun Collection; Norton Company, Minutes, September 21, 1886; April 25, May 10, September 20, 1887; *Worcester Sunday Telegram*, November 20, 1887, p. 7.

81. "Making Emery Wheel Grinders," *Machinery*, 1896, in Norton scrapbook of 1890s clippings; Oakley S. Walker to Aldus Higgins, July 5, 1940; *Worcester Daily Telegram*, December 12, 1899, p. 8.

82. Tymeson, *Norton*, p. 61; Norton Company, Minutes, November 15, 1887.

83. Norton Company, Minutes, June 15, 1886; George Jeppson's comments on the manuscript for Tymeson's *Norton Story*, undated, in Tymeson Papers.

84. George Jeppson interview, June 28, 1950, Tymeson Papers.

85. George Jeppson interview, July 28, 1950, and his notes on Tymeson manuscript, in Tymeson Papers; Charles Allen to Washington Emery Manufacturing Company, June 6, 1885, to Hampden Emery Company, June 6, 1885, and to Ashland Emery Milling Company, July 31, 1885, in Norton letterbook.

86. W. F. Burleigh, "Analysis of Emery and Corundum" (Undergraduate thesis, Worcester Polytechnic Institute, 1892).

87. George Jeppson interview, July 28, 1950, Tymeson Papers.

88. George Jeppson quotes John Jeppson as part of a series of corrections to the first four chapters of Tymeson's manuscript for *The Norton Story*, Tymeson Papers.

89. Oakley Walker's memoirs in *Norton Spirit*, April 1937, p. 5, and June 1937, p. 5; untitled book of twenty-five-year men; Herbert Dodge interview, January 29, 1951, Tymeson Papers.

90. George Jeppson interview, June 28, 1950, and Jeppson notes on Tymeson chapters, in Tymeson Papers.

91. "Factory Cost and Business Methods," *Iron Age*, 80 (July 11, 1907), 142–143; "Making Emery Wheel Grinders," *Machinery*, 1896, in Norton scrapbook of 1890s clippings. For cost accounting and scientific management, see Chandler, *Visible Hand*, pp. 272–281.

92. Henry Duckworth, undated interview, Tymeson Papers.

93. Ibid.

94. George Jeppson interview, June 28, 1950, Tymeson Papers; Hanson, *Swedish-American*, p. 3. See also sources cited in note 49 above.

95. There were 75 who started elsewhere and 18 for whom the data were incomplete. Undated twenty-five-year men's book. See also "Migration Patterns," trans. Helen Winroth, in Hans Norman, *From Bergslagen to North America* (Upsala, Sweden, 1974), pp. 261–270.

96. Eric Olson interview, March 1957, and P. Joel Styffe interview, undated, Tymeson Papers.

97. "Census of Norton Emery Wheel Company Employees, November 1, 1899."

98. Ibid.

99. Edward Anderson interview, undated, Tymeson Papers. See also Norton Mutual Benefit Association, Minute book.

100. John Jeppson interviews, March 11, 1980, and March 20, 1981.

101. Carl Ahlstrom interview, undated, Tymeson Papers.

102. Notes from undated interviews with Nils Nymberg and Joel Styffe, in Norton Archives; "Norton Emery Wheel Programs [for Christmas dinners]"; *Worcester Daily Telegram*, June 24, 1900, p. 20.

103. Norton Company, Minutes, September 21, 1886.

104. Fullerton Waldo, "What Employers Say of Profit-Sharing," *World's Work*, 5 (December 1902), 2853–55.

105. Paul Du Caillu, *The Land of the Midnight Sun* (New York: Harper and Brothers, 1882), II, 462.

106. Daniel Nelson, *Managers and Workers: Origins of the New Factory System*

in the United States, 1880–1920 (Madison: University of Wisconsin Press, 1975), pp. 101–106; Thomas Dublin, *Women at Work: The Transformation of Work and Community in Lowell, Massachusetts, 1826–1860* (New York: Columbia University Press, 1979), esp. pp. 59–60, 77–78; Donald Cole, *Immigrant City: Lawrence, Massachusetts, 1845–1921* (Chapel Hill: University of North Carolina Press, 1963), pp. 21–26, 115; Thomas A. McMullin, "Lost Alternative: The Urban Industrial Utopia of William D. Howland," *New England Quarterly*, 55 (March 1982), 25–38. For similar examples of paternalism by New England manufacturers, see James P. Hanlan, *The Working Population of Manchester, New Hampshire, 1840–1886* (Ann Arbor: UMI Research Press, 1981), pp. 30–45; Tamara K. Hareven, *Family Time and Industrial Time: The Relationships between the Family and Work in a New England Industrial Community* (Cambridge: Cambridge University Press, 1982), pp. 53–57; Edward T. Fairbanks, *The Town of St. Johnsbury, Vermont* (St. Johnsbury: Cowles Press, 1914), esp. pp. 416–418; Thomas R. Navin, *The Whitin Machine Work since 1831: A Textile Machinery Company in an Industrial Village* (Cambridge, Mass.: Harvard University Press, 1950), pp. 166–168; George S. Gibb, *The Whitesmiths of Taunton: A History of Reed and Barton, 1824–1943* (Cambridge, Mass.: Harvard University Press, 1943), pp. 146–149; Charles W. Moore, *Timing a Century: History of the Waltham Watch Company* (Cambridge, Mass.: Harvard University Press, 1945), pp. 43–44.

107. Worcester newspaper clippings for summer 1901, in Norton scrapbook of published materials, vol. 1, p. 33.

108. For patterns of nineteenth-century industrial distribution, see Glenn Porter and Harold Livesay, *Merchants and Manufacturers: Studies in the Changing Structure of Nineteenth Century Marketing* (Baltimore: Johns Hopkins University Press, 1973); Chandler, *Visible Hand*, chaps. 1, 7, 9.

109. Office salary book, 1899–1901; Norton Company, *Catalogs*, 1888, 1900.

110. George I. Alden to Milton P. Higgins, August 31, 1885.

111. Charles Allen to Walter Messer, July 30, 1885, letterbook.

112. Norton Company, Minutes, December 15, 1885; January 19, March 2, 1886; Charles Allen to C. M. Emerson, July 29, 1885, and to Harlan Page, July 29, 1885, letterbook.

113. The dresser debate is in Norton Company, Minutes, April 9, 1886; February 23–April 23, July 16, 1888.

114. Alden, quoted in Norton Company, Minutes, April 9, 1888.

115. Norton Company, *Catalog*, 1888.

116. Norton Company, Minutes, March 1, 3, 1890.

117. For the evolution of manufacturer over merchant, see Porter and Livesay, *Merchants and Manufacturers*.

118. Norton Company, Minutes, January 6, 1894.

119. "Census of Norton Employees, November 1, 1899."

120. Norton Company, *Catalog*, 1888.

121. Charles H. Norton to Aldus Higgins, September 28, 1926, Charles Norton Papers; Charles Allen to Walter Messer, June 11, 1885, and to Brown and Sharpe, June 11, 1885, letterbook.

122. Charles Allen to Jones and Laughlin, August 6, 1885, letterbook.

123. David Spencer to Norton Emery Wheel Company, June 4, 1888.

124. Small excerpt from Sales book for 1891.

125. "How and Where Emery Wheels Are Made," undated and unidentified clipping in 1890s scrapbook; *Worcester Evening Gazette*, January 22, 1903, p. 141.

126. *Worcester Daily Telegram*, April 3, 1893, p. 4.

127. Norton Company, Minutes, June 20, 1891.

128. Ibid., September 28, 1891; *Bilder vom Schutte-Werk und Bemerkenswerte Daten zur Firmengeschichte* (Koln-Deutz: Alfred H. Schutte, 1955?), pp. 46–54.

129. George Jeppson interview, June 1956, Tymeson Papers; Norton Emery Wheel Company, "Annual Report," 1905. A series of typed private annual reports were issued at least for 1905 to 1910. No public, published annual reports appeared until 1962.

130. Oakley Walker to Aldus Higgins, July 5, 1940; Walker memoirs, in *Norton Spirit*, April 1937, p. 5, and June 1937, p. 5.

131. For the confusion, see Norton Company, Minutes, 1887–1890.

132. Charles Allen to Milton P. Higgins, June 4, 1889.

133. *Worcester Daily Telegram*, November 24, 1887, p. 4. See also Worcester Polytechnic Institute, Minutes of the Board of Trustees, November 23, 1887 at Gordon Library, WPI; *Worcester Sunday Telegram*, November 20, 1887, p. 7.

134. Charles Allen to Walter Messer, June 23, 1885, letterbook.

135. Sales and profit data for 1885–1910 are in Norton Company, "Annual Report," 1910. Industry figures are in U.S. Bureau of the Census, *Fifteenth Census, Manufactures*, II, 866. Stock dividends are recorded in Norton Company, Minutes, passim.

136. Tymeson, *Norton Story*, p. 72.

137. For a colorful description of merger and high finance, see Matthew Josephson, *The Robber Barons: The Great American Capitalists, 1861–1901* (New York: Harcourt, Brace, 1934). For more analytical coverage, see Ralph Nelson, *Merger Movements in American Industry, 1895–1956* (Princeton: Princeton University Press, 1959); Thomas Navin and Marian Sears, "The Rise of a Market for Industrial Securities," *Business History Review*, 29 (June 1955), 105–138; Chandler, *Visible Hand*, chap. 10.

138. Norton Company, "Annual Report," 1910.

139. Plant construction data from an untitled date outline of Norton history.

140. *Norton Spirit*, April 1937, p. 5, and June 1937, p. 5.

141. For the Carborundum Company's evolution, see Edward G. Acheson, *A Pathfinder: Discovery, Invention and Industry* (Port Huron, Mich.: Acheson Industries, 1965), chap. 7; Raymond Szymanowitz, *Edward Goodrich Acheson: Inventor, Scientist, Industrialist* (New York: Vantage Press, 1971), chaps. 9–17.

142. Edward Acheson to Charles Allen, March 26, 1895, in 1894–95 letterbook, Acheson Papers, Library of Congress.

143. For the Mellon takeover, see Szymanowitz, *Acheson*, pp. 239–243, 248–257, 292–309, 329–333. For a different view, see David E. Koskoff, *The Mellons: The Chronicle of America's Richest Family* (New York: Thomas Y. Crowell, 1978), pp. 85–88.

144. Department of the Interior, *Mineral Resources*, 1901, p. 807.

145. Collie, *Saga*, pp. 81, 84, 95, 103, 184; Prouty, *Pencil Shavings*, p. 73.

146. James H. Soltow, "Origins of Small Business and the Relationships between Large and Small Firms: Metal Fabrication and Machinery Making in New England, 1890–1957," in Stuart Bruchey, ed., *Small Business in American Life* (New York: Columbia University Press, 1980), pp. 192–211. For a fuller statement, see James Soltow, "Origins of Small Business: Metal Fabricators and Machinery Makers in New England, 1890–1957," *Transactions of the American Philosophical Society*, n.s., 55, pt. 10 (1965), 1–58.

2 The Rise of the Big Firm

1. George Jeppson interview, June 28, 1950, Tymeson Papers; U.S. Bureau of the Census, *Twelfth Census of the United States, 1900: Manufactures*, pt. 1, *United States by Industries*, pp. 3–17.

2. Charles Allen speech, November 3, 1926.

3. Alfred D. Chandler, *The Visible Hand* (Cambridge, Mass.: Harvard University Press, 1977), esp. chaps. 8–10.

4. Robert S. Woodbury, *History of the Grinding Machine*, in his *Studies in the History of Machine Tools* (Cambridge, Mass.: MIT Press, 1972), pp. 97–105, 109–120.

5. The Appleton example was listed in Charles H. Norton, "The Field for Grinding," undated reprint of an article published by the American Society of Mechanical Engineers, and located in the Charles Norton Papers in the Norton Company Archives, p. 2114.

6. Charles H. Norton, "Talk on 'Chatters,' " speech to Norton Company sales conference, June 27, 1919, typescript, p. 3, Norton Papers.

7. Charles Norton to Aldus Higgins, November 23 and December 14, 1922, Norton Papers.

8. Woodbury, *Grinding Machine*, pp. 110–112. For a careful analysis of the application of mass production techniques to metal working, see David Allen Hounshell, "From the American System to Mass Production: The Development of Manufacturing Technology in the United States, 1850–1920" (Ph.D. diss., University of Delaware, 1978).

9. Norton Company, *Salute! Mr. Norton* (Worcester, Mass., 1941), quoted in Woodbury, *Grinding Machine*, p. 118.

10. Woodbury, *Grinding Machine*, pp. 120–133. For a more general study of the automobile's influence on the development of mass production techniques, see Hounshell, "American System," chap. 5.

11. Alfred Chandler, *Giant Enterprise: Ford, General Motors and the Automobile Industry* (New York: Harcourt, Brace and World, 1964), p. xii.

12. Nathan Rosenberg, *Technology and American Economic Growth* (New York: Harper and Row, 1972), p. 107.

13. William G. Pinkstone, *The Abrasive Ages* (Lititz, Pa.: Sutter House, 1974), p. 68.

14. *Norton Spirit*, July 15, 1927, pp. 1–2, 11.

15. *Grits and Grinds*, 7 (January 1916), 2–3; Oscar Knight, "Developments

in Production Grinding in the Automotive Industry," *Journal of the Society of Automotive Engineers*, 13 (November 1923), 389.

16. Kenneth B. Lewis, *The Grinding Wheel: A Textbook of Modern Grinding Practice*, 1st ed. (Concord, N.H.: Rumford Press, 1951), pp. 5–6; William Haynes, *American Chemical Industry*, vol. II, *The World War I Period* (New York: D. Van Nostrand, 1945), chap. 19.

17. U.S. Bureau of the Census, *Fifteenth Census of the United States: 1930, Manufactures: 1929*, II, 866.

18. Woodbury, *Grinding Machine*, pp. 125–133, 153–161.

19. For Charles Norton's career, see Charles H. Norton, "A Brief Autobiography," typescript, August 15, 1922, in Norton Papers; Charles H. Norton, "Reminiscences of Mr. Charles H. Norton," typescript, December 12, 1929, in Norton Papers. For published accounts, see Charles H. Norton, *Etched in Memory* (Plainville, Conn., 1936); and Woodbury, *Grinding Machine*, pp. 97–101.

20. Charles H. Norton, 19-page handwritten memoir, undated, p. 5, Norton Papers.

21. Charles H. Norton, "Cylindrical Grinding Wheels and Machines," *Grits and Grinds*, 2 (June 1910), unpaged.

22. Charles H. Norton, "Reminiscences," pp. 5–8 (part of which is quoted in Woodbury, *Grinding Machine*, pp. 99–100); Charles Norton's 19-page, undated (probably 1922) account of the cylindrical production grinder's evolution, in Norton Papers.

23. Charles Norton to Aldus Higgins, November 23, 1922; Charles Norton, "Reminiscences."

24. Charles Norton, "Cylindrical."

25. Charles Norton, "Reminiscences."

26. Carl Ahlstrom interview, undated, Tymeson Papers; Charles Norton, "Story of the First Machine," typescript, January 12, 1926, Norton Papers.

27. *American Engineer and Railroad Journal*, 77 (August 1903), 287.

28. Charles Norton, speech to WPI freshman class, typescript, February 28, 1927, Norton Papers.

29. Norton Grinding Company, Minute book, December 1909, pp. 98–99.

30. Grinding Company, Minutes, June 20, 1900.

31. Charles Norton, quoted in Mildred Tymeson, *The Norton Story* (Worcester, Mass.: Norton Company, 1953), p. 89.

32. Norton Emery Wheel Company, *Catalogue*, 1901, pp. 150–155.

33. Charles Norton, 19-page handwritten memoir, undated, Norton Papers; Charles Norton, "The Grinding Machine as a Metal Cutting Tool," typescript of an article published in *Machinist*, in Norton Papers; Joseph Horner, "The Norton Grinding Machine," *Engineering*, 74 (October 17, 1902), 505.

34. See, for example, Alfred D. Chandler, "Anthracite Coal and the Beginnings of the Industrial Revolution in the United States," *Business History Review*, 46 (Summer 1972), 141–181.

35. Charles Norton, "Past Accomplishments and Future Possibilities," undated speech to Norton Company sales conference, typescript, Norton Papers, pp. 1–2.

36. Norton Grinding Company, Order book, 1901–1905.

37. W. T. Montague, "Norton Grinding Machines and the Railroad Industry" and "Tool Maintenance and Off Hand Grinding," unidentified articles in Norton Company scrapbooks for published materials, vol. 5; Charles Norton, "Efficient Production."

38. Norton speech to WPI freshmen, February 28, 1927.

39. George Jeppson speech, January 24, 1947, Jeppson Papers; Robert Lawson interview (by author), April 21, 1980.

40. Charles Norton, "The Grinding Machine as a Metal Cutting Tool."

41. Norton, "Autobiography"; "The Shops and Some of the Methods of the Norton Grinding Company," *American Machinist*, 29 (March 1, 1906), 265–269; Norton, "Reminiscences."

42. Charles Norton to Aldus Higgins, November 23, 1922.

43. Charles Norton, untitled, dictated statement, January 12, 1926; *Norton Spirit*, July 15, 1927, pp. 15–16, and April 1929, pp. 3–4.

44. Norton Company, "Brief to Commissioner of Internal Revenue," July 12, 1922.

45. Grinding Company, Minutes, January 1907, p. 61; July 15, 1904, p. 45; March 1906, p. 55; Norton Company, "Brief," July 12, 1922; Norton Company, "Brief to Commissioner of Internal Revenue, Re: Claims for Depreciation of Patents and Contract for the Calendar Year 1917," June 16, 1928, exhibit K.

46. Harry G. Stoddard, *The 70-Year Saga of a New England Enterprise at Industrial Worcester* (New York: Newcomen Society of North America, 1952), pp. 15–16.

47. Norton Grinding Company, Order book, 1901–1905.

48. Woodbury, *Grinding Machine*, pp. 105–106.

49. John C. Spence, "Some Types of Automobile Crankshaft Lathes," *Machinery*, 21 (March 1915), 569; Norton Grinding Company, Order book, 1901–1905.

50. Charles H. Norton, "The Introduction of Cylindrical Grinding and Worcester's Part in the Development of the Art," undated typescript, Norton Papers, p. 7.

51. *Worcester Daily Telegram*, February 24, 1914, p. 18; Norton, "Introduction," p. 10.

52. Norton Company, "Brief," June 16, 1928, exhibit K.

53. Lowell H. Milligan, "Abrasives and Grinding," *Industrial and Engineering Chemistry*, 19 (October 1927), 1127; Charles H. Norton, "The Engineer's Part in Human Progress," speech to New Britain branch of the American Society of Mechanical Engineers, April 25, 1928, in Norton Papers, p. 8; Machine division folder in Tymeson Papers.

54. Charles H. Norton, "The Great Example," undated typescript, Norton Papers, p. 5.

55. "Grinding Large Shells and Projectiles," *Iron Age*, 95 (February 25, 1915), 445–447.

56. George Park interview, October 5, 1979; Norton Company, Minutes, January 7, 1919; Albert Belden interview, undated, Tymeson Papers.

57. Norton Company, "Brief," June 16, 1928, exhibit K.

58. Norton Company, *Two Norton Achievements* (Worcester, Mass., 1926).

59. Charles Norton, "Past Accomplishments," p. 4; Norton Company, "Brief," June 16, 1928, exhibit K.

60. Typescript of 1918 Norton Grinding Company advertisement; *Grits and Grinds*, 2 (June 1910).

61. Grinding Company, Minutes, January 12, 1915; *Grits and Grinds*, 2 (June 1910).

62. Norton Grinding Company, "Directors' Report to Stockholders, January 1, 1911"; "The History of Alfred Herbert Limited," undated typescript, Tymeson Papers.

63. Grinding Company, Minutes, January 1907, p. 61.

64. Ibid., November 1918.

65. Milligan, "Abrasives and Grinding," p. 1127; Norton Company, "Brief," June 16, 1928, exhibit J.

66. Charles H. Norton, "Recent Progress in Cylindrical Grinding," *Iron Age*, 73 (January 7, 1904), 39; Norton, "Grinding Machine as a Metal Cutting Tool."

67. U.S. Department of the Interior, U.S. Geological Survey, *Mineral Resources of the United States*, 1897, p. 524.

68. Muriel F. Collie, *The Saga of the Abrasives Industry* (Greendale, Mass.: The Grinding Wheel Institute and the Abrasive Grain Association, 1951), pp. 82, 84–85.

69. Charles N. Jenks to Mr. Pratt, February 10, 1928; Collie, *Saga*, pp. 89, 100–101.

70. Norton Company sales are from "Comparative Net Sales Growth, 1885–1932"; industry figures for 1899 and 1919 are in Bureau of the Census, *Fifteenth Census, Manufactures*, II, p. 866. Norton's share of association sales is in Henry Duckworth to Charles Allen, November 11, 1919. The association figure was based on reports from twenty-four companies out of sixty listed by the Census.

71. V. L. Eardley-Wilmot, "Artificial Abrasives and Manufactured Abrasive Products and Their Uses," in his *Abrasives: Products of Canada; Technology and Application* (Ottawa: F. A. Acland, 1927–1929), pt. 4, p. 16. Frank J. Tone, "How Chemists and Abrasive Engineers Have Made Quantity Production Possible," *Abrasive Industry*, 6 (February 1925), 47–48; Robert J. Forbes, *Man the Maker* (New York: Henry Schuman, 1950), p. 279.

72. Charles C. Carr, *Alcoa: An American Enterprise* (New York: Rinehart, 1952), pp. 11–13; J. Felton Gibbons, "A Story of the Bauxite Industry," typescript, August 1947, pp. 1–2, in Norton Archives.

73. For the Ampere Company, see Martha Moore Trescott, *The Rise of the American Electrochemicals Industry, 1880–1910* (Westport, Conn.: Greenwood Press, 1981), pp. 70–71, 186–187.

74. General Electro-Chemical Company, Minute book, vol. 1, pp. 1–129; Collie, *Saga*, p. 20.

75. George Jeppson's notes on early draft of *Norton Story*, Tymeson Papers; *Grits and Grinds*, 25 (September–October 1934), 10–11; Tymeson, *Norton Story*, p. 93.

76. Raymond Szymanowitz, *Edward Goodrich Acheson: Inventor, Scientist, Industrialist* (New York: Vantage Press, 1971), pp. 301–309.

77. General Electro-Chemical Company, Minutes, June 27, 1900.

78. Milton P. Higgins to Aldus Higgins, July 11, 1900.

79. Ibid.; Carr, *Alcoa*, p. 53.

80. Milton P. Higgins to Aldus Higgins, July 11, 1900.

81. Norton Company, "Brief to Commissioner of Internal Revenue," July 13, 1922. Norton's exclusive license from the General Electro-Chemical Company, January 1, 1904, is summarized in Norton Company, "Brief," June 16, 1928, 31.

82. Norton Company, "Brief," June 16, 1928, 31.

83. Ibid., exhibit U. The quotation is in Collie, *Saga*, p. 211.

84. Eardley-Wilmot, "Artificial," pp. 20–23.

85. Collie, *Saga*, pp. 132, 204–205, 211–212.

86. Ibid., pp. 25, 142–143; Norton Company, "Briefs," July 12 and 13, 1922; General Electro-Chemical Company, Minutes, June 16, 1916; January 10, April 9, 16, October 10, 1917.

87. For interlocks, see Trescott, *Rise*, pp. 70–73, 105, 185–188, 193. Trescott asserts cooperation between Norton and Carborundum, but offers no evidence. Records of early research work by Norton at Worcester and Niagara Falls show only internal development. See also Eardley-Wilmot, "Artificial," for Norton's use of patents for exclusivity.

88. Collie, *Saga*, pp. 60–61, 143; Norton Company, "Brief," July 12, 1922.

89. R. R. Ridgway to R. B. McMullin, March 12, 1940; Philip Schultz interview, undated, Tymeson Papers.

90. J. B. Glaze, "Review of Research Work: Abrasive Plants—Crystolon," in typescript file headed "Report for Dr. Bancroft of Review of Research Work," at Norton Company Library in Chippawa, Ontario.

91. George Jeppson's notes, Tymeson Papers; P. Joel Styffe interview, undated, Tymeson Papers.

92. Jacobs's patent is U.S. patent no. 659,926, October 16, 1900.

93. Norton Company, *Artificial Abrasives: Their History and Development* (Worcester, 1929), p. 17.

94. Charles Norton, "The Grinding Machine as a Metal Cutting Tool."

95. George Jeppson speech, October 1946, Jeppson Papers; notes on joint monthly conferences among Niagara, Chippawa, and Worcester people, November 7, 1913; R. H. White, "Review of Research Work: Abrasives Plants," in typescript file headed "Report for Dr. Bancroft of Review of Research Work," at Chippawa Library; R. R. Ridgway, "Manufactured Abrasives—Old and New," *Chemical and Engineering News*, 21 (June 10, 1943), 858–862.

96. Eardley-Wilmot, "Artificial," pp. 27–28; "Minutes from Experimental and Off Grade Committee Meetings, 1908–1913," typescript volume in Norton Archives, February 24, 1908.

97. Eardley-Wilmot, "Artificial," p. 26.

98. For early Alundum production techniques, see ibid.; Norton Company, *Artificial Abrasives*; R. H. White, "Review of Research Work"; Norton Company, "Brief," June 16, 1928, 15–17.

99. Norton Company, "Brief," June 16, 1928, 13–14; Eardley-Wilmot, "Artificial," pp. 24–25; Gibbons, "Story," pp. 31–32.

100. Norton Company, "Brief," July 12, 1922; Aldus Higgins to Byrnes and Townsend, November 30, December 2, 4, 1907; U.S. patent no. 775,654, November 22, 1904. See also reissue no. 13,027, November 26, 1909, for patent no. 856,061, June 4, 1907.

101. Gordon Finlay, interview, March 17, 1981; Norton Company, "Brief," June 16, 1928, exhibit U.

102. Norton Company, "Brief," July 12, 1922.

103. "Alundum: Its Manufacture, Characteristics and Use," *Machinery*, 13 (December 1906), 204.

104. For silicon carbide manufacture, see Tone, "How"; Francis A. J. Fitzgerald, "The Plant of the Norton Company at Chippawa, Ontario," *Metallurgical and Chemical Engineering*, 10 (September 1912), 519–521.

105. Ibid.

106. Fitzgerald, "Plant"; joint conference records, May 18, June 23, 24, 1913.

107. "Made in America," *American Monthly Export*, October 24, 1914, in scrapbooks of published material, vol. 3, p. 178.

108. For the evolution of U.S. bauxite mining, see Gibbons, "Story"; Donald H. Wallace, *Market Control in the Aluminum Industry* (Cambridge, Mass.: Harvard University Press, 1937), pp. 103–105; Raymond B. Ladoo and W. M. Myers, *Non-Metallic Minerals*, 2nd ed. (New York: McGraw-Hill, 1951), pp. 83–91.

109. Gibbons, "Story," pp. 10, 13–14, 17, 29; Wallace, *Market Control*, pp. 103–105.

110. "Report on the General Bauxite Situation in Arkansas," August 1906, in file labeled "American Bauxite and Republic Mining Company."

111. Aldus Higgins's work with Republic and the Arkansas fields is documented in the American Bauxite file.

112. Gibbons, "Story," pp. 5–8.

113. Aldus Higgins to Charles Allen, November 21, 1906.

114. Ibid.

115. Ibid.

116. Chandler, *Visible Hand*, pp. 472–473.

117. Gibbons, "Story," pp. 32–33.

118. *Poor's Manual of Industrials and Public Utilities*, 1912, pp. 2772, 3264.

119. For the split, see Norton Company, Minutes, 1910–1912, especially September 30, 1910.

120. Wallace, *Market Control*, pp. 103–105.

121. Copy of contract in Norton Archives.

122. Gibbons, "Story," pp. 35–40; P. G. Savage, "Reports of Exploration for Bauxite in the Guianas," 1916–1920, 2 vols., typescript in Norton Company's research library in Worcester.

123. Norton Company, "Brief," June 16, 1928, exhibit M.

124. The Hall patents were U.S. patents no. 678,732, July 16, 1901, and 677,207, 677,208, 677,209, June 25, 1901. For their significance, see Eardley-Wilmot, "Artificial," pp. 17, 20.

125. Thomas R. Navin, "The 500 Largest American Industrials in 1917," *Business History Review*, 44 (Autumn 1970), 381; "Total Number of Employees at End of Each Year," in Norton Company's Personnel Department; Norton Company's annual reports of condition to the Commonwealth of Massachusetts, 1916–1959, in Corporate Records Division, Baker Library, Harvard Business School.

3 "Catching Up"

1. Mildred Tymeson, *The Norton Story* (Worcester, Mass.: Norton Company, 1953), title of chap. 6.

2. U.S. Department of the Interior, U.S. Geological Survey, *Mineral Resources of the United States*, 1917, pp. 214–215, 232. See also Norton Company, "Brief to Commissioner of Internal Revenue, re: Claims for Depreciation of Patents and Contract for the Calendar Year 1917," June 16, 1928, exhibit N.

3. Muriel F. Collie, *The Saga of the Abrasives Industry* (Greendale, Mass.: The Grinding Wheel Institute and the Abrasive Grain Association, 1951), pp. 143–144.

4. "Comparative Net Sales Growth, 1885–1932"; William C. Wendel, *The Scratch Heard 'Round the World: The Story of Carborundum Company* (Princeton, N.J.: Newcomen Society of North America, 1965), pp. 11–12.

5. Collie, *Saga*, pp. 292–298.

6. Ibid., pp. 319–320.

7. *United States of America* v. *Grinding Wheel Manufacturers Association; Norton Company et al.*, Civil Action no. 6636, District Court for Mass. (1947), Complaint.

8. Earl Hughes interview, September 23, 1980.

9. "Standardization of Grade for Grinding Wheels," *American Machinist*, 40 (May 14, 1914), 877; "Report of Conference between Grinding Machine Manufacturers and Grinding Wheel Manufacturers, October 21, 1913," National Machine Tool Builders' Association *Bulletin*, 6 (December 1913), 14.

10. *Grits and Grinds*, 16 (April 1925), 2.

11. "Standard Grinding Wheels Reduce Inventories and Benefit Users," *Abrasive Industry*, 11 (February 1930), 60.

12. Ibid., pp. 60–61; U.S. Department of Commerce, *Elimination of Waste: Simplified Practice, Grinding Wheels*, Simplified Practice Recommendation no. 45; Collie, *Saga*, pp. 298–306.

13. Collie, *Saga*, pp. 306–312, 325–327, 329–330, 341–343.

14. Ibid., pp. 320–323, 364–368.

15. Alfred D. Chandler, *The Visible Hand* (Cambridge, Mass.: Harvard University Press, 1977), pp. 491–492.

16. George Jeppson interview, June 28, 1950, Tymeson Papers.

17. Norton Company, *Aldus Chapin Higgins, 1872–1948: In Memorium* (Worcester, 1948).

18. Norton Company, Minutes, February 20, 1907; August 16, 19, 1909; December 29, 1910; April 11, November 21, 1911.

19. John Jeppson interview, March 20, 1981.

20. George Jeppson to Aldus Higgins, June 13, 1934, Jeppson Papers.

21. Wallace Howe interview, June 18, 1979.

22. Ralph Gow interview, June 17, 1980.

23. Ibid., June 17, December 4, 1980; Milton Higgins interview, February 5, 1981; John Jeppson interview, March 20, 1981.

24. Milton Higgins interview, February 5, 1981.

25. Aldus Higgins to Charles Allen, January 6, 1938.

26. *Norton Spirit*, June 1949, p. 1.

27. Collie, *Saga*, p. 64; Milton Higgins interview, June 12, 1979.

28. John Jeppson interviews, March 11, 1980; April 2, 1981.

29. Joel Styffe interview, undated, Tymeson Papers; *Norton Spirit*, June 1929, pp. 15–16.

30. *Norton Spirit*, June 1958, p. 1.

31. Collie, *Saga*, passim.

32. Ibid., pp. 126–127, 135.

33. James H. Soltow, "Origins of Small Business and the Relationships between Large and Small Firms: Metal Fabricating and Machinery Making in New England, 1890–1957," pp. 201–202, and Clyde and Sally Griffen, "Small Business and Occupational Mobility in Nineteenth Century Poughkeepsie," p. 139, in Stuart W. Bruchey, *Small Business in American Life* (New York: Columbia University Press, 1980). The Griffens point out that high failure rates and short life spans, especially among small retail firms, restricted intergenerational management as a percentage of total companies. Nevertheless, they found eighty-nine such firms in Poughkeepsie between 1850 and 1880.

34. Chandler, *Visible Hand*, pp. 281–282, 464–468, 491–493.

35. Milton Higgins interview, February 5, 1981.

36. George Jeppson's public service is recorded in his correspondence as works manager, 1917–1919, in the Norton Archives. See also, Naboth Hedin, *George Nathaniel Jeppson, 1873–1962*, reprint from *Yearbook* of the American Swedish Historical Foundation, 1963, in Norton Archives.

37. Ralph Gow, "Memoirs," tape 6, April 3, 1979.

38. Chandler, *Visible Hand*, chaps. 12–13.

39. Norton Emery Wheel Company, "Annual Report," 1905.

40. Norton Company, Minutes, June 20, 1919.

41. Norton Company, Minute Book of Stockholders' Meetings, November 16, 1921.

42. See, for example, Gow, "Memoirs," tape 1, February 1979.

43. Ibid.

44. Donation records are scattered through the Norton Minute books.

45. Civic service by Norton officials is documented in the company scrapbooks and in George Jeppson's papers as works manager for 1917–1919. See also Hedin, *George Jeppson*; Norton Company, *Aldus Higgins: In Memorium; Bulletin of the American Ceramic Society*, 17 (June 1938), 267–268.

46. Gow, "Memoirs," tape 1, February 1979.

47. For example, see George Jeppson to Aldus Higgins, June 13, 1934, with attached notes, Jeppson Papers.

48. Norton Company, Minutes, December 21, 1915.

49. Ibid.

50. W. E. Freeland, "Two Years' Growth of an Abrasive Industry," *Iron Age*, 99 (January 25, 1917), 248–251; "Minutes from Experimental and Off Grade Committee Meetings, 1908–1913," typescript volume in Norton Archives.

51. Norton Emery Wheel Company, "Annual Report," 1905.

52. "Factory Cost and Business Methods," *Iron Age*, 80 (July 11, 1907), 142–143; Henry Duckworth to George Jeppson, June 30, 1919.

53. Henry Duckworth to George Jeppson, June 30, 1919.

54. Norton Company, "Brief," June 16, 1928, exhibits C, D, E.

55. Norton Company, Minutes, January 19, 1910; December 21, 1915; George Jeppson, memorandum, January 7, 1918.

56. Norton Company, Minutes, March 26, 1913; March 15, 1917; June 27, 1920; Norton Company, "Brief to Commissioner of Internal Revenue," July 13, 1922, p. 17.

57. Norton Company, Minutes, January 4, 1916.

58. Norton Company, "Annual Report," 1907; E. H. Fish, "Educational Activities at Norton Companies," National Association of Corporation Schools *Bulletin*, 2 (October 1915), 17–22.

59. George Montague interview, undated, Tymeson Papers.

60. Charles Jinnette interview, undated, Tymeson Papers.

61. *Grits and Grinds*, 5 (March 1914), 2–4.

62. Robert (Joe) Cannon interview, June 14, 1979.

63. Literature for the 1919 and 1920 Norton Company sales conferences, in company scrapbooks of printed materials, vol. 1; interviews with William L. Neilson and W. R. Moore, May 8, 1929, in Norton Company folder, no. 207.07, box 2, Papers of the Manufacturers Research Association, Baker Library, Harvard Business School (hereafter cited as MRA records).

64. *Norton Spirit*, October 1923, pp. 1, 3.

65. Milton Higgins interviews, July 16, December 2, 1980; Neilson and Moore interviews, May 8, 1929, in MRA records. Sales manuals and bulletins can be found in Norton Company scrapbooks.

66. Milton Higgins interview, December 2, 1980.

67. Aldus Higgins, *Messages from Management* (Worcester, 1947), p. 9; Howard Dunbar, *Bargain Day in Machinetoolville* (Worcester, 1925); typescript copy of speech by Howard Dunbar, undated.

68. H. K. Dodge in *Selling Magazine*, July 1907, p. 35.

69. Numerous scrapbooks of company material printed for the trade and a complete run of *Grits and Grinds* are in the Norton Company Archives.

70. Milton Higgins interview, February 24, 1981; Milton Higgins, "Market Research," speech to St. Wulstan Society, March 13, 1981.

71. Data on formation and responsibilities of various departments can be found in George Jeppson's correspondence as works manager and in Tymeson, *Norton Story*, pp. 124–126.

72. George Jeppson to Henry Duckworth, November 20, 1918; George Jeppson to Carl Dietz, November 16, 1918.

73. T. S. Green to George Jeppson, January 25, 1917; George Jeppson, memorandum, December 11, 1919; Norton Company, Minutes, June 4, 1918.

74. George Jeppson to Sales Department, December 6, 1919; Wallace Montague to George Jeppson, December 18, 1919.

75. Alfred D. Chandler, *Giant Enterprise: Ford, General Motors, and the Automobile Industry* (New York: Harcourt, Brace and World, 1964), pp. 71–92.

76. Aldus Higgins to William L. Neilson, December 6, 1920; Charles Allen to William L. Neilson, June 4, 1921, Tymeson Papers; "Comparative Net Sales Growth, 1885–1932."

77. Aldus Higgins to William L. Neilson, June 14, 1921, Tymeson Papers.

78. Norton Company, Minutes, February 17, April 30, 1920; Aldus Higgins quoted in *Norton Spirit*, May 1922, p. 3; May–June 1931, p. 8.

79. Norton Company, Minutes, June 21, 1921; Robert Lawson interview, July 21, 1980.

80. Aldus Higgins to William L. Neilson, June 14, 1921, Tymeson Papers; Norton Company, Minutes, December 27, 1922.

81. Norton Company's annual reports to the Commonwealth of Massachusetts, in Corporate Records Division, Baker Library, Harvard Business School, 1942–1945.

82. Orello S. Buckner interview, May 1957, Tymeson Papers.

83. Aldus Higgins to William L. Neilson, June 14, 1921, Tymeson Papers.

84. Alfred D. Chandler, *Strategy and Structure* (Cambridge, Mass.: MIT Press, 1962), pp. 122–123, 174–185, 360–361; Alfred D. Chandler and Stephen Salsbury, *Pierre S. du Pont and the Making of the Modern Corporation* (New York: Harper and Row, 1971), pp. 504, 549–554.

85. Henry Duckworth quoting Donaldson Brown's *The New Way to Net Profits* in "Budgetary Control Is Explained to Foremen," *Norton Spirit*, March 1929, p. 3.

86. Ellis W. Hawley, "Herbert Hoover, the Commerce Secretariat, and the Vision of an Associative State, 1921–1928," *Journal of American History*, 61 (June 1974), pp. 116–140.

87. *Norton Spirit*, April 1929, pp. 9–10; October 1949, p. 8; August 1952, p. 5.

88. For Norton's forecasting, see Duckworth, "Budgetary Control"; discussions by Stephen Foster and H. J. Griffing, August 6, 1929, in Market Research Group B file, MRA records.

89. Duckworth, "Budgetary Control," p. 5.

90. Ibid.; Foster discussion, August 6, 1929, MRA records.

91. Aldus Higgins in *Norton Spirit*, April 1938, p. 4.

92. Milton Higgins interview, August 7, 1980; Ralph Gow interview, June 17, 1980.

93. Duckworth, "Budgetary Control," p. 5.

94. "Total Number of Employees at End of Each Year," in Norton Company's Personnel Department.

95. W. Irving Clark interview, undated, Tymeson Papers.

96. J. C. Spence to George I. Alden, November 1, 1917; "Nationalities in Plant," typed sheet in Works Manager's Papers, September 1, 1917.

97. Henry Duckworth to George Jeppson, November 22, 1917.

98. E. H. Fish to George Jeppson, May 18, 1917.

99. George Jeppson to Legal Department, November 22, 1917; George Jeppson, "Women Employees," April 27, 1917; George Jeppson to Charles Allen, March 1, 1918; George Jeppson to Norton Mutual Benefit Association, July 11, 1918.

100. George Jeppson to Bertram Hildebrant, November 19, 1917; Waldemar Rosedale to George Jeppson, July 23, 1918.

101. David Brody, *Workers in Industrial America* (New York: Oxford University Press, 1980), pp. 12–26.

102. For accounts of the strike, see William E. Zeuch, "An Investigation of the Metal Trades Strikes of Worcester, 1915" (Master's thesis, Clark University, 1916); John Spence to Morse Twist Drill Company, November 22, 1917; *Worcester Sunday Telegram*, October 10, 1915, p. 2.

103. John Spence to Morse Twist Drill Company, November 22, 1917.

104. Ibid.

105. Zeuch, "Strikes," pp. 32, 34–36.

106. Alden quoted in *Worcester Sunday Telegram*, October 10, 1915, p. 2.

107. Robert Lawson interview, July 21, 1980; John Spence to George Jeppson, June 11, 1919.

108. George Jeppson to Charles Allen, November 1, 1919.

109. George Jeppson to John Spence, December 13, 1917. See also Jeppson to Spence, June 5, 6, 16, July 1, 1919.

110. George Jeppson to Charles Allen, July 6, 25, 1917. I am also indebted to James Hanlan of Worcester Polytechnic Institute for the loan of his records of Norton Company employee cards.

111. Hanlan records.

112. The spy episode is documented in the Works Manager's Papers for 1917–1919, especially those files labeled J-8, G-7, B-24, S-7, M-50, H-17, Germans from Interned Ships, and Germans.

113. John Jeppson interview, March 11, 1980.

114. George Jeppson to George Merryweather, May 31, 1918.

115. George Jeppson to Charles Allen, August 9, 1917.

116. Ibid., April 5, 1917.

117. *Grits and Grinds*, 2 (June 1910).

118. Aldus Higgins quoted in *Iron Age*, 89 (April 11, 1912), 914.

119. George Jeppson speech to foremen's banquet, February 16, 1917.

120. Zeuch, "Strikes."

121. W. Irving Clark, *Norton Service to Employees* (Worcester, n.d.), p. 36; see also Clark to George Jeppson, November 8, 1918.

122. W. Irving Clark and Edward B. Simmons, "The Dust Hazard in the Abrasive Industry," *Journal of Industrial Hygiene*, 7 (August 1925), 345–351; Clark, "Clinical Aspects, Diagnosis and Treatment of Pneumononiosis," *Journal of Industrial Hygiene and Toxicology*, 18 (October 1936), 537–549; Leroy U. Gardner and Donald E. Cummings, "The Reaction to Fine and Medium Sized Quartz and Aluminum Oxide Particles, Silicotic Cirrhosis of the Liver," *American Journal of Pathology*, 9 (suppl., 1933), 751–763.

123. W. Irving Clark, *Health Service in Industry* (New York: Macmillan, 1922); Clark, "Medical Treatment for Employees," *Southern Machinery*, January 1912, pp. 73–77; Clark, "The Physical Examination of Workers," *Safety*, March 1913, pp. 64–65.

124. Clark, *Health Service*, p. 4. See also Clark, "Keeping Workmen in Repair," *System*, 24 (September 1913), 263–269.

125. Perry R. MacNeille, "First Aid Hospitals for Industrial Plants," *Modern Hospital*, June 1914, p. 355.

126. J-8 (Burns detective) to L. Letherman, April 24, 1917.

127. John Jeppson interview, March 11, 1980; E. H. Fish to George Jeppson, August 22, 1917.

128. *Worcester Evening Post*, June 13, 1930, p. 32; Service Department file.

129. W. Irving Clark, "Old Workers in Industry Remain in Good Health," *Nation's Health*, 7 (December 1925), 1.

130. Clifford Anderson, "Recreation for Industrial Workers," p. 3, in Norton Company, *Norton Service* (Worcester, n.d.).

131. George Jeppson to Charles Allen, August 11, 1919.

132. George Jeppson, "Rowing," November 5, 1919.

133. For sports and hobbies, see Anderson, "Recreation"; *Worcester Daily Telegram*, May 9, 1920, p. C4; Carl Leafe's report to the Service Department, October 29, 1919.

134. Jeppson, "Rowing."

135. *Norton Spirit*, August 1965, p. 1.

136. Clifford Anderson, "Indian Hill: An Industrial Village," in *Norton Service*, p. 2.

137. Ibid., "Housing Plans of the Norton Companies," *The Review*, 13 (August 1916), 353–365.

138. "Conference with Mr. Grosvenor Atterbury," July 3, 1917, in Works Manager's Papers.

139. *Norton Spirit*, October 20, 1926, p. 1; John Jeppson interview, March 11, 1980.

140. Stuart D. Brandes, *American Welfare Capitalism, 1880–1940* (Chicago: University of Chicago Press, 1976); Brody, *Workers*, chap. 2; Kim McQuaid, "Corporate Liberalism in the American Business Community, 1920–1940," *Business History Review*, 52 (Autumn, 1978), 342–368.

141. Brandes, *Capitalism*, p. 9.

142. For other examples of New England firms perpetuating nineteenth-century paternalism in twentieth-century corporate welfare, see Tamara K. Hareven, *Family Time and Industrial Time: The Relationship between the Family and Work in a New England Industrial Community* (Cambridge: Cambridge University Press, 1982), chap. 3; Dorothy Bowler Laverty, *Millinocket: Magic City of Maine's Wilderness* (Freeport, Me.: Bond Wheelwright Company, 1973).

143. Excerpt from *American Machinist*, 58 (April 12, 1923), in scrapbooks of trade publications about Norton, vol. 15; *Worcester Gazette*, September 18, 1926, p. 18; *Norton Spirit*, June 1930, p. 10.

144. Ralph Gow, "Memoirs," tape 2, February 1979; Milton Higgins interview, February 5, 1981.

145. "The Norton Community," *Magazine of Management*, January–February 1948, p. 7.

146. Kendall Birr, "Industrial Research Laboratories," in Nathan Reingold, *The Sciences in the American Context: New Perspectives* (Washington, D.C.: Smithsonian Institution Press, 1979), pp. 199–200.

147. Milton Higgins to Charles Allen, June 1, 1906; Milton Higgins's notes, dated July 1905, in Norton Company Archives.

148. Ross Purdy to George Jeppson, November 26, 1918.

149. Purdy in unattributed article titled "Norton Research Laboratory," in scrapbooks of published materials about Norton, vol. 3, p. 170.

150. Ross Purdy to Charles Allen, April 23, 1919.

151. Wallace Howe interview, February 6, 1981.

152. Report by Ross Purdy, September 8, 1914, in file RE 25-1 at Norton Company Library, Chippawa, Ontario.

153. Ross Purdy, "Compression Strength of Grains of Various Abrasives," May 7, 1914, pp. 14–15, at Chippawa Library.

154. Loring Coes, *Abrasives* (New York: Springer-Verlag, 1971).

155. Newman Thibault interview, March 3, 1981; see also Gordon Finlay interview, March 17, 1981.

156. Baalis Sanford interview, February 25, 1981.

157. Isabelle Chaffin to Ross Purdy, January 11, 1919.

158. George Jeppson to Ross Purdy, March 27, 1918.

159. Charles Allen, Aldus Higgins, and George Jeppson, "New Division of Research Work," December 16, 1916, in Works Manager's Papers.

160. Wallace Howe interview, February 6, 1981; Max Wheilden interview, May 20, 1980; Ralph Gow interview, December 4, 1980.

161. "Application of B Process to Plant Production," pp. 14459–460, film 4, in Worcester research records at Norton's library in Worcester (hereafter cited as Worcester research records).

162. Ralph Gow, "Memoirs," tape 6, April 3, 1979.

163. Wallace Howe interview, June 18, 1979; see also Neuman Thibault interview, March 31, 1981; Ralph Gow, "Memoirs," tape 6, April 3, 1979.

164. Baalis Sanford interview, February 25, 1981.

165. Wallace Howe interview, June 18, 1979; Charles Hudson interview, undated, Tymeson Papers.

166. Ross Purdy to George Jeppson, February 8, 1915; Hugo Beth to George Jeppson, June 6, 1919; Ross Purdy, Charles Hudson, Milton Beecher, et al. to George Jeppson, May 20, 1919; Norman Monks, Ralph Gustafson, and Bob Werme, joint interview, April 2, 1981; Lowell Milligan interview, undated, Tymeson Papers.

167. Donald Chisholm, "Norton Pulpstone Development," typescript memoir, 1981.

168. For development of Norbide, see *Grits and Grinds*, 25 (September–October 1934), 1–8; Raymond Ridgeway, "Boron Carbide: A New Crystalline Abrasive and Wear Resistant Product," *Transactions of the Electrochemical Society*, 56 (1934), 293–308.

169. For Norton's work with diamond wheels, see Baalis Sanford interview, February 25, 1981; *Grits and Grinds*, 25 (November–December 1934), 1–4, and

30 (November–December 1939), 7–8; "Index Report of Norton Diamond-Bakelite Grinding Wheels," August 25, 1934, research file TIC 34.0006, in Worcester research records.

170. "Index Report"; A. A. Klein, memorandum, December 17, 1942, pp. 23089–90, film 5, in Worcester research records; Tymeson, *Norton Story*, p. 276.

171. *Grits and Grinds*, 22 (January 1931), 1–3; L. H. Milligan and Warren H. Turner, "Bond Glasses for Vitrified Alundum Wheels," May 25, 1927, research file TIC 27.0014; "Application of B Process to Plant Production," undated, pp. 1457–471, film 4, Worcester research records.

172. Wallace Howe interview, February 6, 1981; Norman Monks, Ralph Gustafson, and Bob Werme, joint interview, April 2, 1981.

173. Wallace Howe interviews, June 18, 1979; February 6, 1981.

174. Ibid.; Norman Monks, Ralph Gustafson, and Bob Werme, joint interview, April 2, 1981.

175. Milton Higgins interview, August 7, 1980.

176. W. C. Wickenden, "Comparative Statements of Norton Company and Carborundum," March 18, 1955, in file of supplementary data for the Board of Directors. For the 1919 share, see Henry Duckworth to Charles Allen, November 12, 1919.

177. *Norton Spirit*, February 1942, p. 4; George Jeppson speech to ten- and fifteen-year people, May 27, 1942, Jeppson Papers.

178. George Jeppson speech, May 27, 1942; "Total Number of Employees at End of Each Year," in Norton Company Personnel Department.

4   Challenges to the Family Firm

1. Robert S. Woodbury, *History of the Grinding Machine*, pp. 135–161, and *History of the Milling Machine*, pp. 91–100, in his *Studies in the History of Machine Tools* (Cambridge, Mass.: MIT Press, 1972).

2. U.S. Bureau of the Census, *Seventeenth Census of the United States: 1950, Population*, II, pt. 21, p. 9.

3. William L. Neilson interview, September 1955, Tymeson Papers.

4. Earl Hughes interview, September 23, 1980.

5. Kenneth J. Moynihan, "Swedes and Yankees in Worcester Politics: A Protestant Partnership," p. 8, typescript of a paper presented at the Joint Conference of the Victorian Society in America and the National Archives, Washington, D.C., March 1979.

6. For foreign plant expansion, see chap. 5.

7. See, for example, *Metallurgical and Chemical Engineering*, 9 (May 1911), 257–258.

8. George Jeppson interview, June 28, 1950, Tymeson Papers.

9. "Refractory Conferences Minute Book, 1908–1910"; M. F. Beecher, "Development of Refractory Department," October 5, 1917, in Works Manager's Papers; catalogs in Norton scrapbooks.

10. Milton Higgins interviews, June 12, 1979; December 2, 1980; Clayton Jenks to George Jeppson, September 16, 1919.

11. Ross Purdy to George Jeppson, August 3, 15, 1919.

12. William R. Moore to Ralph Johnson, January 7, 1954, in file of supporting documents for Board of Directors meetings; William L. Neilson and W. R. Moore interviews, May 8, 1929, in Norton Company folder, no. 207.07, box 2, MRA records.

13. Howard Dunbar, typescript autobiography, July 23, 1951, in Tymeson Papers; Norton Grinding Company, Minutes of Board of Directors meetings, November 1918, June 20, 1919.

14. Woodbury, *Grinding Machine*, pp. 135–142.

15. Norton Company, "Brief to Commissioner of Internal Revenue, re: Claims for Depreciation of Patents and Contract for the Calendar Year 1917," June 16, 1928, p. 22.

16. Dunbar typescript, July 23, 1951.

17. Woodbury, *Grinding Machine*, pp. 151–161.

18. Robert Lawson interview, July 21, 1980. See also *Heim Grinder Company* v. *Fafnir Bearing Company*, 13 Federal Reporter, 2nd ser., 408 (1926). Fafnir was unsuccessfully defended by the Detroit Machine Tool Company, the Norton subsidiary that had manufactured and sold Fafnir the centerless machine at issue.

19. Robert Lawson interview, July 21, 1980; Norton Company, "Brief," June 16, 1928, p. 42.

20. Dunbar typescript, July 23, 1951; Robert Lawson interview, July 21, 1980; "Putting the Shop in Order Increases Plant Capacity," *Grits and Grinds*, 22 (May 1931), 1–12.

21. Herbert S. Indge, "Refinement of Ground Surfaces," *Mechanical Engineering*, 60 (November 1938), 807–812; H. J. Griffing, "Lapping," *The Tool Engineer*, 7 (April 1939), 32–33; "How Flat Can You Get?" *Fortune*, 42 (December 1950), 115–122.

22. *Grits and Grinds*, 22 (December 1931), 5.

23. Milton Higgins interview, February 24, 1981; Behr-Manning Corporation, "Sharpening Stones: Their History and Development," typescript, Tymeson Papers; "Affiliates" folder, Tymeson Papers.

24. Behr-Manning Corporation, *Lecture on Coated Abrasives* (Troy, N.Y., 1946); Behr-Manning Corporation, *History of Behr Manning in the Coated Abrasive Industry* (Troy, N.Y., 1954); A. J. Sidford, "Rough Notes on the History of the Sandpaper Business," typescript, revised April 1944, Behr-Manning Archives at Watervliet.

25. Donald Kelso, "Early Days of Coated Abrasives," undated typescript in Mrs. Kelso's possession; Donald and Florence Kelso, "Autobiography," undated manuscript in Mrs. Kelso's possession.

26. Kelso, "Early Days," pp. 7–9.

27. Ibid., pp. 9–10.

28. Sidford, "Rough Notes," pp. 1, 3, 4, 23.

29. Ibid.; Elmer Schacht, "Notes Used in Lecture Given to 'Know Behr-Manning' Conference Group on December 1, 1949," typescript, Behr-Manning Archives, p. 25.

30. U.S. Bureau of the Census, *Fifteenth Census of the United States: 1930, Manufactures: 1929*, II, p. 1354.

31. Histories of the early industry and its firms are fragmentary. The best sources are Sidford, "Rough Notes"; Kelso, "Early Days"; Schacht, "Notes"; Kelso and Kelso, "Autobiography."

32. Bureau of the Census, *Fifteenth Census, Manufactures,* II, 1354; Schacht, "Notes."

33. Virginia Huck, *Brand of the Tartan: The 3M Story* (New York: Appleton-Century-Crofts, 1955), pp. 42, 93.

34. Kelso, "Early Days," pp. 10–11.

35. Sidford, "Rough Notes," p. 2.

36. Huck, *Brand*, pp. 44, 57, 59.

37. Elmer Schacht, "Standards and Tests Benefit Coated Abrasive Users," *Abrasive Industry*, 12 (March 1931), 23–26.

38. Huck, *Brand*, p. 89; *Grits and Grinds,* 22 (January 1931), 5; A. J. Sidford, "After 40 Years," *Grits and Grinds,* 28 (November–December 1937), 11–12. The Kelso, Schacht, and Sidford accounts are again the best general primary sources.

39. Maximilian Pesnel interview, undated, Tymeson Papers.

40. Elmer Schacht interviews, August 15, 1980; March 11, 1981; *Speed Grits,* 2 (March 1920), 1–4.

41. Sidford, "Rough Notes," pp. 10–11; Kelso, "Early Days," p. 15; Huck, *Brand*, pp. 96–99.

42. Huck, *Brand*, pp. 92–100.

43. Ibid., pp. 82–83, 100–101.

44. Norton Company, *Norton Folks Contribute to Industry* (Worcester, 1944); Sidford, "Rough Notes," pp. 6–7.

45. For Schacht's work on electrocoating, see Schacht interviews, August 17, 1980; November 11, 1980; *Grits and Grinds,* 27 (January–February 1936), 10–12.

46. "Order of Material in Electrocoating Publicity Collection," typescript file, Behr-Manning Archives; Behr-Manning (Mass.), Minutes, January 17, 1934.

47. Daniel Nelson, *Managers and Workers: Origins of the New Factory System in the United States, 1880–1920* (Madison: University of Wisconsin Press, 1975).

48. Huck, *Brand*, pp. 75–77.

49. Elmer Schacht interviews, August 17, 1980; March 11, 1981; Kelso, "Early Days," pp. 9–10.

50. Huck, *Brand*, pp. 60–69; Henry Merrill interview, October 3, 1980.

51. Behr-Manning Corporation (Del.), Minutes, October 17, 1928; Behr-Manning Company (N.Y.), Minutes, August 15, September 16, 1928; Henry Merrill interview, October 3, 1980; 3M Company, *Annual Report,* 1930, 1946.

52. Waterproof patent license from 3M to Behr-Manning, June 23, 1930, Behr-Manning Archives. For 3M's early days, see Huck, *Brand*, especially chaps. 1–13.

53. Elmer Schacht interviews, August 17, November 11, 1980; Henry Merrill interview, October 3, 1980.

54. Huck, *Brand*, pp. 195–197.

55. Elmer Schacht interview, August 15, 1980; "Patent License Agreement Related to Electrocoated Sandpaper, September 13, 1932," Behr-Manning Archives.

56. Henry Merrill interview, October 3, 1980.

57. Behr-Manning (Mass.), Minutes, September 21, 1932; *U.S.* v. *General Electric Company*, 272 U.S. 476 (1926).

58. Henry Merrill interview, October 3, 1980.

59. For export and foreign manufacture, see Kelso, "Early Days," pp. 17–18, 21; Donald Kelso interview, June 14, 1979.

60. For a discussion of the Webb-Pomerene Act and American foreign enterprise, see Mira Wilkins, *The Maturing of Multinational Enterprise: American Business Abroad from 1914 to 1970* (Cambridge, Mass.: Harvard University Press, 1974), pp. 49–50, 63, 68–69, 88.

6l. Kelso, "Early Days," p. 17; Donald Kelso interview, June 14, 1979.

62. Elmer Schacht interviews, August 17, 1980; March 11, 1981; Behr-Manning (N.Y.), Minutes, August 15, September 19, 1928.

63. Randall Manchester interview, October 2, 1980; Elmer Schacht interview, March 11, 1981; Behr-Manning (Mass.), Minutes, August 17, 1937.

64. Kelso, "Early Days," p. 17; Donald Kelso interview, June 19, 1979.

65. Donald Kelso interview, June 19, 1979.

66. Ibid.

67. Max Pesnel interview, undated, Tymeson Papers; F. E. Gallagher to W. J. Magee, November 5, 1935, in tax file at Watervliet vault.

68. Elmer Schacht interview, March 11, 1981.

69. Henry Merrill interview, October 3, 1980.

70. George Link, Jr., to John D. Gaffey, October 28, 1963, in Legal Department vault in Worcester.

71. Huck, *Brand*, chaps. 15–20; 3M Company, *Annual Reports*, 1930, 1935.

72. Elmer Schacht interview, August 17, 1980; Donald Kelso interview, June 19, 1979; Henry Merrill interview, October 3, 1980.

73. Behr-Manning (Mass.), Minutes, May 3, 1928; March 18, October 17, 1931; January 17, 1934.

74. Elmer Schacht interview, August 17, 1980.

75. Behr-Manning (N.Y.), Minutes, May 29 through September 10, 1931.

76. Ibid., May 23, 1928.

77. Lee Hoogstoel interview, March 10, 1981; Lee Hoogstoel, "Memoirs," March 9, 1981, in Hoogstoel's possession; Behr-Manning, *History*, pp. 5–6.

78. Elmer Schacht interview, August 15, 1980; Henry Merrill interview, October 3, 1980.

79. Elmer Schacht interview, August 15, 1980; Henry Merrill interview, October 3, 1980.

80. For the development of product engineering and belt sanding, see Dirck Olton interview, October 1, 1980; Elmer Schacht interviews, August 17, November 11, 1980; Henry Merrill interview, October 3, 1980; Lee Vorce, "Abrasive Belt Polishing," *Steel*, 137 (September 5, 12, 19, 1955), 84–89, 102–104, 132–134; Stan L. Johnson, "New Abrasive Methods Cut Costs," *Metal Finishing*, 48 (March 1950), 78–80.

81. Johnson, "New Abrasive," pp. 78–80.

82. Henry Merrill interview, October 3, 1980.

83. Ibid.; Elmer Schacht interview, August 15, 1980; Milton Higgins interview, February 5, 1981.

84. Lee Hoogstoel, typescript lecture dated June 19, 1953, in Hoogstoel's possession; Behr-Manning Company, sales catalog, 1951.

85. Henry Merrill interview, October 3, 1980; Elmer Schacht interview, August 17, 1980.

86. For dividends, see Behr-Manning (Mass.), Minutes, August 29, November 11, 1947; December 13, 1946; April 16, 1954; January 18, 1957. Industry share data is from a chart headed "Norton Coated Abrasive Market Share," in "Presentation to Norton Coated Abrasive Division," by Boston Consulting Group, July 1973.

87. Elmer Schacht interview, August 15, 1980.

88. Ibid.

5   Worcesterites Abroad

1. Mira Wilkins, *The Emergence of Multinational Enterprise: American Business Abroad from the Colonial Era to 1914* (Cambridge, Mass.: Harvard University Press, 1970), p. 110. This book and its sequel, *The Maturing of Multinational Enterprise: American Business Abroad from 1914 to 1970* (Cambridge, Mass.: Harvard University Press, 1974), are the best sources on the evolution of American multinationals.

2. Wilkins, *Emergence*, chaps. 4–9.

3. Ibid., pp. 70, 207.

4. Ibid., pp. 83, 91, 103.

5. Ibid., pp. 201, 212–214, 110.

6. Walter C. Gold, "Grinding Wheels," *Metal Industry*, 13 (November 1915), 450–452; Leonard Kellenberger interview, May 2, 1981.

7. *Worcester Daily Telegram*, August 5, 1886, p. 2.

8. Norton Company, Minutes, September 28, 1891.

9. Norton Company, "Annual Report," 1910; George Jeppson interview, June 1956, Tymeson Papers.

10. *American Machinist*, 44 (March 2, 1916), 395; notes on Norton in England, Tymeson Papers.

11. "The History of Alfred Herbert Limited," undated typescript, Tymeson Papers.

12. Swen Pulson III interview, March 25, 1981; Norton Company, Minutes, September 28, 1891.

13. Swen Pulson III interview, March 25, 1981; Norton Company, Minutes, September 28, 1891.

14. Copy of Alfred Herbert–Norton contract in Norton Company, Minutes, December 12, 1913.

15. The Million-dollar estimate assumes that foreign sales were 25 percent of total revenue, the average for 1903–1910. Norton Company, "Annual Re-

port," 1910. See also Henry Sheehan interview, undated, Tymeson Papers; *Norton Spirit*, November 1955, p. 9.

16. Charles Allen, quoted in an excerpt from *Machinery* (1907), in scrapbooks of publications about Norton, vol. 5, p. 185.

17. Unidentified articles in scrapbooks, vol. 1, pp. 37–38.

18. Otto Schutte interview, May 1956, Tymeson Papers; excerpt from *Iron Age*, July 17, 1893, in scrapbooks, vol. 3, p. 209; Alexander Luchars, "The German Machine Tool and Related Industries," undated, unidentified article in the president's file, Works Manager's Papers for 1919; "A European Machinery House," *Machinery*, 13 (December 1906), 208–209; *Bilder vom Schutte-Werk und Bemerkenswerte Daten zur Firmengeschichte* (Coln-Deutz: Alfred H. Schutte, 1955?), pp. 46–59.

19. Norton Company, Minutes, June 19, 1907; January 17, 1913; Norton Accounting Department to C. H. Griffin, April 21, 1924. Tymeson says the fee was 6 percent in "Made in Germany," pp. 11–12, a chapter in "Norton Behr-Manning Overseas, Inc.," typescript, February 14, 1958, Tymeson Papers (hereafter cited by author's name and chapter title).

20. William L. Neilson interview, September 1955, Tymeson Papers; Tymeson, "Made in Germany," pp. 12–13.

21. Norton Company, Minutes, January 16, 1912; January 1, April 8, November 11, 1913; Accounting Department to C. H. Griffin, April 1, 1924. Marks were converted to dollars at the 4.2-to-1 gold rate.

22. For Norton in Germany during World War I, see *Norton Spirit*, February 1915, p. 1; Otto Lof to Martin Lof, February 20, 1917; Otto Lof to Charles Allen, April 18, 1919; Accounting Department to C. H. Griffin, April 1, 1924; Norton Company, Minutes, March 6, 1917.

23. William L. Neilson to Norton Company, September 20, 1919; Carl Dietz to Norton Company, December 11, 1919; Otto Lof to Charles Allen, April 18, 1919; Accounting Department to C. H. Griffin, April 1, 1924; ledger sheets for DNG, February 1, 1922; January 1, 1924, in Norton Company Archives.

24. Wilkins, *Maturing*, pp. 32, 51.

25. Carl Dietz to Norton Company, December 27, 1919.

26. Aldus Higgins to William L. Neilson, December 6, 1920, Tymeson Papers.

27. William L. Neilson to Norton Company, July 7, September 20, 1919; Carl Dietz to Norton Company, December 11, 1919; Otto Lof, memorandum, April 22, 1919.

28. Carl Dietz to Norton Company, December 11, 1919; Aldus Higgins to William L. Neilson, December 6, 1920, Tymeson Papers; Otto Bjorklund interview, undated, Tymeson Papers; Leonard Kellenberger interview, May 2, 1981; Arne Lundgren, Leonard Buhre, Bertil Linquist, Gosta Johnson joint interview, May 12, 1981; Hugo Timonen interview, May 13, 1981.

29. Carl Dietz to Norton Company, December 11, 1919; Otto Lof, memorandum, April 22, 1919.

30. Aldus Higgins to William L. Neilson, December 6, 1920, Tymeson Papers.

31. For the French story, see Carl Dietz to Norton Company, December

27, 1919; George Jeppson, undated memorandum, in "M" file of Works Manager's Papers for 1919; "History of Compagnie des Meules Norton," June 3, 1947, in Norton Archives; Tymeson, "Two Years in the Making."

32. For the Japanese story, see Charles Allen to Norton Company, September 19, 1917; Hiroshima files in Works Manager's Papers for 1918 and 1919; "Hiroshima Records" and "Documents: The Hiroshima Grinding Wheel Company, Limited," 2 vols. in Norton Archives.

33. Pierre Baruzy to William L. Neilson, December 10, 1919, Tymeson Papers.

34. For Canada, see Carl Dietz to Charles Allen, November 12, 1918; Tymeson, "Humming in Hamilton."

35. Pierre Baruzy to William L. Neilson, December 10, 1919.

36. William L. Neilson interview, September 1955, Tymeson Papers.

37. Norton Company, Minutes, October 21, 1919; "Hiroshima Records" and "Documents."

38. Wilkins, *Maturing*, p. 51.

39. Aldus Higgins in *Norton Spirit*, May–June 1931, p. 8.

40. Aldus Higgins to William L. Neilson, December 6, 1920; June 14, 1921, Tymeson Papers; Tymeson, "Its Own Salvation," p. 3.

41. Aldus Higgins to William L. Neilson, June 14, 1921, Tymeson Papers.

42. Hiroshima files in Works Manager's Papers, especially letters and reports by Orello Buckner.

43. Ross Purdy to George Jeppson, August 17, 1919.

44. Orello Buckner to T. G. Nee, April 5, 1919.

45. Tymeson, "The Best Record for Timing"; Herbert Stanton interview, September 1955, Tymeson Papers. For Australia, see Tymeson, "Unlimited is an Audacious Word"; John Adams interviews, September 27, October 1, 1979.

46. Lewis Greenleaf, in Behr-Manning (Mass.), Minutes, October 16, 1935. For the Italian acquisition, see *Norton Spirit*, August 1935, p. 4; Nino Barberis interview, May 4, 1981; Angelo D'Imporzano interview, May 4, 1981.

47. *Norton Spirit*, May 1938, p. 4; September 1938, p. 4.

48. Wilkins, *Maturing*, pp. 416–422.

49. Ibid., pp. 422–435.

50. Ted Meyer interview, March 25, 1981; *Norton Spirit*, June 1937, pp. 1, 6–7.

51. Ralph Gow interview, June 20, 1979; Pierre Baruzy interview, April 26, 1981; Angelo D'Imporzano interview, May 4, 1981; Tom Green interview, March 30, 1981; George Jeppson, "W. Lacoste Neilson," January 19, 1937. See also Tymeson chaps. on England, Germany, Italy, and France.

52. Ralph Gow interview, June 20, 1979; Tymeson chaps. on England, Germany, and France.

53. *Norton Spirit*, June 1937, pp. 1, 6–7; Ted Meyer interview, March 25, 1981; Ed Van der Pyl interview, June 14, 1979; Tymeson chaps., passim.

54. George Jeppson, "W. Lacoste Neilson," January 19, 1937; Tymeson, "Made in Germany," p. 14.

55. Aldus Higgins to William L. Neilson, June 14, 1921, Tymeson Papers.

56. Ted Meyer interview, March 25, 1981; Ralph Gow interview, June 20, 1979; Armand Lefebvre interview, April 29, 1981.

57. Tom Green interview, March 30, 1981; Ralph Gow interview, June 20, 1979.

58. Armand Lefebvre interview, April 29, 1981.

59. Ralph Gow interview, June 20, 1979.

60. Louis Camarra, series of conversations, April–May 1981; Tom Green interview, March 30, 1981.

61. Pierre Baruzy interview, April 26, 1981; Tom Green interview, March 30, 1981; Eric Becker interview, May 11, 1981; Otto Schutte interview, May 1956, Tymeson Papers.

62. Angelo D'Imporzano interview, May 4, 1981; Nino Barberis interview, May 4, 1981.

63. Aldus Higgins, quoted in *Norton Spirit*, August 1935, p. 4.

64. Aldus Higgins, quoted in *Norton Spirit*, September 1938, p. 4.

65. Otto Schutte interview, May 1956, Tymeson Papers.

66. Eric Becker interview, May 11, 1981; Ted Meyer interview, March 25, 1981; Otto Schutte interview, May 1956, Tymeson Papers.

67. For the DNG–World War II story, see folder in Norton Archives labeled "Compagnie des Meules Norton: Reports by Otto Schutte," which contains a number of letters by Schutte and the French managers; Otto Schutte, "D.N.G., 1939–1946"; folder of documents headed "Denazification of Otto Schutte"; "Otto Schutte, 1945–1947," a file of documents and letters; Otto Schutte's corrections to the Tymeson manuscript, "Norton Behr-Manning Overseas," Tymeson Papers. Also helpful were interviews with Ted Meyer, March 25, 1981, and Eric Becker, May 11, 1981. The material is summarized in Steven Koblik, "Business as Usual," unpublished, in Jeppson Papers, and in Tymeson, "Potential Promise."

68. Schutte, "D.N.G.: 1939–1946," p. 28.

69. Angelo D'Imporzano interview, May 4, 1981, and Nino Barberis interview, May 4, 1981, are supplements to materials listed in note 67.

70. In addition to sources listed in note 67, see Pierre Baruzy interview, April 26, 1981; Armand Lefebvre interview, April 19, 1981; Pierre Baruzy, "Four Years of Occupation . . . Four of Struggle," 1945; "History of Compagnie," June 3, 1947; Tymeson, "The Common Good."

71. Otto Schutte corrections to Tymeson, "Potential Promise," in typescript titled "Revisions of German Plant Story," pp. 3–4, Tymeson Papers.

72. Otto Schutte to Bert Stanton, August 15, 1940.

73. Baruzy, "Four Years"; Ralph Gow to Bert Stanton, February 22, 1945, translates and quotes Didier.

74. Schutte, "D.N.G.: 1939–1946," p. 17.

75. Ibid., p. 20. See also Leonard Kellenberger interview, May 2, 1981; Arne Lundgren and Gosta Johnson, joint interview, May 12, 1981; Hugo Timonen interview, May 13, 1981.

76. Hugo Timonen interview, May 13, 1981.

77. Otto Schutte to Pierre Baruzy, October 8, 1945.

78. Otto Schutte to Bert Stanton, May 15, 1946.

79. See sources cited in note 69.

80. Ralph Gow to Bert Stanton, February 22, 1945, quoting Didier.

81. Baruzy, "Four Years."

82. Otto Schutte to Andrew Holmstrom, October 29, 1957.

83. Pierre Baruzy to Bert Stanton, November 9, 1944.

84. Milton Higgins interview, August 7, 1980.

85. Account books for Mole Norton, CMN, and DNG, 1938–1951.

86. Otto Schutte, "D.N.G.: 1939–1946," p. 8; Otto Schutte to Bert Stanton, July 4, 1945.

87. Milton Higgins interview, August 7, 1980; DNG account book.

88. Milton Higgins interview, August 7, 1980.

89. Ibid.

90. Tymeson, "A Pottery Maker Becomes a Wheel Maker," p. 16; French data supplied by Armand Lefebvre, April 19, 1981; Jack Ewer interviews, August 1955, Tymeson Papers, and March 26, 1981, with the author.

91. "Norton Behr-Manning Overseas, Inc.," undated sheet in file of supporting data for NBMO's directors, in Legal Department.

92. Herbert Stanton interview, undated, Tymeson Papers; M. N. Pilsworth, Norton counsel, to Bert Stanton, February 10, 1948, in file of supporting documents for Norton Company's Board of Directors; Jack Ewer interview, March 26, 1981; John Manning (a manager at Welwyn) interview, April 24, 1981.

93. Primary sources for Durex were Donald Kelso interviews, June 14, 19, 1979; Donald Kelso, "Early Days of Coated Abrasives," undated typescript in Mrs. Kelso's possession; Donald and Florence Kelso, "Autobiography," undated manuscript in Mrs. Kelso's possession; *United States of America* v. *Minnesota Mining and Manufacturing Company, Behr-Manning Corporation, The Carborundum Company, Armour and Company, Durex Abrasives Corporation, and the Durex Corporation,* Civil Action no. 8119, District Court for Mass. (1950), case record, at Federal Archives and Records Center, Waltham, Mass. See also Jules Schaetzel interview, October 1955, Tymeson Papers.

94. A. J. Sidford to Henry Elliot, March 6, 1939, Government's exhibit 63 of the *Durex* case.

95. Kelso, "Autobiography," unpaged.

96. Donald Kelso interview, June 14, 1979.

97. Ibid.

98. Robert Young to Donald Kelso, October 18, 1932, Defendants' exhibit 55, *Durex*.

99. Robert Young, Report to Directors, November 15, 1932, pp. 173–174 of Defendants' Motion for Judgment, *Durex*.

100. Robert Young to Donald Kelso, May 24, 1934, Defendants' exhibit 123, *Durex*.

101. Durex Abrasives Corporation, Minutes, November 26, 1935, Defendants' exhibit 536, *Durex*.

102. "Abrasive Dollar Sales," exhibit 11-B of Government Document G-38, *Durex*.

103. Robert Young, Report to Durex Abrasives Corporation Directors, April 14, 1944, Government document G-58, *Durex.*

104. Robert Young to F. J. Tone, April 29, 1943, Government document G-43a, *Durex.*

105. A. J. Sidford to Robert Young, May 8, 1948, Government document G-43a, *Durex.*

106. Louis Camarra conversation with author, May 4, 1981.

107. Behr-Manning (Mass.), Minutes, July 8, 1936.

6   The Third Generation

1. For the Machine Division's experience in World War II, see Norton Company, *Salute! Mr. Norton* (Worcester, 1941); "Production for National Defense," *Grits and Grinds,* 32 (March 1941), 1–6; *Machine Sales News*, March 1, 1942.

2. For abrasives operations during the war, see "Norton Company in World War II," typescript prepared for the historical section of the Army Ordnance Association, May 1944; Norton Company, *Norton Folks Contribute to Industry* (Worcester, 1944).

3. Milton Higgins interview, August 7, 1980.

4. Norton Company, "Norton in World War II"; Wallace Howe interview, February 11, 1981; Milton Higgins interview, August 7, 1980.

5. Kenneth Lewis, *The Grinding Wheel: A Textbook of Modern Grinding Practice,* 1st ed. (Concord, N. H.: Rumford Press, 1951), p. 5; W. C. Wickenden, "Comparative Statements: Norton Company and Carborundum," March 18, 1955; Norton Company's annual reports of condition to the Commonwealth of Massachusetts, in Corporate Records Division, Baker Library, Harvard Business School, 1945; Chart of consolidated sales, 1937–1961, from John Jeppson, "Your Future at Norton Company," typescript of speech, October 10, 1962, Jeppson Papers.

6. Milton Higgins interviews, June 20, 1979; July 6, December 10, 1980; Ralph Gow interview, June 20, 1979; John Jeppson interview, March 20, 1981; Newman Thibault interview, March 13, 1981; "It's No Longer Just Grind, Grind at Norton," *Fortune,* 58 (August 1963), 168.

7. Ibid.

8. Milton Higgins interview, June 12, 1979.

9. Milton Higgins, quoted in *Norton Spirit,* May 1949, p. 4.

10. Ibid., September 1955, p. 8.

11. John Jeppson interview, April 2, 1981.

12. John Jeppson interview, undated, Tymeson Papers; John Jeppson interview, April 2, 1981.

13. Muriel F. Collie, *The Saga of the Abrasives Industry* (Greendale, Mass.: The Grinding Wheel Institute and the Abrasive Grain Association, 1951), p. 69.

14. Ralph Gow interview, December 4, 1980.

15. George Jeppson speech, August 12, 1950, Jeppson Papers.

16. Ralph Gow interviews, June 20, 1979; June 17, December 4, 1980.

17. Fairman Cowan interview, January 15, 1980; John Jeppson interview, March 20, 1981; Ralph Gow interview, June 20, 1979; Milton Higgins interview, December 10, 1980.

18. Ralph Gow interview, December 4, 1980.

19. The best sources for Higgins-Gow management are Ralph Gow, "Memoirs," a series of tapes dictated February–April 1979; numerous interviews with Ralph Gow and Milton Higgins cited in this chapter; interviews with John Jeppson, March 20, 1981; Fairman Cowan, January 15, 1980; Curt Clark, July 23, 1980; Everett Hicks, September 23, 1980.

20. Ralph Gow interview, June 20, 1979; John Jeppson interview, March 20, 1981; Milton Higgins interview, December 10, 1980; Everett Hicks interview, September 23, 1980.

21 John Jeppson, "Your Future at Norton Company," October 10, 1962, Jeppson Papers.

22. Ralph Gow interview, December 4, 1980.

23. Ibid., June 20, 1979.

24. Ibid.

25. Robert Cushman interview, March 23, 1981.

26. Fairman Cowan interview, January 15, 1980.

27. *Norton Spirit*, April 1967, p. 1.

28. Mildred Tymeson, *The Norton Story* (Worcester: Norton Company, 1953), p. vi.

29. For the tornado, see Francis J. Burgoyne, "How to Plan for Unexpected Disasters," *Safety Maintenance*, 119 (June 1960), 14–18, 47; Elliott B. Knowlton, "Disaster and Public Relations," *Public Relations Journal*, 9 (September 1953), 12–14.

30. *Norton Spirit*, September 1953, p. 1.

31. George Jeppson, speech to Grinding Wheel Manufacturers Association, September 9, 1943, Jeppson Papers.

32. Ibid.; George Jeppson speech, May 14, 1945; Aldus Higgins, *Editorials from "The Norton Spirit"* (Worcester, n.d.), p. 6; *Norton Spirit*, August 1945, p. 4.

33. George Jeppson speech, December 26, 1945, Jeppson Papers.

34. Wickenden, "Comparative Statements," March 18, 1955.

35. George Jeppson speech, December 26, 1945, Jeppson Papers.

36. George Jeppson to Aldus Higgins, March 23, 1945.

37. Wallace Howe interview, June 18, 1979.

38. For plant 7 project and the General Development Committee, see Wallace Howe interviews, June 18, 1979; February 11, 1981; Ed Van der Pyl interview, undated, Tymeson Papers; George Jeppson to Aldus Higgins, March 23, 1945; John Jeppson interview, March 20, 1981; *Norton Spirit*, September 1948, pp. 1–2; David Reid interview, June 13, 1979; John Jeppson, "Report on Audit of Processes Program," August 13, 1946, Jeppson Papers.

39. Wallace Howe interview, June 18, 1979.

40. George Jeppson to Aldus Higgins, March 23, 1945.

41. Ibid.

42. Norton Company, "Norton in World War II," p. 22.

43. George Jeppson, "Talk to Committee on Development Work and New Processes," July 29, 1946, Jeppson Papers.

44. John Jeppson, "Report," August 13, 1946, Jeppson Papers.

45. For development of the manufacturing process, see David Reid interview, June 13, 1979; Wallace Howe interviews, June 18, 1979; February 11, 1981; John Jeppson interview, March 20, 1981; Elwell Ljungberg interview, November 13, 1980.

46. *Norton Spirit,* September 1948, pp. 1–2.

47. Gordon Finlay interview, March 17, 1981; "Schoelkopf Medal Presentation to Raymond R. Ridgeway," May 17, 1943; Laboratory report in Norton Library at Worcester, TIC 46.0008.

48. Gordon Finlay interview, March 17, 1981; "Research" file, Tymeson Papers.

49. Everett Hicks interview, September 23, 1980; *Norton Spirit,* (June 1951), p. 1.

50. Ralph Gow interview, June 20, 1979.

51. George Jeppson to Clifford Anderson, July 30, 1919.

52. Wallace Howe interview, June 18, 1979; John Jeppson interview, March 20, 1981; *Norton Spirit,* February 1960, p. 2.

53. David Reid interview, June 13, 1979.

54. Wallace Howe interview, June 18, 1979; Gordon Finlay interview, March 17, 1981; W. C. Wickenden, "Comparative Statements," March 18, 1955.

55. For Norton's role in the development of synthetic diamonds, see Gordon Finlay interview, March 17, 1981; Max Whielden interview, May 20, 1981; P. W. Bridgman, "History and Present Status of the Bridgman Project as of December 1, 1945," typescript in Norton Library at Worcester, TIC 45.0022.

56. John Jeppson interview, March 20, 1981.

57. Ellis W. Hawley, *The New Deal and the Problems of Monoply: A Study in Economic Ambivalence* (Princeton: Princeton University Press, 1966).

58. Everett Hicks to Milton Higgins, October 20, 1945. For limitation of price control by patents and the evolution of per se rules for price fixing, see A. D. Neale, *The Antitrust Laws of the United States of America: A Study of Competition Enforced by Law* (Cambridge: Cambridge University Press, 1970), especially pp. 32–40, 303–313.

59. Earl Hughes interview, September 23, 1980; *United States of America* v. *Grinding Wheel Manufacturers Association; Norton Company; the Carborundum Company; Bay State Abrasive Products Company, Inc.; Simonds Abrasive Company; Macklin Company,* Civil Action no. 6636, District Court for Mass. (1947), Complaint, Answers and Final Judgment. The abrasive grain case was *United States of America* v. *Abrasive Grain Association, Norton Company et al.,* Civil Action no. 3672, District Court for Western N. Y. (1948). Neither case was reported in the Federal Supplement.

60. Ralph Gow interview, December 4, 1980; W. T. Kneisner to Milton Higgins, April 1, 1947.

61. For the antitrust cases, see the several folders in Norton's Legal Department containing charges, decrees, letters, and other documents.

62. Prentice Coonley to Milton Higgins, February 28, 1947.

63. Joseph Welch to T. Ewing Montgomery, July 21, 1947.

64. Prentice Coonley to Milton Higgins, April 1, 1947.

65. "Preliminary Survey re List Prices," undated typescript in Norton's Legal Department. See also W. J. Magee to J. N. Welch, June 13, 1947.

66. Joseph Welch to W. T. Kneisner, July 25, 1947; Milton Higgins interview, December 10, 1980.

67. Ralph Gow to J. N. Welch, May 28, 1953; Everett Hicks to Milton Higgins, October 20, 1945; Everett Hicks interview, September 23, 1980. See also antitrust compliance folders in Legal Department for discussions of quantity pricing and its implementation.

68. W. C. Wickenden, "Comparative Statements," March 18, 1955; Milton Higgins interview, August 7, 1980; John Jeppson, "Your Future at Norton Company," October 10, 1962.

69. John Jeppson interview, March 20, 1981; Ralph Gow interview, June 20, 1979; David A. Loehwing, "Scratching the Surface: Abrasive Makers Are Beginning to Tap Rich New Markets," *Barrons*, 48 (June 24, 1968), 3.

70. Robert Cushman, memorandum, December 19, 1958.

71. In addition to a small file in Norton's Legal Department, see *United States of America* v. *Minnesota Mining and Manufacturing Company*, 92 F. Supp. 947, District Court for Mass. (1950), case record, at Federal Archives and Records Center, Waltham, Mass.

72. For NBMO during Kelso's tenure, see Donald and Florence Kelso, "Autobiography"; Donald Kelso interviews, June 14, 19, 1979; Ralph Gow interviews, April 4, 1979; July 1, 1980; Milton Higgins interviews, June 12, 1979; February 12, 28, 1981. An interview, March 3, 1981, and extensive conversations, April 21–May 15, 1981, with Louis Camarra, a retired vice-president who spent thirty-five years in Norton's foreign business, provided both overview and details. See also International Management Association, *Case Studies in Foreign Operation* (New York, 1957), pp. 107–155; Wilfred Place interview, April 28, 1981; Fairman Cowan interview, January 15, 1980; Elmer Schacht interview, August 15, 1980; Ted Meyer interview, March 25, 1981; Gene Uhler interview, May 28, 1981. Mildred Tymeson's "Norton Behr-Manning Overseas, Inc.," February 14, 1958, typescript, Tymeson Papers, gives a sketchy overview.

73. Donald Kelso, "History and Policies of Foreign Operations," in International Management Association, *Case Studies*, p. 113.

74. Wilfred Place, "Norton Operations Overseas," typescript of speech, May 4, 1960.

75. Kelso, "History and Policies," pp. 109–117.

76. Ibid., p. 111.

77. Milton Higgins interview, February 12, 1981.

78. Bernard Meyer interview, April 17, 1981.

79. Kelso, "History and Policies," p. 115.

80. Frank Ryan, "Marketing and Merchandising," in International Management Association, *Case Studies*, pp. 118–119.

81. Conversation with Louis Camarra, April 28, 1981.

82. Paul Gaillour and Georges Bykhovetz, joint interview, April 27, 1981; Ted Meyer interview, March 25, 1981; Gene Uhler interview, May 28, 1981.

83. Fairman Cowan interview, January 15, 1980; Donald Kelso interview, June 19, 1979.

84. Louis Camarra interview, March 3, 1981.

85. Paine, Webber, Jackson and Curtis, and Goldman, Sachs and Co., *Prospectus: Norton Company,* September 28, 1962, p. 8; *Norton Spirit,* November 1951, p. 4. Market share and profit data for NBMO, 1952–1954, are in supporting documents for NBMO Board of Directors for 1955.

86. Fairman Cowan interview, January 15, 1980; Alfredo Povedano interview, September 25, 1979; Elmer Schacht interview, March 11, 1981; Louis Camarra conversation, May 12, 1981; R. H. Harris to the Executive Committee of the Board of Directors of Norton Company, March 15, 1961; Donald Kelso to Executive Committee, December 6, 1961; Donald Kelso to Florencio Casale, April 6, 1962; Donald Kelso to Norton Board of Directors, June 28, 1962. The last four letters are in the supporting documents for Norton's Board of Directors.

87. Louis Camarra conversations, April 21, 28, 1981; Wilfred Place and Réné Longfier, joint interview, April 28, 1981.

88. Alfred D. Chandler, *Strategy and Structure* (Cambridge, Mass.: MIT Press, 1962), especially chap. 7.

89. "It's No Longer," p. 118; Estabrook and Company, *Basic Study: Norton Company* (Boston and New York, January 12, 1965), p. 1, in Norton Archives.

90. Milton Higgins interviews, June 12, 1979; December 10, 1980; John Jeppson interview, April 2, 1981; Ralph Gow, "Memoirs," tape 2, February 1979; Ralph Gow interview, July 1, 1980.

91. Ralph Gow, "Memoirs," tape 2, February 1979.

92. Ibid.

93. Ibid.

94. Fairman Cowan interview, January 15, 1980; "It's No Longer," p. 118.

95. Fairman Cowan interview, January 15, 1980.

96. Ibid.; Curt Clark interview, July 23, 1980.

97. Richard Nichols interview, April 8, 1981.

98. Milton Higgins interviews, December 10, 1980; February 12, 1981.

99. Milton Higgins, "Comments at Stockholders Meeting," August 6, 1962.

100. Paine, Webber and Goldman, Sachs, *Prospectus,* p. 4; John Jeppson, "Your Future at Norton Company"; Milton Higgins interview, December 10, 1980; Ralph Gow, "Memoirs," tape 2, February 1979.

7 "Buying the Unknown with Confidence"

1. Alfred D. Chandler, *Strategy and Structure* (Cambridge, Mass.: MIT Press, 1962), especially chaps. 2–3.

2. For a colorful account, see John Brooks, *The Go-Go Years* (New York: Weybright and Talley, 1973). A more analytical approach is found in Robert Sobel, *The Age of Giant Corporations* (Westport, Conn.: Greenwood Press, 1972), chaps. 7–8.

3. Everett Hicks interview, September 23, 1980.

4. For refractory development, see William Fallon interview, June 13, 1979; Bill Moore to Ralph Johnson, May 7, 1951; Bill Moore to Ralph Gow, May 18, 1951. The last two items are in the supporting data for Norton's Board of Directors, hereafter cited as Supporting Data.

5. Ralph Gow, quoted in *Norton Spirit*, February 1955, p. 2. For products, see *Norton Spirit*, June 1955, p. 4; February 1957, p. 1. See also W. C. Wickenden, "Comparative Statements: Norton Company and Carborundum," March 18, 1955.

6. For divisionalization, see *Norton Spirit*, October 1956, pp. 1, 5; December 1956, p. 8; Milton Higgins, "Changes in Organization," September 14, 1956, Supporting Data.

7. *Norton Spirit*, December 1956, p. 8.

8. John Dingle interview, April 22, 1981.

9. Robert Cushman interview, May 26, 1981; Milton Higgins, "Changes in Organization," September 14, 1956.

10. Ralph Gow interview, December 4, 1980.

11. Allan Hardy to Board of Directors, January 20, 1965, Supporting Data.

12. Gordon Finlay interview, March 17, 1981; Ed Lowe interview, March 19, 1981; Terry Lapp interview, March 17, 1981.

13. Ralph Gow interview, December 4, 1980.

14. Milton Higgins, quoted in "It's No Longer Just Grind, Grind at Norton," *Fortune*, 58 (August 1963), 118.

15. Milton Higgins interview, February 12, 1981.

16. For National Research, see Richard Nichols interview, April 8, 1981; John Jeppson interview, April 2, 1981; Robert Stauffer interview, May 19, 1981; Allan Hardy interview, April 9, 1981; Fairman Cowan interviews, January 15, 1980; March 4, 1981; Ralph Gow interviews, April 2, 1979; July 1, December 4, 1980; *Norton Spirit*, April 1963, p. 3; "It's No Longer"; Norton Company, *Explanatory Statement in Connection with Proposed Consolidation of National Research Corporation into Norton Company* (Worcester, 1963).

17. "It's No Longer," p. 121.

18. Robert Stauffer interview, May 19, 1981; Milton Higgins to Norton shareholders, March 3, 1964, p. 5, Supporting Data.

19. Fairman Cowan interview, January 15, 1980; Norton Company, *Explanatory Statement*; Estabrook and Company, *Basic Study: Norton Company*, January 12, 1965, in Norton Archives.

20. John Jeppson interview, April 2, 1981; John Jeppson, quoted in "Shake-Up at Norton," *Forbes*, 100 (December 1, 1967), 44.

21. Fairman Cowan interview, January 15, 1980.

22. Richard Nichols interview, April 8, 1981; Robert Stauffer interview, May 19, 1981; "It's No Longer"; G. L. Martin to Fairman Cowan, May 18, 1965.

23. Brooks, *Go-Go Years*, especially chap. 7; Sobel, *Age*, pp. 196–209; Andrew Tobias, *The Funny Money Game* (Chicago: Playboy Press, 1971).

24. Brooks, *Go-Go Years*, p. 128.

25. Richard Nichols interview, April 8, 1981; Milton Higgins interview, February 12, 1981.

26. Robert Stauffer interview, May 19, 1981.

27. Milton Higgins, quoted in "It's No Longer," p. 121.

28. Ibid., p. 118.

29. Folder labeled "Stockholders Meetings" in Legal Department.

30. For the silicon carbide debacle, see P. F. Schlaikjer to Board of Directors, December 14, 1966, Supporting Data.

31. Harry Brustlin interview, May 20, 1981.

32. Bruce Henderson, "Norton's Corporate Development," August 1964, Supporting Data.

33. For Clipper and its acquisition, see Ralph Gow interviews, April 2, 1979; December 4, 1980; Milton Higgins interview, February 12, 1981; Fairman Cowan interview, March 4, 1981; "Agreement for Purchase and Sale," January 20, 1964, Supporting Data; Norton Company, *Annual Reports*, 1963, 1964.

34. For USS merger, see Robert Hunter interview, May 21, 1981; John Phipps and Ralph Gross, joint interview, April 13, 1981; Arthur D. Little, Inc., "Evaluation of the Tower Packings and Vinyl Tubing Businesses of U.S. Stoneware," February 1966, Supporting Data; "History of CPPD," *Norton Nuggets*, 1 (1979); Ralph Gow interviews, April 2, 1979; December 4, 1980.

35. Robert Hunter interview, May 21, 1981.

36. Robert Hunter to Board of Directors, August 16, 1966, Supporting Data.

37. Ralph Gow interview, December 4, 1980.

38. Norton Company, *Annual Reports*, 1963, 1964, 1966.

39. Norton Company, *Annual Report,* 1963, p. 5; Fairman Cowan to Board of Directors, May 19, 1966, Supporting Data.

40. Donald Melville interview, April 17, 1981; Helen Delage, "Norton Abrasives: Handsome Payoff from R and D," *Magazine of Wall Street*, 120 (April 1, 1967), 16–19.

41. Arthur D. Little, "Evaluation"; Robert Hunter speech, June 8, 1970.

42. Hugh S. Ferguson to Board of Directors, January 22, 1964; January 20, 1965, Supporting Data; Allan Hardy to Board of Directors, January 19, 1966; January 19, 1967, Supporting Data.

43. Unsigned report on Clipper to Board of Directors, November 1966, Supporting Data.

44. Allan Hardy's monthly report to Board of Directors, September 26, 1967, Supporting Data.

45. "Norton Company: Continuing a Successful Diversification beyond Abrasives," *Business Week,* July 9, 1979, p. 81.

46. Hugh Ferguson to Board of Directors, January 20, 1965, Supporting Data; "Smoothing the Rough Spots," *Barrons,* 44 (June 1, 1964), 8.

47. Allan Hardy to Board of Directors, September 26, 1967, Supporting Data.

48. Sobel, *Age,* pp. 208–209; Brooks, *Go-Go Years,* pp. 180–181; Tobias, *Funny Money,* pp. 154–174.

49. Ralph Gow interview, December 4, 1980; Milton Higgins interview, February 12, 1981.

50. Everett Hicks interview, September 23, 1980.

51. John Dingle interview, April 22, 1981.

52. Robert Cushman interview, March 30, 1981. See, for example, Theodore

Levitt, *Innovation in Marketing: New Perspectives for Profit and Growth* (New York: McGraw-Hill, 1962), especially chap. 3.

53. Allan Hardy interview, April 9, 1981.

54. John Jeppson interview, April 2, 1981; Robert Stauffer interview, May 19, 1981; Newman Thibault interview, March 31, 1981.

55. For slower growth, see John Jeppson to Norton Distributors Advisory Council, May 12, 1960; John Jeppson to District Sales Managers Meeting, October 3, 1960; John Jeppson to Norton R and D Conference, September 10, 1965. All items are in the Jeppson Papers.

56. William Fallon to Board of Directors, June 21, 1973, Supporting Data. For growth rates in the 1950s and 1960s, see "Grinding Wheel Non-Diamond Industry Growth, 1920–1979," chart from W. P. Densmore at Norton's Worcester offices; chart labeled "Grinding Wheel Physical Volume and the GNP," in Henderson, "Norton's Corporate Development."

57. John Berry, "Comeback at Carborundum," *Dun's Review*, 87 (April 1966), 36–39; "Why Eaton Likes Carborundum," *Business Week*, November 21, 1977, pp. 116–117.

58. Robert Cushman to Supervisors Meeting, March 9, 1960.

59. John M. Nelson to Board of Directors, June 14, 1967, Supporting Data; Robert Cushman to Board of Directors, May 18, 1966, Supporting Data.

60. David A. Loehwing, "Scratching the Surface: Abrasive Makers Are Beginning to Tap Rich New Markets," *Barrons*, 48 (June 24, 1968), 3.

61. John M. Nelson to Board of Directors, July 19, 1967, Supporting Data.

62. John Jeppson interview, March 20, 1981; Harry Brustlin interview, May 20, 1981; "Norton Company (A)," Harvard Business School case, Industrial Marketing, 259R, in Norton Archives.

63. Wickenden, "Comparative Statements," March 18, 1955; Robert Cushman to Board of Directors, February 17, 1966, Supporting Data.

64. John M. Nelson to Board of Directors, February 18, 1971, Supporting Data.

65. John Jeppson to Norton Distributors Advisory Council, May 12, 1960, Jeppson Papers.

66. Norton Company, *Annual Reports*, especially 1967, 1969–1971; Paine, Webber, Jackson and Curtis, and Goldman, Sachs and Company, *Prospectus: Norton Company*, September 28, 1962, p. 4.

67. H. G. Duane, memorandum, June 8, 1962, Supporting Data.

68. Sales for 1960 were $63.9 million. J. E. Cotter to Board of Directors, July 17, 1964, Supporting Data. Sales for 1968 were $99.5 million, $32.3 million for abrasive materials and $67.2 million for grinding wheels. Annual division reports to Board of Directors, January 1969, Supporting Data.

69. For abrasive machining, see *Norton Spirit*, March 1962, pp. 1–2; *Business Week*, February 9, 1963, p. 76; "Abrasive Industry Sets Sights for Rough Grind," *Iron Age*, 197 (March 10, 1966), 108.

70. John Manning interview, April 24, 1981.

71. Eric Becker and Norbert Hoffer, joint interview, May 11, 1981.

72. Harry Duane interview, May 27, 1981.

73. Donald and Florence Kelso, "Autobiography," undated typescript in Mrs. Kelso's possession; William Fallon interview, June 13, 1979; Fairman

Cowan interview, January 15, 1980; Donald Kelso interview, June 19, 1979; Milton Higgins interview, February 12, 1981.

74. Donald Kelso to NBMO's Board of Directors, March 27, 1959; A. M. Warren, "Product Supply Source Alternatives," December 20, 1966, NII Supporting Data; Milton Higgins interview, February 12, 1981; Louis Camarra conversation, April 21, 1981.

75. Louis Camarra conversation, April 28, 1981; Wilfred Place and Réné Longfier, joint interview, April 28, 1981; Angelo D'Imporzano interview, May 4, 1981.

76. Paine, Webber and Goldman, Sachs, *Prospectus,* p. 8; Norton Company, *Annual Report,* 1970, p. 1.

77. Louis Camarra conversation, April 27, 1981; Georges Bykhovetz interview, April 27, 1981; Harry Duane interview, May 27, 1981; Stanley Berman interview, April 17, 1981.

78. Georges Bykhovetz interview, April 27, 1981.

79. Annual division reports to Board of Directors, 1963–1971, Supporting Data; Boston Consulting Group, "Presentation to Norton Coated Abrasives Division," July 1973, Supporting Data.

80. For Behr-Manning's decline, see Boston Consulting Group, "Presentation"; Elmer Schacht interview, March 11, 1981; Edwin Evans interview, October 2, 1980; Dirck Olton interview, October 1, 1980; Henry Merrill interview, October 3, 1980; Harry Brustlin interview, May 20, 1981; Lee Hoogstoel interview, March 10, 1981; Randall Manchester interview, October 2, 1980; Charles Smith interview, April 1, 1981; John Jeppson interview, April 2, 1981; Milton Higgins interview, February 5, 1981; Gene Uhler interview, May 28, 1981; Strategic Guidance Committee, untitled review of Coated Abrasives Division, May 1974.

81. Elmer Schacht interview, March 11, 1981.

82. Henry Merrill interview, October 3, 1980.

83. Ibid.

84. Ibid.; Strategic Guidance Committee, untitled review, May 1974; Boston Consulting Group, "A Strategic Assessment of the Coated Abrasives Division," September 1973, Supporting Data.

85. For the tape venture, see Lee Hoogstoel interview, March 10, 1981; Elmer Schacht interviews, August 15, November 11, 1980; Edwin Evans interview, October 2, 1980; Henry Merrill interview, October 3, 1980; "New Product Reshapes Company," *Business Week,* October 12, 1957, pp. 120–126.

86. Elmer Schacht interview, November 11, 1980.

87. Behr-Manning sales manual, April 1958, section A.P. 13.

88. Henry Merrill interview, October 3, 1980.

89. Henderson, "Norton's Corporate Development." For market share, see J. A. Bump to Board of Directors, August 19, 1970, Supporting Data.

90. For market share, see Boston Consulting Group, "Presentation."

91. Edwin Evans to Board of Directors, January 18, 1966, Supporting Data.

92. For the strike, see Edwin Evans interview, October 2, 1980; Henry Merrill interview, October 3, 1980; Charles Smith interview, April 1, 1981; *Troy Times Record,* May 15–17, 23, June 9, 15, 25, 27, 1966. Mr. Olszowy refused to discuss the issue.

93. Edwin Evans to Board of Directors, September 12, 1966; Henry Merrill interview, October 3, 1980; Charles Smith interview, April 1, 1981.

94. Boston Consulting Group, "Presentation."

95. Harry Seifert conversation, November 13, 1979.

96. Milton Higgins interview, February 5, 1981.

97. This quotation and all quotations in the next three paragraphs are from Henderson, "Norton's Corporate Development."

98. Ibid.; "Shake-Up"; "Big Wheel in Worcester," *Forbes*, 91 (June 15, 1963), 41–42.

99. Chandler, *Strategy and Structure*, especially chaps. 6–7.

100. John Jeppson interview, May 27, 1981.

101. For reorganization, see Norton Company, *Annual Reports*, 1967–1969; *Norton Spirit*, May 1967, p. 1; February 1969, p. 1.

102. John M. Nelson to Board of Directors, March 20, 1969, Supporting Data.

103. Brief backgrounds of appointees are in Norton Company, *Annual Reports*, 1967–1969.

104. For Robert Cushman's career and promotion, see Robert Cushman interview, March 23, 1981; John Jeppson interview, May 27, 1981; *Norton Spirit*, January 1961, p. 1.

105. Robert Cushman interview, March 30, 1981.

106. Ibid. For the evolution of the Norton Plan, see also "Norton Company (A)"; David Reid interview, June 13, 1979; Harry Brustlin interview, May 20, 1981; "Distributors Fight for Their Take," *Business Week*, January 8, 1966, p. 33; *Business Week*, March 16, 1968, p. 37.

107. Harry Brustlin interview, May 20, 1981.

108. Robert Cushman interview, March 30, 1981.

109. John M. Nelson to Board of Directors, February 20, 1969, Supporting Data; see also Robert Cushman to Board of Directors, February 17, March 18, July 21, 1965, Supporting Data.

110. Robert Cushman interview, March 23, 1981; see also Richard Flynn interview, April 21, 1981, for an analysis of Cushman's leadership.

111. Ralph Gow interview, December 4, 1980; see also Ralph Gow interview, July 1, 1980.

112. Milton Higgins interview, February 5, 1981; John Jeppson interview, May 27, 1981; Allan Hardy interview, April 9, 1981; Robert Cushman interview, March 23, 1981.

8 Farewell to the Family Firm

1. Robert Cushman, "Norton Company: Corporate Objectives," June 4, 1971, Cushman Papers (in his possession).

2. John Jeppson, "Announcement of Corporate Strategy," Bermuda Conference, November 8, 1968, Supporting Data.

3. John Jeppson, speech at Taormina Conference, June 16, 1969.

4. Robert Cushman interview, March 23, 1981.

5. The three-paragraph discussion of Cushman's early plans is taken from his speech, "Who is Management?" September 7, 1966; and his untitled talk

to managers and supervisors, April 28, 1967, in Cushman Papers. See also Cushman interviews, March 23, 30, May 26, 1981.

6. Robert Cushman, quoted in *Boston Globe*, May 20, 1980, p. 51.

7. For evolution of strategic planning, see "Norton Company (A, B, C, D, E)," Harvard Business School cases, ICH 14C2 BC297; ICH 14C3 BC298, BC300; 9-114-020 BC 301; 1-377-044. John Jeppson interview, May 27, 1981; Robert Cushman interviews, March 23, 30, May 26, 1981.

8. Ralph Gow to division heads, January 18, 1966, Supporting Data.

9. Milton Higgins interview, December 2, 1980.

10. B. Charles Ames, "Payoff from Product Management," *Harvard Business Review*, 41 (November–December 1963), 141–152.

11. Robert Cushman, quoted in "Norton Company (A)," p. 8.

12. Robert Cushman interview, May 26, 1981.

13. Ibid.; John Jeppson interview, May 27, 1981; "Report of Product Line Study Committee to Executive Committee," February 14, 1968, Supporting Data.

14. Robert Cushman interview, March 23, 1981.

15. Harry B. Duane to John F. Dingle, October 15, 1969, Supporting Data.

16. For Boston Consulting Group strategy, see Robert Cushman, "President's Report," *Norton Spirit*, Spring 1977, pp. 2–3; "Norton Company (C, D)"; "Norton Company (E): "Strategic Planning for Diversified Business Operations," Harvard Business School case, 1-377-044; Cushman, "Corporate Strategy: Planning for the Future," speech to North American Society for Corporate Planning, October 19, 1978; Cushman, "Memorandum: Corporate Strategy," March 26, 1968, Cushman Papers; Cushman, "Current Corporate Strategic Concepts and Practices," speech to Board of Directors, December 12, 1975, Cushman Papers.

17. Richard Flynn interview, April 21, 1981.

18. Alfred D. Chandler, *Strategy and Structure* (Cambridge, Mass.: MIT Press, 1962).

19. Robert Cushman, "Corporate Strategy," October 19, 1978, p. 2.

20. For the evolution of the Strategic Guidance Committee, see "Norton Company (C and D)"; Cushman, "President's Report"; Cushman, "Current," December 12, 1975; Cushman, "Corporate Strategy," October 19, 1978; Cushman interview, March 23, 1981.

21. Robert Cushman, quoted in *Boston Globe*, May 20, 1980, p. 51; Robert Cushman interview, March 21, 1983.

22. For Schoeffler's contribution, see Cushman, "Current," December 12, 1975; "Norton Company (D)."

23. Robert Cushman interview, March 23, 1981.

24. Ibid., March 30, 1981.

25. Ibid., March 23, 1981.

26. *Norton Spirit*, May 1970, p. 5; see also *Norton Spirit*, May 1971, pp. 2–3; "Norton Aligns Its Top Jobs with Its Markets," *Business Week*, August 7, 1971, pp. 80–82.

27. *Norton Spirit*, May 1974, p. 3; Robert Cushman, "Corporate Objectives: Short Term," April 9, 1971, Supporting Data. Earnings per share and all

subsequent unattributed financial data can be found in the appropriate annual report.

28. For financial tools, see John Dingle interview, April 22, 1981. Numerous examples of capital project forms and post audits can be found in the supporting data for the Board of Directors in the 1970s.

29. J. I. Olson speech, in Norton Company, *Second World Management Conference*, October 6–8, 1971, Worcester, 1971, pp. 68–69.

30. George Bernardin speech, in Norton Company, *Second World*, pp. 70–72.

31. For personnel management, see Robert Cushman interview, March 23, 1981; "Norton Company (C)"; "Descriptive Summary of the Norton Management Incentive Plan," January 1967, Supporting Data; W. F. Lionett to Executive Committee, January 27, 1971, Supporting Data.

32. "Norton Company (C)," p. 4.

33. For example, see Norton Company, *Second World; Norton Spirit*, Spring 1977, December 1976; "Norton Management Conference: A Special Report for Norton Employees," June 1–4, 1971; "Announcement of Corporate Strategy Statements," November 8, 1968, Supporting Data; Cushman, "Norton Company: Corporate Objectives."

34. Harry Duane interview, May 27, 1981. Also helpful were Stanley Berman interview, April 17, 1981; Bernard Meyer interview, April 17, 1981; Louis Camarra conversations, April 21–May 15, 1981; Duane's memoranda: "Norton Company Abrasives Operations," September 12, 1980; "Style of Management: Teaching of Management Science," September 12, 1980; "Organizational Philosophy and Resolution of Organizational Problems," September 12, 1980; "Creativity," August 28, 1980; "Profit Variance Analysis," September 7, 1980; "Norton Plan," September 3, 1980, all in Duane's possession.

35. "How Norton Went POP," *Business Abroad*, 95 (April 1970), 21–23; Harry Duane, in *Wall Street Transcript*, June 17, 1978, pp. 13, 598.

36. Duane, "Style of Management."

37. Duane, "Organizational Philosophy"; "Freedom Within Bounds," August 28, 1980.

38. H. B. Duane to Board of Directors, May 18, 1967, Supporting Data.

39. Robert Cushman interview, May 26, 1981; Harry Duane interview, May 27, 1981.

40. Stanley Berman interview, April 17, 1981; Harry Duane interview, May 27, 1981; Harry Duane, "Profit Opportunities in Abrasives," April 13, 1972, Supporting Data.

41. For Japan, see Harry Duane interview, May 27, 1981; Stanley Berman interview, April 17, 1981; H. B. Duane to Board of Directors, September 28, 1967, Supporting Data; H. B. Duane, "Riken Corundum Company Ltd.: Joint Venture," January 8, 1969, Supporting Data; H. B. Duane, "Bonded Abrasives Joint Venture with Kure Grinding Wheel Manufacturing Company Ltd., Kure, Japan," October 14, 1970, Supporting Data; Strategic Guidance Committee, untitled review of Japanese operations, December 3, 1975; Duane, "Japanese Abrasives Operations."

42. H. B. Duane, "Overall Strategy: Japan," December 31, 1968, Supporting Data.

43. Stanley Berman interview, April 17, 1981.

44. For Brazilian operations, see Alfredo Povedano interview, September 25, 1979; H. B. Duane to J. F. Dingle, October 15, 1969, Supporting Data; J. F. Dingle to Board of Directors, October 14, 1969, Supporting Data; Strategic Guidance Committee, reviews of Brazilian operations, June 1975, June 1977; Duane, "Brazil."

45. For Australia, see John Adams interviews, September 27, October 1, 1979; H. B. Duane to Board of Directors, March 19, 1970, Supporting Data; Duane, "Modernization of Bonded Abrasives Facility, Australian Abrasives, Auburn, Australia," October 8, 1970, Supporting Data; Duane, "Australian Abrasives (Pty) Ltd.," September 21, 1980. For South Africa, see William Campbell-Pitt interview, October 7, 1980; Duane, "South Africa," September 8, 1980; "Proposed Acquisition: Blane Group by Norton-Isando," February 2, 1971, Supporting Data. For Spain, see J. F. Dingle to Board of Directors, November 13, 1973, Supporting Data; B. F. Meyer to Executive Committee, March 7, 1973, Supporting Data; Robert Cushman speech, April 25, 1975.

46. Norton Company, *Second World,* pp. 35–36; Robert Cushman speech, April 22, 1976.

47. For sourcing, see Harry Duane interview, May 27, 1981; Stanley Berman interview, April 17, 1981; "Coated Abrasives Planning: Conflans," October 1969, Supporting Data; Louis Camarra conversations, April 26, 27, 28, 1981; Duane, "European Bonded Abrasives," September 3, 1980.

48. H. B. Duane to Board of Directors, April 12, 1974. For zirconia-alumina, see also "Zirconia Alumina Abrasive Grain: Additional Facilitiies at Chippawa, Canada," 1974, Supporting Data; Newman Thibault interview, March 31, 1981; Thibault, "History of the Development of Alumina-Zirconia Abrasives of the ZA-ZS Types," undated manuscript in Thibault's possession.

49. Robert Cushman speech, April 22, 1976; "Zirconia Alumina Abrasive Grain," 1974.

50. Duane, "Norton Company Abrasives Operations."

51. Robert Cushman interview, March 23, 1981. For the 40 percent target, see Cushman, "Norton Company: Corporate Objectives."

52. For divestments, see Donald Melville interview, April 17, 1981; Norton Company, *Annual Reports,* especially 1969–1972; pamphlets of president's speeches to annual meetings.

53. B. H. McLachlan, "A Background Study Concerning Investment in a Foreign Tool Plant," July 17, 1961, Supporting Data; Everett Hicks interview, September 23, 1980; Ralph Gow interview, April 2, 1979; Robert Lawson interview, July 21, 1980; Fairman Cowan interview, January 15, 1980; Allan Hardy interview, April 9, 1981.

54. Robert Lawson interview, July 21, 1980.

55. Ibid.; Everett Hicks interview, September 23, 1980; T. J. Englund to Robert Cushman, November 25, 1964, Supporting Data.

56. Donald Melville interview, April 17, 1981.

57. Donald Melville speech, in Norton Company *Second World,* pp. 44–48; Robert Cushman speech, April 25, 1974, Cushman Papers.

58. For the evolution of diversified products, see "Norton Company (D)"; Donald Melville interview, April 17, 1981; Robert Cushman interview, March 23, 1981; Cushman and Melville talks in pamphlets of speeches at annual meetings. See also Norton Company's annual reports for the 1970s.

59. Strategic Guidance Committee, untitled review of Industrial Ceramics Division, October 1974. See also *Norton Spirit,* May 1971, pp. 2–3; William P. Densmore, "New Business Opportunities in Advanced Ceramic Technology," speech to annual meeting, April 8, 1971.

60. W. P. Densmore to Board of Directors, January 9, 1969; *Norton Spirit,* Winter 1977, p. 5.

61. For U.S. Stoneware, see Robert Hunter interview, May 21, 1981; John Phipps and Ralph Gross, joint interview, April 13, 1981.

62. For sealants' development, see Norton Company, *Second World,* pp. 48–53.

63. Robert Cushman, "Acquisition Program," speech, October 26, 1972, Cushman Papers.

64. For Griffin's work I have relied heavily on John P. Dory, *The Domestic Diversifying Acquisition* (Ann Arbor: UMI Research Press, 1978), pp. 26–45.

65. For the development of safety products, see Donald Melville interview, April 17, 1981; Donald Melville to Board of Directors, May 17, 1973, Supporting Data; Strategic Guidance Committee, reviews of safety products, September 1974, January 1976.

66. Strategic Guidance Committee, review, September 1974.

67. Robert Cushman, speech to annual meeting, April 22, 1976; Strategic Guidance Committee, review, January 1976.

68. Sales and profit data are from annual reports. See also Donald Melville speech, in Norton Company, *Second World,* pp. 44–46.

69. Donald Melville interview, April 17, 1981; Robert Cushman interview, March 23, 1981; Melville, speech to annual meeting, April 26, 1973.

70. Donald Melville interview, April 17, 1981.

71. Ibid.; W. G. Fallon to Board of Directors, June 21, 1973, Supporting Data.

72. R. J. Hoover to Board of Directors, April 13, May 15, 1974, Supporting Data.

73. W. G. Fallon to Board of Directors, June 21, 1973, Supporting Data; Harry Duane to Board of Directors, April 12, 1974, Supporting Data; Al Cotton to Robert Cushman, November 1, 1976.

74. Strategic Guidance Committee, review of Japanese operations, December 1975.

75. For Behr-Manning's problems, see Charles Smith interview, April 1, 1981; Gene Uhler interview, May 28, 1981; W. P. Midghall to Executive Committee, May 7, 1975, Supporting Data; "Norton Company: Strategic Planning for Diversified Business Operations"; Strategic Guidance Committee, reviews of coated operations, May 1974, June 1, 1976, May 1, 1978; Robert Cushman interview, March 30, 1981; John Nelson interview, April 14, 1981; Boston Consulting Group, "A Strategic Assessment of the Coated Abrasive Division," September 1973, Supporting Data.

76. John Jeppson interview, April 2, 1981.

77. Robert Cushman, quoted in "Norton Aligns," p. 82.

78. Cushman, "Current Corporate Strategic Concepts and Practices."

79. *Norton Spirit*, Spring 1977, pp. 4–8.

80. Robert Cushman, speech to annual meeting, April 27, 1978.

81. For Christensen's history, see Frank Christensen interview, April 14, 1981; *Norton Spirit*, Spring 1977, pp. 4–8.

82. Frank Christensen interview, April 14, 1981.

83. Arthur D. Little, "Assessment of the Diamond Drilling and Corehead Industry and Christensen's Part in That Market," November 1976, Supporting Data; "Christensen Historical Review," 1976, exhibit 3, Supporting Data.

84. Frank Christensen interview, April 14, 1981; Daniel D. Nossiter, "Justice vs De Beers," *Barrons*, 61 (March 30, 1981), 9, 24–26.

85. Richard Flynn interview, April 21, 1981; Robert Cushman interview, March 23, 1981.

86. Kenneth Zeitz to Board of Directors, February 19, 1976, Supporting Data; Zeitz interview, March 23, 1981.

87. In supporting data for the Board of Directors, see Salomon Brothers to Norton Company, December 1, 1976; Arthur D. Little, "Assessment"; "Standard and Poor's Oil-Gas Drilling and Services: Basic Analysis," October 7, 1976; "Standard and Poor's Oil-Gas Drilling and Services: Current Analysis," December 9, 1976. See also *Norton Spirit*, Spring 1977, p. 4.

88. Frank Christensen interview, April 14, 1981.

89. Ibid.; Kenneth Zeitz interview, March 23, 1981; Robert Cushman interview, March 23, 1981.

90. John Nelson interview, April 14, 1981; Frank Christensen interview, April 14, 1981.

91. John Nelson interview, April 14, 1981.

92. For the development of downhole tools, see ibid.; Christensen, Inc., *A Report: Building on Success. Christensen World Management Conference* (Salt Lake City, June 4–6, 1979), especially the presentations by John Nelson and Frank Flarity; "Christensen, Inc.: Investment Propsal for Down Hole Tools," May 9, 1977, Supporting Data; Strategic Guidance Committee, review of Christensen, June 1979.

93. John Nelson, "Strategic Concepts," in Christensen, *A Report*; Strategic Guidance Committee, review, June 1979.

94. Norton Company, *Annual Report*, 1980.

95. Ibid., 1977; *Norton Spirit*, February 1973, p. 2.

96. For the development of Norton's accountability program, see Tom Green interview, April 9, 1981; Robert Cushman interview, March 30, 1981; annual statement issued with the annual report and titled variously *Accountability*, *Response*, and *Social Investments*, 1973–1980; Deborah Nabham, "Internship with the Public Relations Department of Norton Company: Charitable Donations," January 23, 1979, paper in Nabham's possession; Norton Company, *The Norton Policy of Business Ethics* (n.d.); Robert Cushman, "The Norton Company Faces the Payoffs Problem," *Harvard Business Review*, 54 (September–October 1976), 6–7.

97. Norton Company, *Norton Policy of Business Ethics* (Worcester, 1976), pp. 2–3.

98. Norton Company, *Annual Report*, 1973; "Number of Employees," April 1, 1959.

99. Norton Company, *Response*, 1973, p. 1.

100. Tom Green interview, April 9, 1981.

101. Norton Company, *Response*, 1975, p. 1.

102. See Robert Cushman speech, in Norton Company, *Second World*, pp. 92–97; "Statement Respecting Norton Company's Investment in South Africa," 1971, Supporting Data; "Consolidation and Decentralization of Three of Our Existing Hand-Tool Plants," July 27, 1973, Supporting Data; C. P. Guise Brown to I. J. Hetherington, September 14, 1976, Supporting Data.

103. Theodore J. Purcell and James Weber, *Institutionalizing Corporate Ethics: A Case History*, The Presidents Association, The Chief Executives Officers' Division, American Management Association, Special Study no. 71 (1979).

104. Robert Cushman interview, March 30, 1981.

105. Norton Company, *Annual Reports*, 1979: *Strategy Seventies*, p. 2; 1980, p. 2; 1975, pp. 1, 3.

106. Norton Company, *Annual Reports*, 1979: *Strategy Seventies*, p. 2; *Strategy Eighties*, p. 1.

Conclusion

1. See Alfred D. Chandler, *The Visible Hand* (Cambridge, Mass.: Harvard University Press, 1977), chaps. 12–13; Chandler, *Strategy and Structure* (Cambridge, Mass.: MIT Press, 1962).

2. For English firms, see Leslie Hannah, *The Rise of the Corporate Economy: The British Experience* (Baltimore: Johns Hopkins University Press, 1976); Leslie Hannah, ed., *Management Strategy and Business Development: An Historical and Comparative Study* (London: Macmillan, 1976), especially Hannah, "Business Development and Economic Structure in Britain since 1880," pp. 1–19, Hannah, "Strategy and Structure in the Manufacturing Sector," pp. 184–202, and Alfred D. Chandler, "The Development of Modern Management Structure in the U.S. and U.K.," pp. 22–51; Chandler and Herman Daems, eds., *Managerial Hierarchies: Comparative Perspectives on the Rise of the Modern Industrial Enterprise* (Cambridge, Mass.: Harvard University Press, 1980), especially Daems, "The Rise of the Modern Industrial Enterprise: A New Perspective," pp. 203–223. For Japan, see Shigeaki Uasuoka, "The Social Background of Zaibatsu in Japan," in Paul Uselding, ed., *Business and Economic History*, 2nd ser., 6 (1977), pp. 84–90.

3. For an excellent analysis, see Chandler, *Strategy and Structure*.

4. For conglomerates, see Robert Sobel, *The Age of Giant Corporations* (Westport, Conn.: Greenwood Press, 1972), especially chaps. 8–9; see also Norman Berg, "Corporate Role in Diversified Companies," in B. Taylor and K. Macmillan, eds., *Business Policy: Teaching and Research* (New York: Wiley, 1973), pp. 298–347.

5. Norton Company, *Annual Report*, 1980, p. 3.

6. See, for example, "Tinkering with Geneen's Growth Machine at ITT," *Business Week*, May 15, 1978, pp. 58–64; "Textron: Shaking Up the Divisions to Enliven a Sluggish Performance," *Business Week*, May 26, 1980, pp. 88–93;

Thomas O'Hanlon, "A Rejuvenated Litton Is Once Again Off to the Races," *Fortune*, 100 (October 8, 1979), 154–164.

7. William K. Hall, "SBUs: Hot New Topic in the Management of Diversification," *Business Horizons*, 21 (February 1978), 17–25. For a view that emphasizes the differences, see Robert A. Pitts, "Toward a Contingency Theory of Multibusiness Organization Design," *Academy of Management Review*, 5 (April 1980), 203–210.

8. Robert Cushman, "Corporate Strategy: Planning for the Future," speech to the North American Society for Corporate Planning, October 19, 1978, Boston, Mass., p. 2.

9. For a review of performance in the 1970s, see Norton Company, *Annual Report*, 1979; for the objectives, see Norton Company, *Second World Management Conference Report*, October 6–8, 1976 (Worcester, 1976).

10. Fairman Cowan interview, March 17, 1983.

11. For a good summary, see Hugh G. J. Aitken, "The Entrepreneurial Approach to Economic History," in George Rogers Taylor and Lucius F. Ellsworth, eds., *Approaches to American Economy History* (Charlottesville: University of Virginia Press, 1971), pp. 1–16.

12. Chandler, *Visible Hand*.

13. Alfred D. Chandler and Stephen Salsbury, *Pierre S. du Pont and the Making of the Modern Corporation* (New York: Harper and Row, 1971); Chandler, ed., *Giant Enterprise: Ford, General Motors and the Automobile Industry: Sources and Readings* (New York: Harcourt, Brace and World, 1964); Virginia Huck, *Brand of the Tartan: The 3M Story* (New York: Appleton-Century-Crofts, 1955).

14. Terrence E. Deal and Allan A. Kennedy, *Corporate Cultures: The Rites and Rituals of Corporate Life* (Reading, Mass.: Addison Wesley, 1982), especially chaps. 1–5. The quotations are from pp. 4 and 23.

15. Chandler and Salsbury, *du Pont*; Chandler, *Giant Enterprise*; Allan Nevins and Frank E. Hill, *Ford: The Times, the Man, the Company* (New York: Scribner's, 1954); Huck, *Brand*.

16. See Harold Livesay, *Andrew Carnegie and the Rise of Big Business* (Boston: Little, Brown, 1975), especially chaps. 7–8; Charles Cheape, *Moving the Masses* (Cambridge, Mass.: Harvard University Press, 1980), especially chaps. 2, 6.

17. Robert H. Hayes and William J. Abernathy, "Managing Our Way to Economic Decline," *Harvard Business Review*, 58 (July–August 1980), 67–77; Robert H. Hayes, "Why Japanese Factories Work," *Harvard Business Review*, 59 (July–August 1981), 57–66; William G. Ouchi, *Theory Z: How American Business Can Meet the Japanese Challenge* (New York: Avon, 1981), especially pp. 178–179; Steve Lohr, "Overhauling American Business Management," *New York Times Magazine*, January 4, 1981, pp. 14ff.; "The Penalties of Short-Term Corporate Strategies," *Business Week*, June 30, 1980, pp. 70–72; David Vogel, "America's Management Crisis," *New Republic*, 184 (February 7, 1981), 21–23.

Index

Abrasive grain, 18, 20; emery, 20, 74–75, 79, 85; processing, 37–38, 240, 286; silicon carbide, 55, 74, 84; aluminum oxide, 74, 76–78

Abrasive Grain Association, 99, 246

Abrasive machining, 287

Abrasives, 2, 13. *See also* Artificial abrasives; Bonded abrasives; Coated abrasives; Emery wheels

Abrasives Material Company, 19, 29, 56, 95

Abrasives Materials Division, 298, 335, 349

Abrasives Group, 296, 312, 318, 322–323; performance, 325–327, 334–336

Abrasives Marketing Group, 325

Acheson, Edward, 54–55, 73, 77

Acquisitions, 160, 330, 340; Behr-Manning Company, 160, 176–181; National Research Corporation, 267–269; Clipper Company, 272; U.S. Stoneware, 272–274; rationalization of, 331–333, 340; Christensen Company, 339–341

Adams, John, 322, 324

Administration: informality, 43–44, 112, 116, 118, 124, 133, 205, 227, 232–233, 251–254, 258, 263, 274, 300–301; organization and structure, 51–52, 93–94, 108, 113, 232–233, 264–266, 292–298, 300; professional management, 106–108, 257, 295–301, 305, 316–318; project approach, 112–113, 144, 197, 204;

emphasis on financial controls, 113, 227–228, 280–281, 293; personnel requirements, 257, 277–278, 281, 296–298

Advanced Materials Group, *see* Diversified Products Group

Ahlstrom, Carl, 41, 42, 44

Alden, George I.: founding of Norton Company, 29, 32; career, 31, 32, 99; management, 45, 46, 51, 52, 53; president, 128, 157

Allen, Charles, 111, 132; career, 26, 29, 32, 103, 150–151; founding of Norton Company, 29; management, 31, 32, 46–47, 51–52, 99, 102–103, 142, 153; character and personality, 32, 33, 52; preservation of family firm, 40–41, 101, 139, 140; sales operations, 47–50; friendship with C. H. Norton, 47, 65; emphasis on abrasives manufacture, 54, 88; overseas operations, 192–193, 201, 207

Allen, Thomas, 95

Allison, John, 251, 253

Aluminum Company of America, 76; bauxite holdings, 85–90

Aluminum oxide, 74, 76–78. *See also* Alundum; Artificial abrasives

Alundum, 155–156; origins, 74, 76–78; product and process development, 77–78, 80–84, 90–92; Norton Company leadership in, 78–79, 81–83; markets, 79–80; characteristics, 81–82;

413

Research and development: origins, 39, 118, 141–143; laboratory functions, 141–144; limitations, 142–143, 144–145, 242; application and theory, 142–143, 145–149, 326, 330–331, 362; Niagara Falls and Chippawa laboratories, 142, 147, 240; process improvements, 145–146, 148, 240; impact, 146–149; product development, 146, 147, 240, 326; laboratory and handicraft production, 148–149
Resin bonds, 145, 182
Richardson, Henry, 19, 20
Ridgway, Robert, 81, 142, 143, 144, 147, 240
Riken Corundum Company, 323
Riley Stoker Company, 31, 103
Rokide coatings, 264
Roslund, John, 26, 40
Ryan, Frank, 251

Safety Products Division, 332, 334, 337, 350
Salaries, 45, 46, 47, 101
Sales Department, 45, 115–118; distributorships, 116, 299–300; branch offices and warehouses, 116, 299, 325; pricing, 117, 118, 244, 245, 246, 247, 299. *See also* Bonded abrasives marketing; Norton Plan
Sales Record Department, 123
Salomon Brothers, 340
Sandon Incorporated, 330, 331
Sandpaper, *see* Coated abrasives
Sanford, Baalis, 143, 147
Saunders, Lewis, 81, 86, 108, 148; Alundum development, 80–81, 82; research and grain operations, 112, 119, 142, 144
Sawyer, W. H., 34
Schacht, Elmer, 168, 170, 181, 188; Behr-Manning leadership, 231, 289–290, 291, 292; foreign operations, 252, 253–254, 255
Schaetzel, Jules, 223, 249
Schoeffler, Sidney, 313–314
Schuchardt and Schutte, 50, 193, 194, 196, 200
Schuchardt, Bernhard, 196, 199
Schutte, Alfred, 105, 196, 199, 206, 211

Schutte, Otto: career, 207–208, 216; management of DNG, 211–212, 252; operations during World War II, 211–216
Sealants Division, 330
Seifert, Harry, 271, 293
Service Department, 131, 133
Sheehan, Henry, 195
Shonfeld, Ray, 331
SIA, 287, 336
Siebe Gorman Holdings PLC, 350
Silicon carbide (carborundum), 55, 74, 84
Simonds Abrasives Company, 95
Sloan, John, 25, 50, 192
Smith, C. O., 72, 153
Smith, George, 45, 47
Soderberg, Otto, 22
Sondering Schleifmittel, 213
Sourcing, 325
South African operations, 249, 254, 289, 324, 346
Southern Bauxite Company, 85
Space blankets, 269, 276, 277, 281
Spanish operations, 324
Speare, Alden, and Sons Company, 75, 79
Spence, John, 72, 108, 157, 159, 160; labor attitudes, 128, 133
Springfield Emery Wheel Company, 19
Standard Abrasives Company, 173
Stanton, Herbert, 150, 214, 216; overseas administration, 206, 218, 249
Stauffer, Robert, 268, 277, 281, 282, 296, 315, 316; business planning, 306, 307
Sterling Emery Wheel Company, 19, 56
Stock ownership: by founder families, 29, 32, 108–110, 258; employee stock, 47, 111–112, 234, 258, 259–260; public sale, 259–260, 267, 269, 270–271, 343
Strategic Guidance Committee, 312–314, 357
Strategic Planning Institute, 313–314
Strong and Trowbridge, 193
Styffe family, 41, 105, 126; Hjalmar, 39, 149; Joel, 44, 148, 181
Supercon Division, 269–270, 277, 281, 327
Swedish community in Worcester, 33, 154–155
Swedish Folk Fest, *see* Family outing

HARVARD STUDIES IN BUSINESS HISTORY

(Some of these titles may be out of print. Write to Harvard University Press for information and ordering.)